Destiny's HAND

Written by Nunzio DeFilippis and Christina Weir
Illustrated by Melvin Calingo

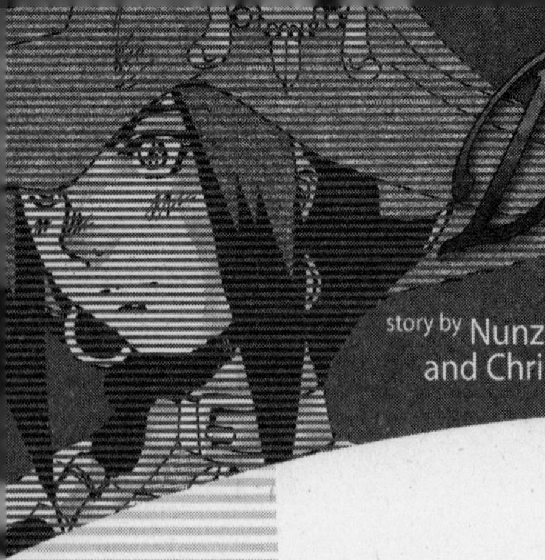

Destiny's HAND

VOLUME 1

story by Nunzio DeFilippis and Christina Weir art by Melvin Calingo

STAFF CREDITS

toning	**Pat Aguasin**
lettering / graphic design	**Jon Zamar**
	Gabe Dela Cruz
cover design	**Nate Legaspi**
assistant editor	**Adam Arnold**
editor	**Jason DeAngelis**
publisher	**Seven Seas Entertainment**

This is a work of fiction. Names, characters, places, and incidents are the products of the author's imagination or are used fictitiously. Any resemblance to actual events, locales, or persons, living or dead, is entirely coincidental.

Visit us online at www.gomanga.com.

ISBN 1-933164-11-5

Printed in Canada

First printing: May, 2006

10987654321

Table of Contents

Volume 1

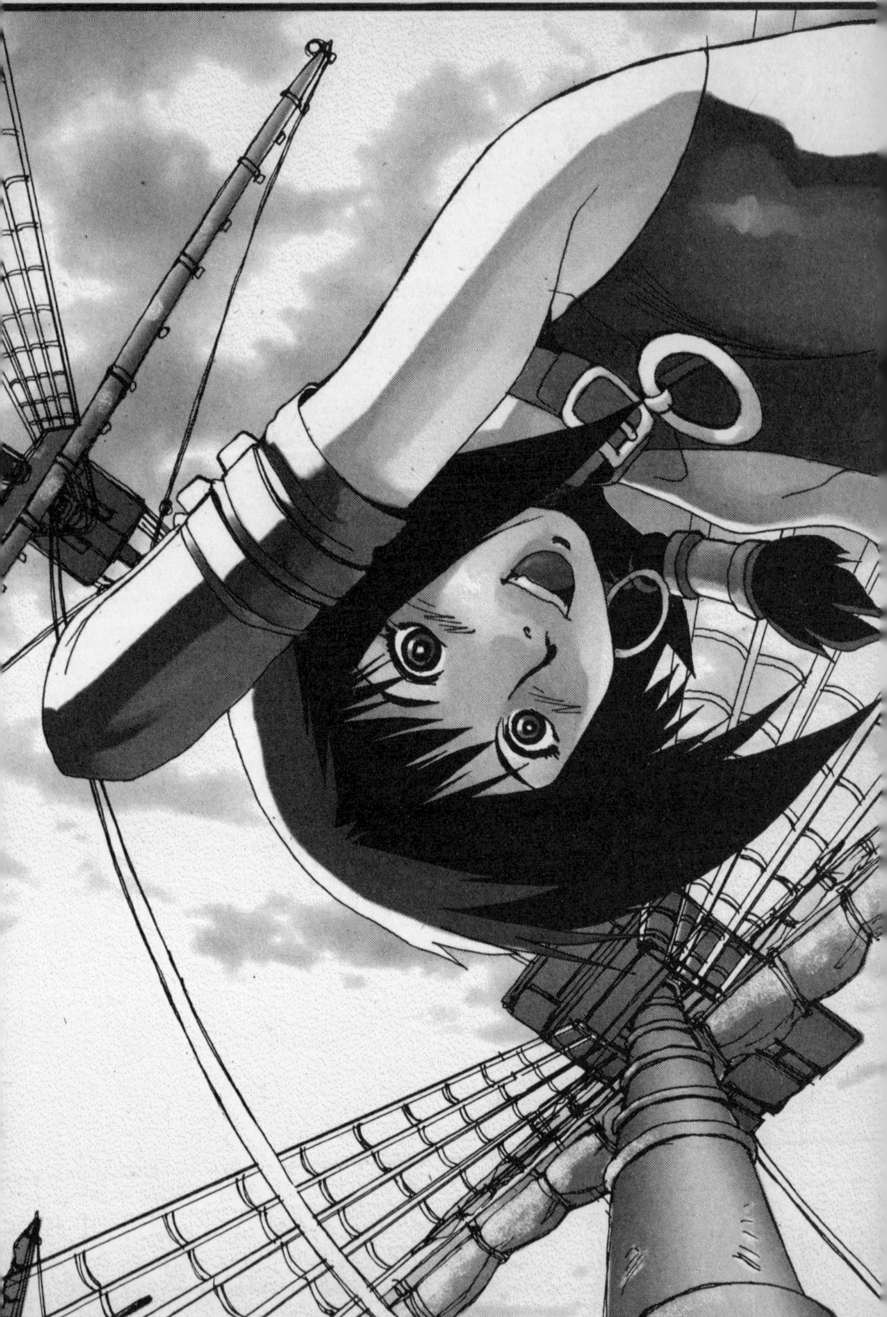

CHAPTER 1
Runaway Child

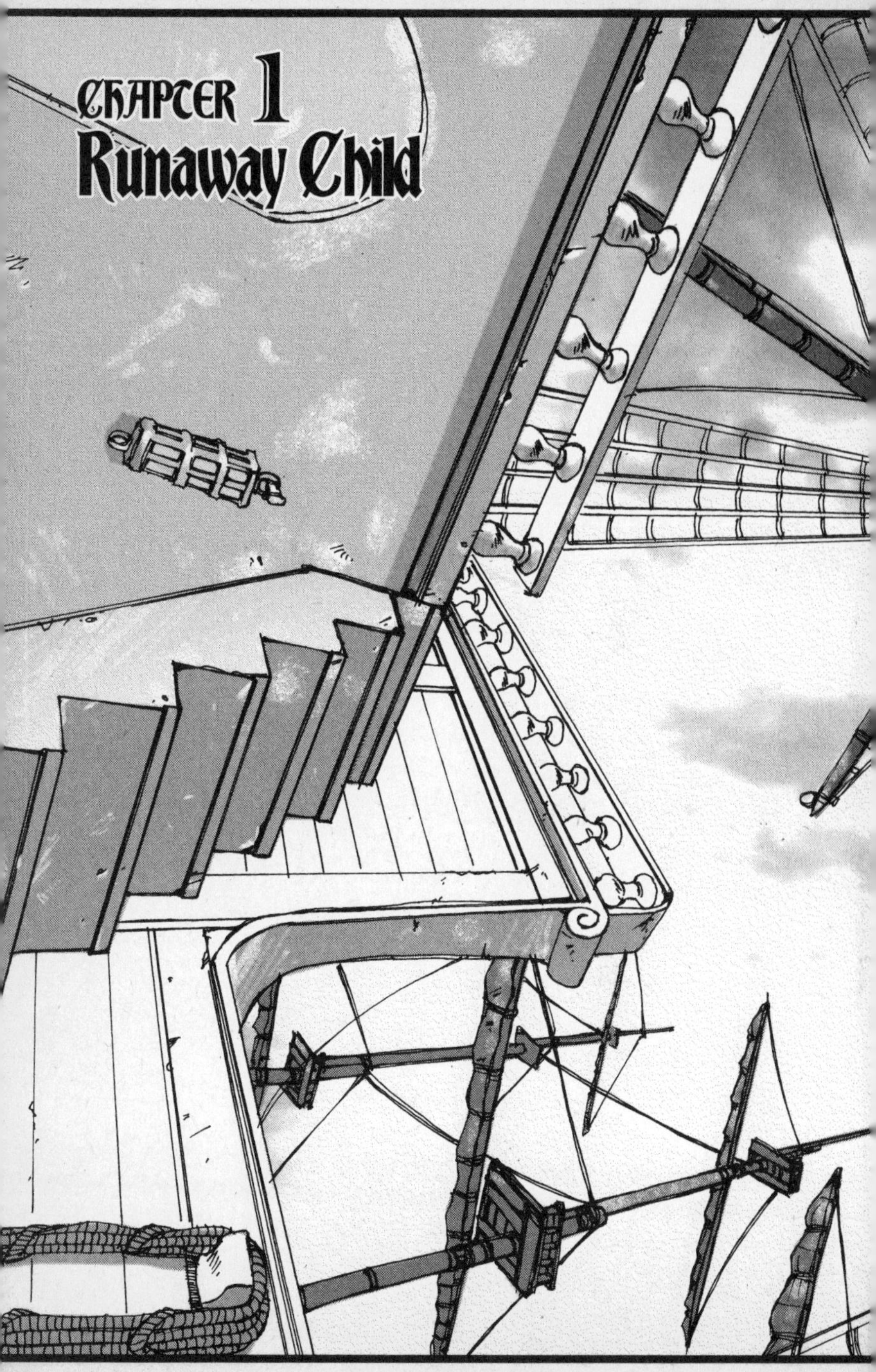

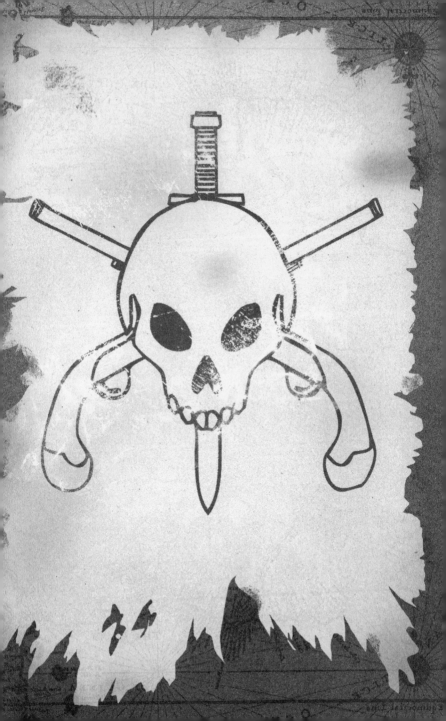

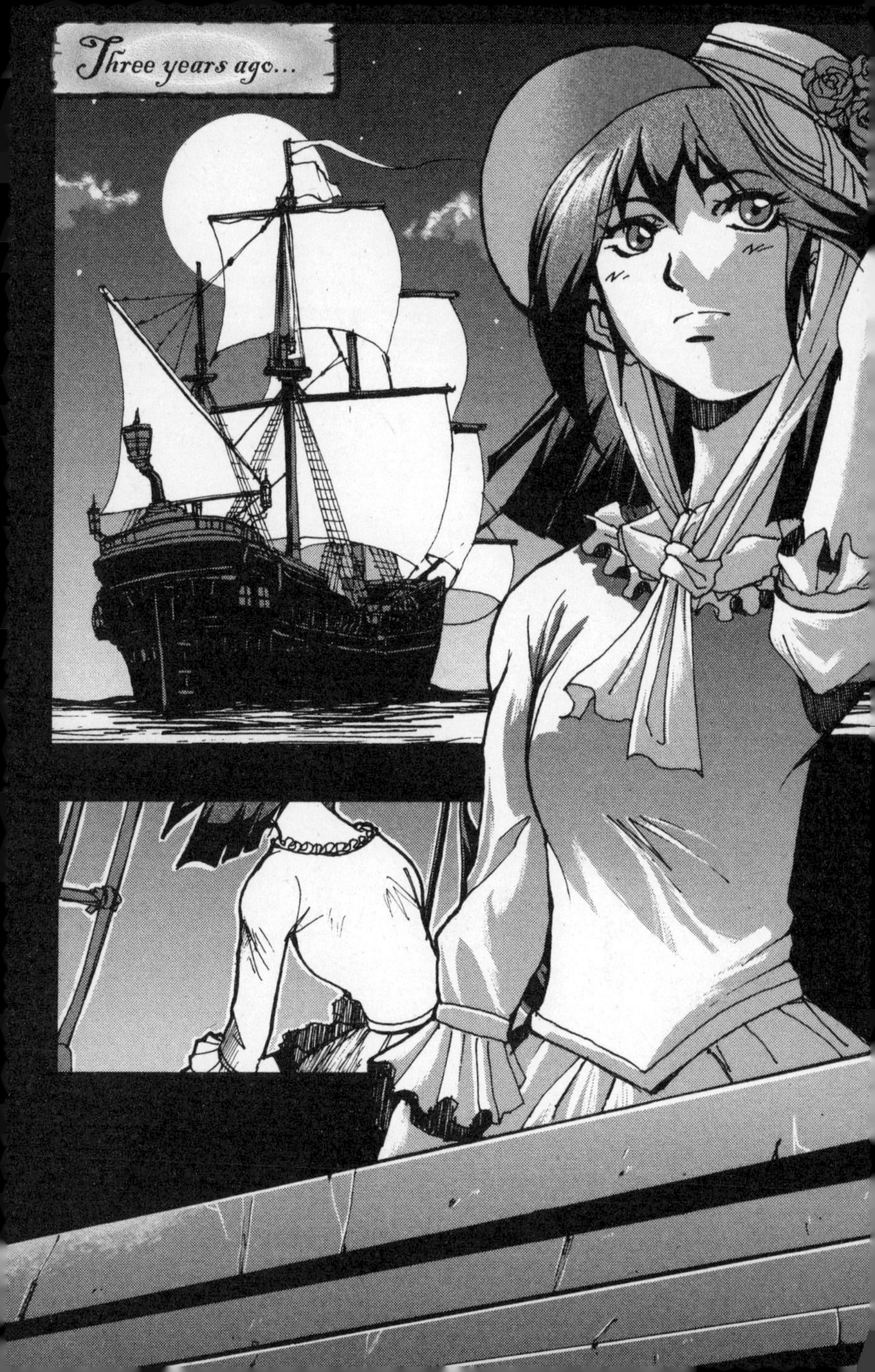
Three years ago...

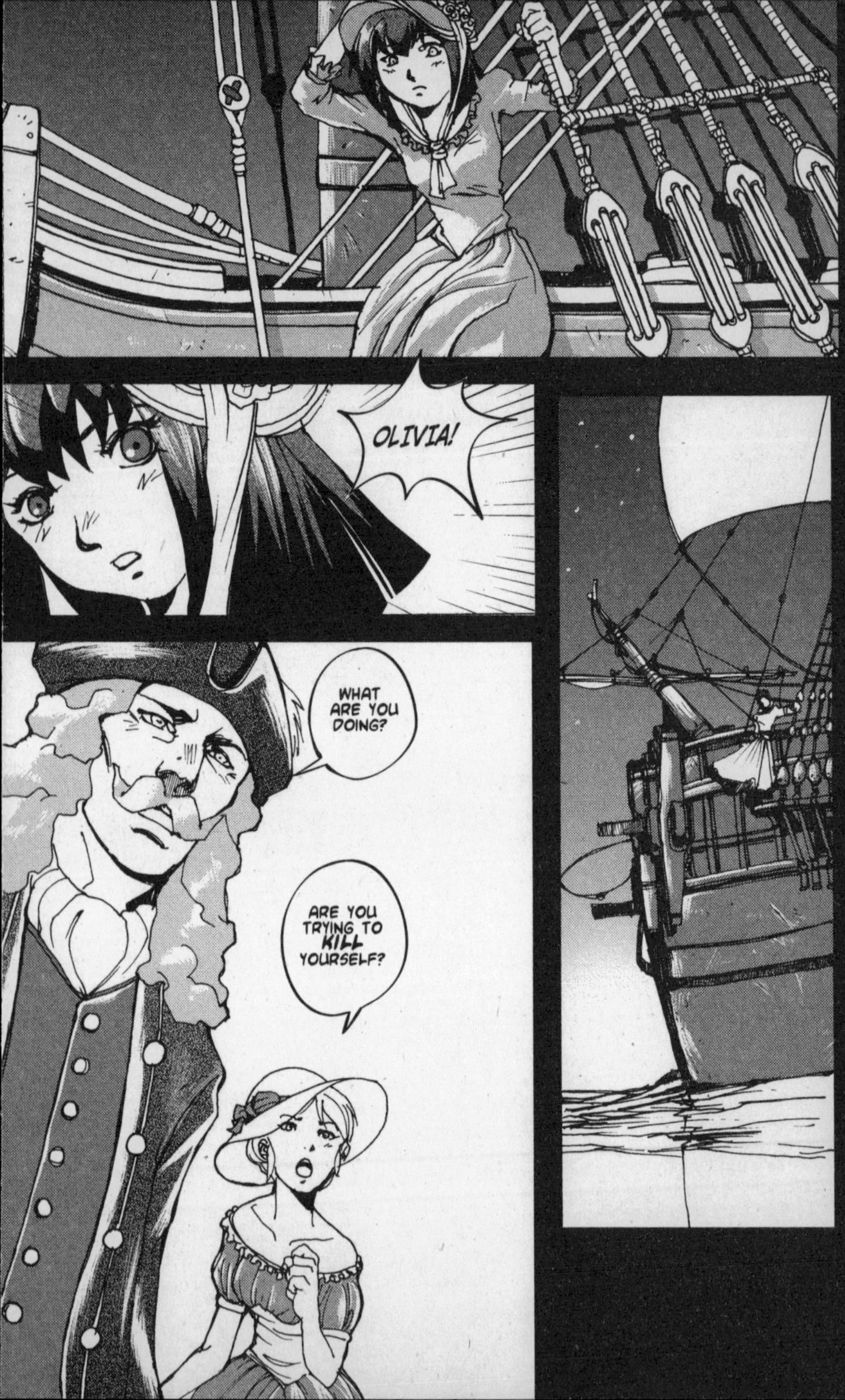
OLIVIA!
WHAT ARE YOU DOING?
ARE YOU TRYING TO KILL YOURSELF?

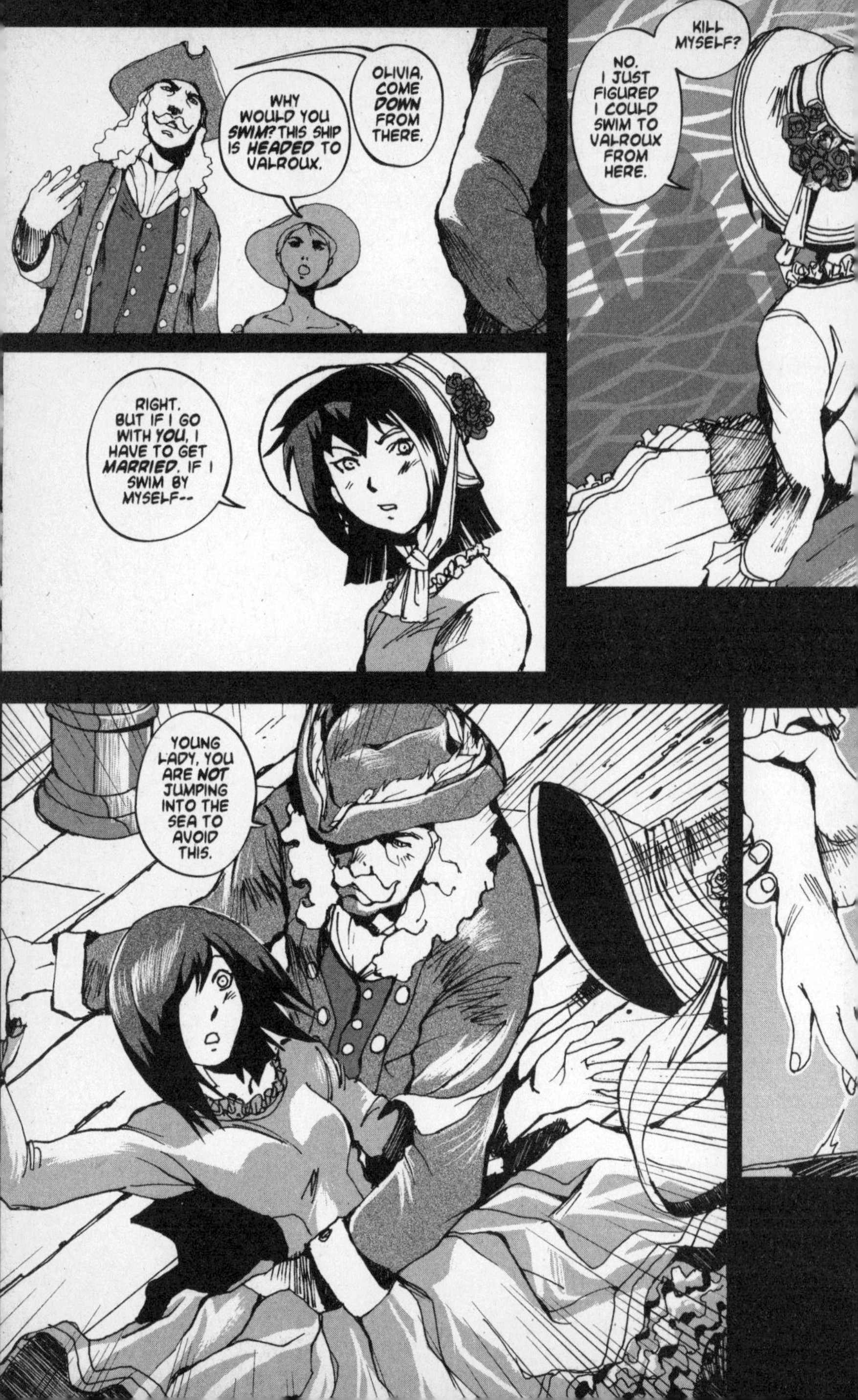
KILL MYSELF?
NO. I JUST FIGURED I COULD SWIM TO VALROUX FROM HERE.
OLIVIA, COME DOWN FROM THERE.
WHY WOULD YOU SWIM? THIS SHIP IS HEADED TO VALROUX.
RIGHT. BUT IF I GO WITH YOU, I HAVE TO GET MARRIED. IF I SWIM BY MYSELF--
YOUNG LADY, YOU ARE NOT JUMPING INTO THE SEA TO AVOID THIS.

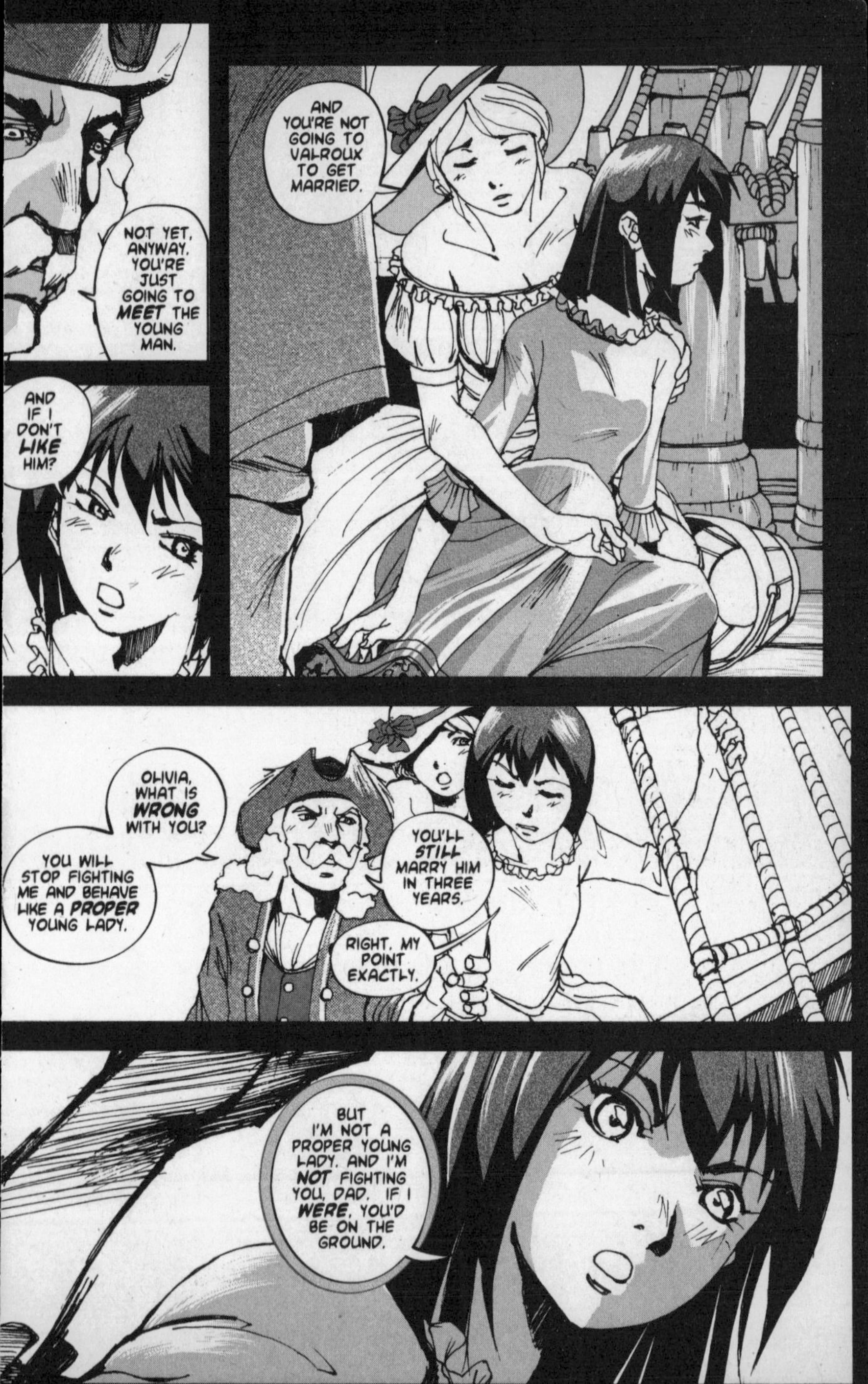
AND YOU'RE NOT GOING TO VALROUX TO GET MARRIED.
NOT YET, ANYWAY. YOU'RE JUST GOING TO *MEET* THE YOUNG MAN.
AND IF I DON'T *LIKE* HIM?
YOU'LL *STILL* MARRY HIM IN THREE YEARS.
RIGHT. MY POINT EXACTLY.
OLIVIA, WHAT IS *WRONG* WITH YOU?
YOU WILL STOP FIGHTING ME AND BEHAVE LIKE A *PROPER* YOUNG LADY.
BUT I'M NOT A PROPER YOUNG LADY. AND I'M *NOT* FIGHTING YOU, DAD. IF I *WERE*, YOU'D BE ON THE GROUND.

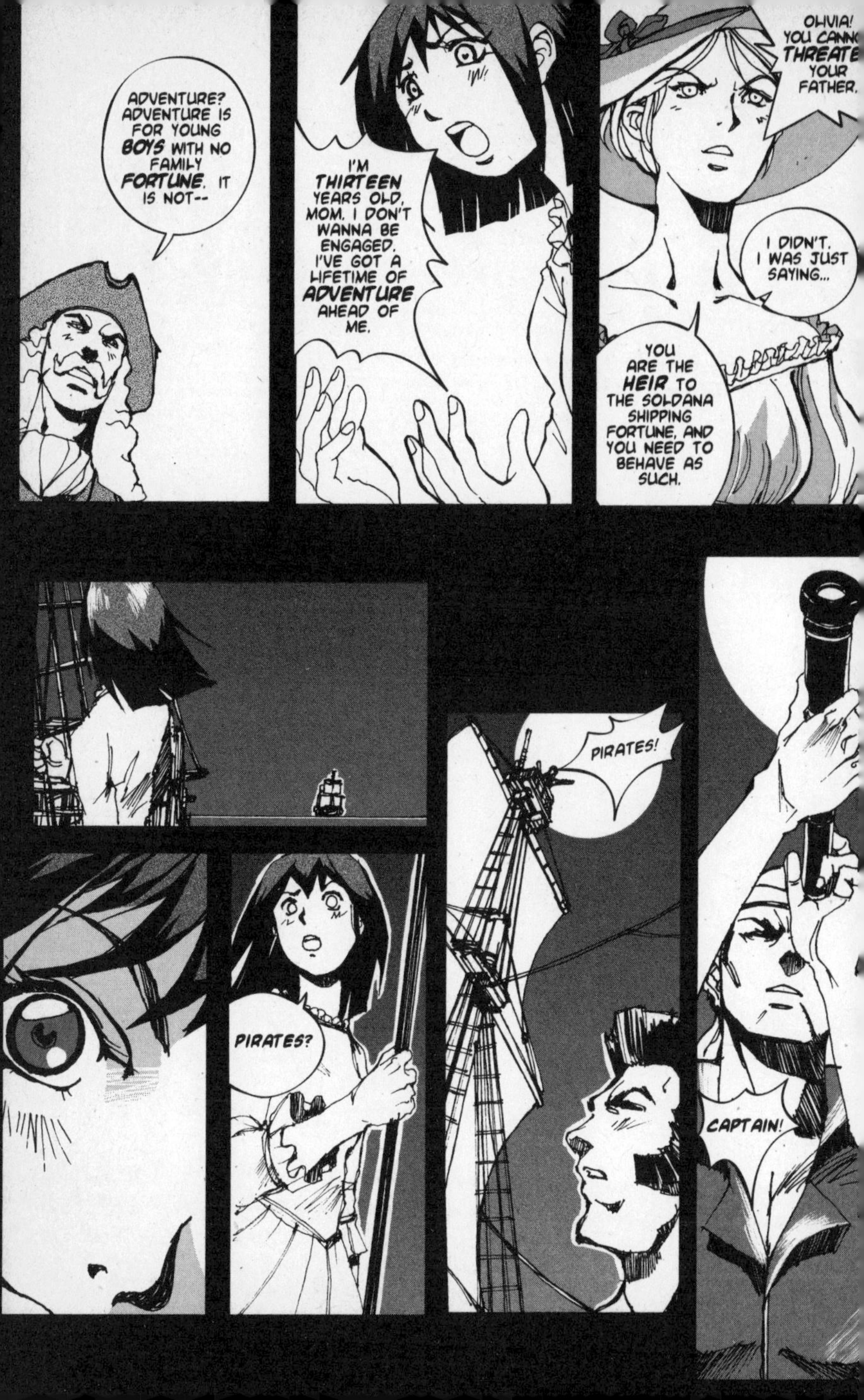
OLIVIA! YOU CANN THREATE YOUR FATHER.
I DIDN'T. I WAS JUST SAYING...
YOU ARE THE HEIR TO THE SOLDANA SHIPPING FORTUNE, AND YOU NEED TO BEHAVE AS SUCH.
I'M THIRTEEN YEARS OLD, MOM. I DON'T WANNA BE ENGAGED. I'VE GOT A LIFETIME OF ADVENTURE AHEAD OF ME.
ADVENTURE? ADVENTURE IS FOR YOUNG BOYS WITH NO FAMILY FORTUNE. IT IS NOT--
CAPTAIN!
PIRATES!
PIRATES?

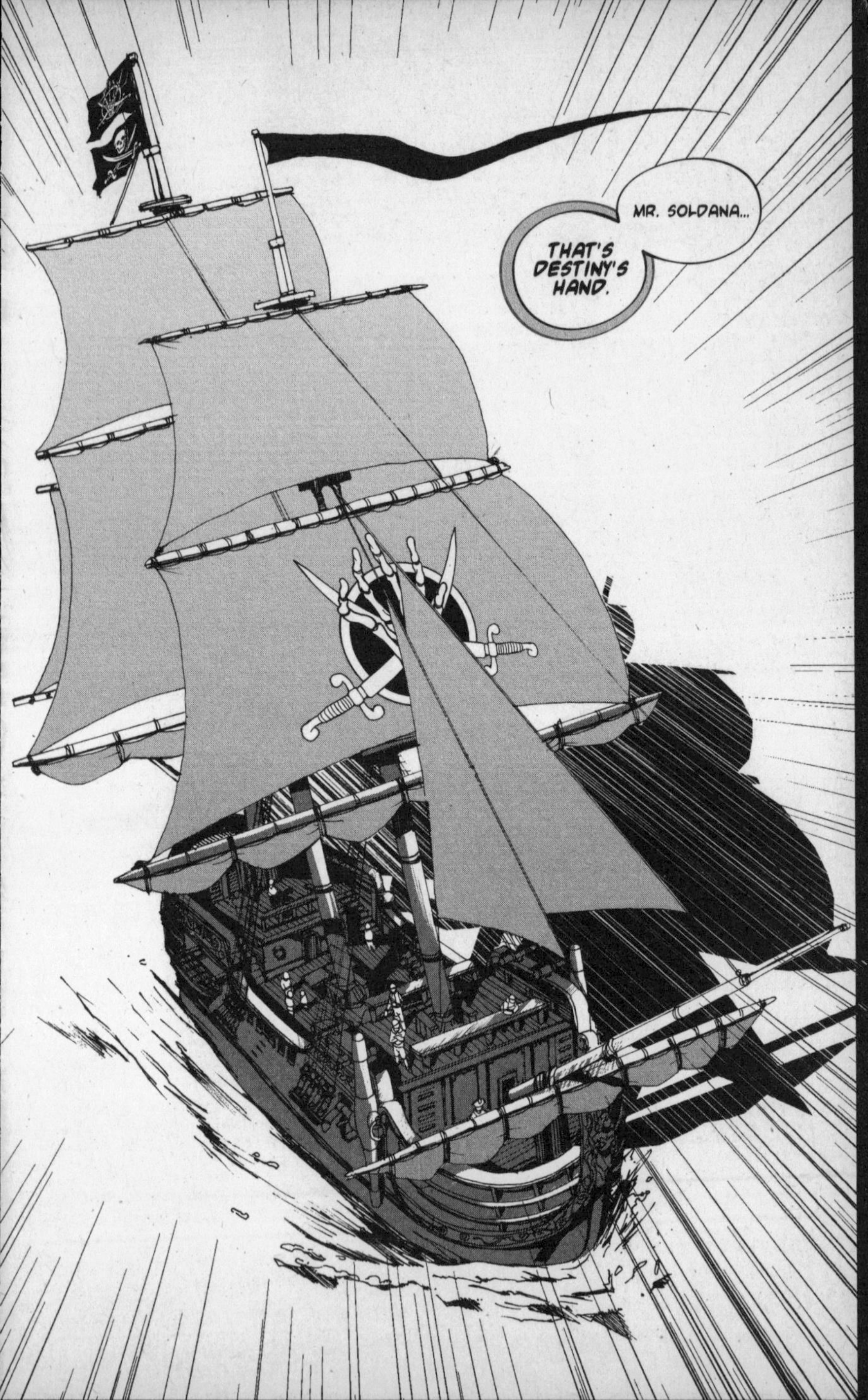
MR. SOLDANA...
THAT'S DESTINY'S HAND.

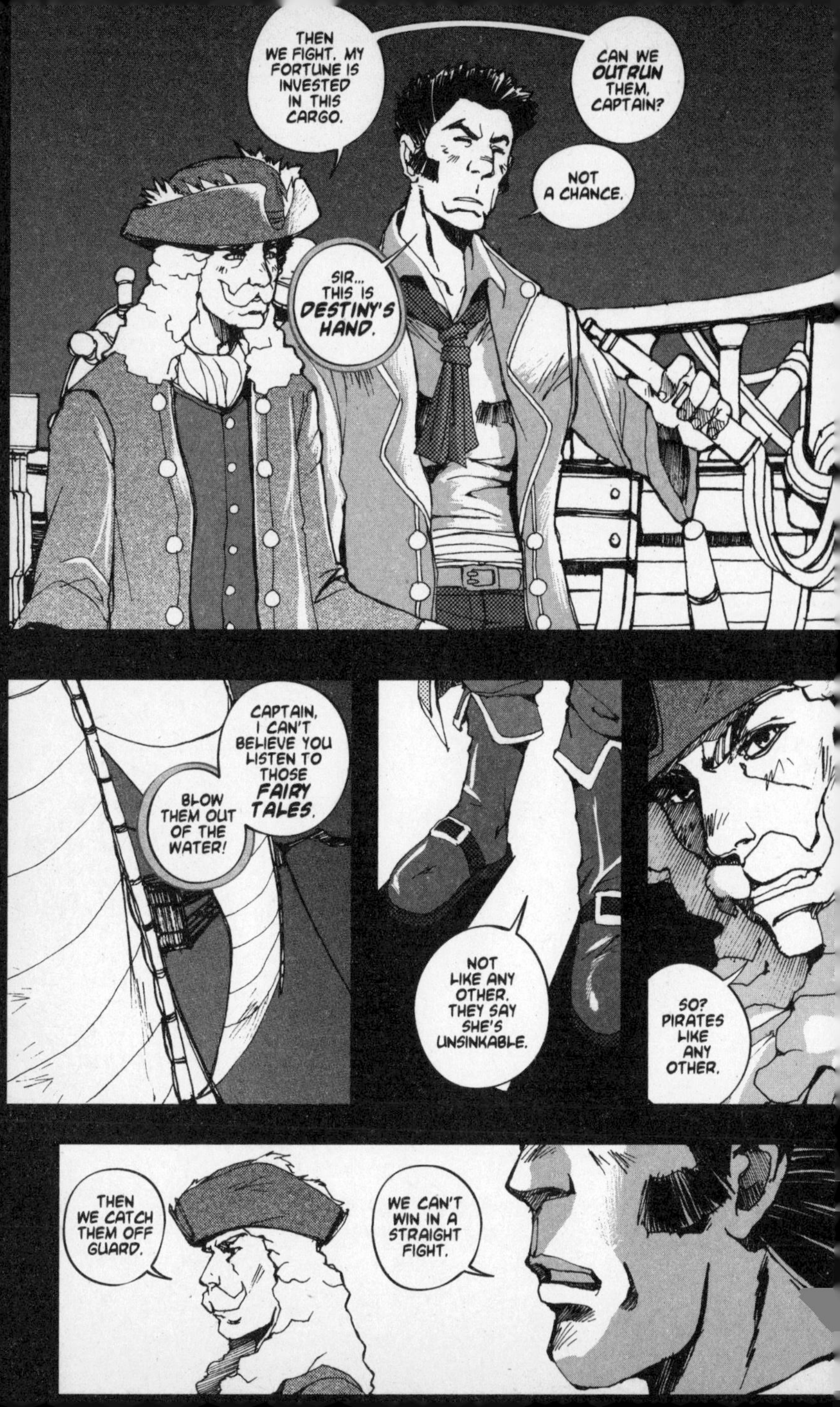
CAN WE OUTRUN THEM, CAPTAIN?
NOT A CHANCE.
THEN WE FIGHT. MY FORTUNE IS INVESTED IN THIS CARGO.
SIR... THIS IS DESTINY'S HAND.
SO? PIRATES LIKE ANY OTHER.
NOT LIKE ANY OTHER. THEY SAY SHE'S UNSINKABLE.
CAPTAIN, I CAN'T BELIEVE YOU LISTEN TO THOSE FAIRY TALES.
BLOW THEM OUT OF THE WATER!
WE CAN'T WIN IN A STRAIGHT FIGHT.
THEN WE CATCH THEM OFF GUARD.

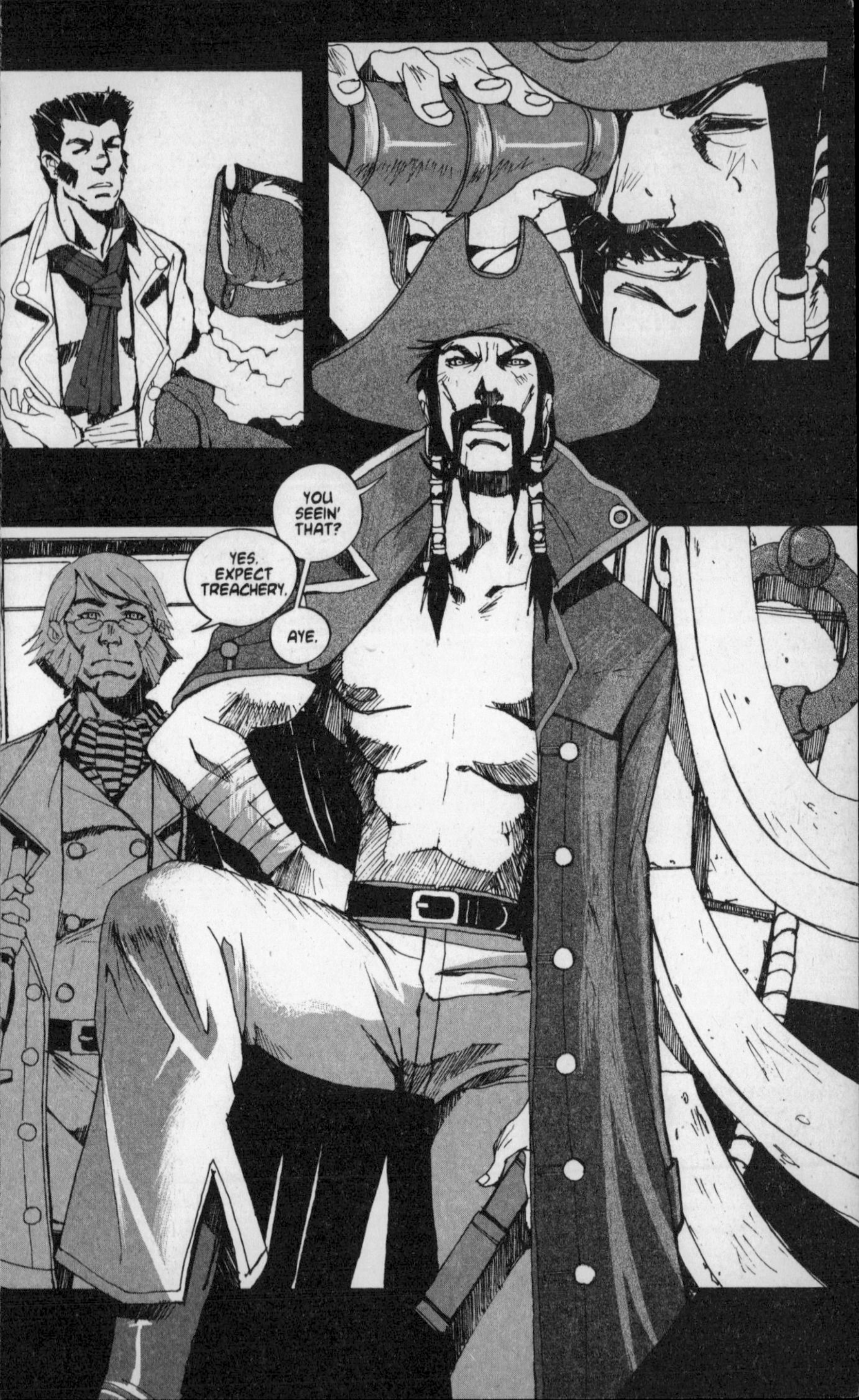
YOU SEEIN' THAT?
YES. EXPECT TREACHERY.
AYE.

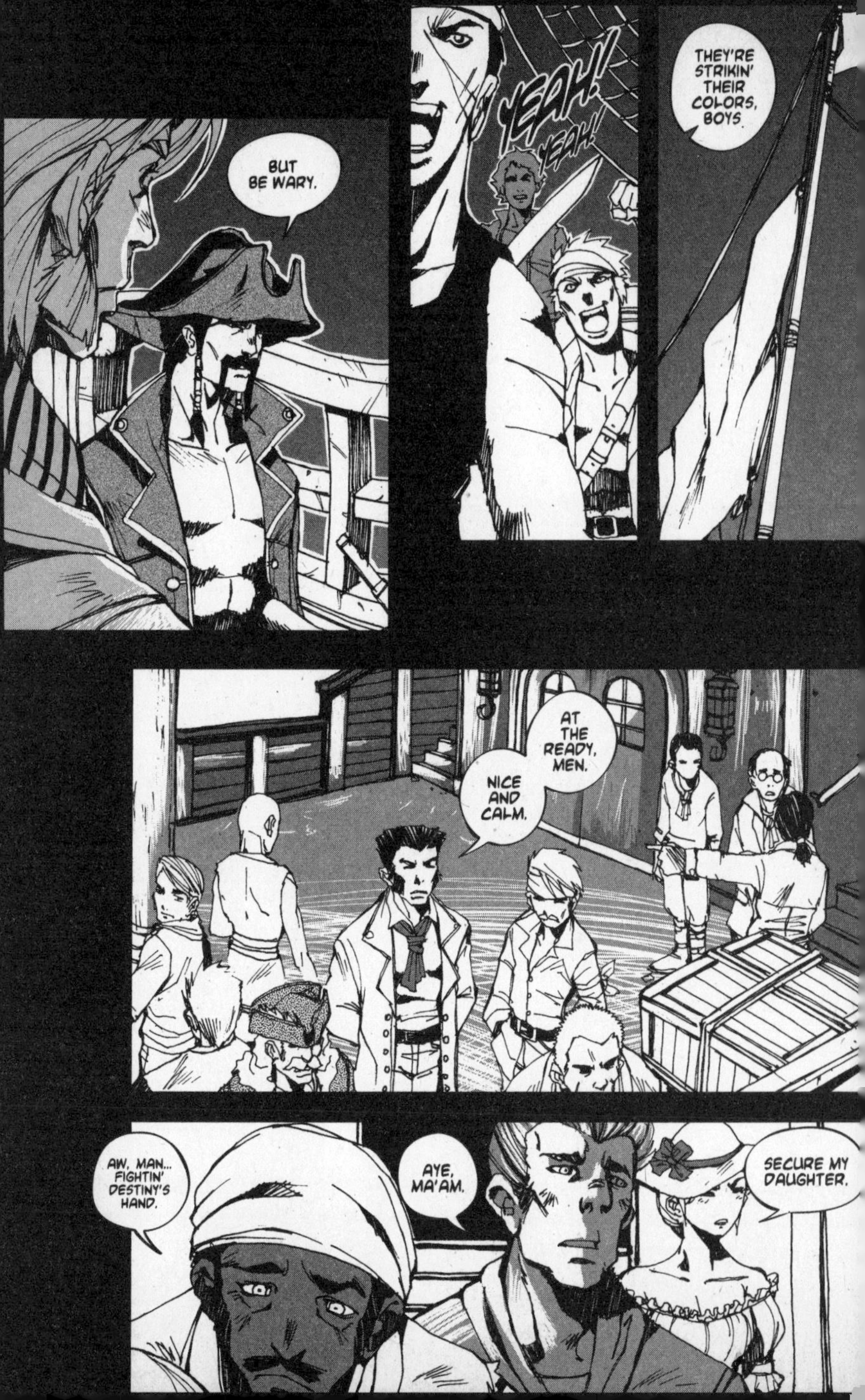
THEY'RE STRIKIN' THEIR COLORS, BOYS.
YEAH! YEAH!
BUT BE WARY.
AT THE READY, MEN.
NICE AND CALM.
SECURE MY DAUGHTER.
AYE, MA'AM.
AW, MAN... FIGHTIN' DESTINY'S HAND.

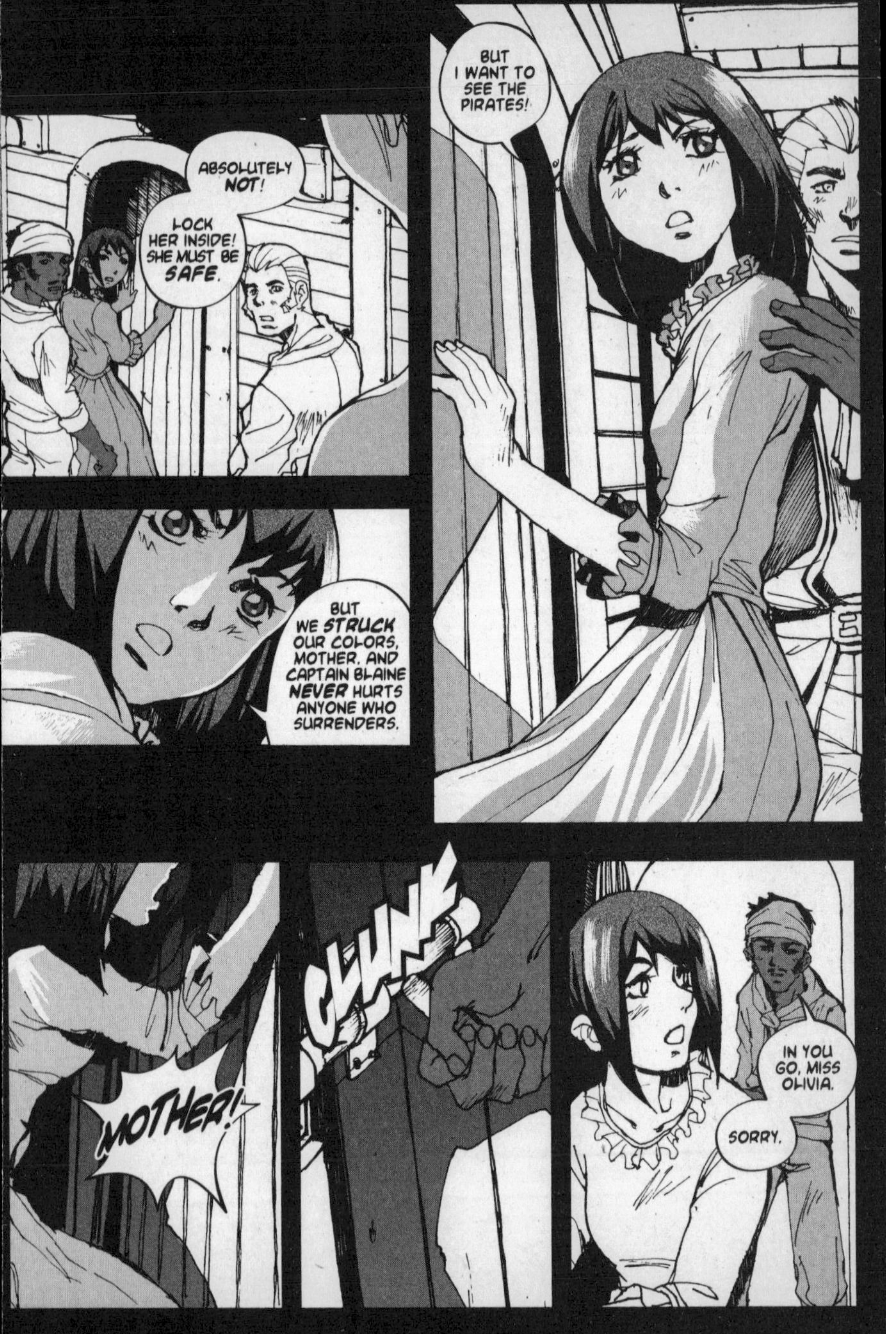
BUT I WANT TO SEE THE PIRATES!
ABSOLUTELY NOT!
LOCK HER INSIDE! SHE MUST BE SAFE.
BUT WE STRUCK OUR COLORS, MOTHER. AND CAPTAIN BLAINE NEVER HURTS ANYONE WHO SURRENDERS.
IN YOU GO, MISS OLIVIA.
SORRY.
CLUNK
MOTHER!

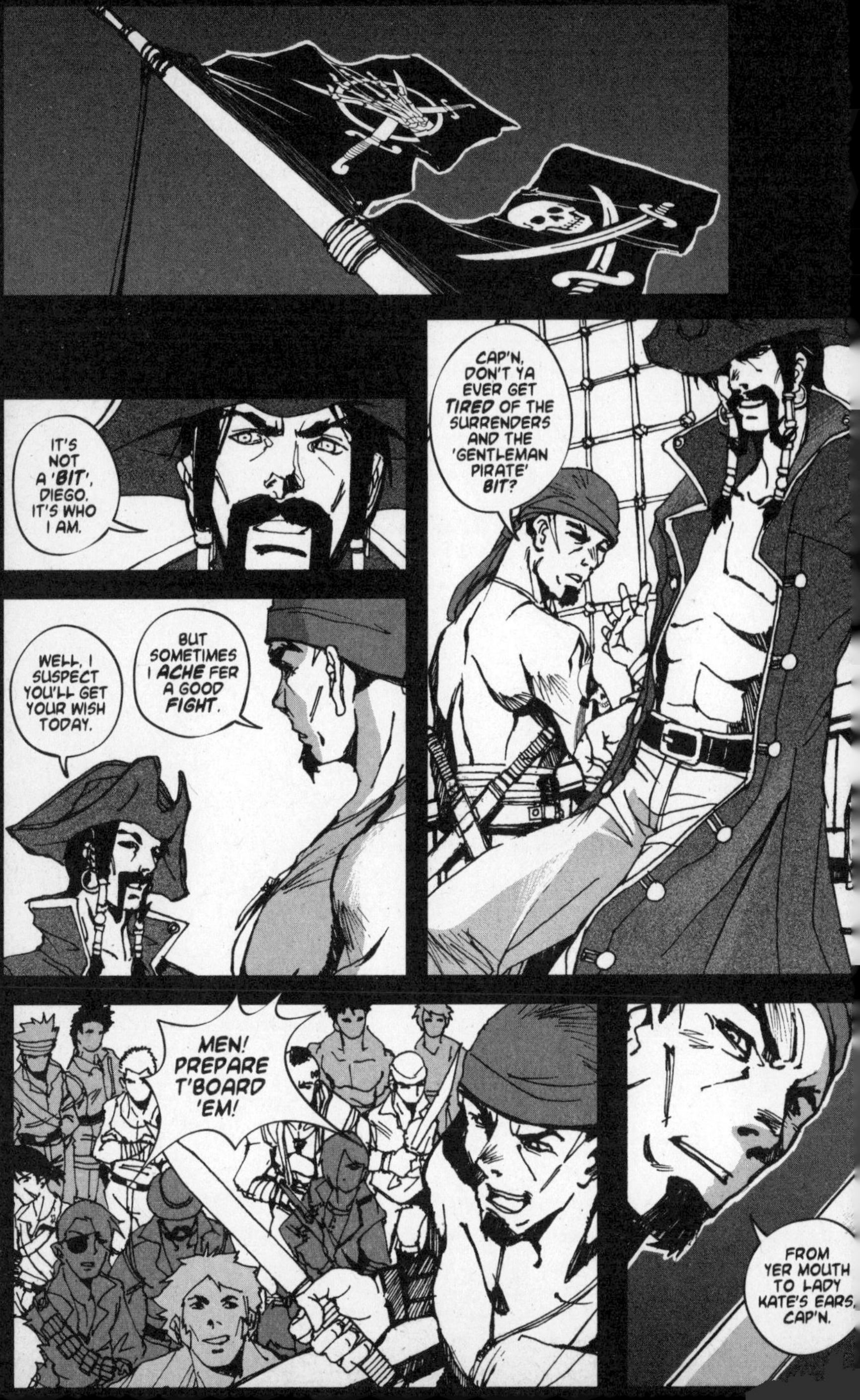
CAP'N, DON'T YA EVER GET TIRED OF THE SURRENDERS AND THE 'GENTLEMAN PIRATE' BIT?
IT'S NOT A 'BIT', DIEGO. IT'S WHO I AM.
BUT SOMETIMES I ACHE FER A GOOD FIGHT.
WELL, I SUSPECT YOU'LL GET YOUR WISH TODAY.
FROM YER MOUTH TO LADY KATE'S EARS, CAP'N.
MEN! PREPARE T'BOARD 'EM!

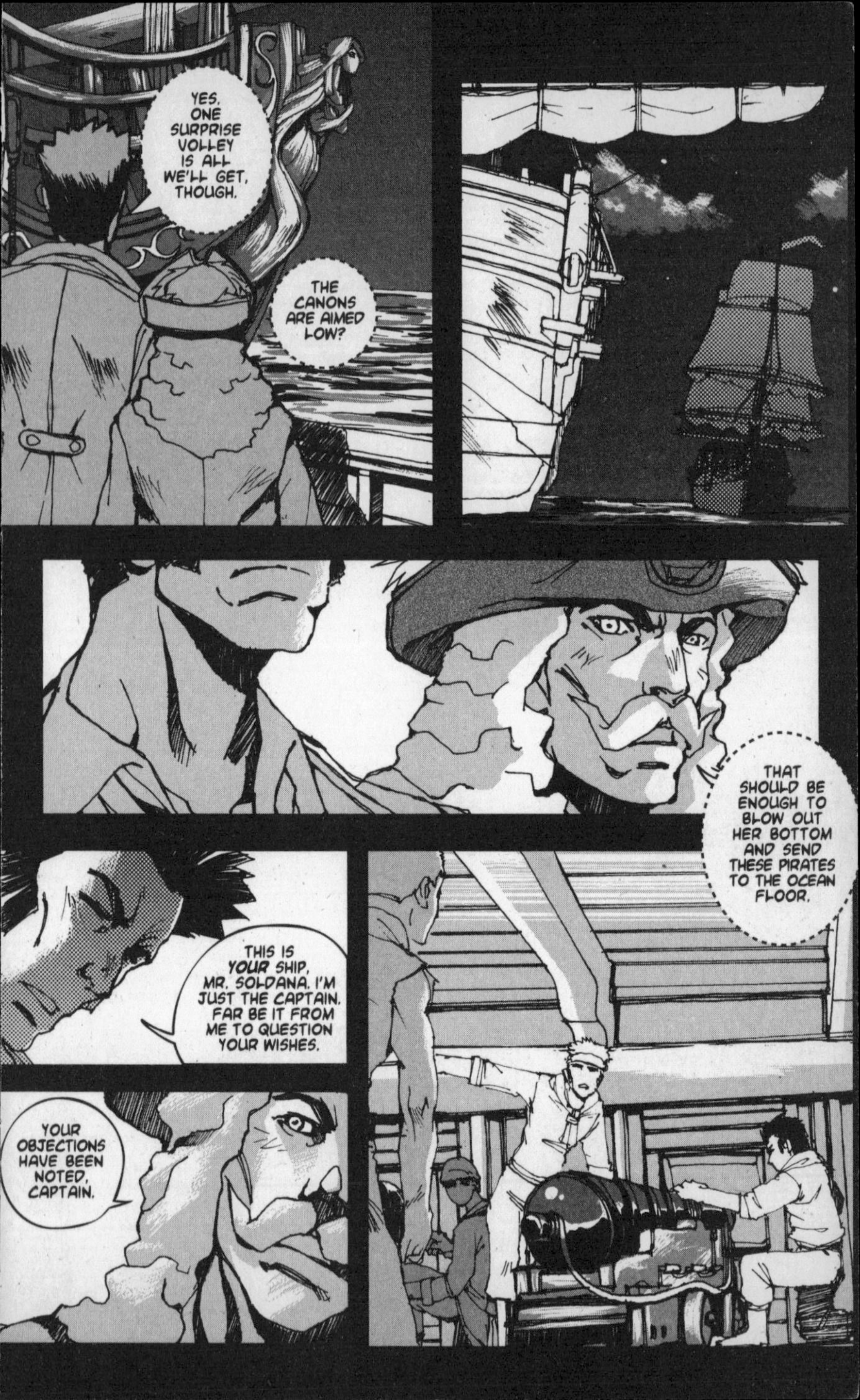
YES. ONE SURPRISE VOLLEY IS ALL WE'LL GET, THOUGH.
THE CANONS ARE AIMED LOW?
THAT SHOULD BE ENOUGH TO BLOW OUT HER BOTTOM AND SEND THESE PIRATES TO THE OCEAN FLOOR.
THIS IS ***YOUR*** SHIP, MR. SOLDANA. I'M JUST THE CAPTAIN. FAR BE IT FROM ME TO QUESTION YOUR WISHES.
YOUR OBJECTIONS HAVE BEEN NOTED, CAPTAIN.

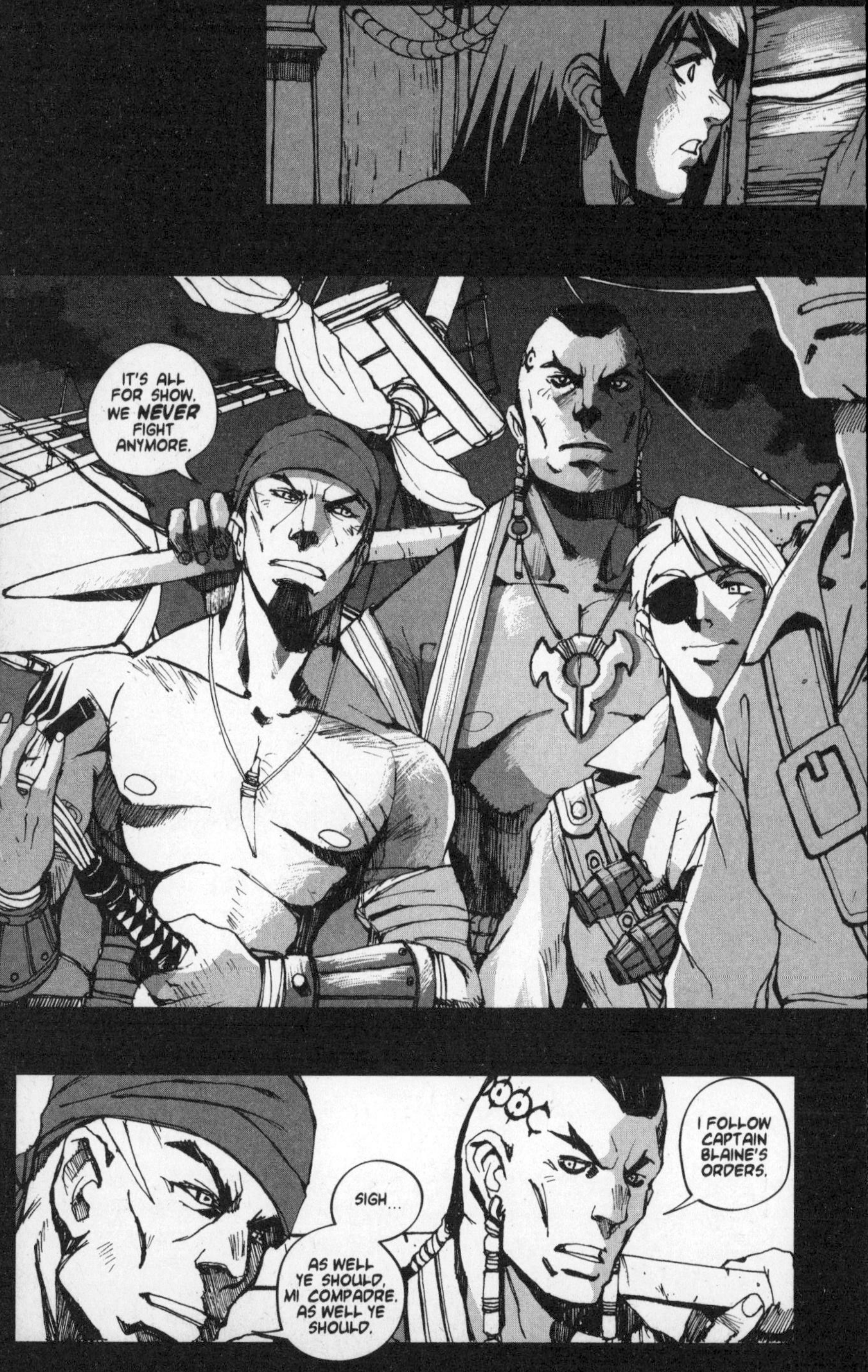
IT'S ALL FOR SHOW. WE **NEVER** FIGHT ANYMORE.
I FOLLOW CAPTAIN BLAINE'S ORDERS.
SIGH...
AS WELL YE SHOULD, MI COMPADRE. AS WELL YE SHOULD.

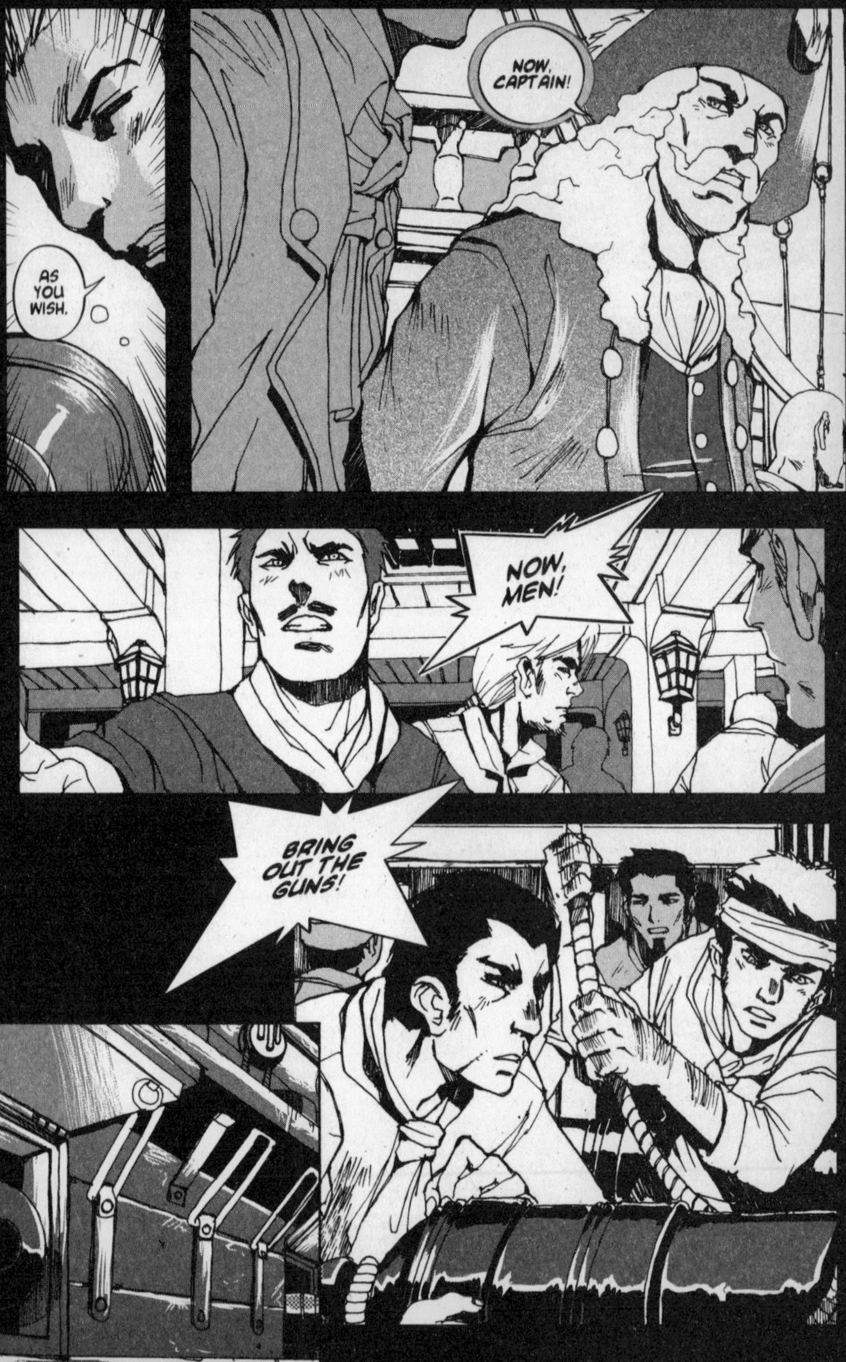
NOW, CAPTAIN!
AS YOU WISH.
NOW, MEN!
BRING OUT THE GUNS!

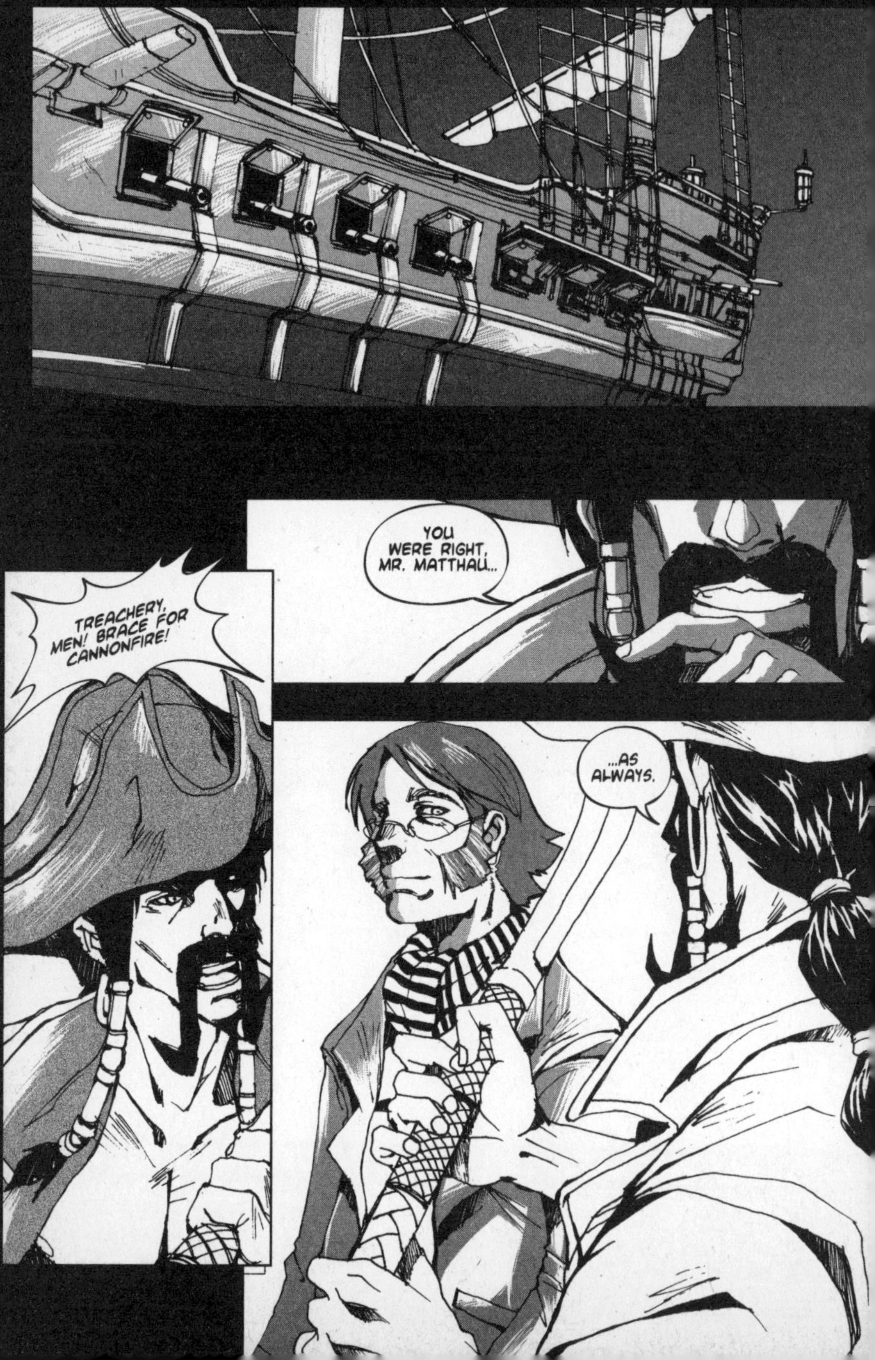
YOU WERE RIGHT, MR. MATTHAU...
...AS ALWAYS.
TREACHERY, MEN! BRACE FOR CANNONFIRE!

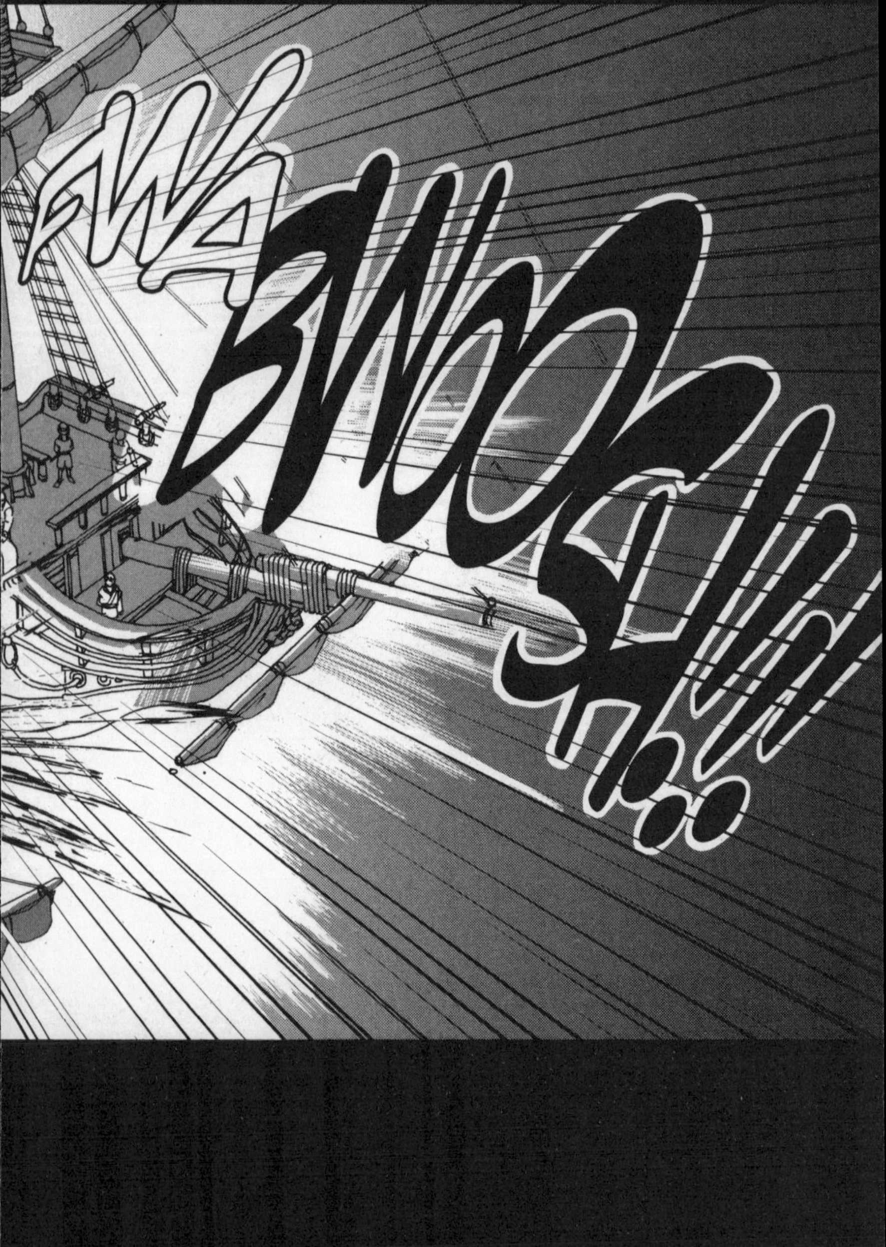
FWA
BWOOSH!!

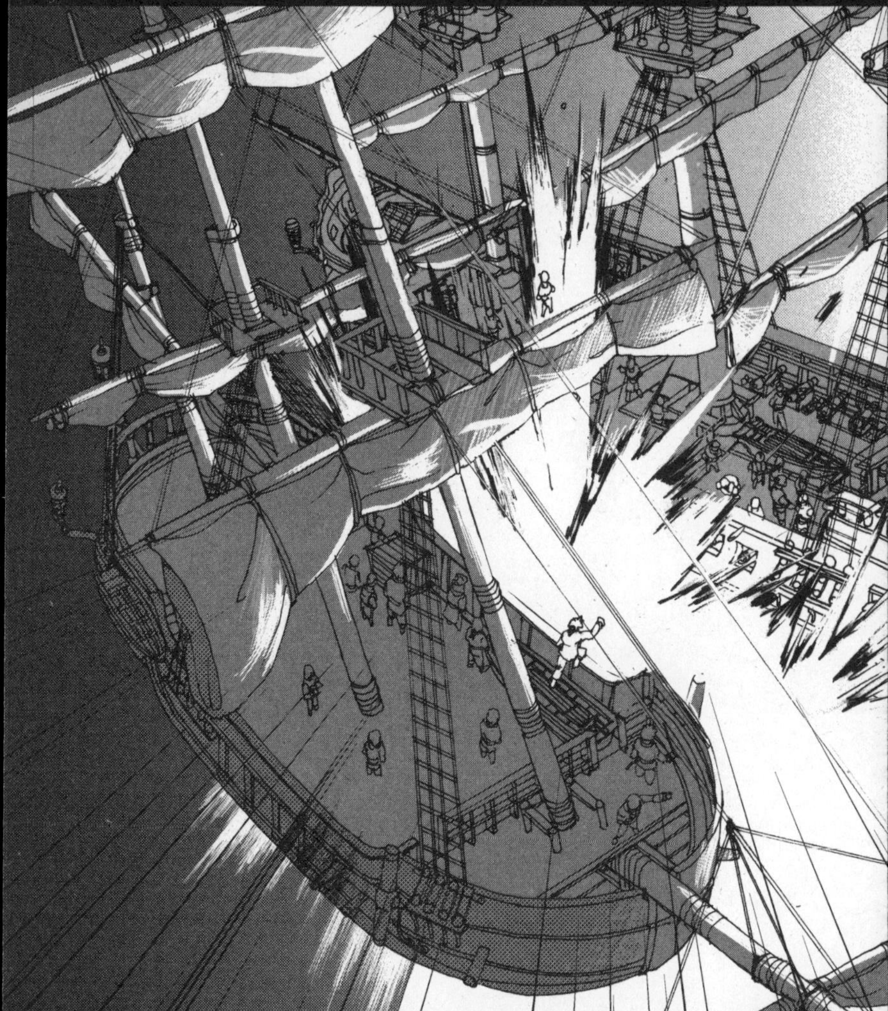

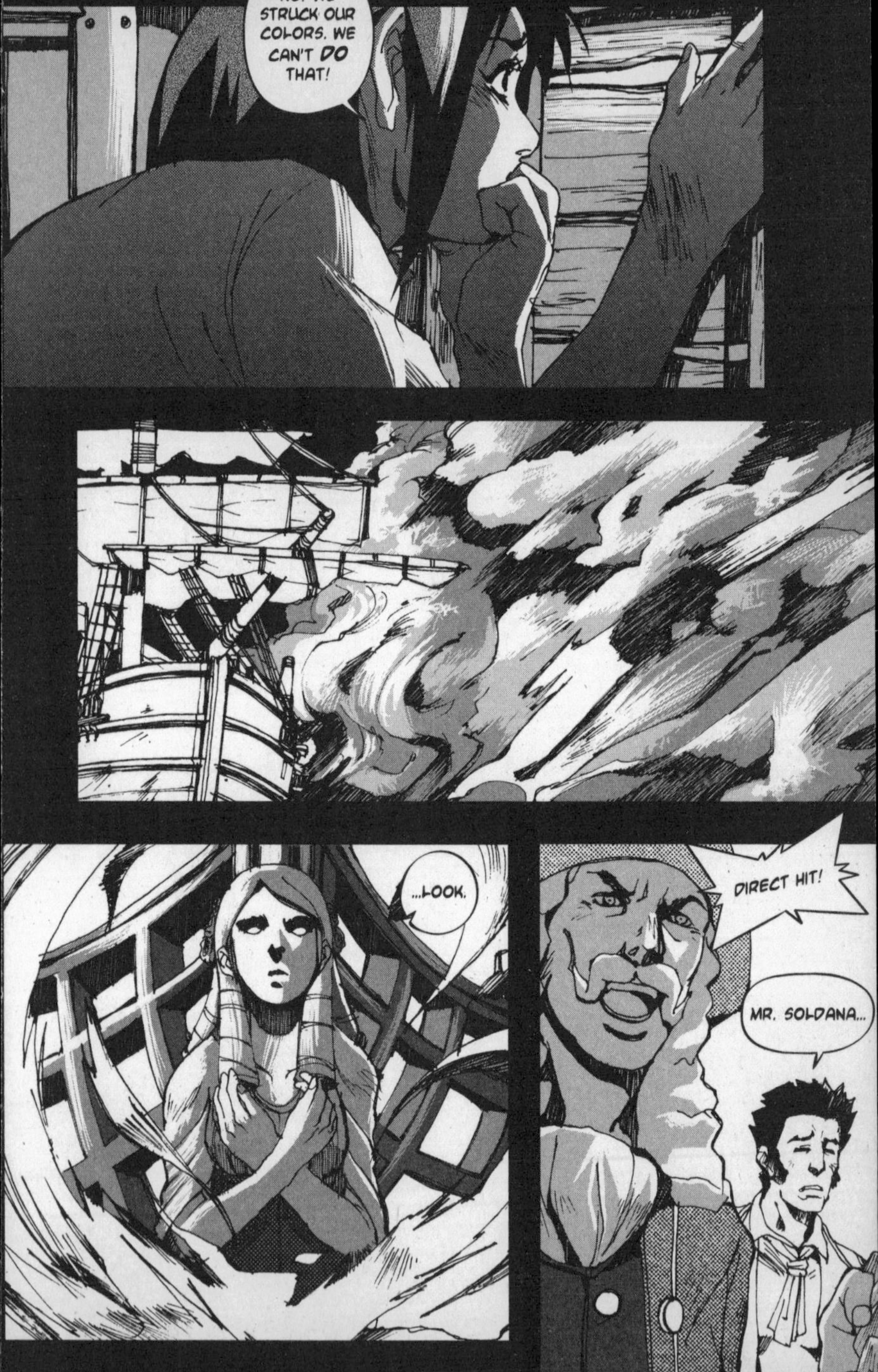
NO! WE STRUCK OUR COLORS. WE CAN'T DO THAT!
DIRECT HIT!
MR. SOLDANA...
...LOOK.

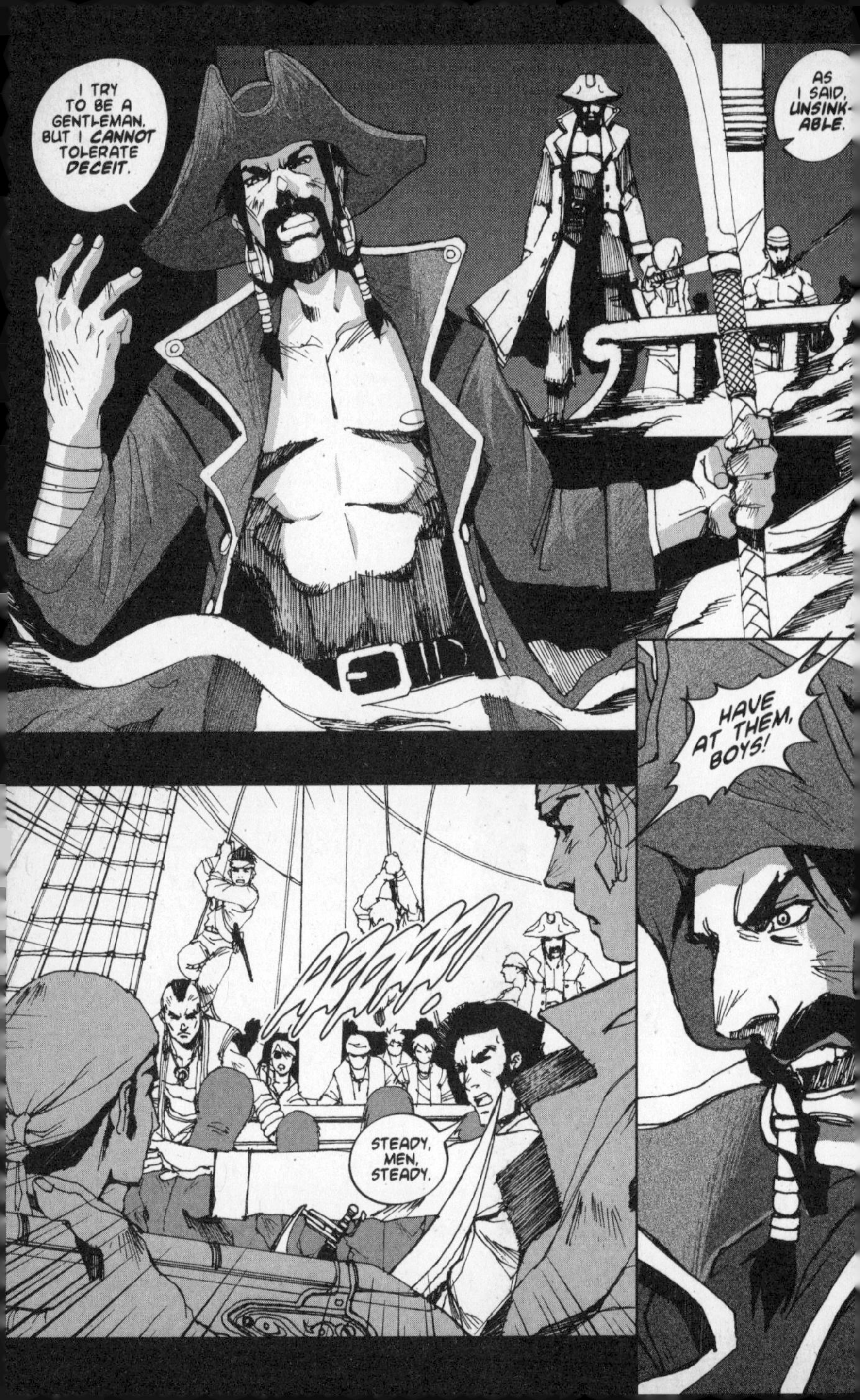
AS I SAID, UNSINKABLE.
I TRY TO BE A GENTLEMAN. BUT I CANNOT TOLERATE DECEIT.
HAVE AT THEM, BOYS!
STEADY, MEN, STEADY.

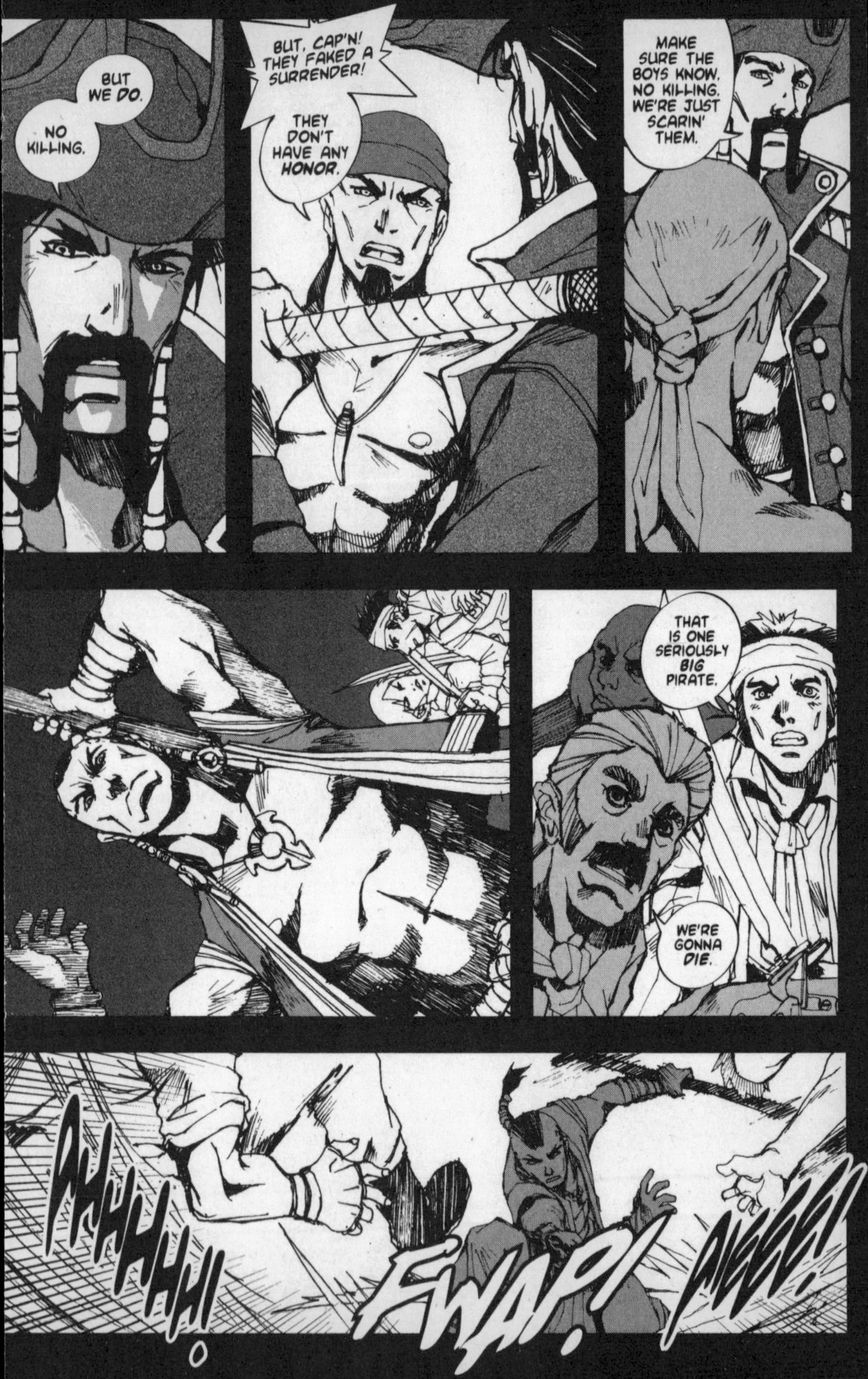
MAKE SURE THE BOYS KNOW. NO KILLING. WE'RE JUST SCARIN' THEM.
BUT, CAP'N! THEY FAKED A SURRENDER!
THEY DON'T HAVE ANY HONOR.
BUT WE DO.
NO KILLING.
THAT IS ONE SERIOUSLY BIG PIRATE.
WE'RE GONNA DIE.
FWAP!

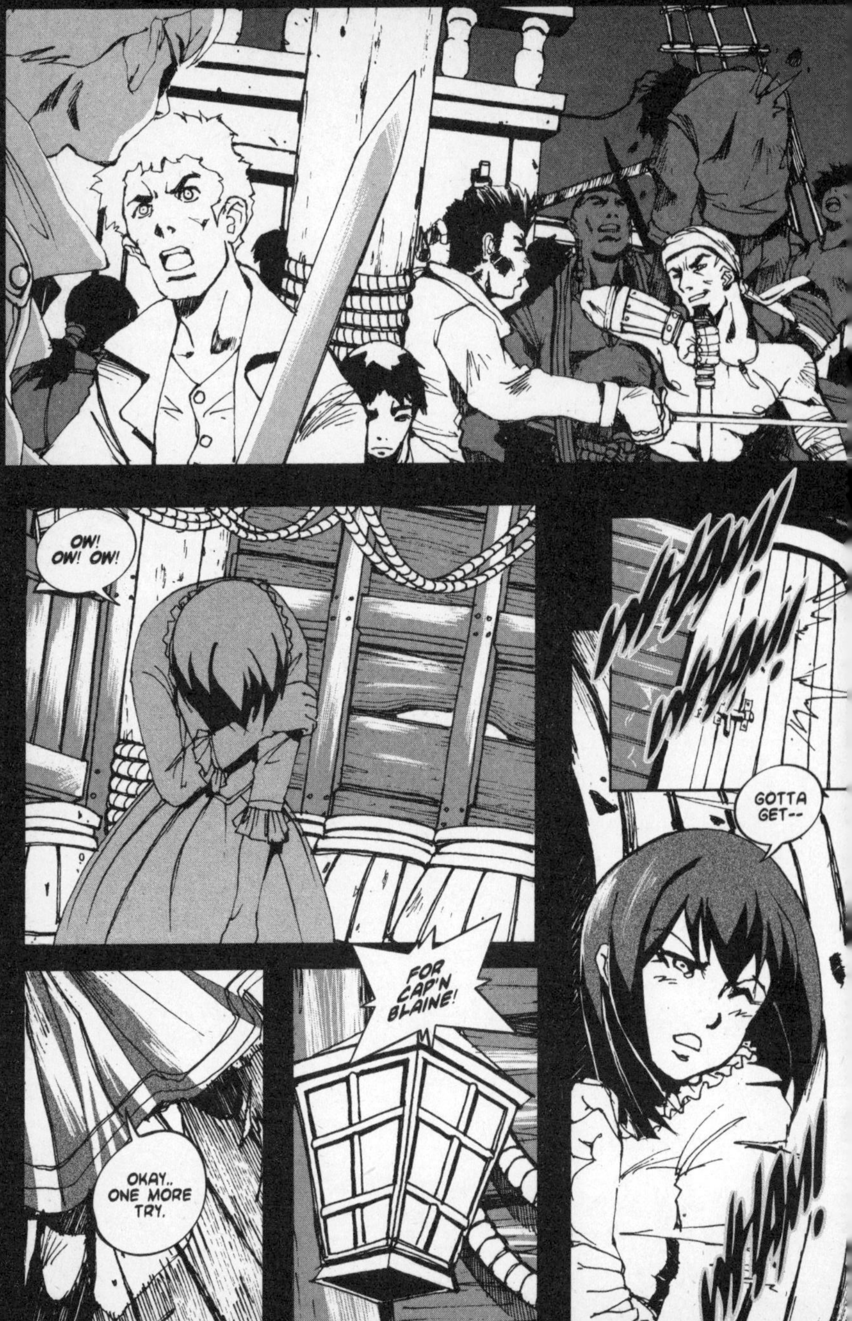
WHAM! WHAM!
OW! OW! OW!
GOTTA GET--
WHAM!
FOR CAP'N BLAINE!
OKAY.. ONE MORE TRY.

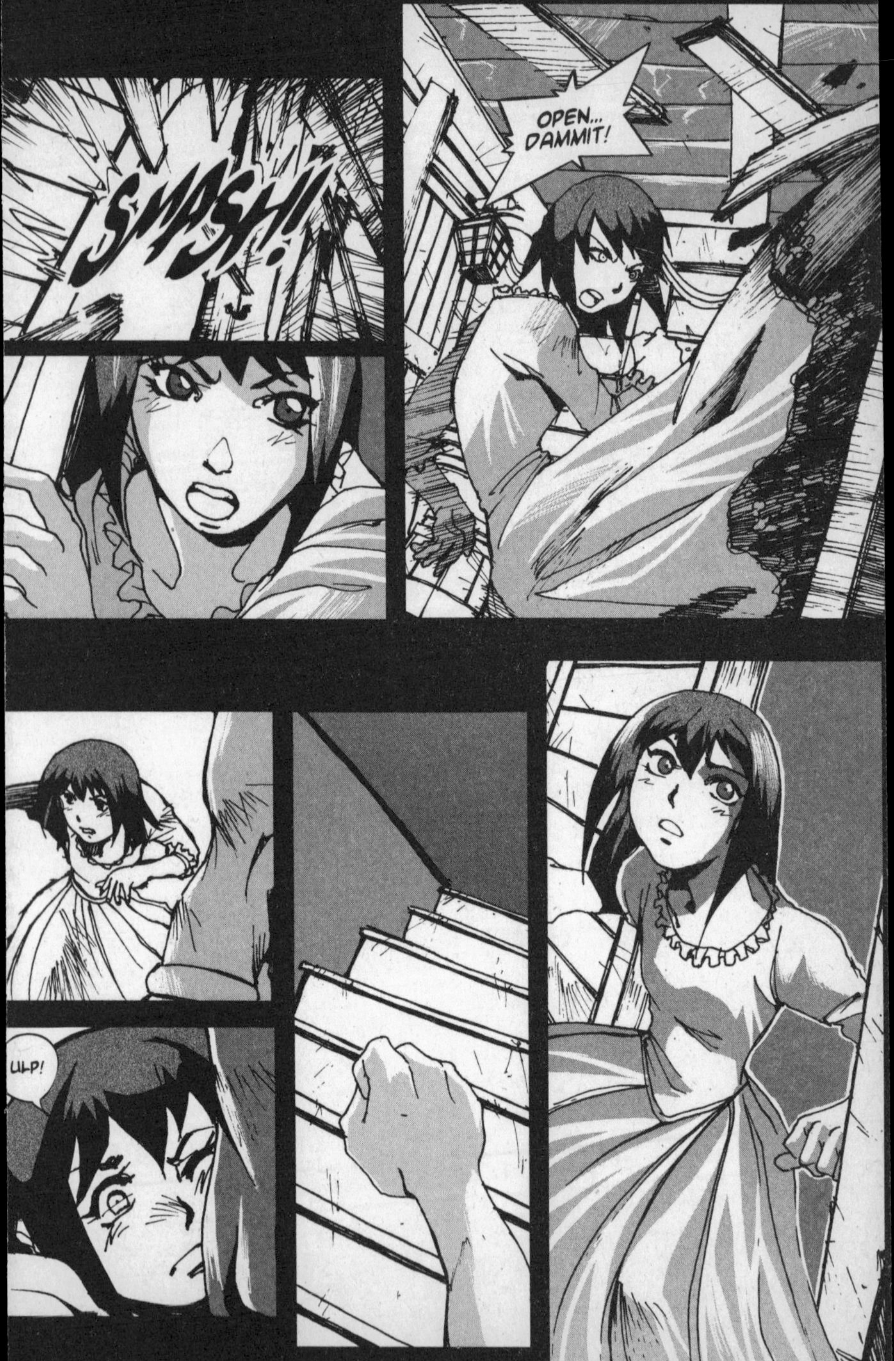
OPEN... DAMMIT!
SMASH!!
ULP!

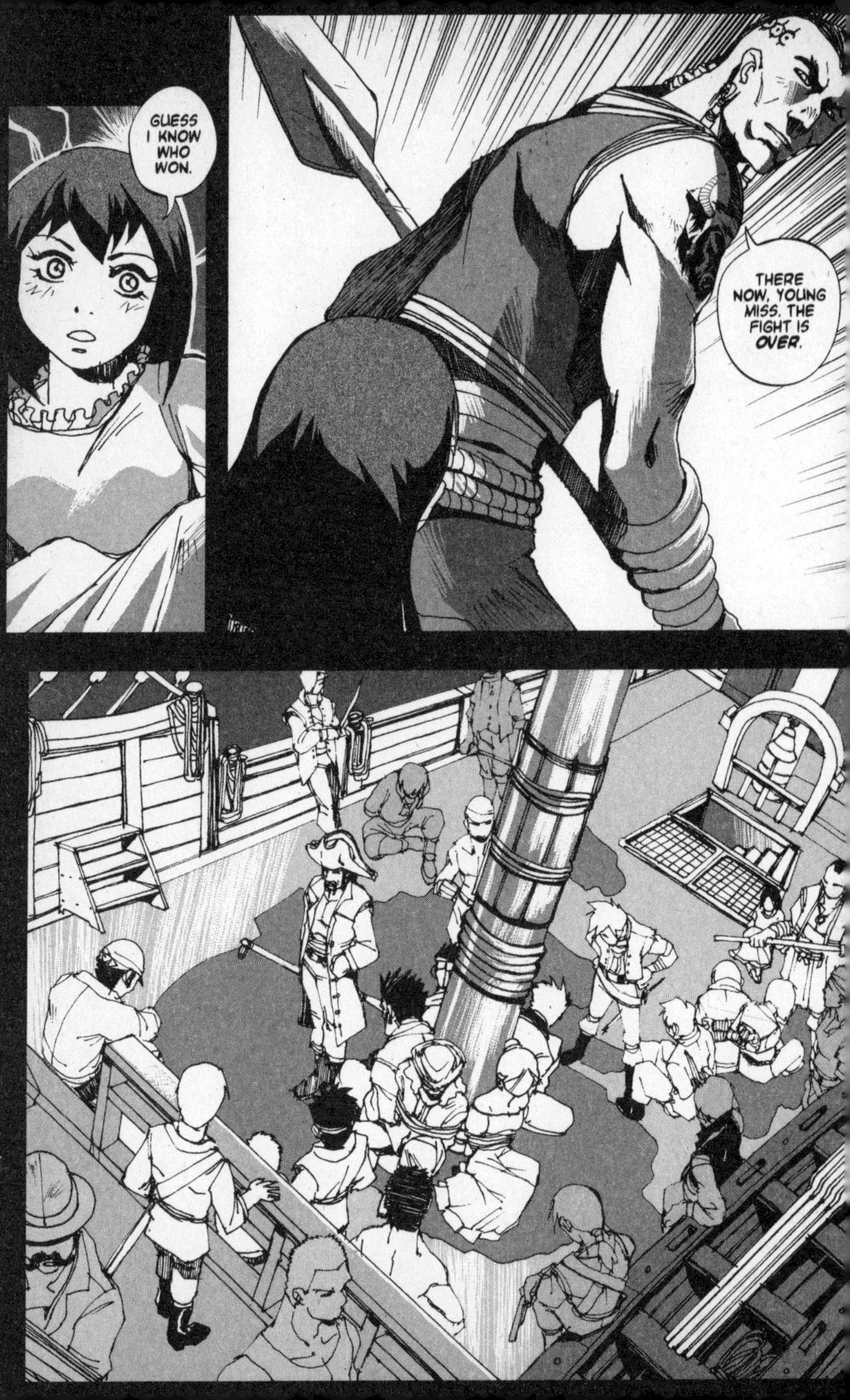
THERE NOW, YOUNG MISS. THE FIGHT IS *OVER*.
GUESS I KNOW WHO WON.

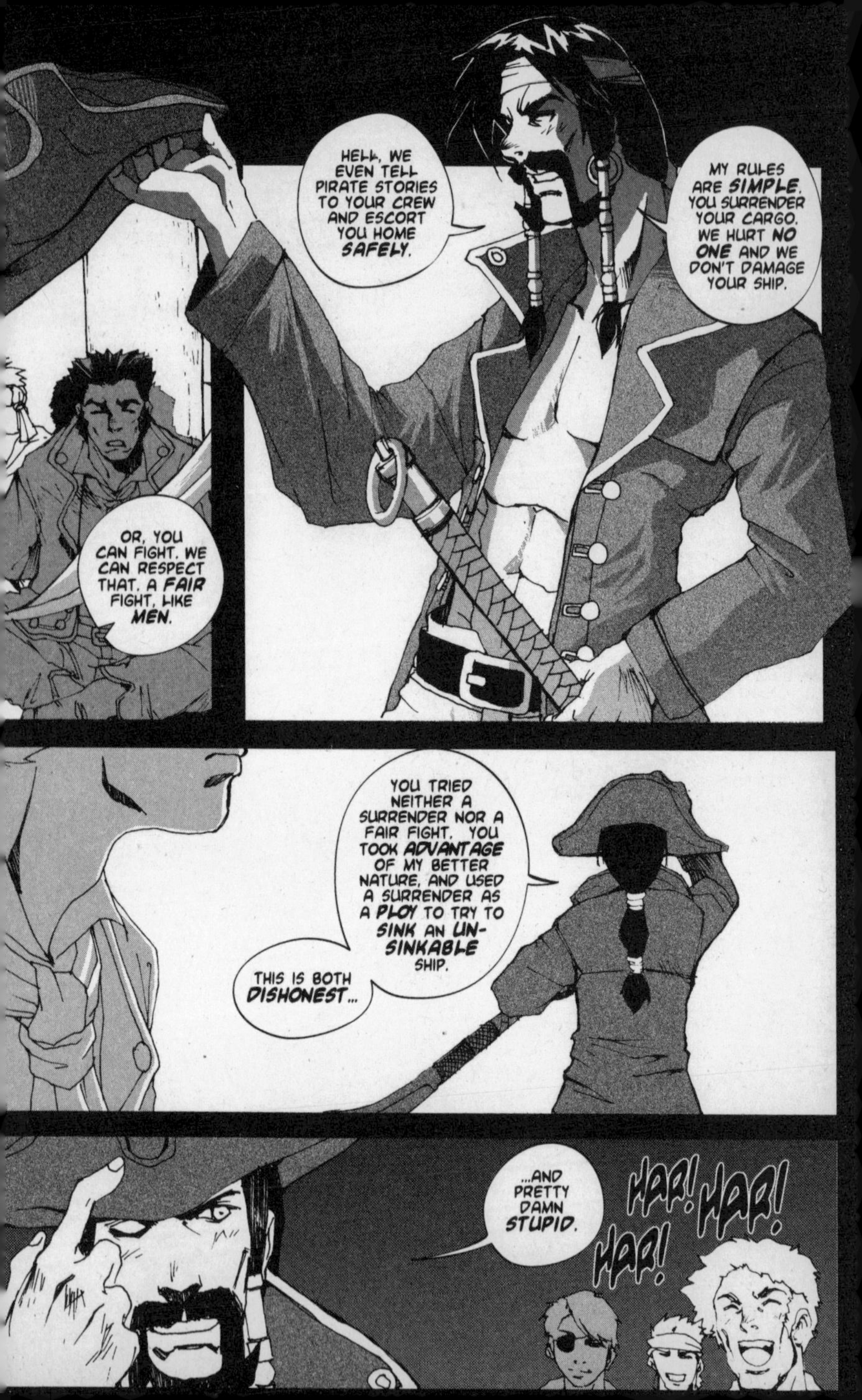
MY RULES ARE SIMPLE. YOU SURRENDER YOUR CARGO. WE HURT NO ONE AND WE DON'T DAMAGE YOUR SHIP.
HELL, WE EVEN TELL PIRATE STORIES TO YOUR CREW AND ESCORT YOU HOME SAFELY.
OR, YOU CAN FIGHT. WE CAN RESPECT THAT. A FAIR FIGHT, LIKE MEN.
YOU TRIED NEITHER A SURRENDER NOR A FAIR FIGHT. YOU TOOK ADVANTAGE OF MY BETTER NATURE, AND USED A SURRENDER AS A PLOY TO TRY TO SINK AN UN-SINKABLE SHIP.
THIS IS BOTH DISHONEST...
...AND PRETTY DAMN STUPID.
HAR! HAR! HAR!

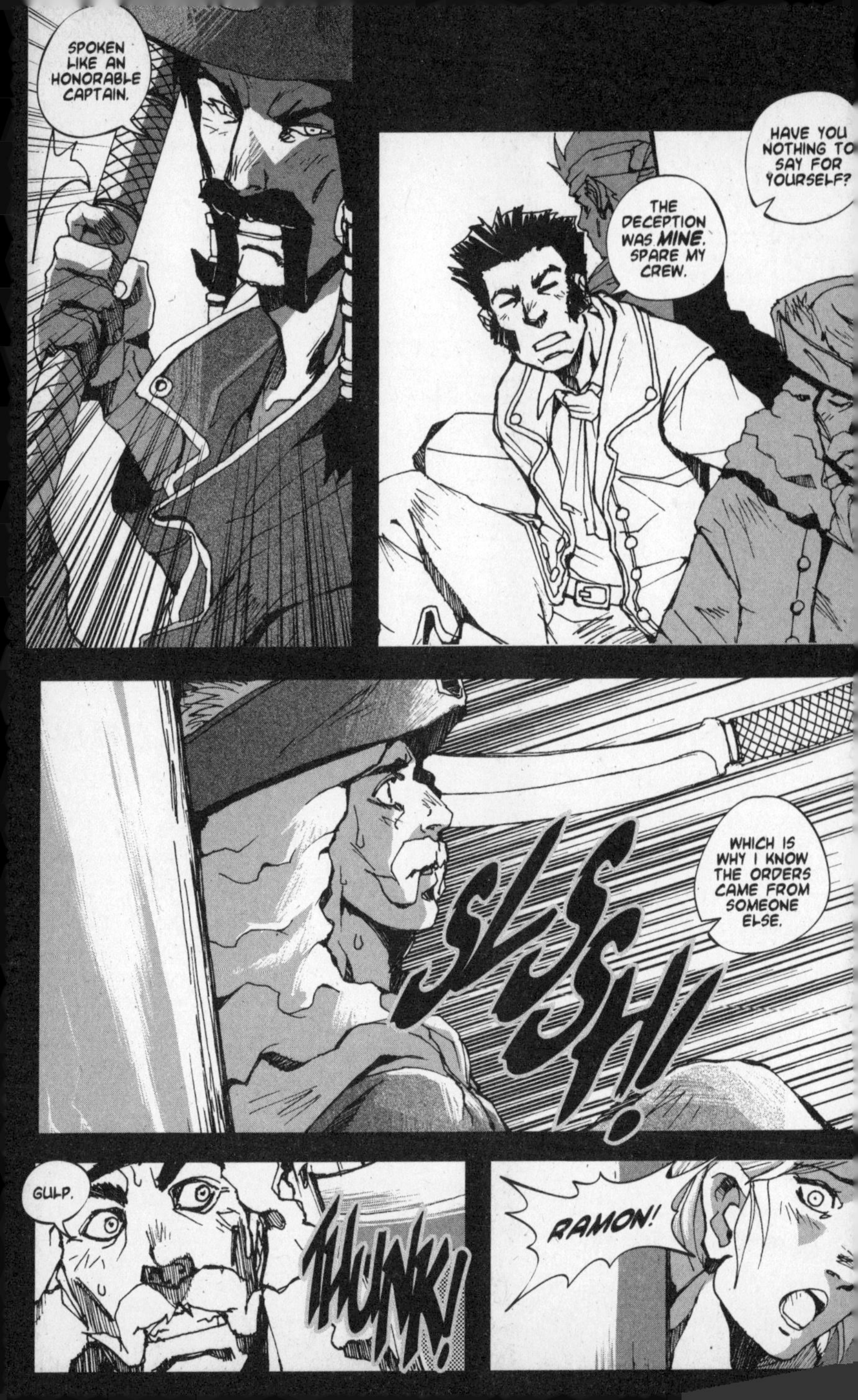
HAVE YOU NOTHING TO SAY FOR YOURSELF?
THE DECEPTION WAS MINE. SPARE MY CREW.
SPOKEN LIKE AN HONORABLE CAPTAIN.
WHICH IS WHY I KNOW THE ORDERS CAME FROM SOMEONE ELSE.
RAMON!
GULP.
THUNK!

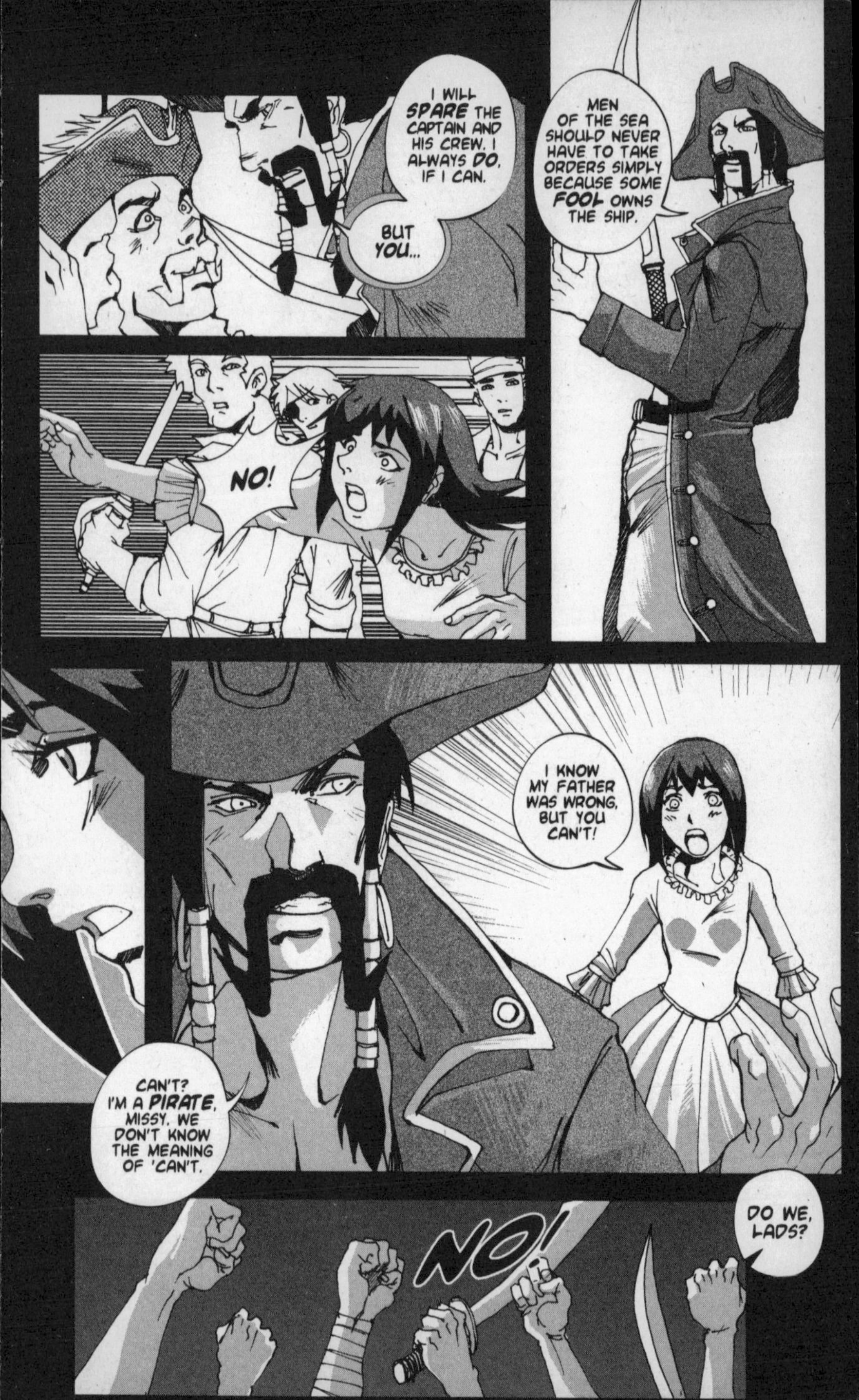
MEN OF THE SEA SHOULD NEVER HAVE TO TAKE ORDERS SIMPLY BECAUSE SOME FOOL OWNS THE SHIP.
I WILL SPARE THE CAPTAIN AND HIS CREW. I ALWAYS DO, IF I CAN.
BUT YOU...
NO!
I KNOW MY FATHER WAS WRONG, BUT YOU CAN'T!
CAN'T? I'M A PIRATE, MISSY. WE DON'T KNOW THE MEANING OF 'CAN'T.
DO WE, LADS?
NO!

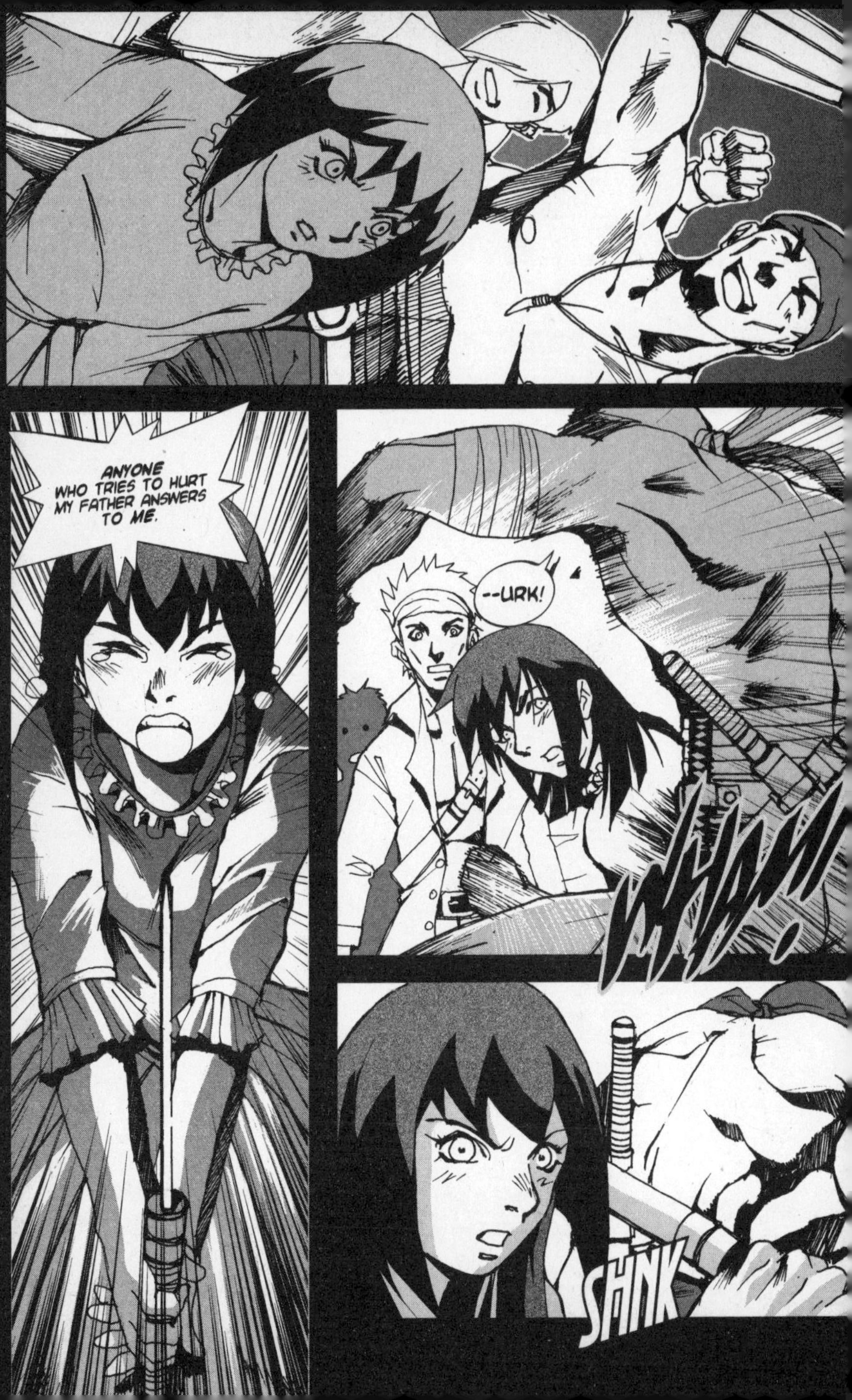
--URK!
SHNK
ANYONE WHO TRIES TO HURT MY FATHER ANSWERS TO ME.

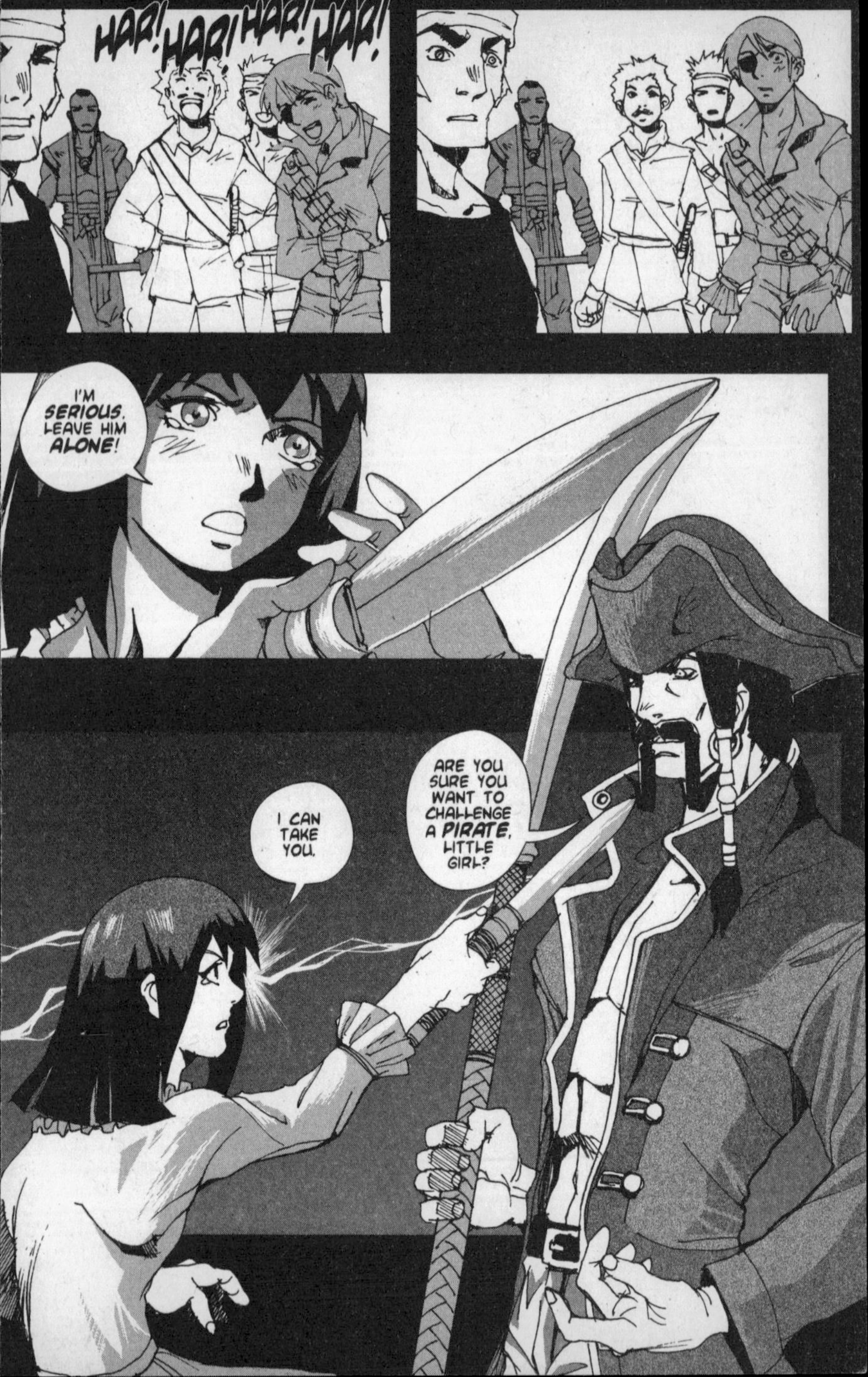
HAR! HAR! HAR! HAR!
I'M SERIOUS. LEAVE HIM ALONE!
ARE YOU SURE YOU WANT TO CHALLENGE A PIRATE, LITTLE GIRL?
I CAN TAKE YOU.

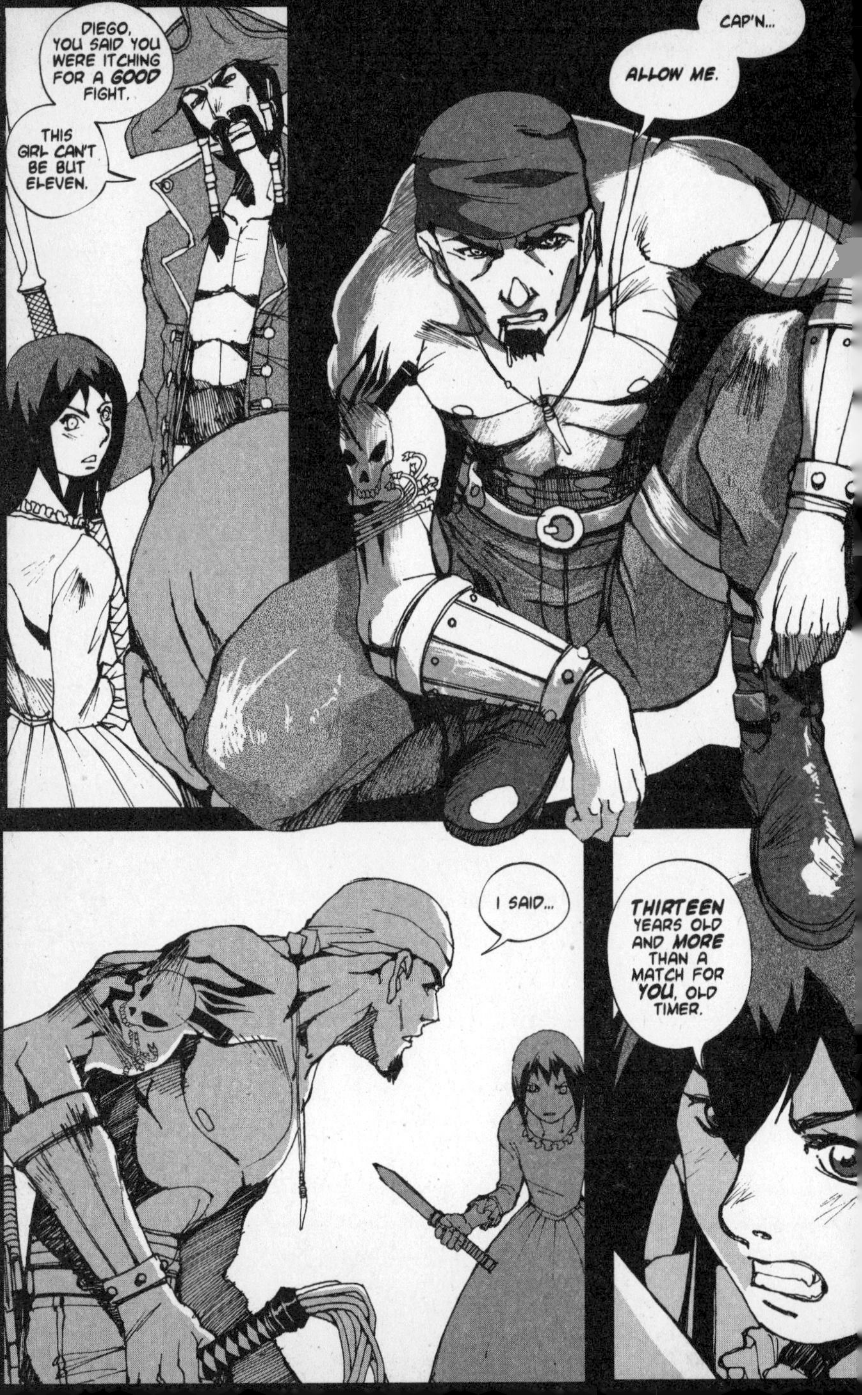
DIEGO, YOU SAID YOU WERE ITCHING FOR A GOOD FIGHT.
THIS GIRL CAN'T BE BUT ELEVEN.
CAP'N...
ALLOW ME.
I SAID...
THIRTEEN YEARS OLD AND MORE THAN A MATCH FOR YOU, OLD TIMER.

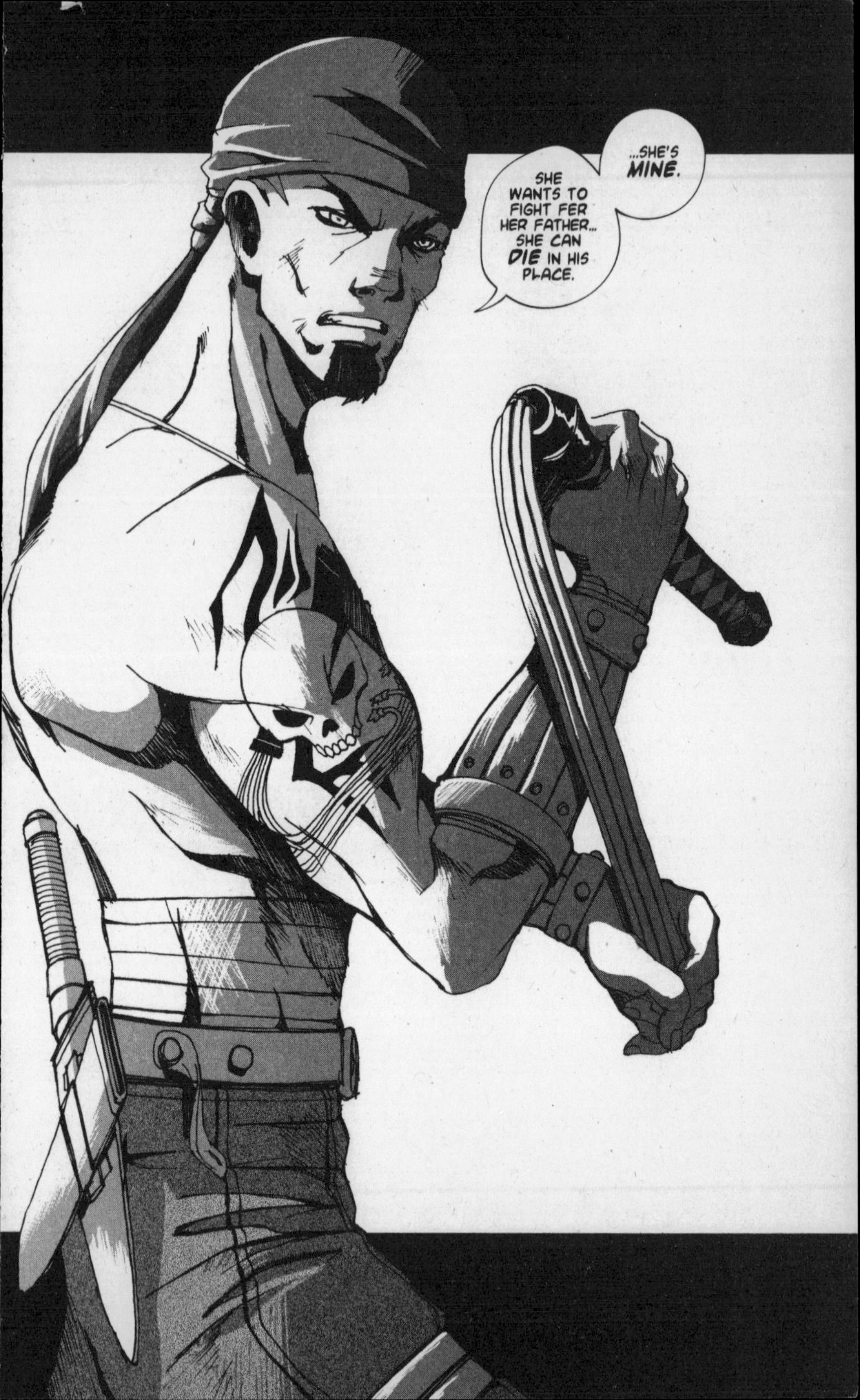
SHE WANTS TO FIGHT FER HER FATHER... SHE CAN DIE IN HIS PLACE.
...SHE'S MINE.

CHAPTER 2
Call Of The Sea

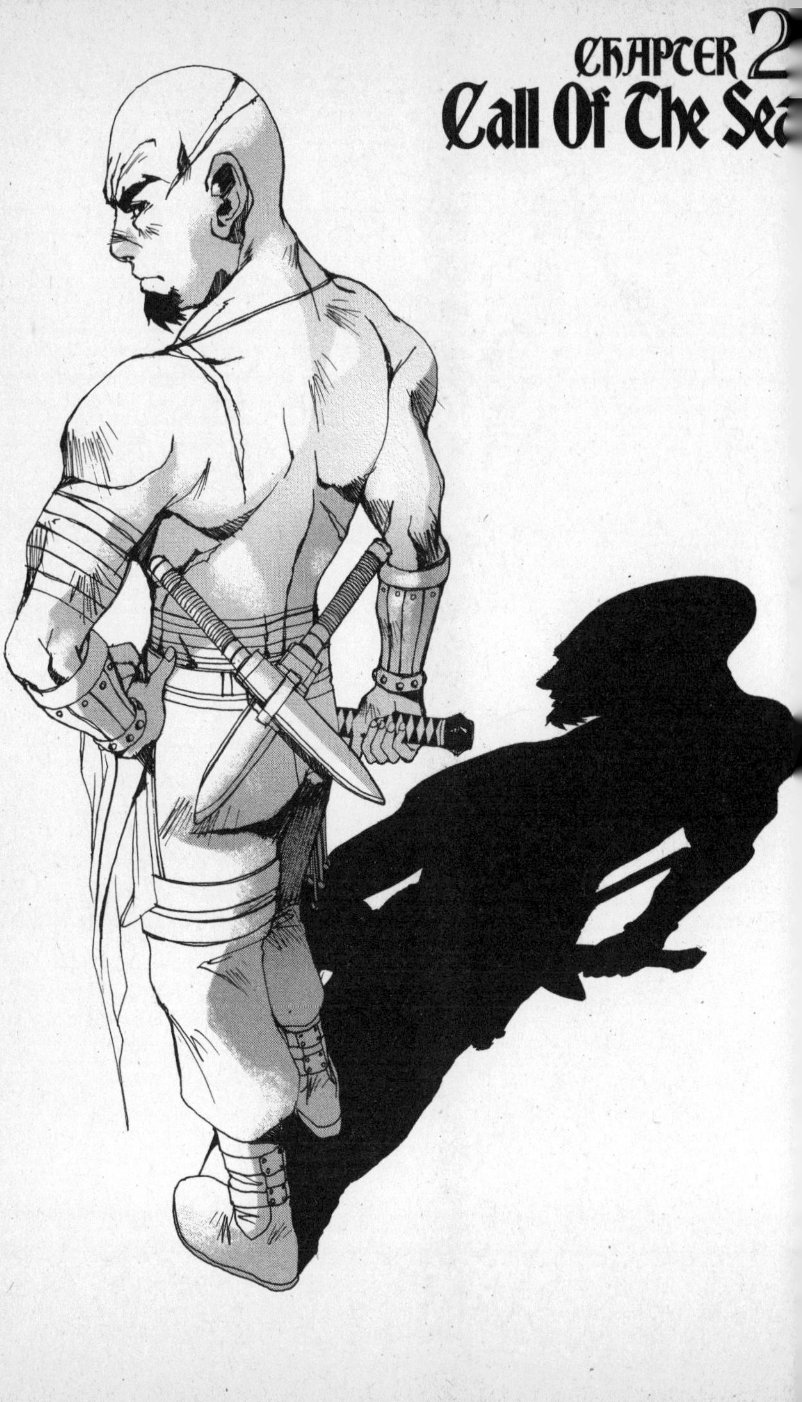

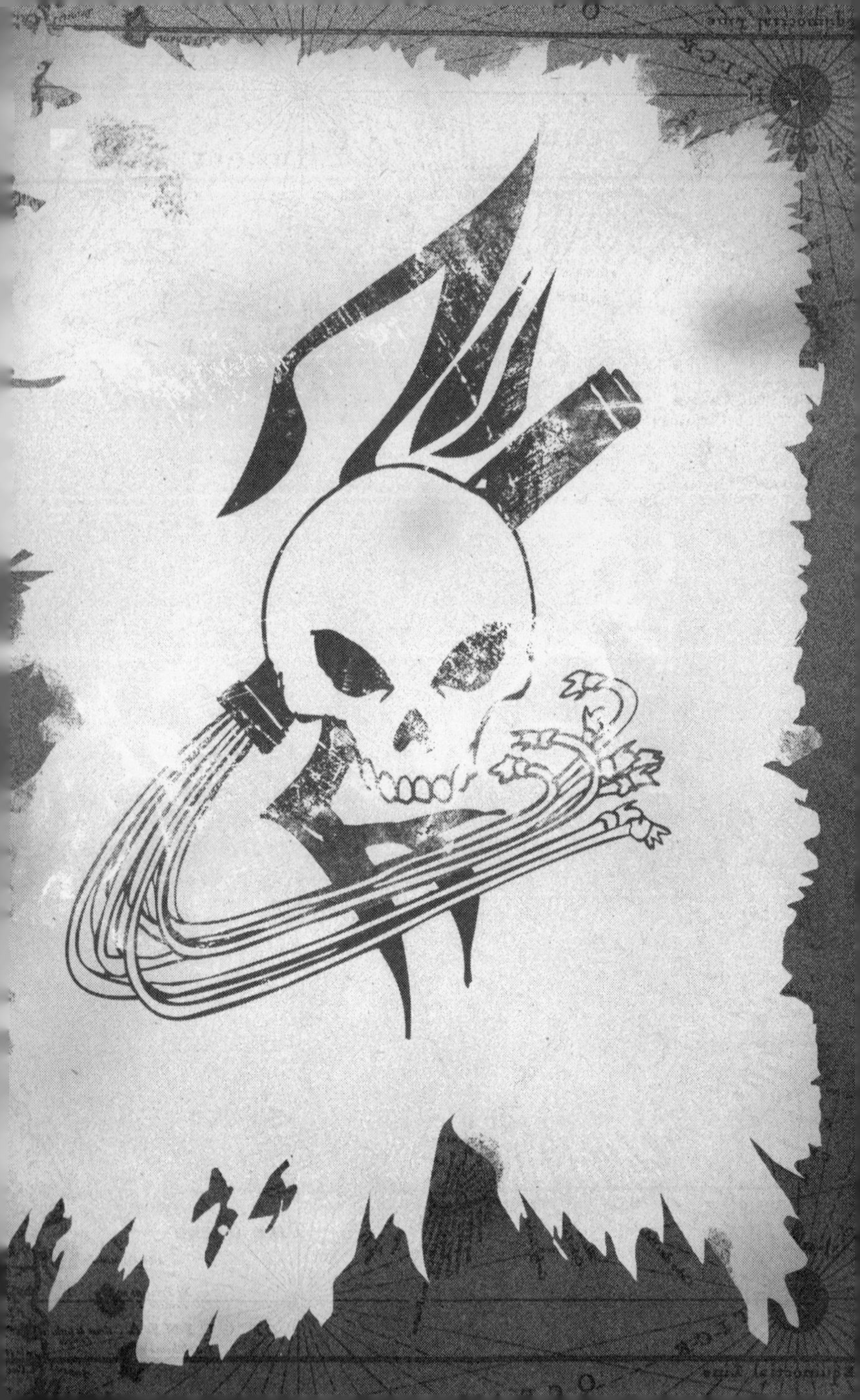

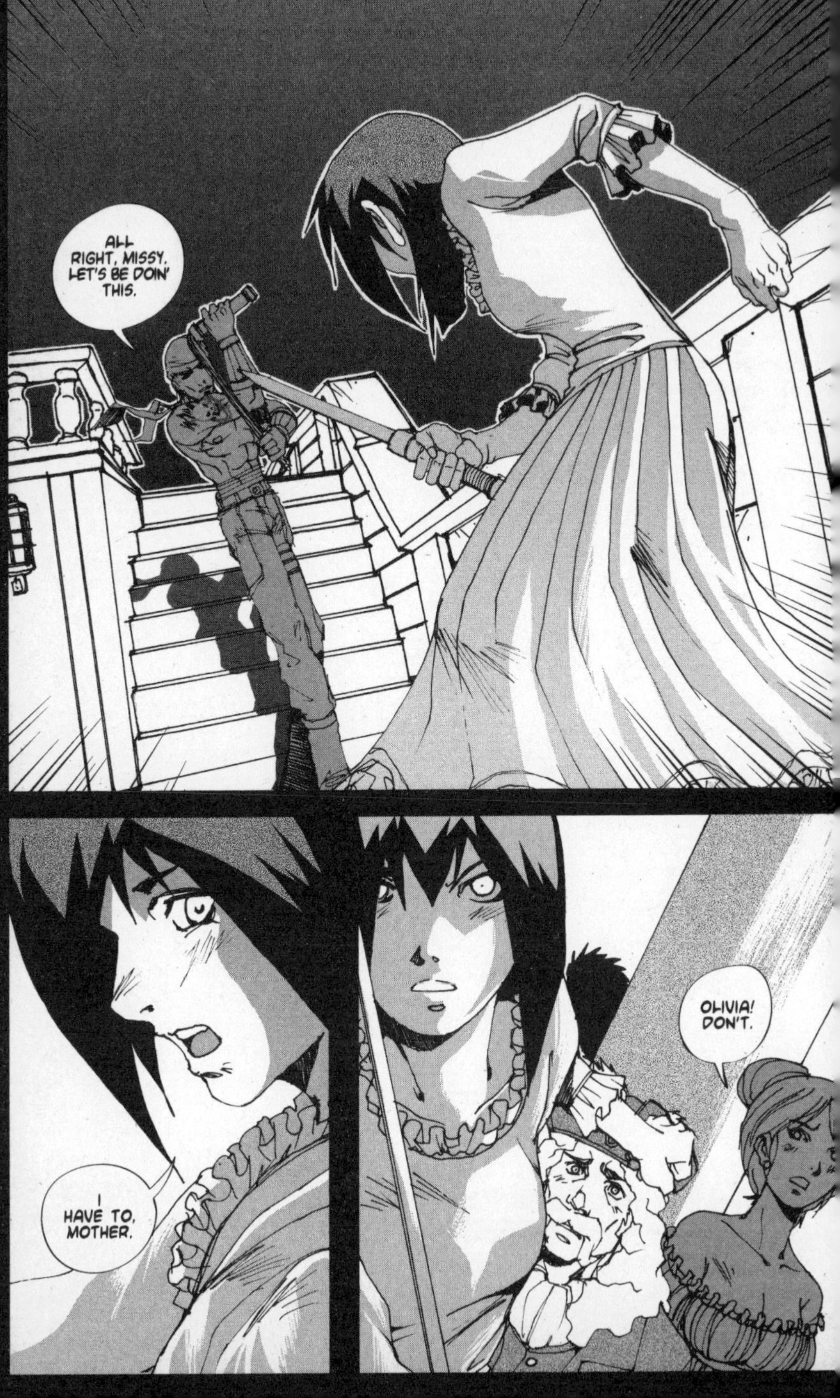
ALL RIGHT, MISSY. LET'S BE DOIN' THIS.
OLIVIA! DON'T.
I HAVE TO, MOTHER.

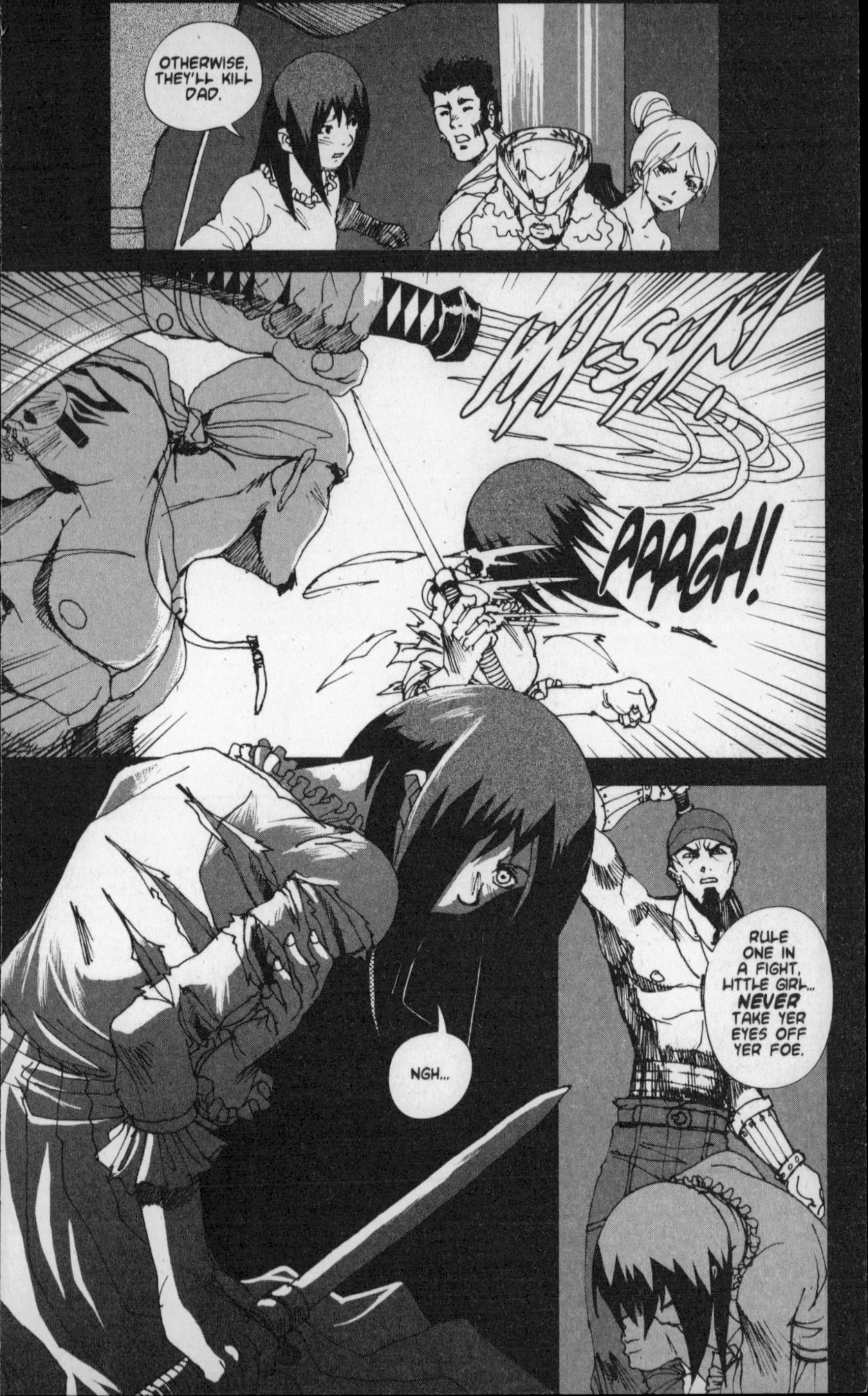
OTHERWISE, THEY'LL KILL DAD.
PAAGH!
RULE ONE IN A FIGHT, LITTLE GIRL... **NEVER** TAKE YER EYES OFF YER FOE.
NGH...

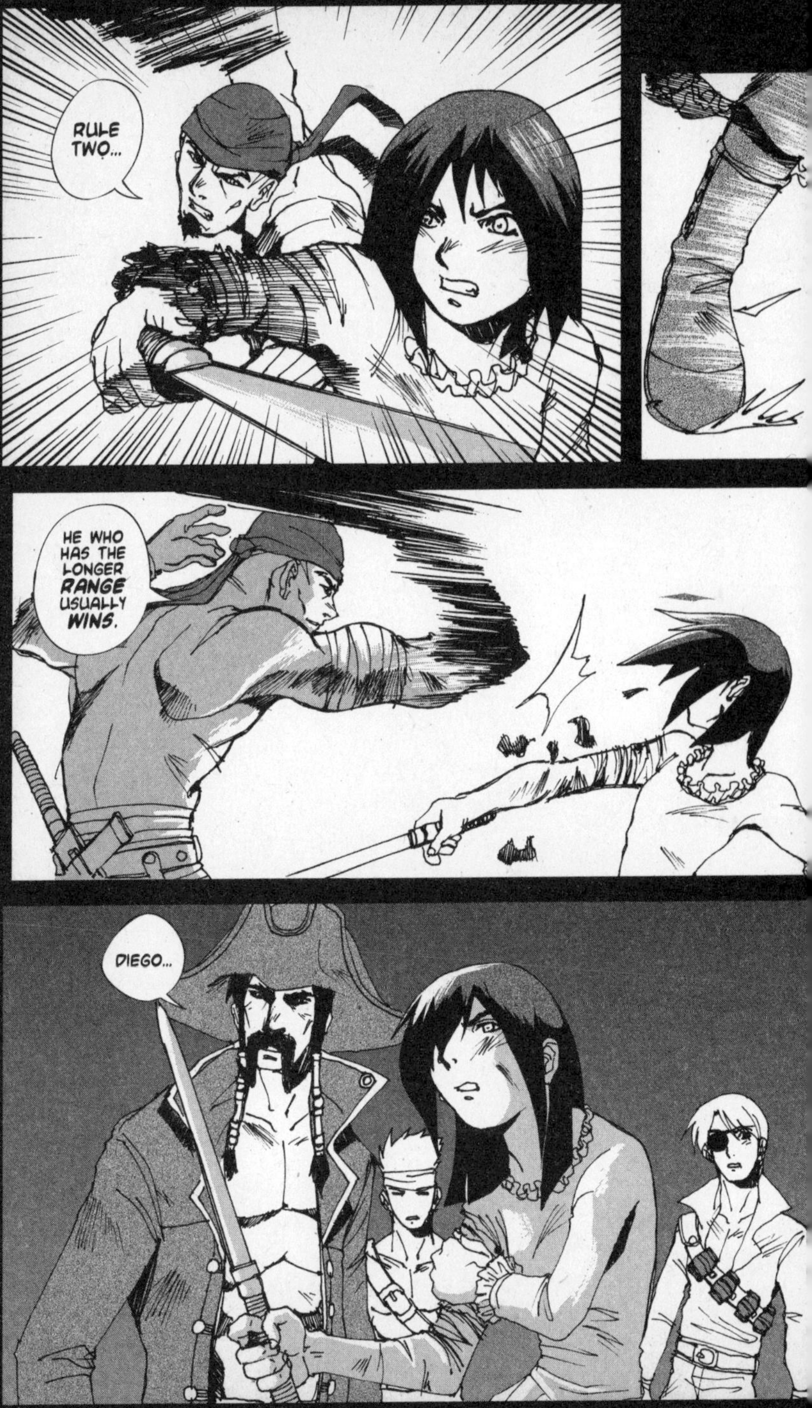
RULE TWO...
HE WHO HAS THE LONGER RANGE USUALLY WINS.
DIEGO...

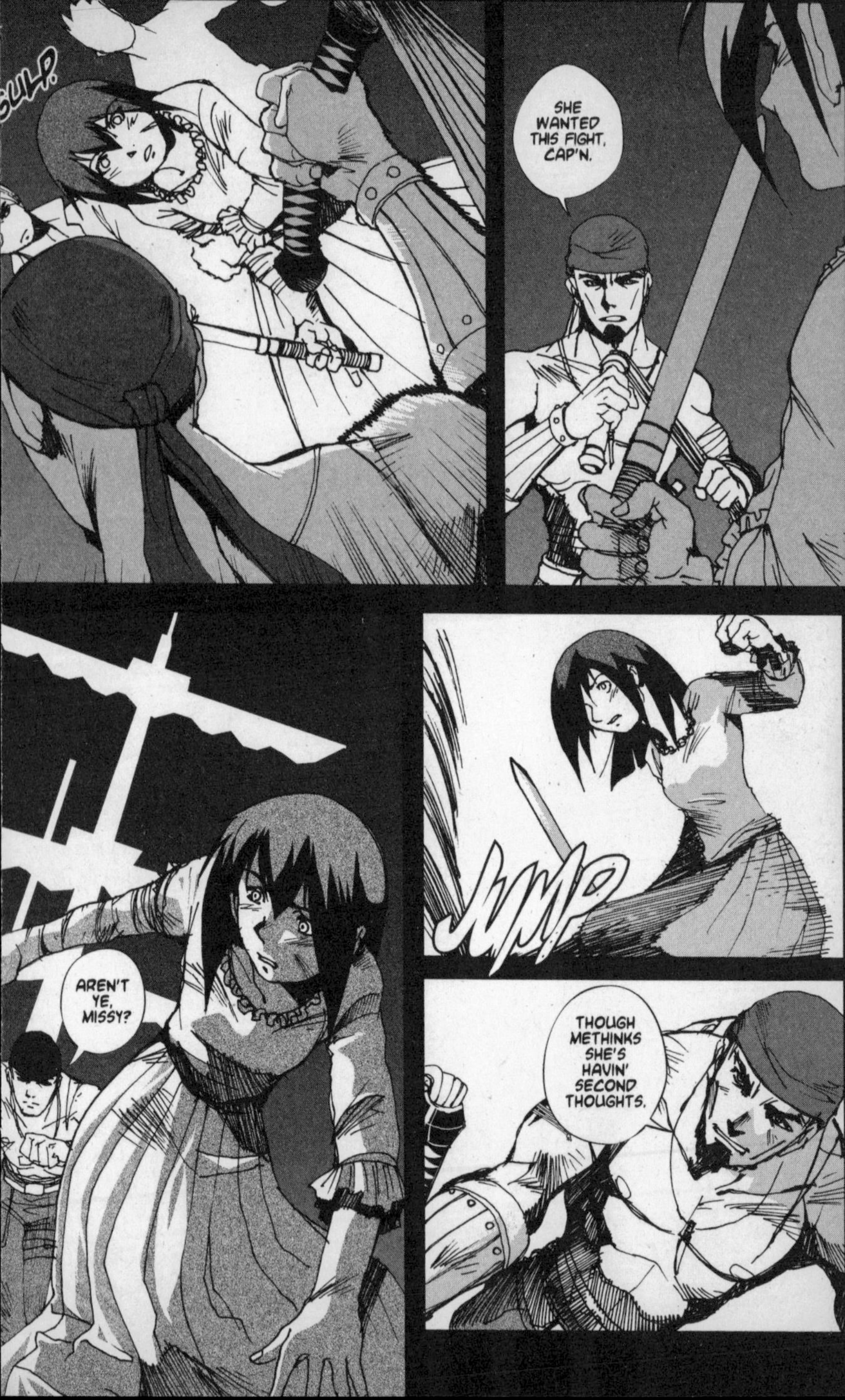
SHE WANTED THIS FIGHT, CAP'N.
GULP
JUMP
THOUGH METHINKS SHE'S HAVIN' SECOND THOUGHTS.
AREN'T YE, MISSY?

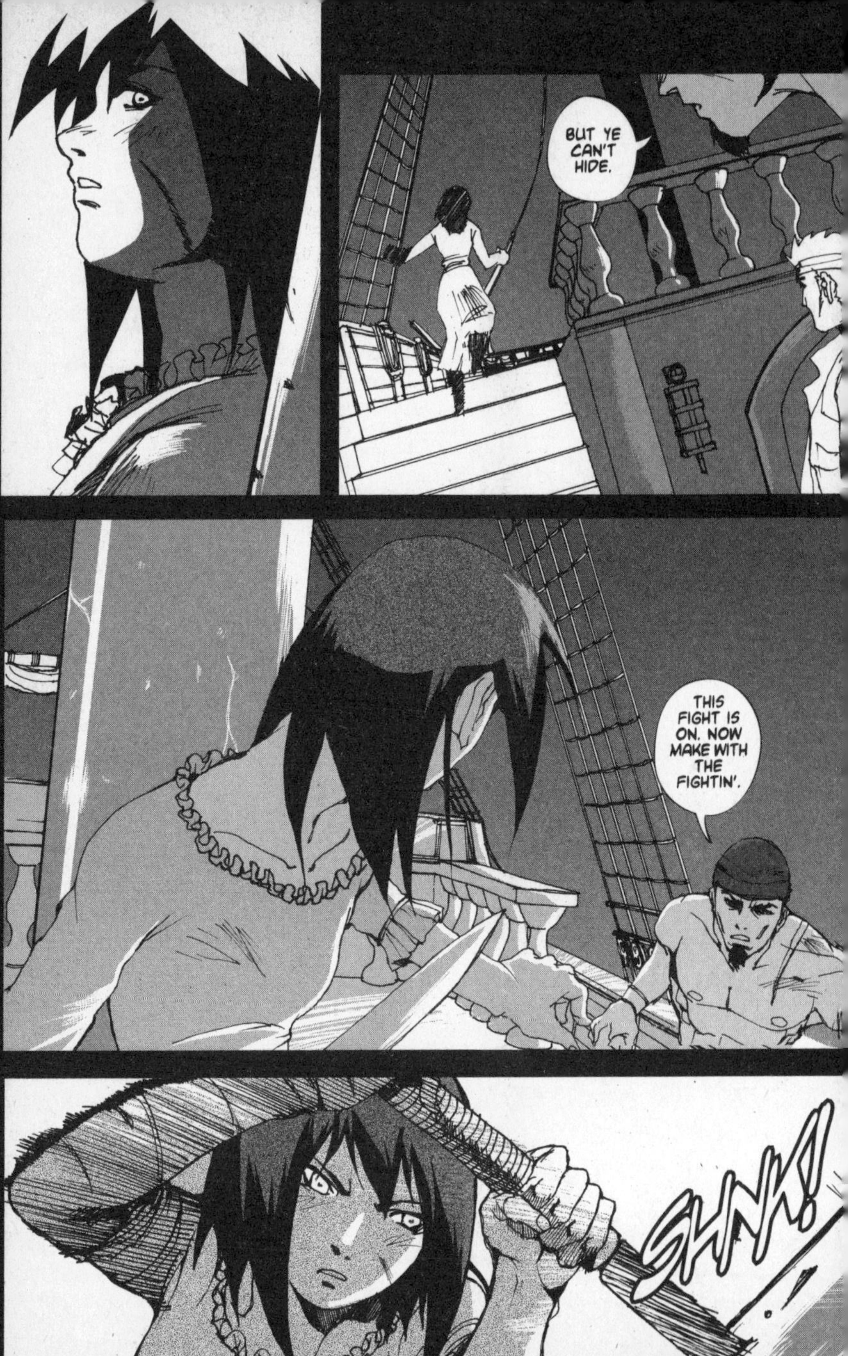
BUT YE CAN'T HIDE.
THIS FIGHT IS ON. NOW MAKE WITH THE FIGHTIN'.
SHNK!

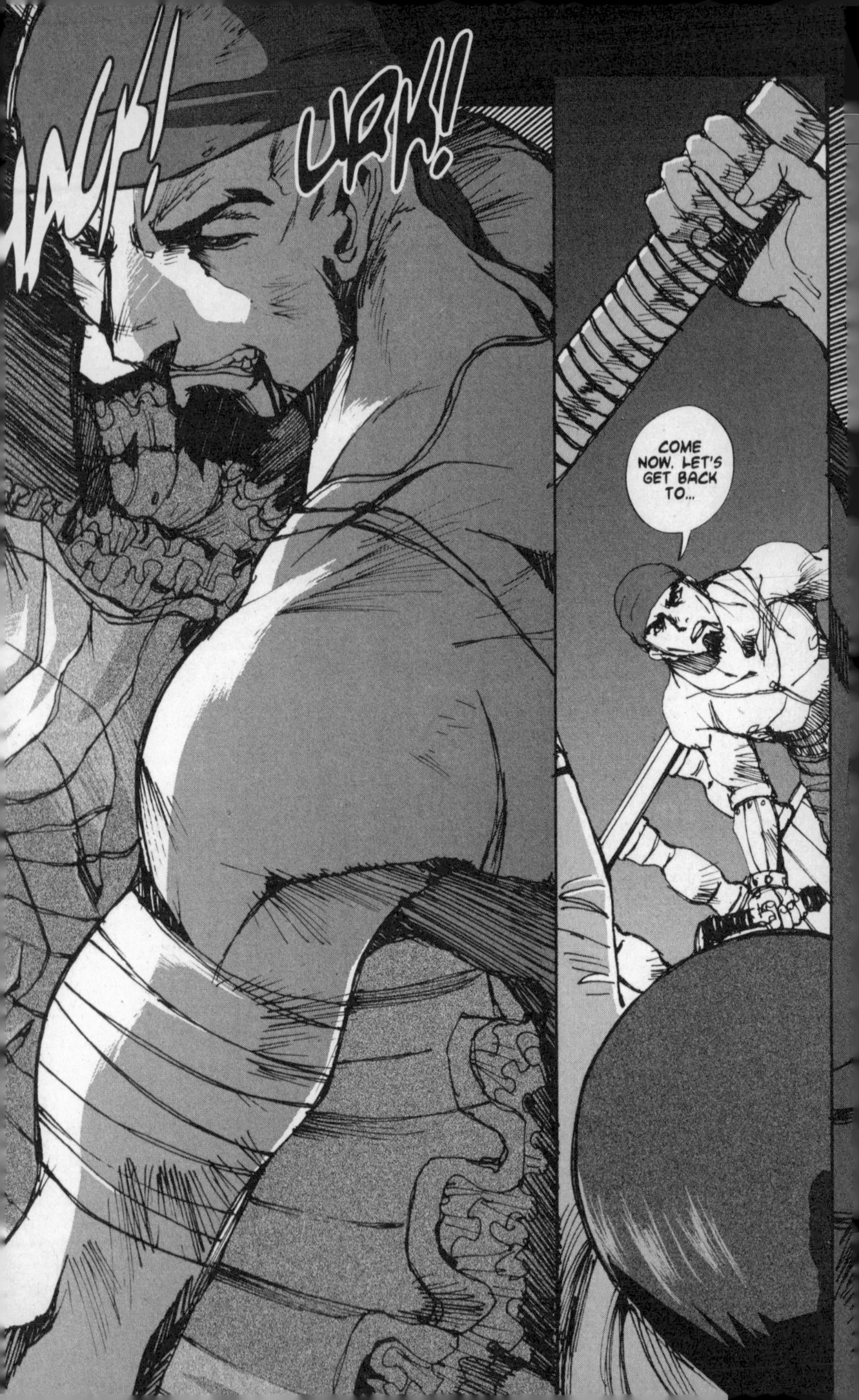
COME NOW. LET'S GET BACK TO...

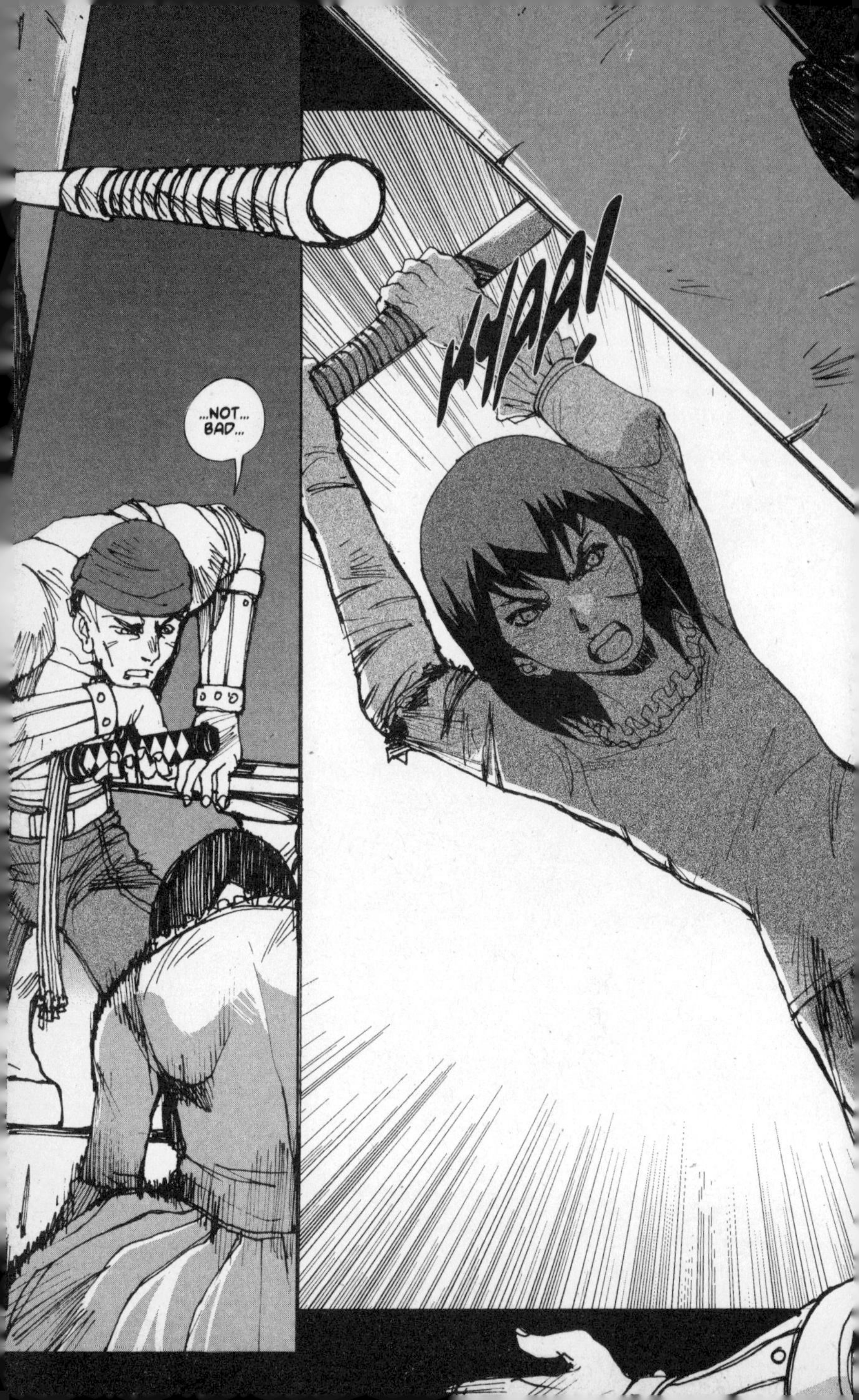
HYAA!
...NOT... BAD...

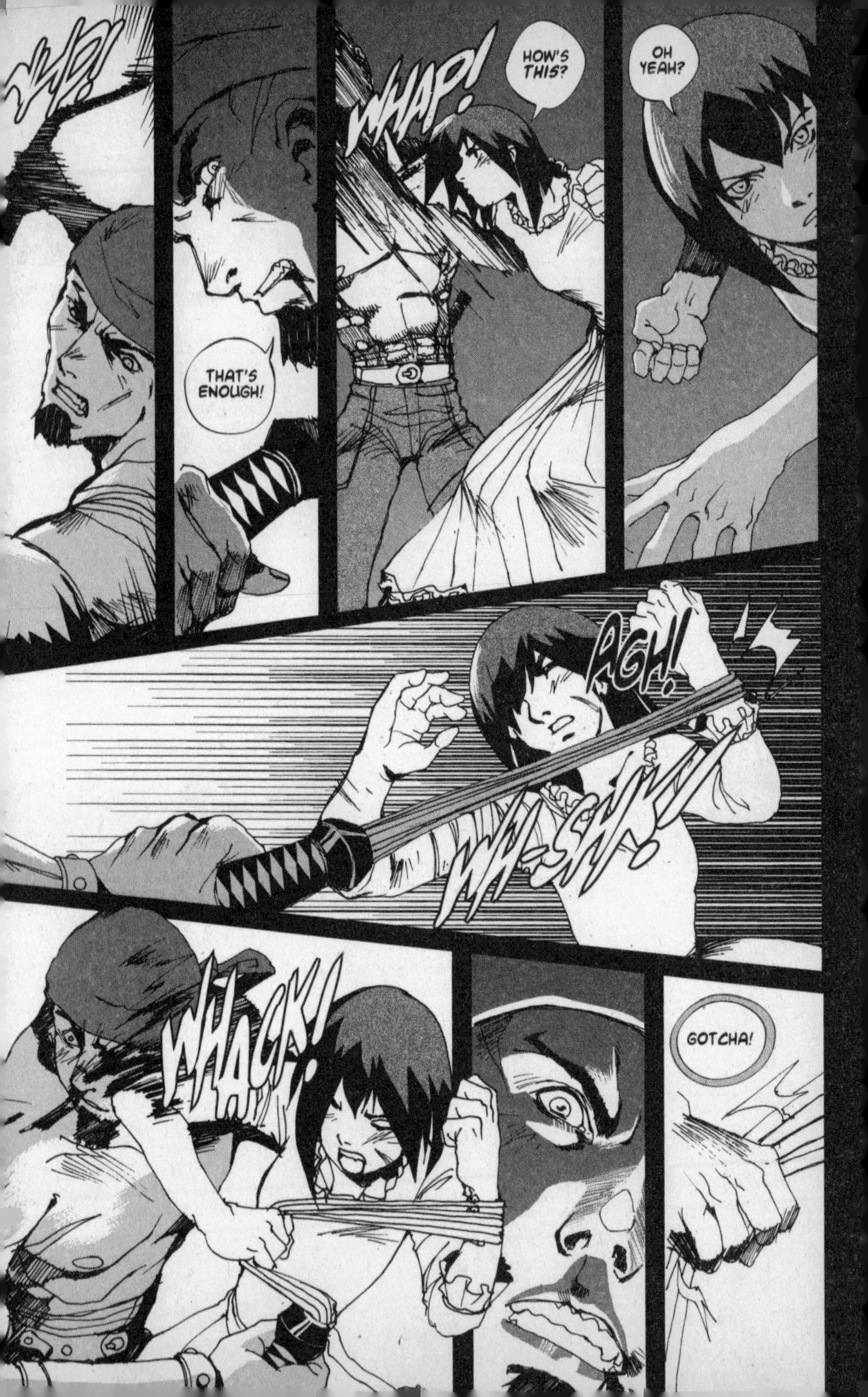
OH YEAH?
HOW'S THIS?
WHAP!
THAT'S ENOUGH!
AGH!
GOTCHA!
WHACK!

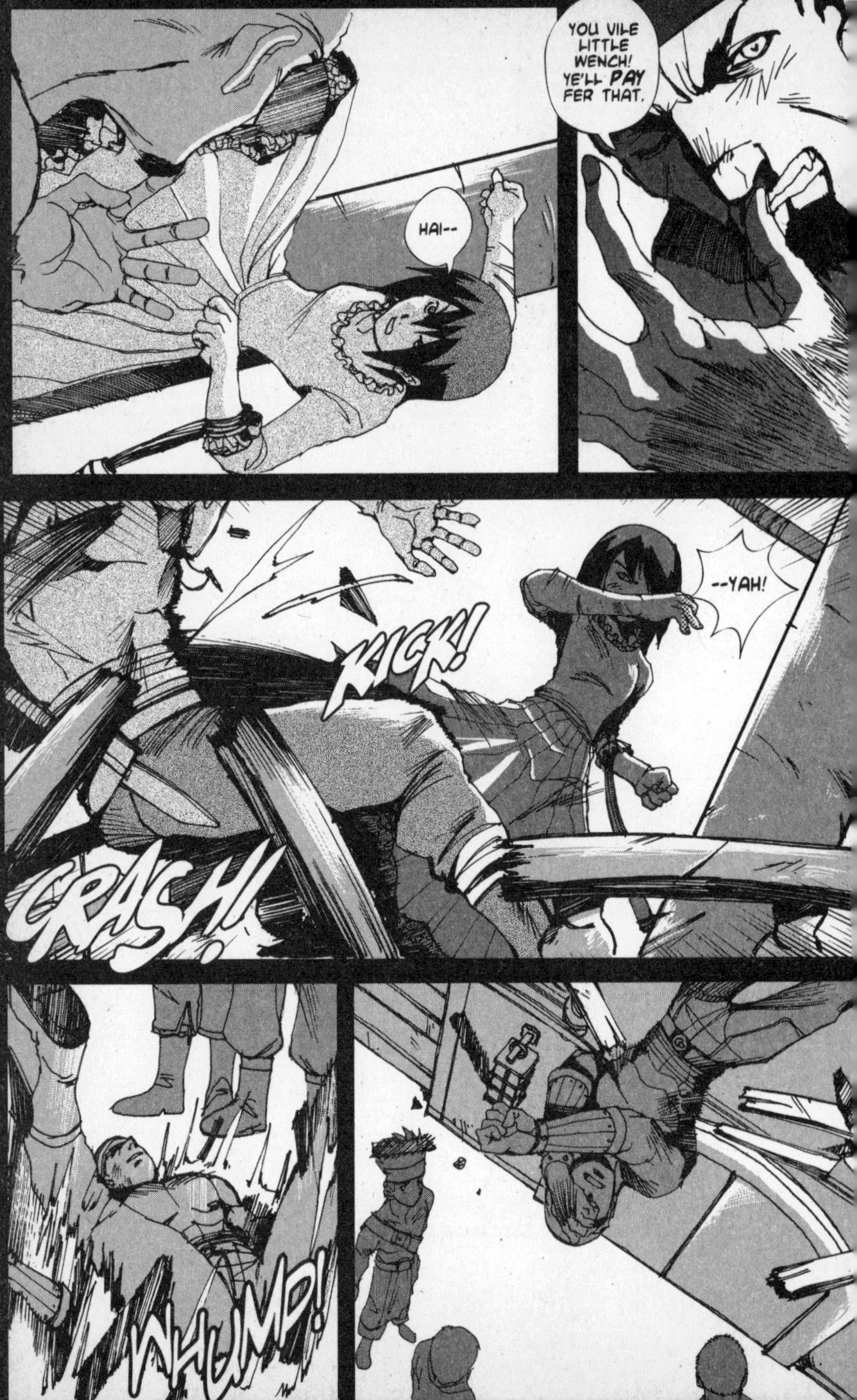
YOU VILE LITTLE WENCH! YE'LL PAY FER THAT.
HAI--
--YAH!
KICK!
CRASH!
WHUMP!

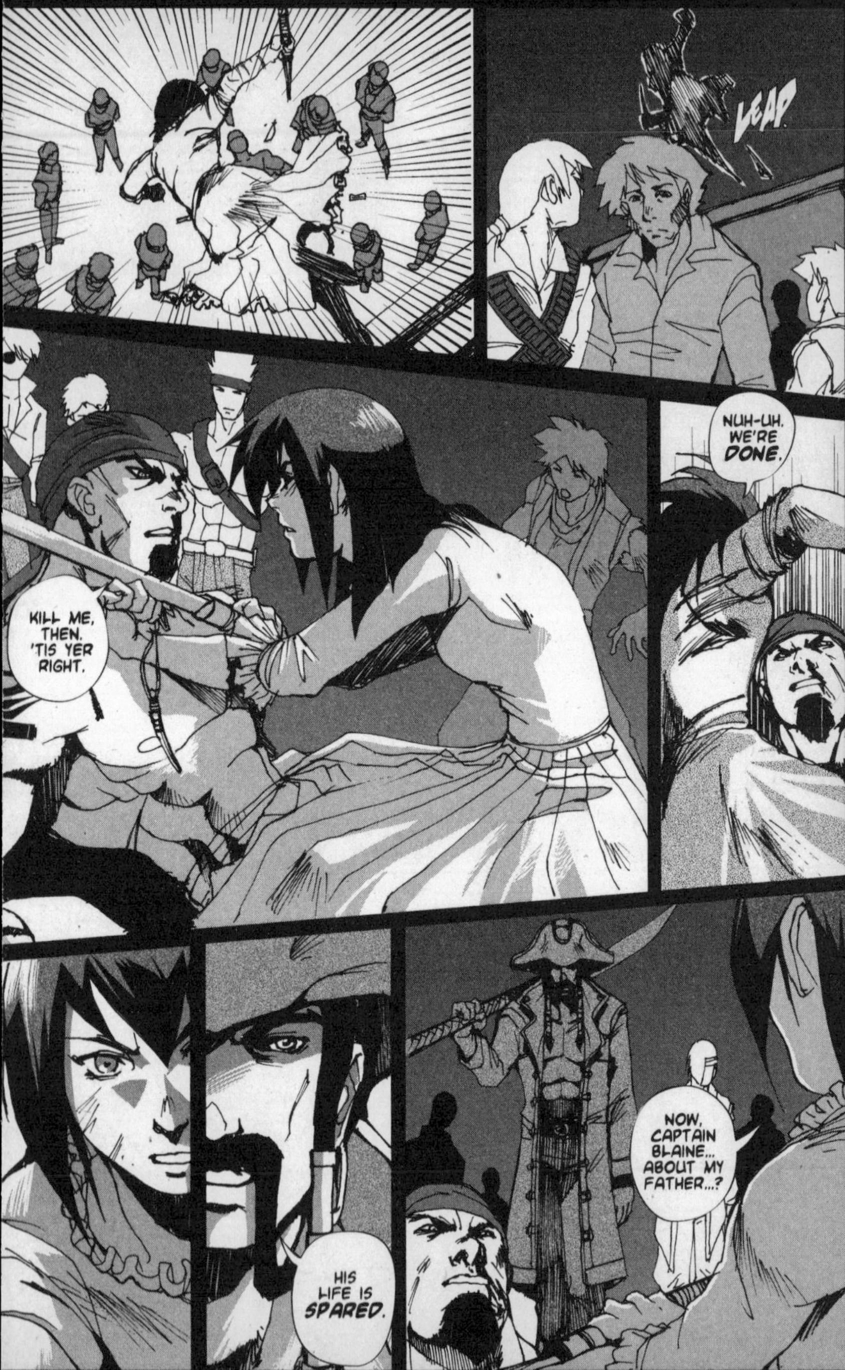
LEAP
NUH-UH. WE'RE DONE.
KILL ME, THEN. 'TIS YER RIGHT.
NOW, CAPTAIN BLAINE... ABOUT MY FATHER...?
HIS LIFE IS SPARED.

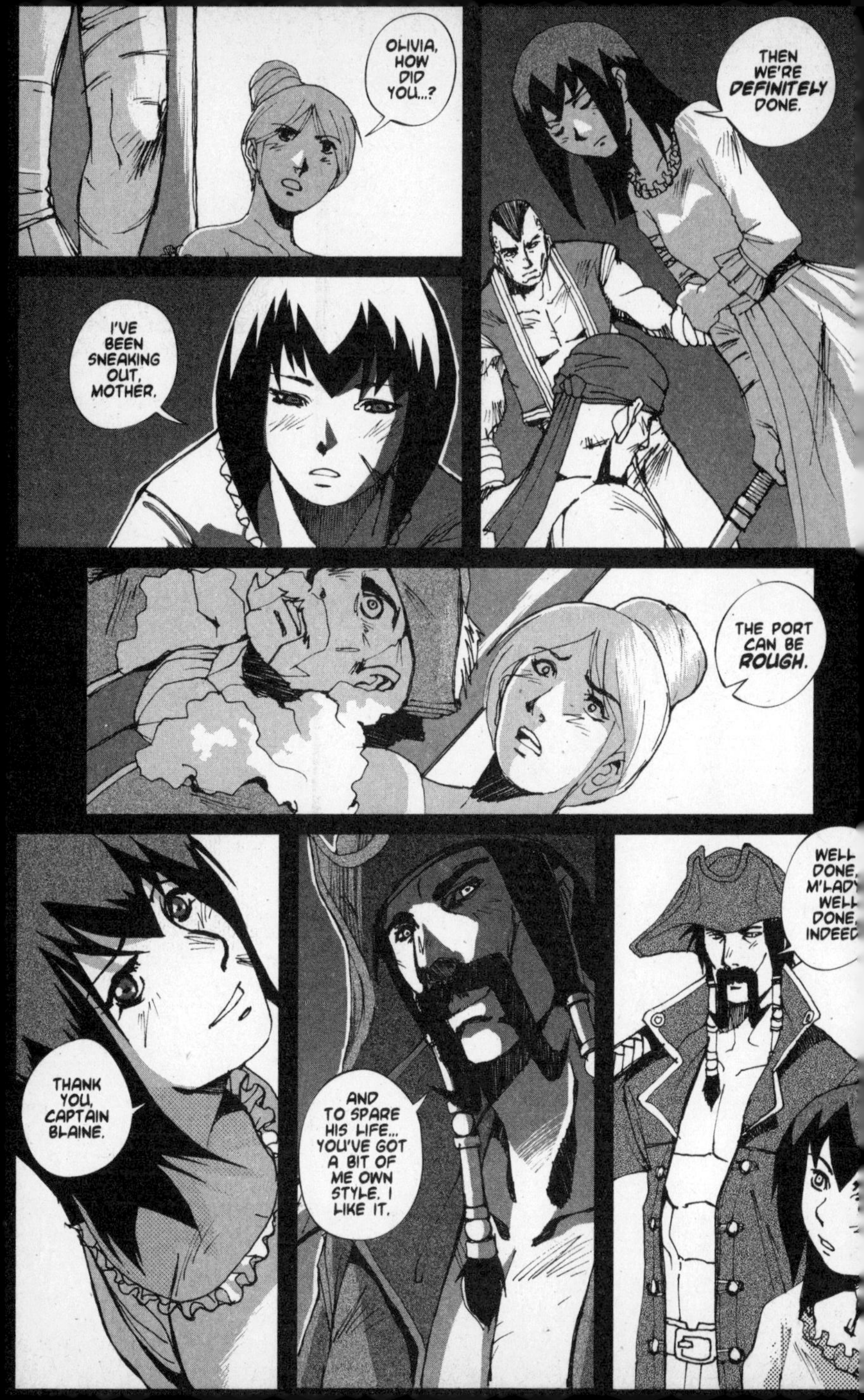
THEN WE'RE DEFINITELY DONE.
OLIVIA, HOW DID YOU...?
I'VE BEEN SNEAKING OUT, MOTHER.
THE PORT CAN BE ROUGH.
WELL DONE, M'LADY WELL DONE, INDEED
AND TO SPARE HIS LIFE... YOU'VE GOT A BIT OF ME OWN STYLE. I LIKE IT.
THANK YOU, CAPTAIN BLAINE.

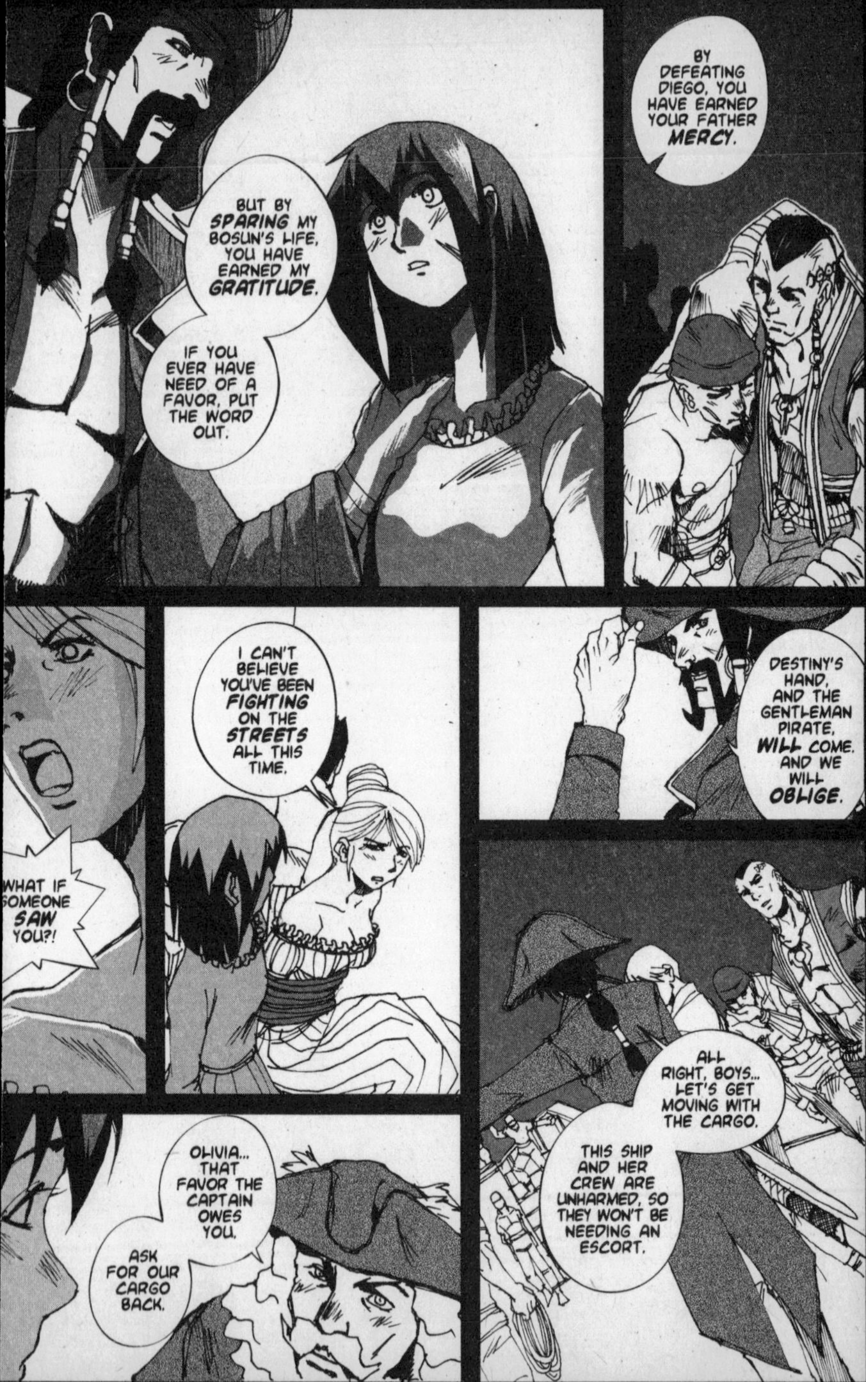
BY DEFEATING DIEGO, YOU HAVE EARNED YOUR FATHER MERCY.
BUT BY SPARING MY BOSUN'S LIFE, YOU HAVE EARNED MY GRATITUDE.
IF YOU EVER HAVE NEED OF A FAVOR, PUT THE WORD OUT.
DESTINY'S HAND, AND THE GENTLEMAN PIRATE, WILL COME. AND WE WILL OBLIGE.
ALL RIGHT, BOYS... LET'S GET MOVING WITH THE CARGO.
THIS SHIP AND HER CREW ARE UNHARMED, SO THEY WON'T BE NEEDING AN ESCORT.
I CAN'T BELIEVE YOU'VE BEEN FIGHTING ON THE STREETS ALL THIS TIME.
WHAT IF SOMEONE SAW YOU?!
OLIVIA... THAT FAVOR THE CAPTAIN OWES YOU.
ASK FOR OUR CARGO BACK.

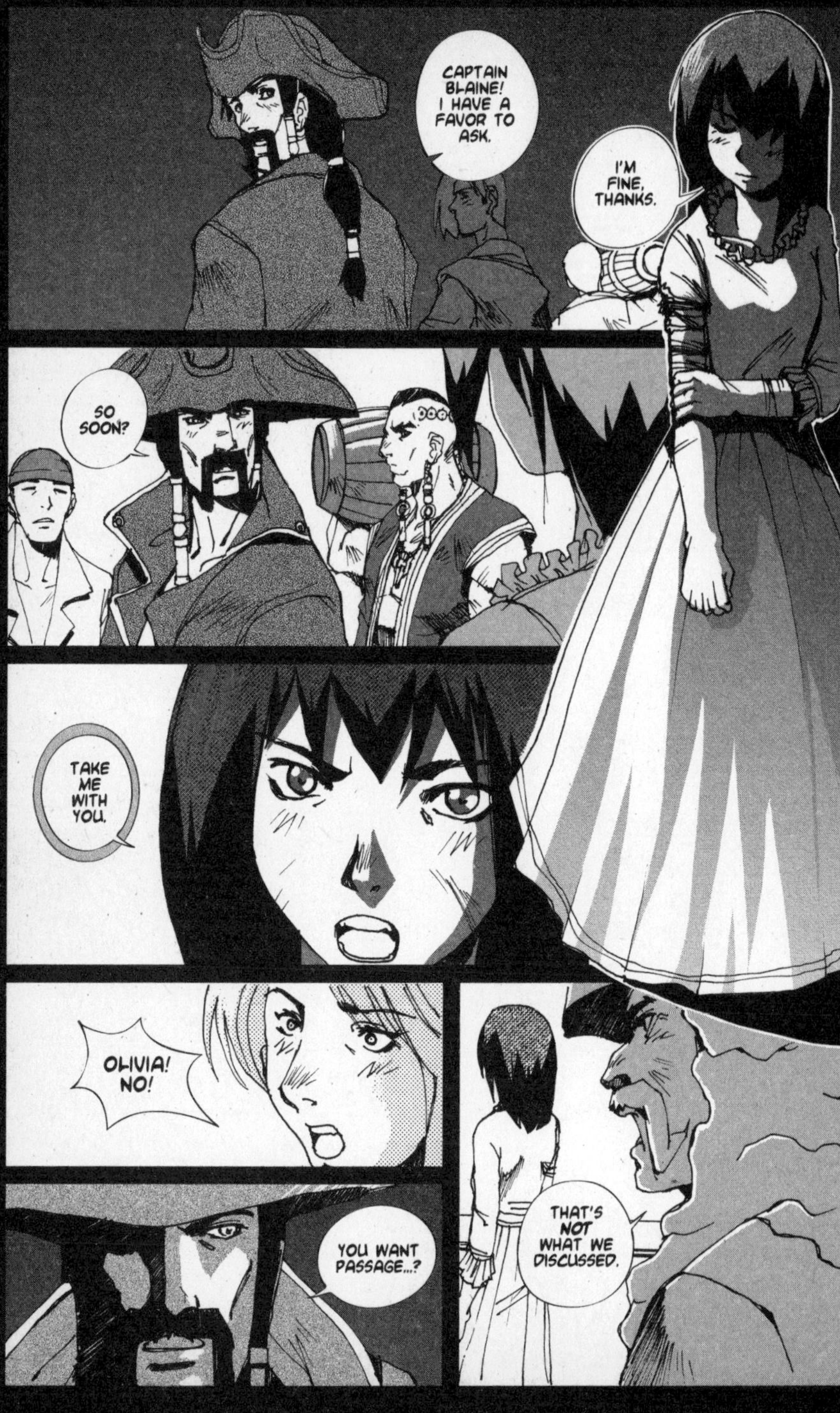
I'M FINE, THANKS.
CAPTAIN BLAINE! I HAVE A FAVOR TO ASK.
SO SOON?
TAKE ME WITH YOU.
THAT'S **NOT** WHAT WE DISCUSSED.
OLIVIA! NO!
YOU WANT PASSAGE...?

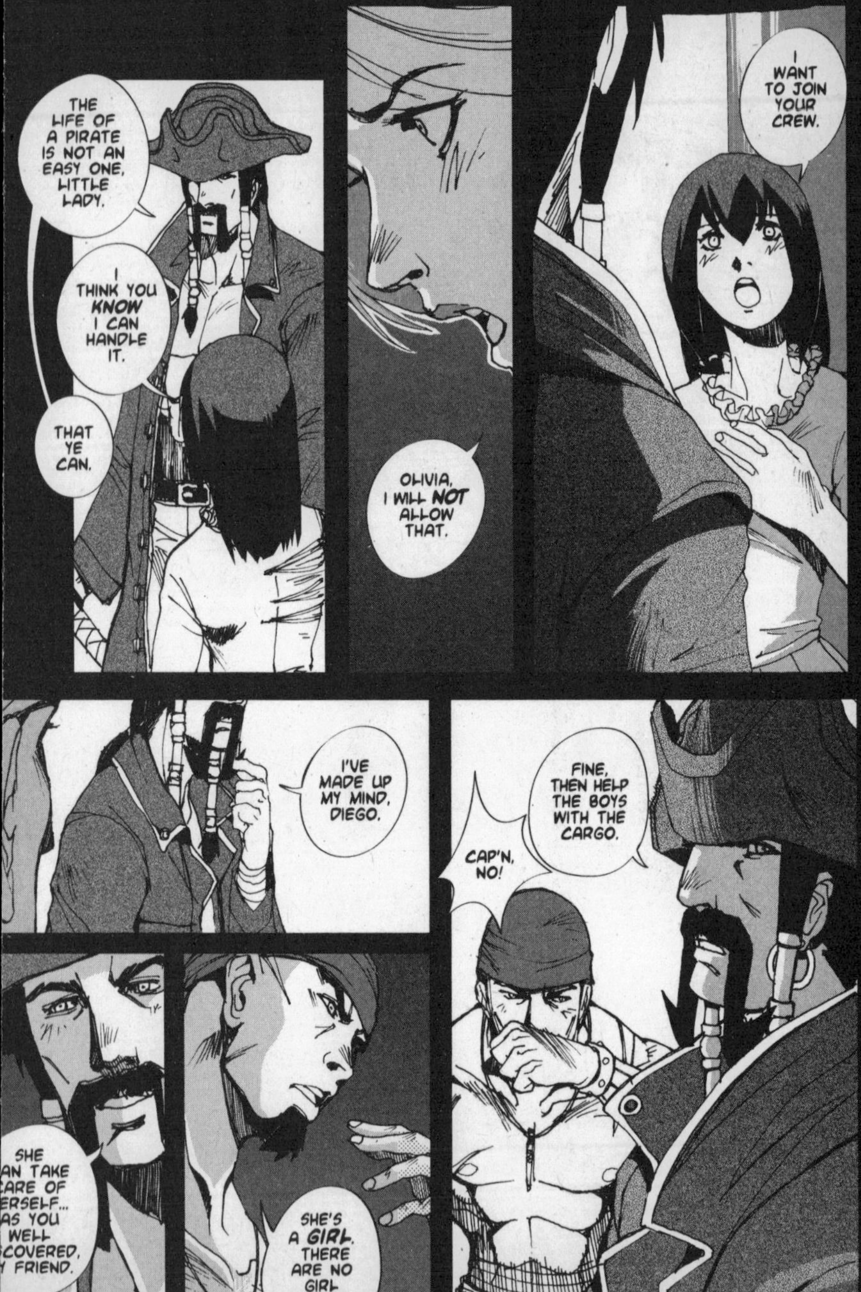
I WANT TO JOIN YOUR CREW.
OLIVIA, I WILL **NOT** ALLOW THAT.
THE LIFE OF A PIRATE IS NOT AN EASY ONE, LITTLE LADY.
I THINK YOU **KNOW** I CAN HANDLE IT.
THAT YE CAN.
FINE, THEN HELP THE BOYS WITH THE CARGO.
CAP'N, NO!
I'VE MADE UP MY MIND, DIEGO.
SHE'S A **GIRL**. THERE ARE NO GIRL PIRATES.
SHE AN TAKE ARE OF ERSELF... AS YOU WELL SCOVERED, Y FRIEND.

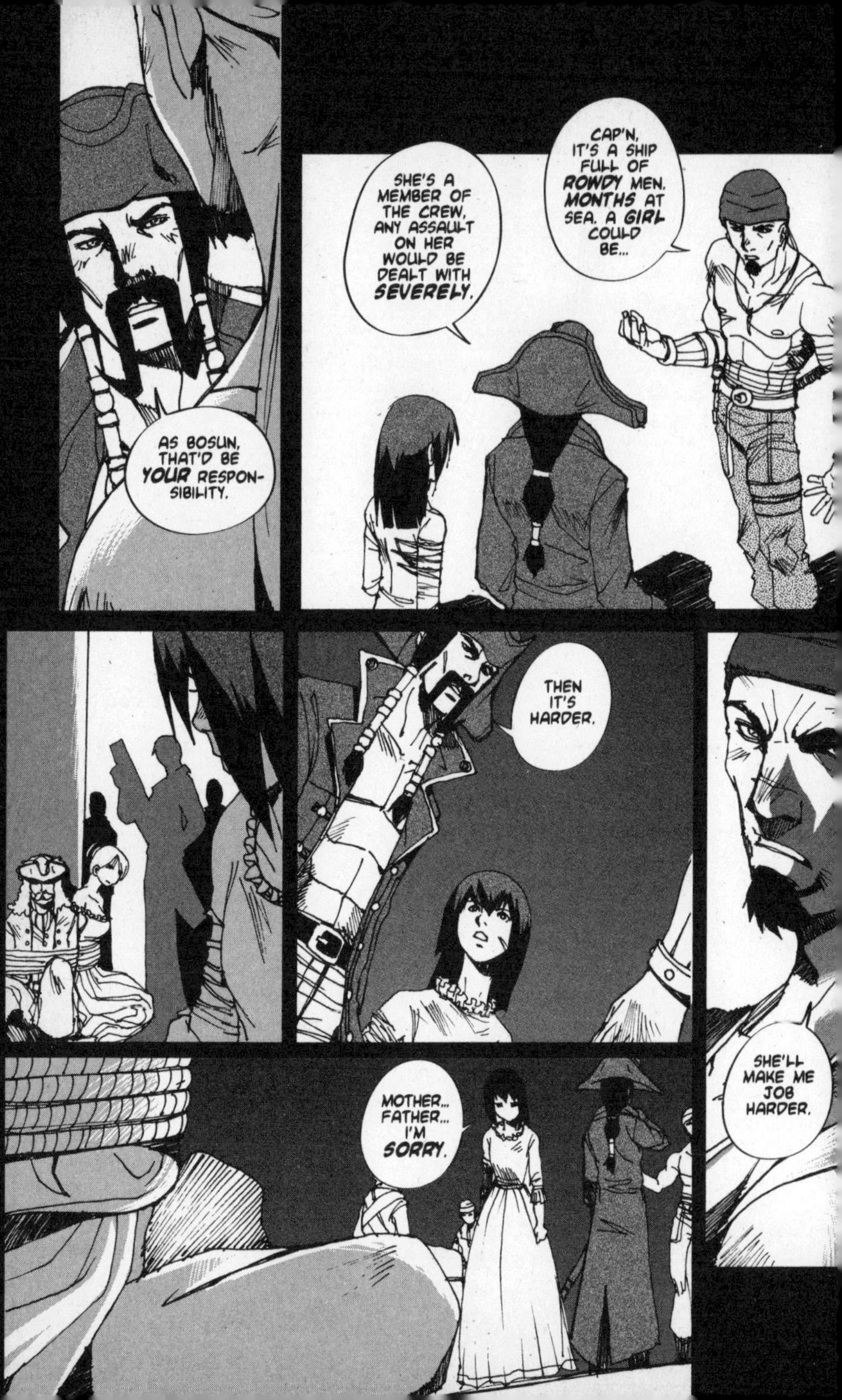
CAP'N, IT'S A SHIP FULL OF ROWDY MEN. MONTHS AT SEA. A GIRL COULD BE...
SHE'S A MEMBER OF THE CREW, ANY ASSAULT ON HER WOULD BE DEALT WITH SEVERELY.
AS BOSUN, THAT'D BE YOUR RESPONSIBILITY.
SHE'LL MAKE ME JOB HARDER.
THEN IT'S HARDER.
MOTHER... FATHER... I'M SORRY.

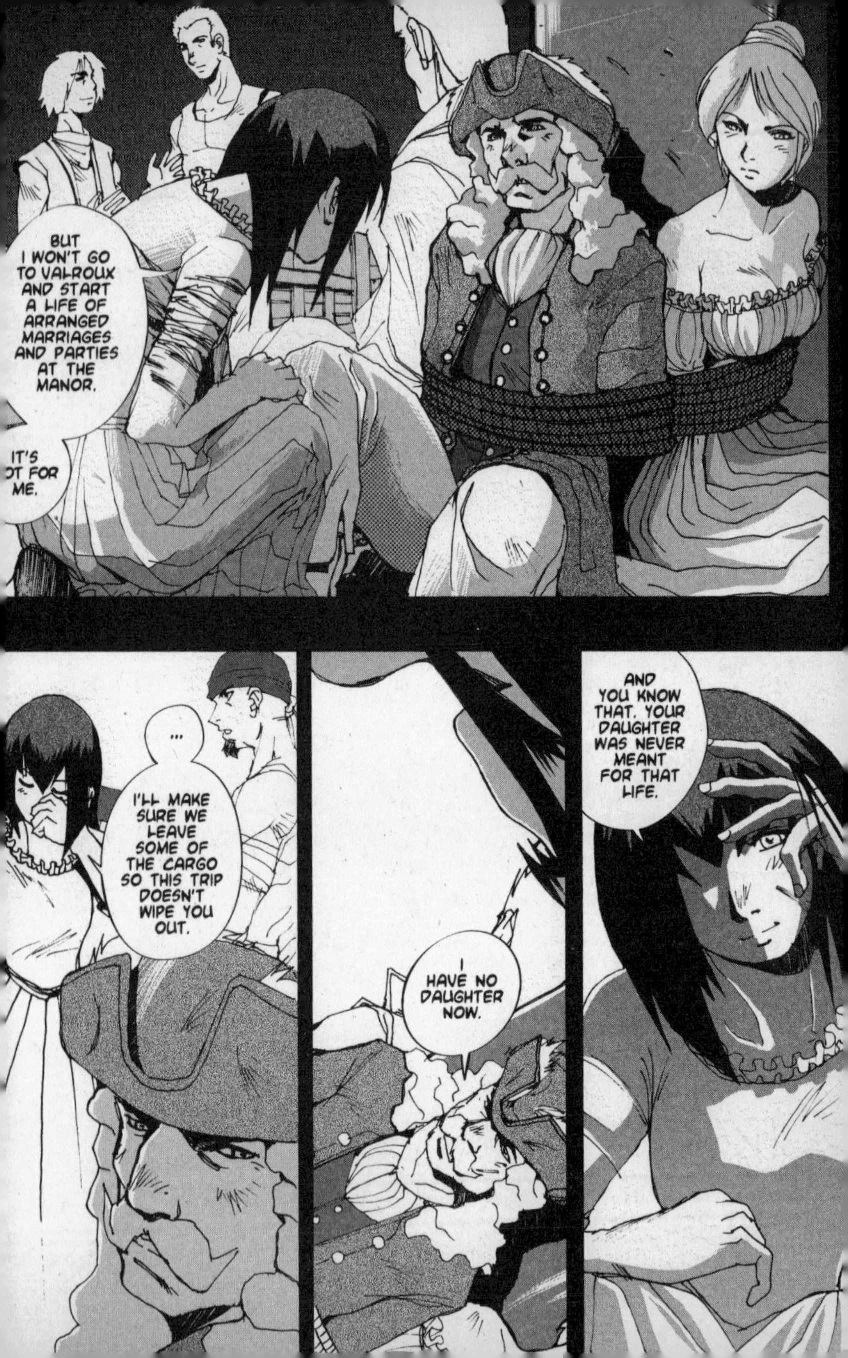
BUT I WON'T GO TO VALROUX AND START A LIFE OF ARRANGED MARRIAGES AND PARTIES AT THE MANOR.
IT'S OT FOR ME.
AND YOU KNOW THAT. YOUR DAUGHTER WAS NEVER MEANT FOR THAT LIFE.
I HAVE NO DAUGHTER NOW.
...
I'LL MAKE SURE WE LEAVE SOME OF THE CARGO SO THIS TRIP DOESN'T WIPE YOU OUT.

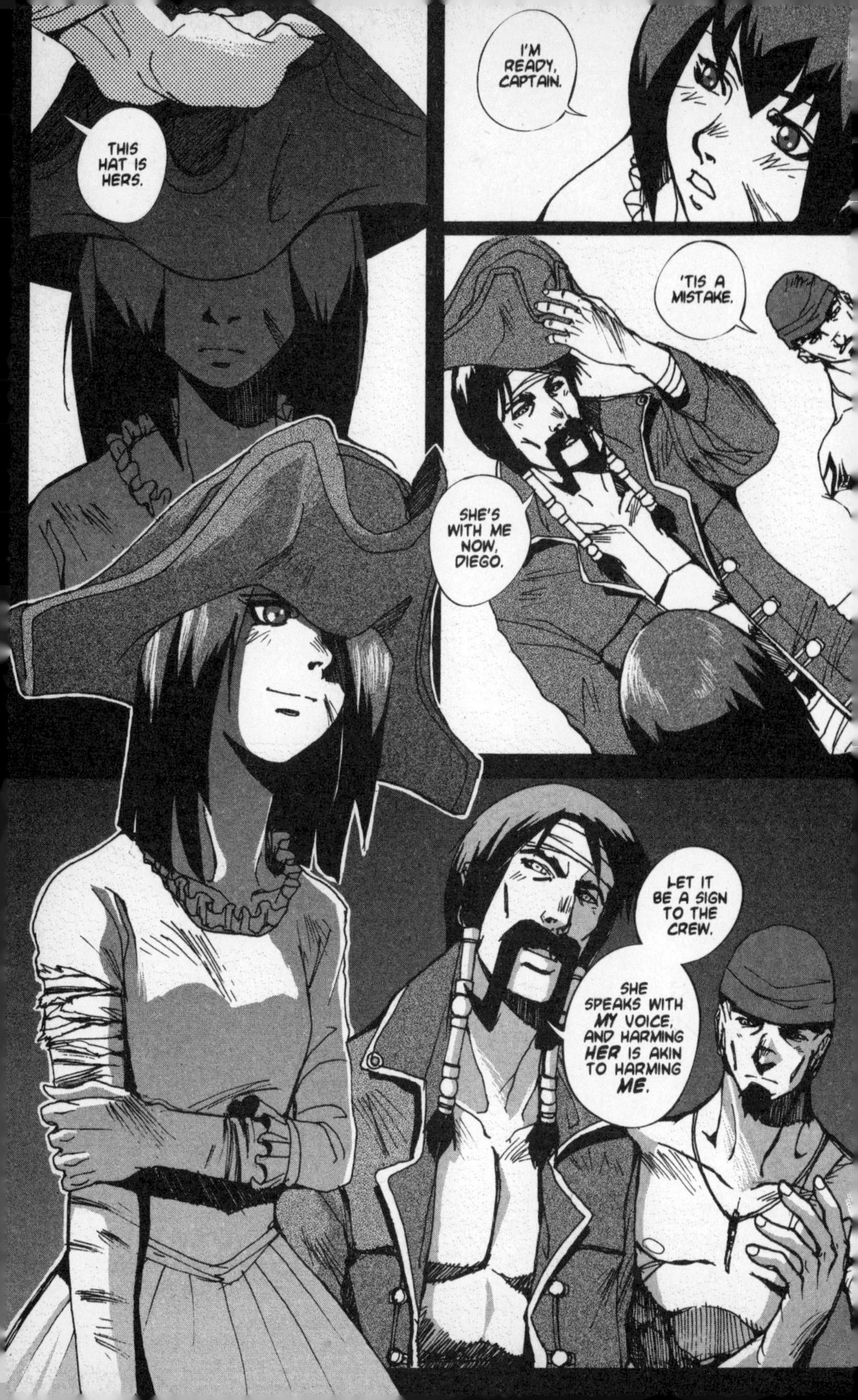
I'M READY, CAPTAIN.
'TIS A MISTAKE.
SHE'S WITH ME NOW, DIEGO.
THIS HAT IS HERS.
LET IT BE A SIGN TO THE CREW.
SHE SPEAKS WITH **MY** VOICE, AND HARMING **HER** IS AKIN TO HARMING **ME**.

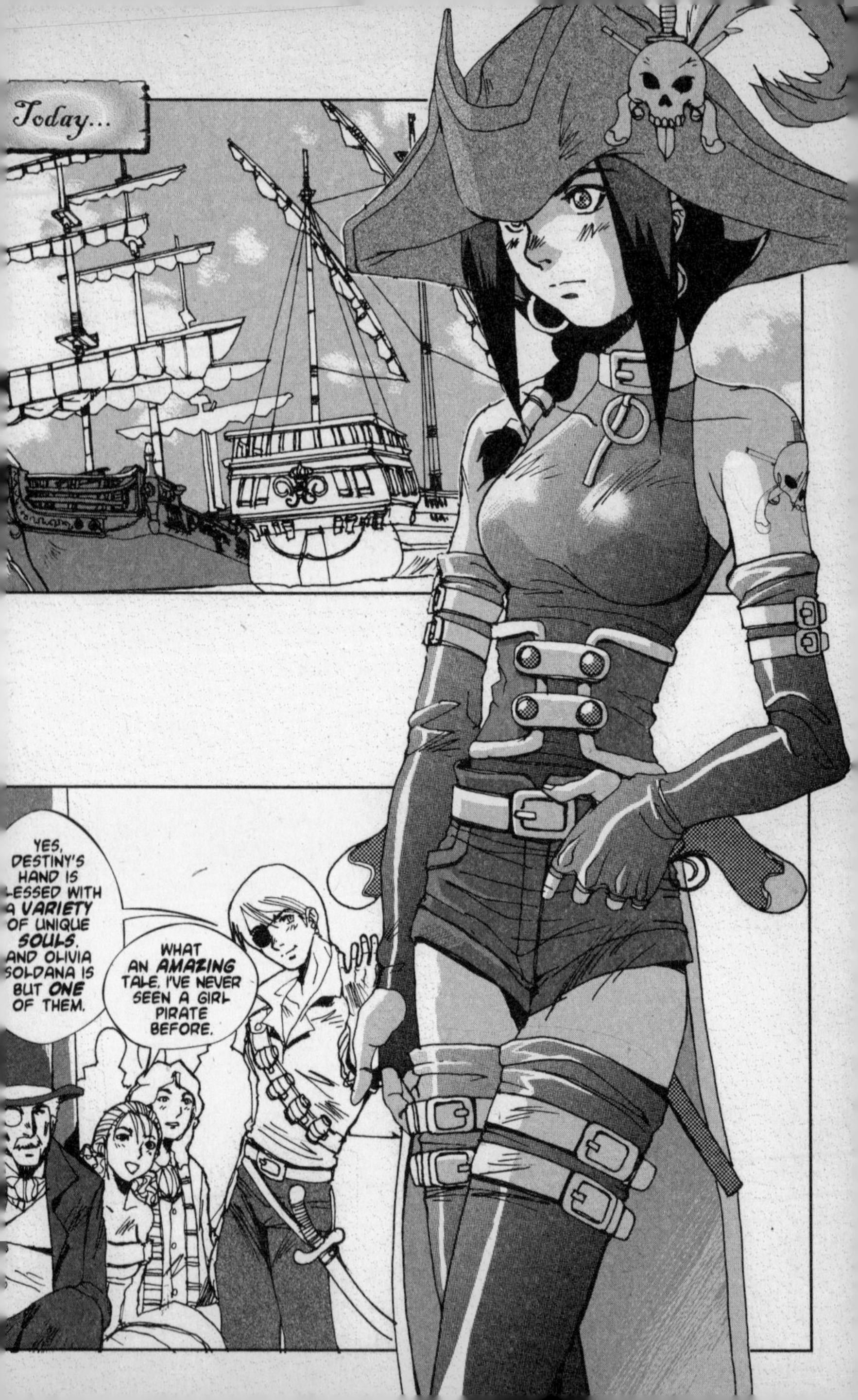
Today...
WHAT AN **AMAZING** TALE. I'VE NEVER SEEN A GIRL PIRATE BEFORE.
YES, DESTINY'S HAND IS LESSED WITH A **VARIETY** OF UNIQUE **SOULS**, AND OLIVIA SOLDANA IS BUT **ONE** OF THEM.

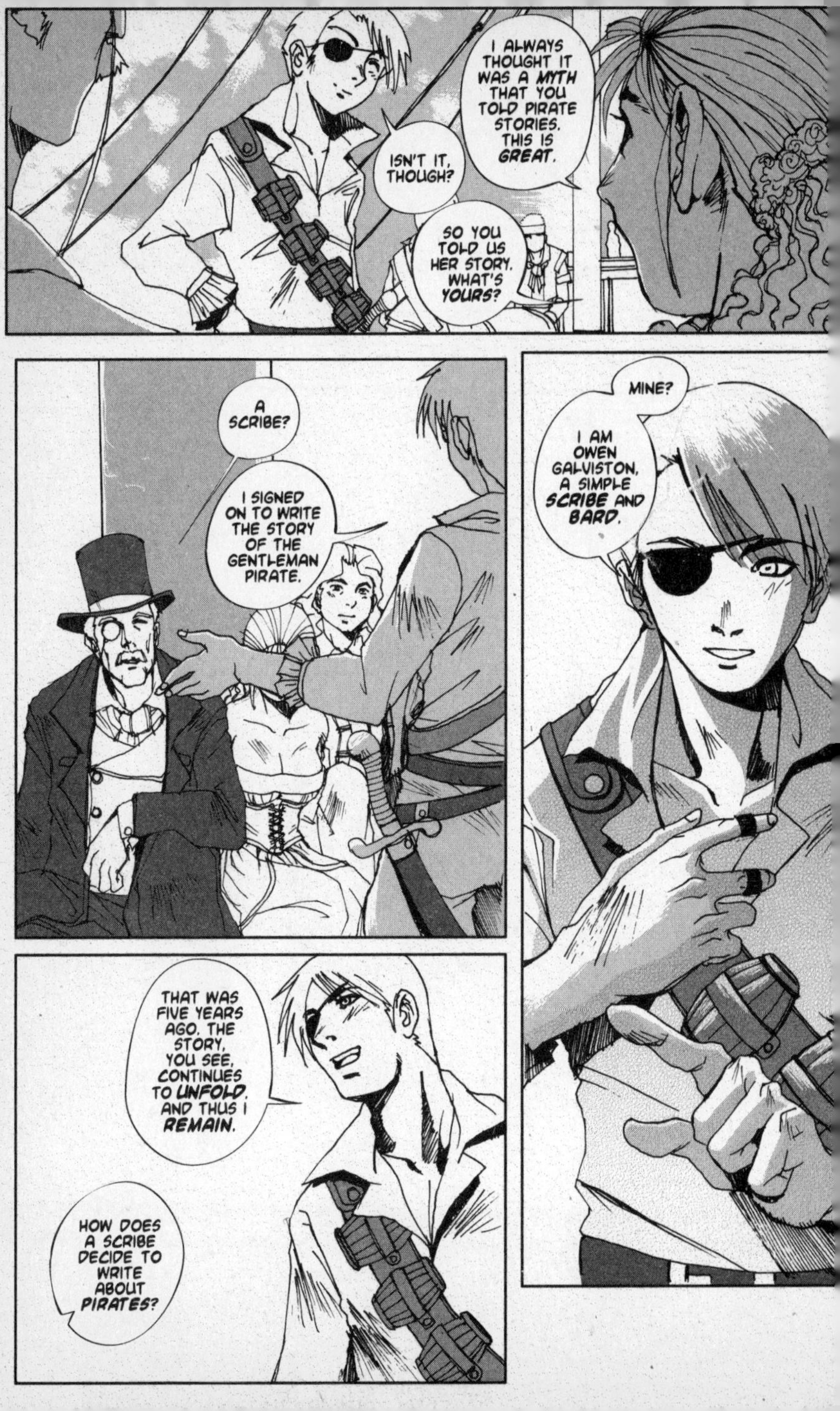
I ALWAYS THOUGHT IT WAS A MYTH THAT YOU TOLD PIRATE STORIES. THIS IS GREAT.
ISN'T IT, THOUGH?
SO YOU TOLD US HER STORY. WHAT'S YOURS?
MINE?
I AM OWEN GALVISTON, A SIMPLE SCRIBE AND BARD.
A SCRIBE?
I SIGNED ON TO WRITE THE STORY OF THE GENTLEMAN PIRATE.
THAT WAS FIVE YEARS AGO. THE STORY, YOU SEE, CONTINUES TO UNFOLD. AND THUS I REMAIN.
HOW DOES A SCRIBE DECIDE TO WRITE ABOUT PIRATES?

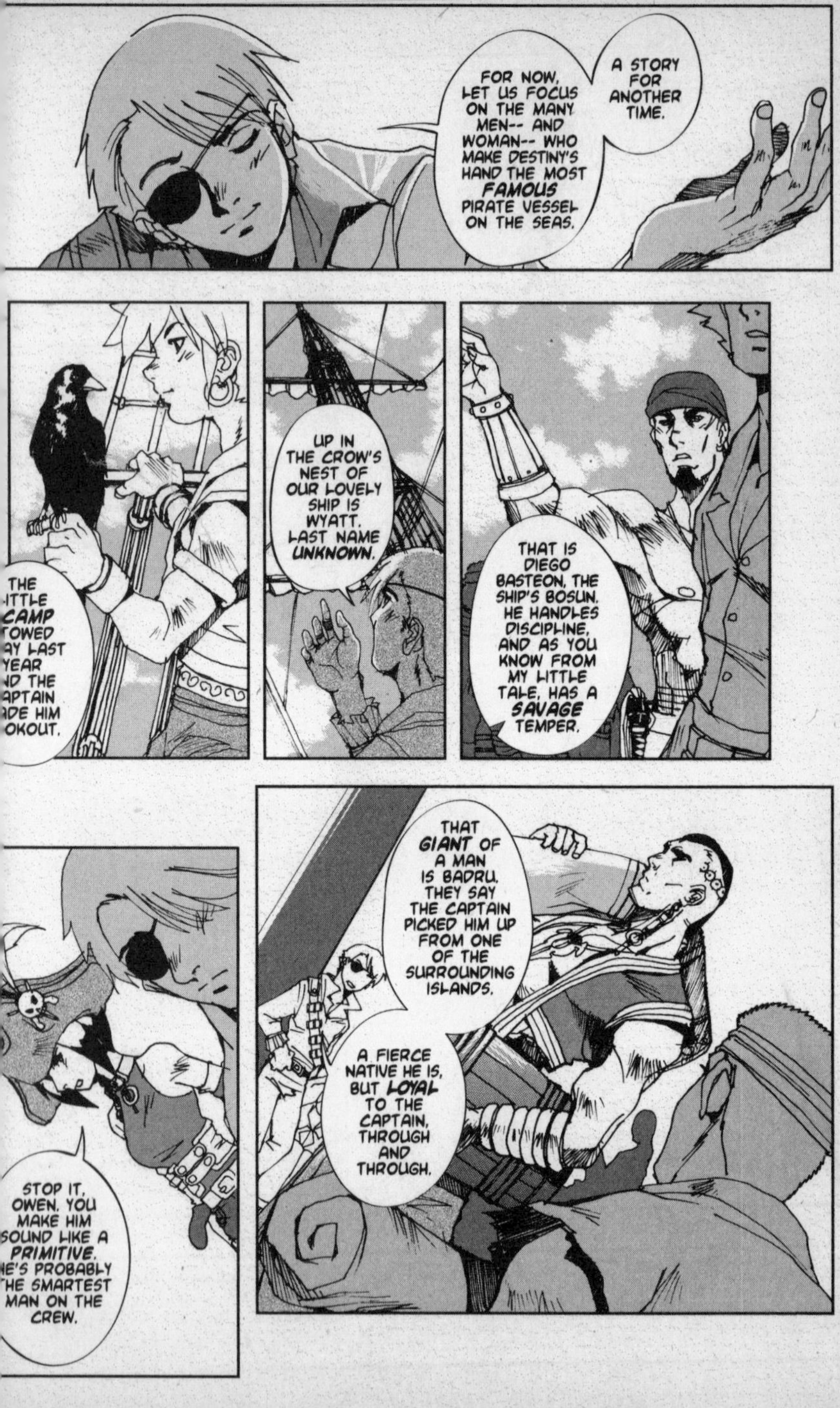
A STORY FOR ANOTHER TIME.
FOR NOW, LET US FOCUS ON THE MANY MEN-- AND WOMAN-- WHO MAKE DESTINY'S HAND THE MOST **FAMOUS** PIRATE VESSEL ON THE SEAS.
THAT IS DIEGO BASTEON, THE SHIP'S BOSUN. HE HANDLES DISCIPLINE, AND AS YOU KNOW FROM MY LITTLE TALE, HAS A **SAVAGE** TEMPER.
UP IN THE CROW'S NEST OF OUR LOVELY SHIP IS WYATT. LAST NAME **UNKNOWN**.
THE ITTLE **CAMP** TOWED AY LAST YEAR ND THE APTAIN ADE HIM OKOUT.
THAT **GIANT** OF A MAN IS BADRU. THEY SAY THE CAPTAIN PICKED HIM UP FROM ONE OF THE SURROUNDING ISLANDS.
A FIERCE NATIVE HE IS, BUT **LOYAL** TO THE CAPTAIN, THROUGH AND THROUGH.
STOP IT, OWEN. YOU MAKE HIM SOUND LIKE A **PRIMITIVE**. E'S PROBABLY THE SMARTEST MAN ON THE CREW.

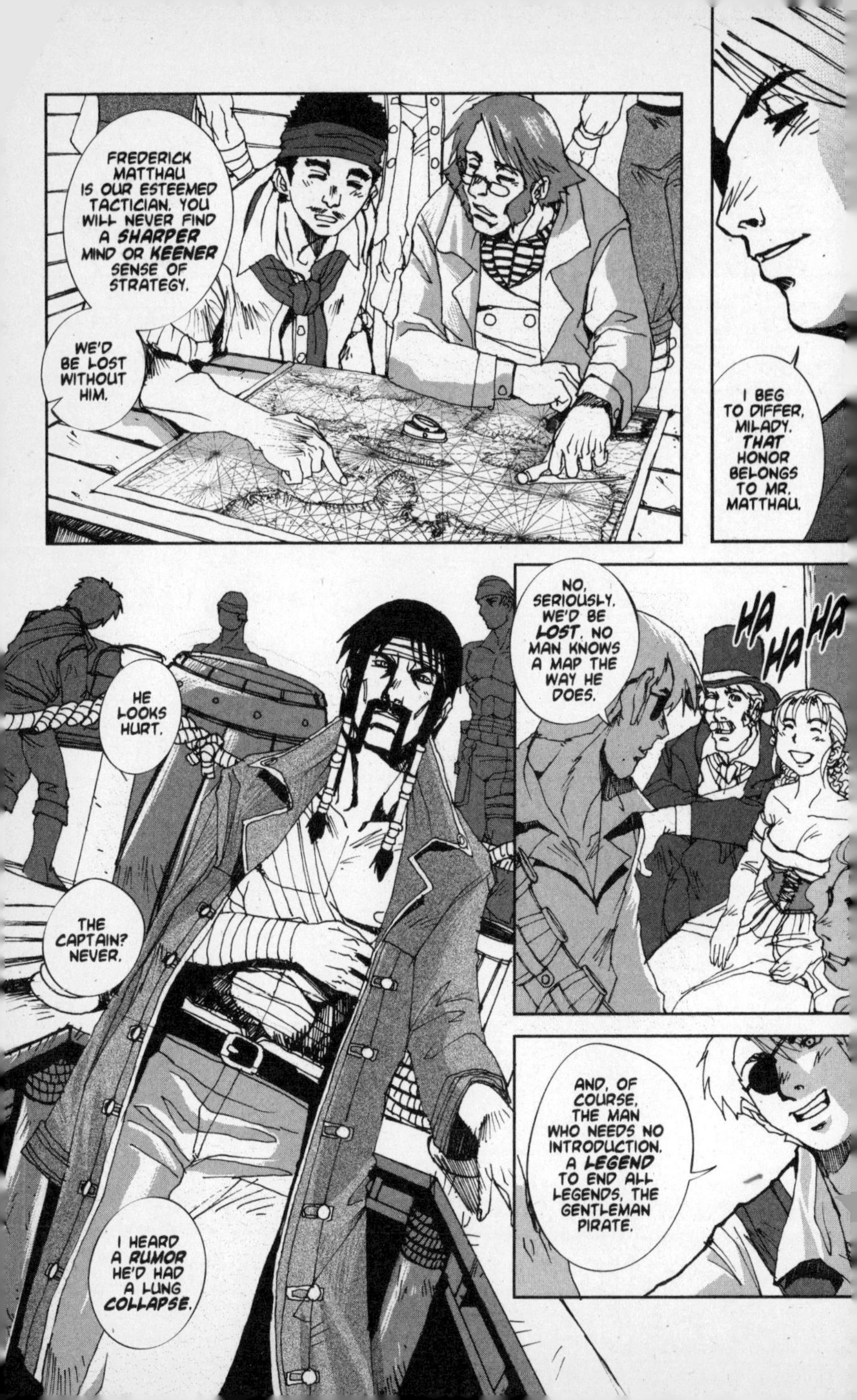
I BEG TO DIFFER, MILADY. THAT HONOR BELONGS TO MR. MATTHAU.
FREDERICK MATTHAU IS OUR ESTEEMED TACTICIAN. YOU WILL NEVER FIND A SHARPER MIND OR KEENER SENSE OF STRATEGY.
WE'D BE LOST WITHOUT HIM.
NO, SERIOUSLY. WE'D BE LOST. NO MAN KNOWS A MAP THE WAY HE DOES.
HA HA HA HA
AND, OF COURSE, THE MAN WHO NEEDS NO INTRODUCTION. A LEGEND TO END ALL LEGENDS, THE GENTLEMAN PIRATE.
HE LOOKS HURT.
THE CAPTAIN? NEVER.
I HEARD A RUMOR HE'D HAD A LUNG COLLAPSE.

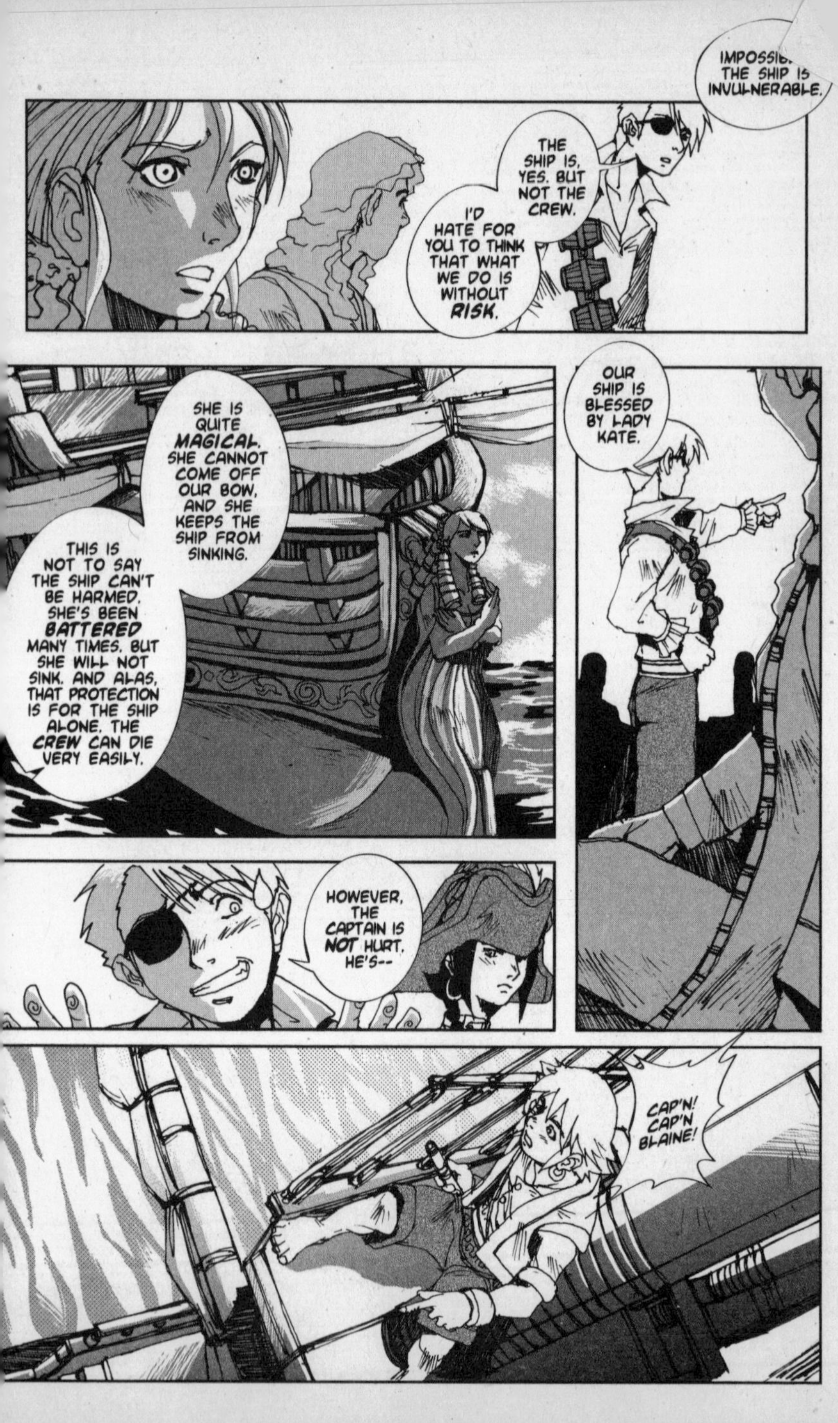
IMPOSSIB THE SHIP IS INVULNERABLE.
THE SHIP IS, YES. BUT NOT THE CREW.
I'D HATE FOR YOU TO THINK THAT WHAT WE DO IS WITHOUT RISK.
OUR SHIP IS BLESSED BY LADY KATE.
SHE IS QUITE MAGICAL. SHE CANNOT COME OFF OUR BOW, AND SHE KEEPS THE SHIP FROM SINKING.
THIS IS NOT TO SAY THE SHIP CAN'T BE HARMED. SHE'S BEEN BATTERED MANY TIMES. BUT SHE WILL NOT SINK. AND ALAS, THAT PROTECTION IS FOR THE SHIP ALONE. THE CREW CAN DIE VERY EASILY.
HOWEVER, THE CAPTAIN IS NOT HURT. HE'S--
CAP'N! CAP'N BLAINE!

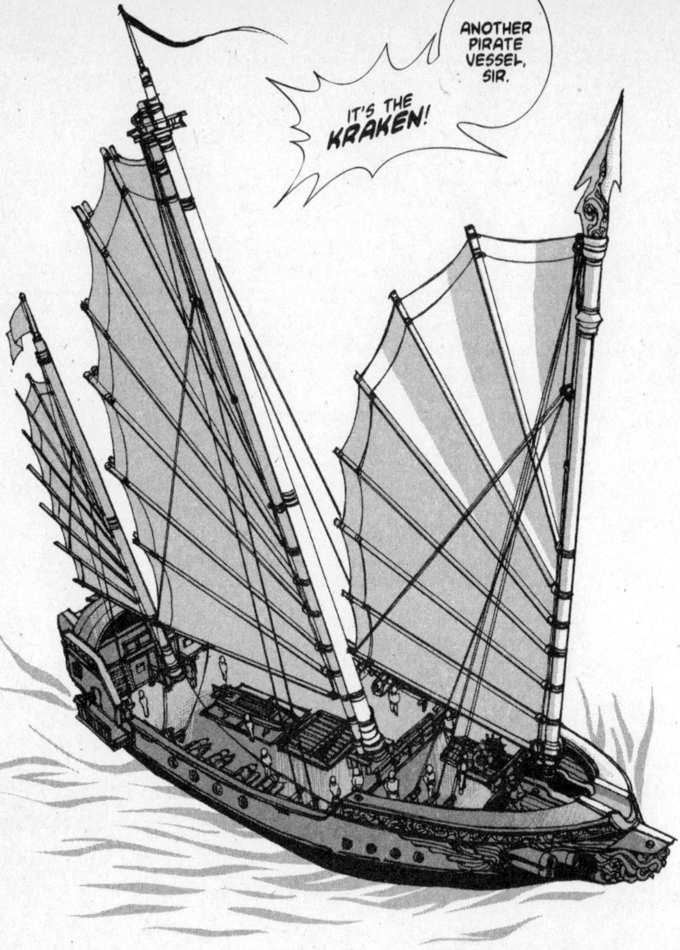
ANOTHER PIRATE VESSEL, SIR.
IT'S THE *KRAKEN*!

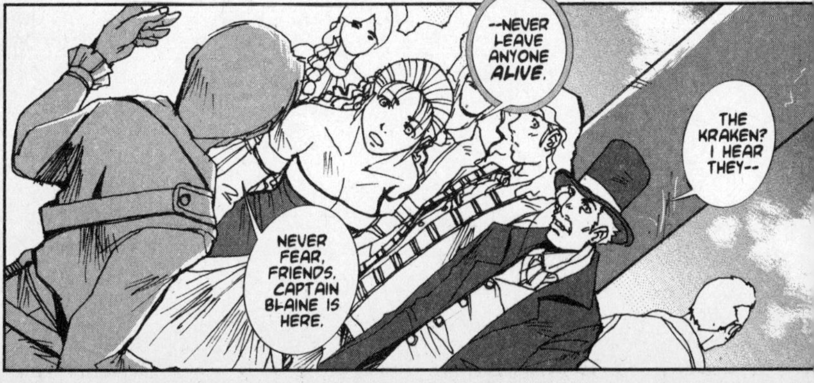
THE KRAKEN? I HEAR THEY--
--NEVER LEAVE ANYONE *ALIVE*.
NEVER FEAR, FRIENDS, CAPTAIN BLAINE IS HERE.

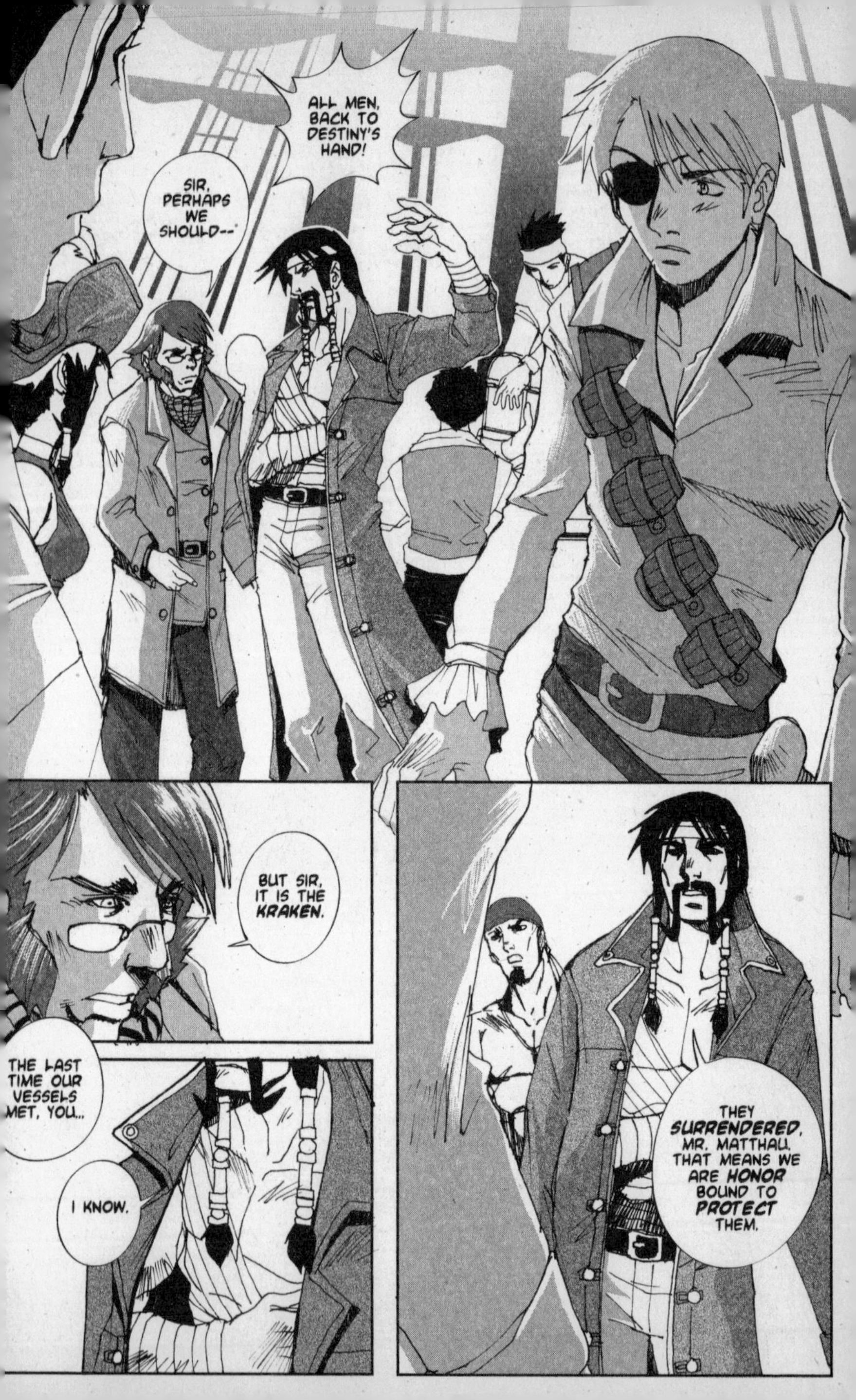
ALL MEN, BACK TO DESTINY'S HAND!
SIR, PERHAPS WE SHOULD--
THEY SURRENDERED, MR. MATTHAU. THAT MEANS WE ARE HONOR BOUND TO PROTECT THEM.
BUT SIR, IT IS THE KRAKEN.
THE LAST TIME OUR VESSELS MET, YOU...
I KNOW.

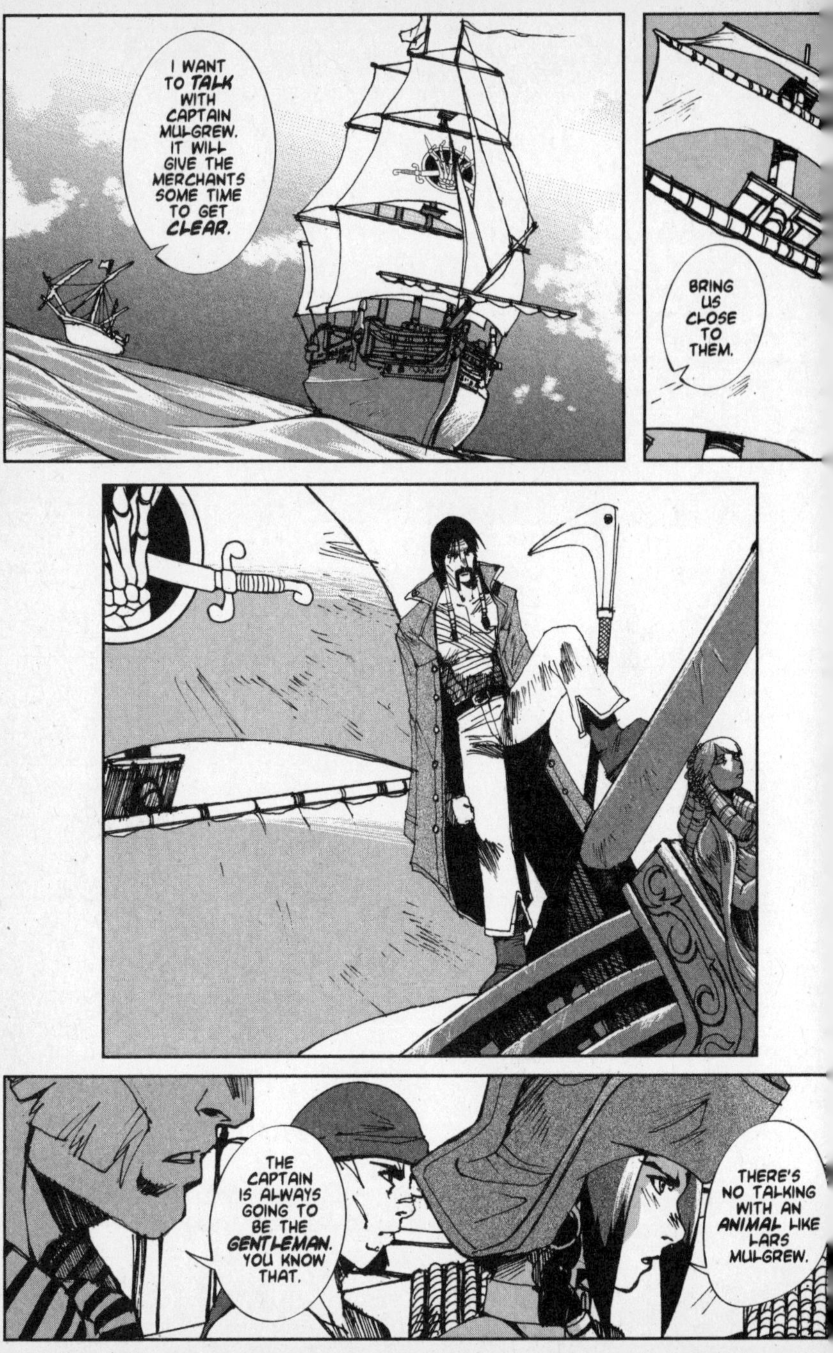
BRING US CLOSE TO THEM.
I WANT TO TALK WITH CAPTAIN MULGREW. IT WILL GIVE THE MERCHANTS SOME TIME TO GET CLEAR.
THERE'S NO TALKING WITH AN ANIMAL LIKE LARS MULGREW.
THE CAPTAIN IS ALWAYS GOING TO BE THE GENTLEMAN. YOU KNOW THAT.

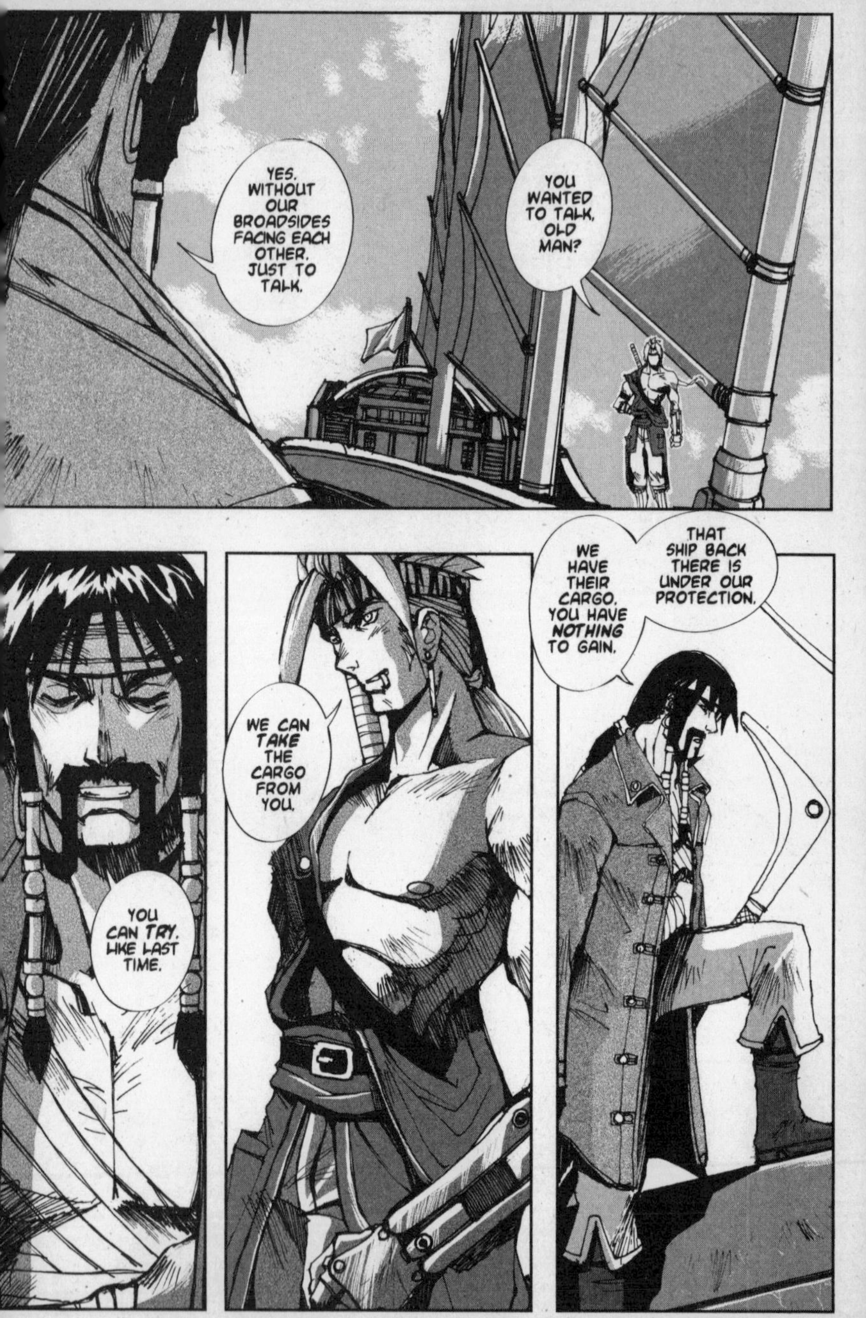
YOU WANTED TO TALK, OLD MAN?
YES. WITHOUT OUR BROADSIDES FACING EACH OTHER. JUST TO TALK.
THAT SHIP BACK THERE IS UNDER OUR PROTECTION.
WE HAVE THEIR CARGO. YOU HAVE NOTHING TO GAIN.
WE CAN TAKE THE CARGO FROM YOU.
YOU CAN TRY. LIKE LAST TIME.

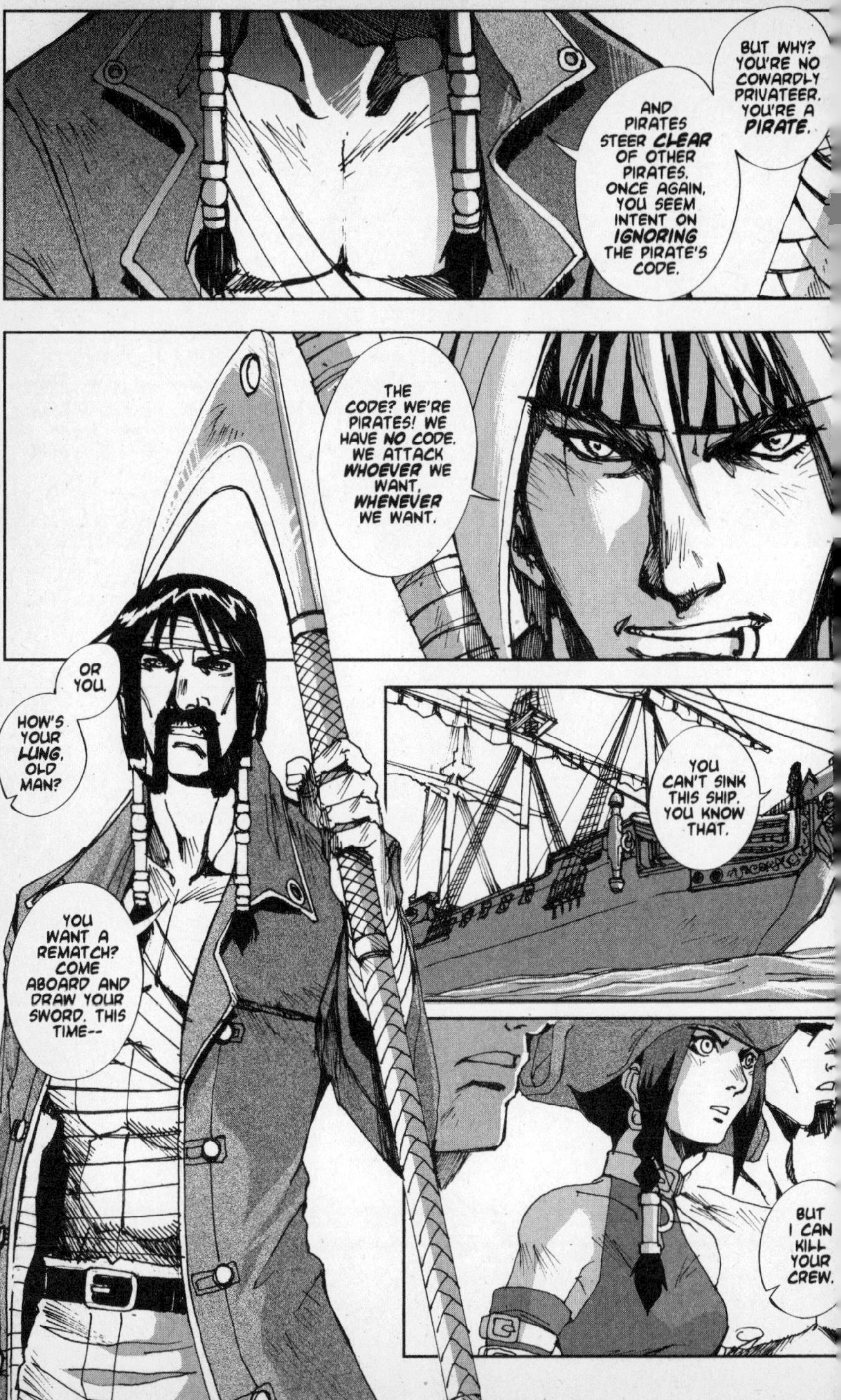
BUT WHY? YOU'RE NO COWARDLY PRIVATEER. YOU'RE A PIRATE.
AND PIRATES STEER CLEAR OF OTHER PIRATES. ONCE AGAIN, YOU SEEM INTENT ON IGNORING THE PIRATE'S CODE.
THE CODE? WE'RE PIRATES! WE HAVE NO CODE. WE ATTACK WHOEVER WE WANT, WHENEVER WE WANT.
YOU CAN'T SINK THIS SHIP. YOU KNOW THAT.
BUT I CAN KILL YOUR CREW.
OR YOU.
HOW'S YOUR LUNG, OLD MAN?
YOU WANT A REMATCH? COME ABOARD AND DRAW YOUR SWORD. THIS TIME--

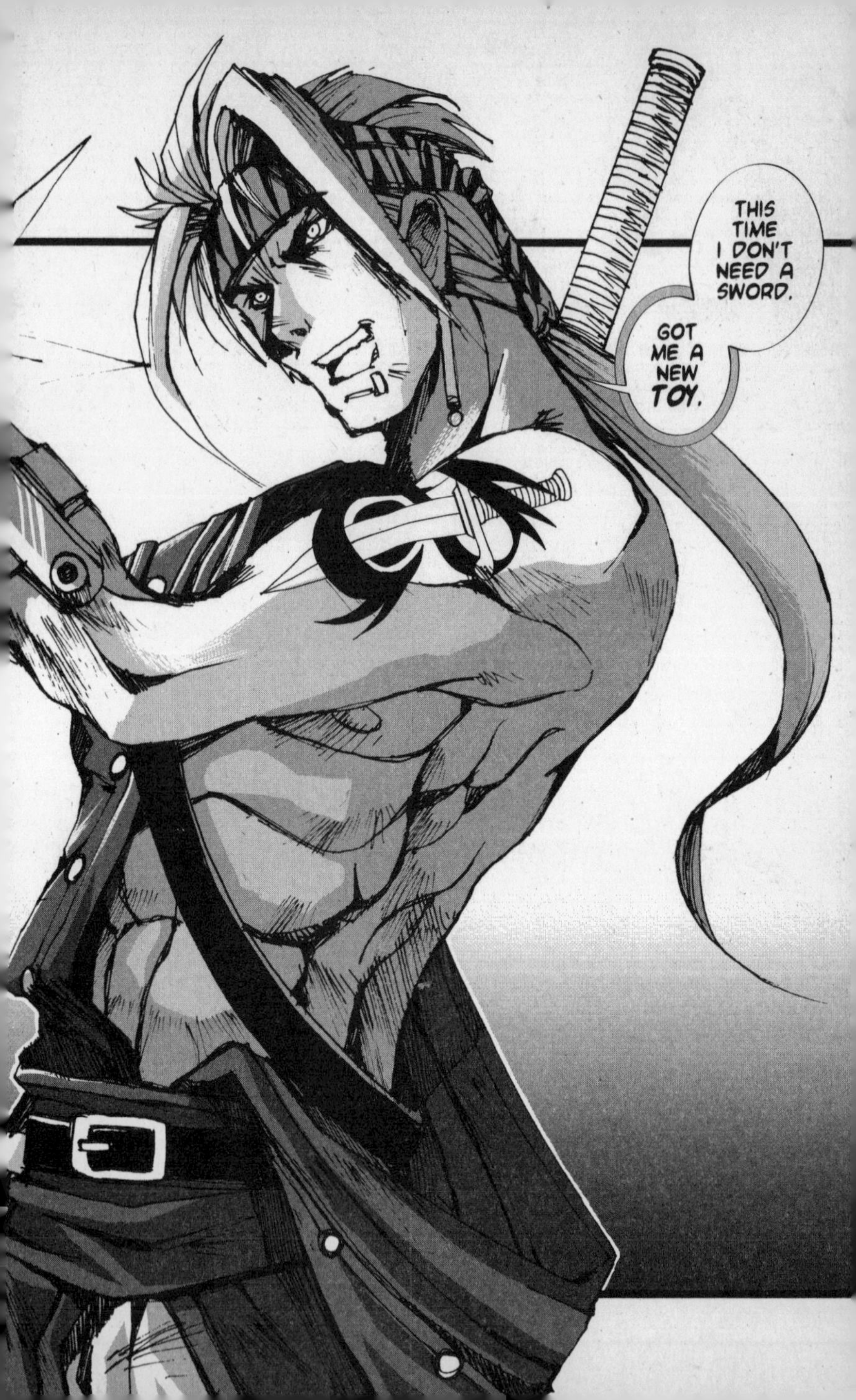
THIS TIME I DON'T NEED A SWORD.
GOT ME A NEW TOY.

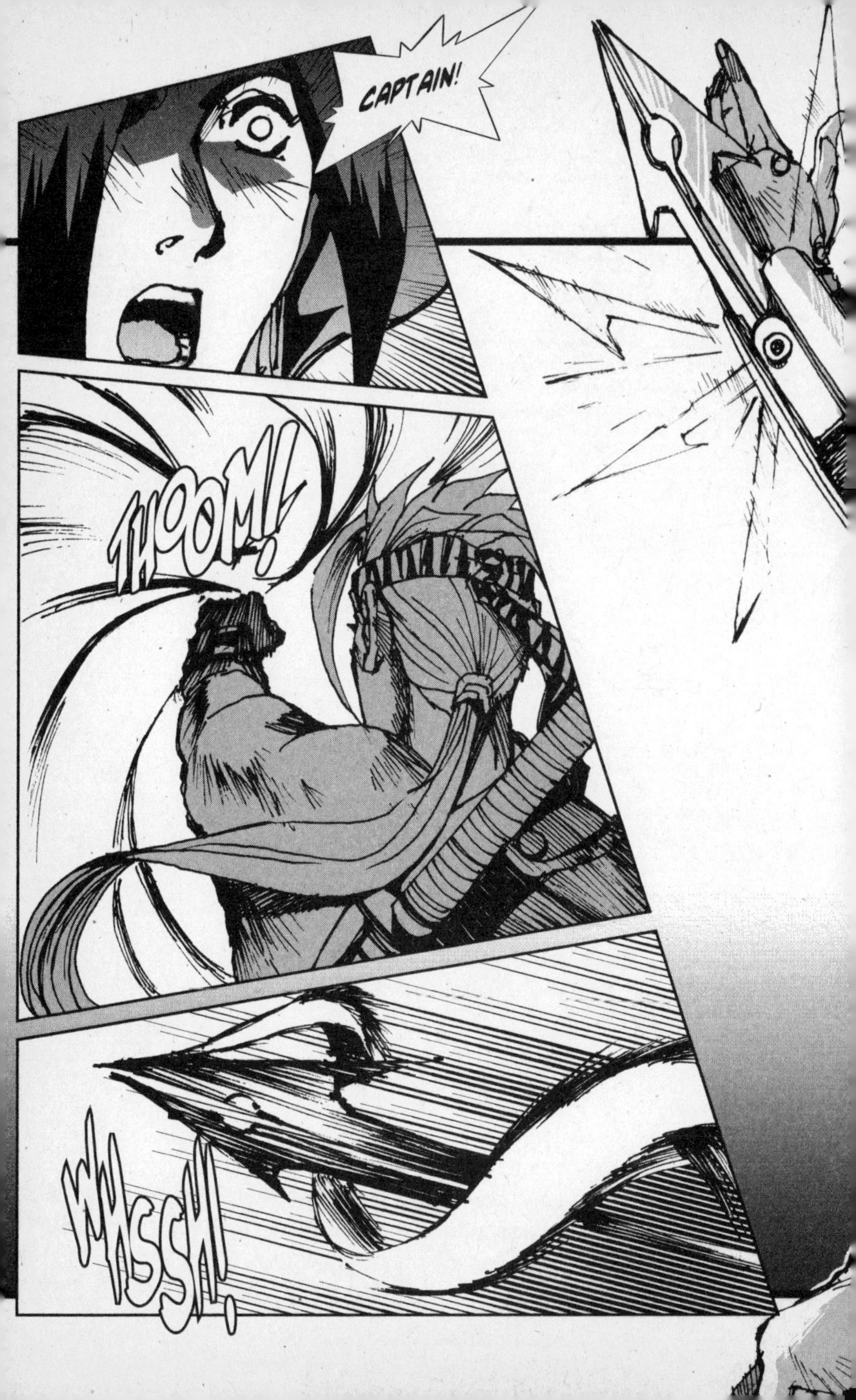
CAPTAIN!
THOOM!!
WHSSH!!

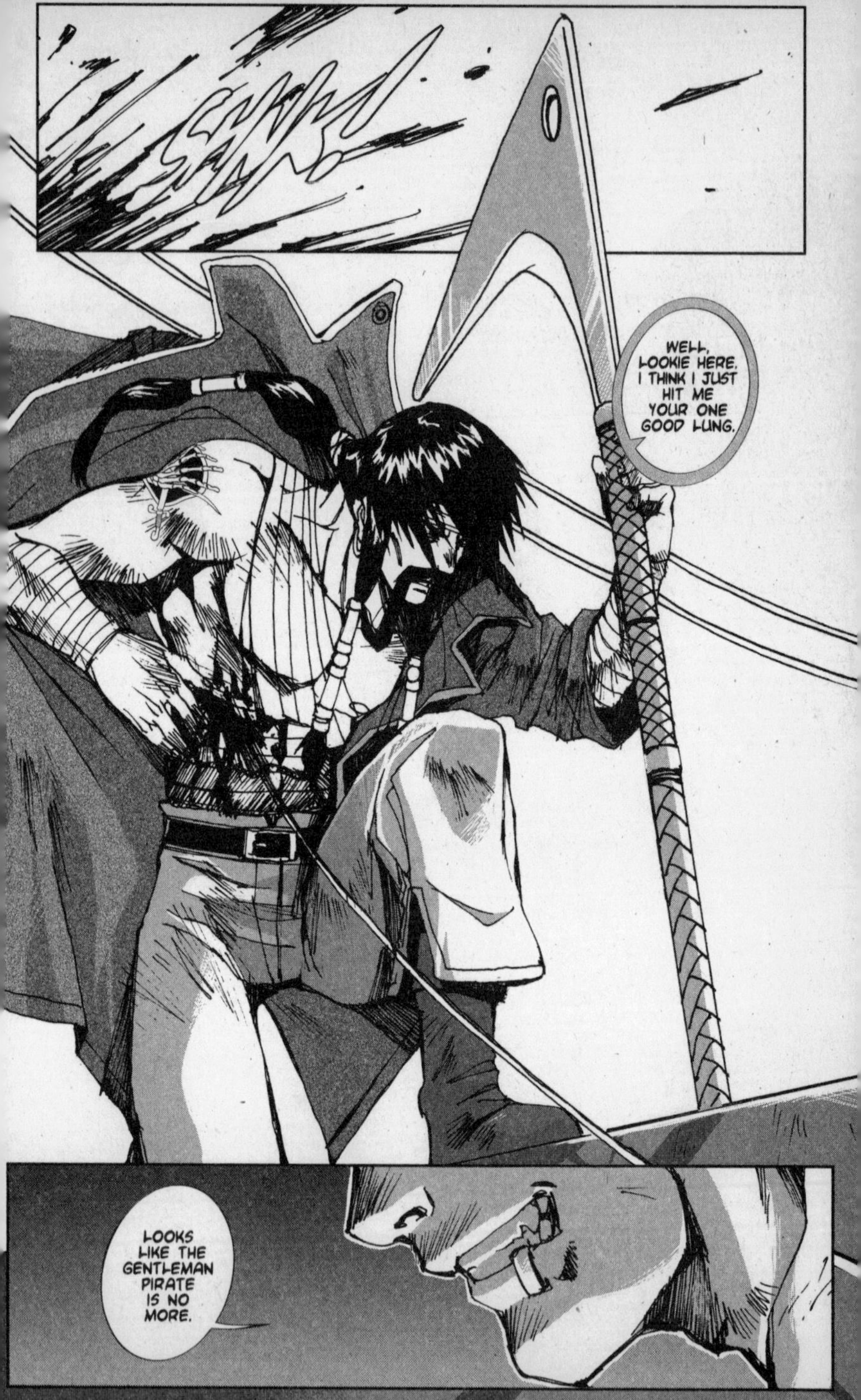
WELL, LOOKIE HERE. I THINK I JUST HIT ME YOUR ONE GOOD LUNG.
LOOKS LIKE THE GENTLEMAN PIRATE IS NO MORE.

CHAPTER 3
Dead Seas

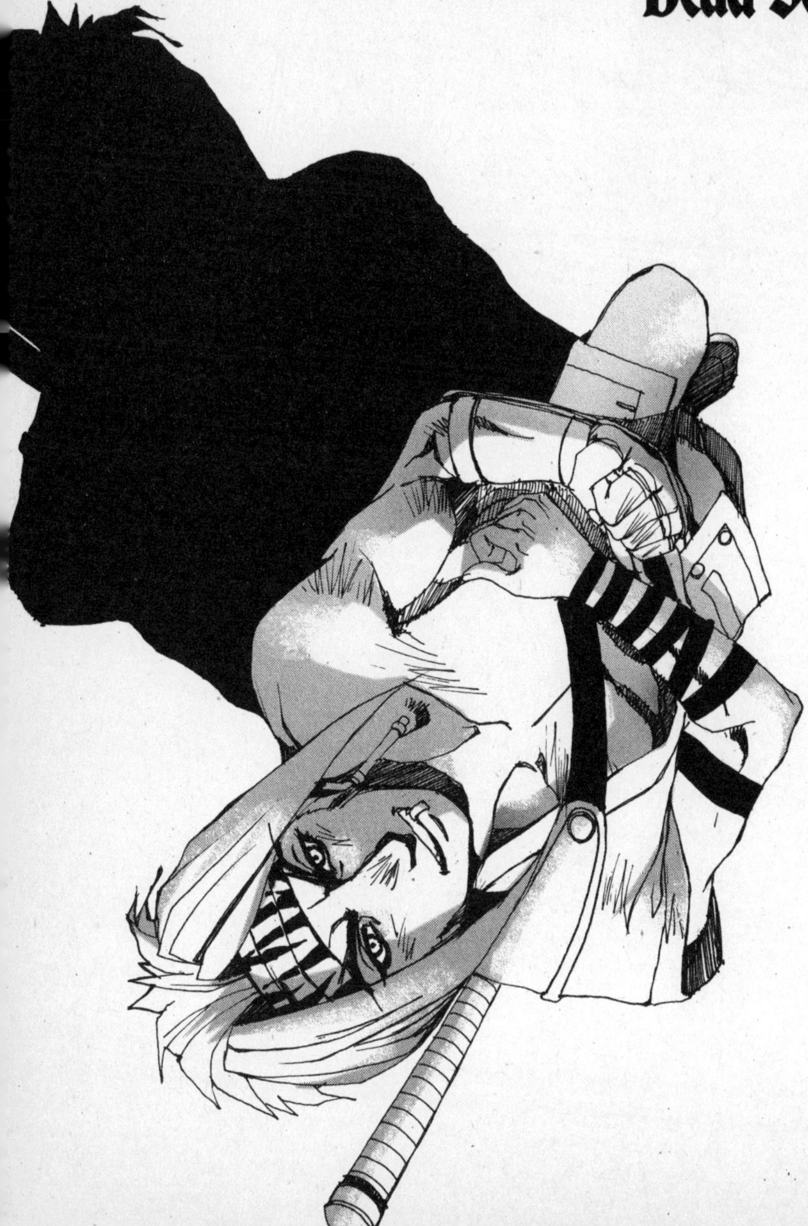

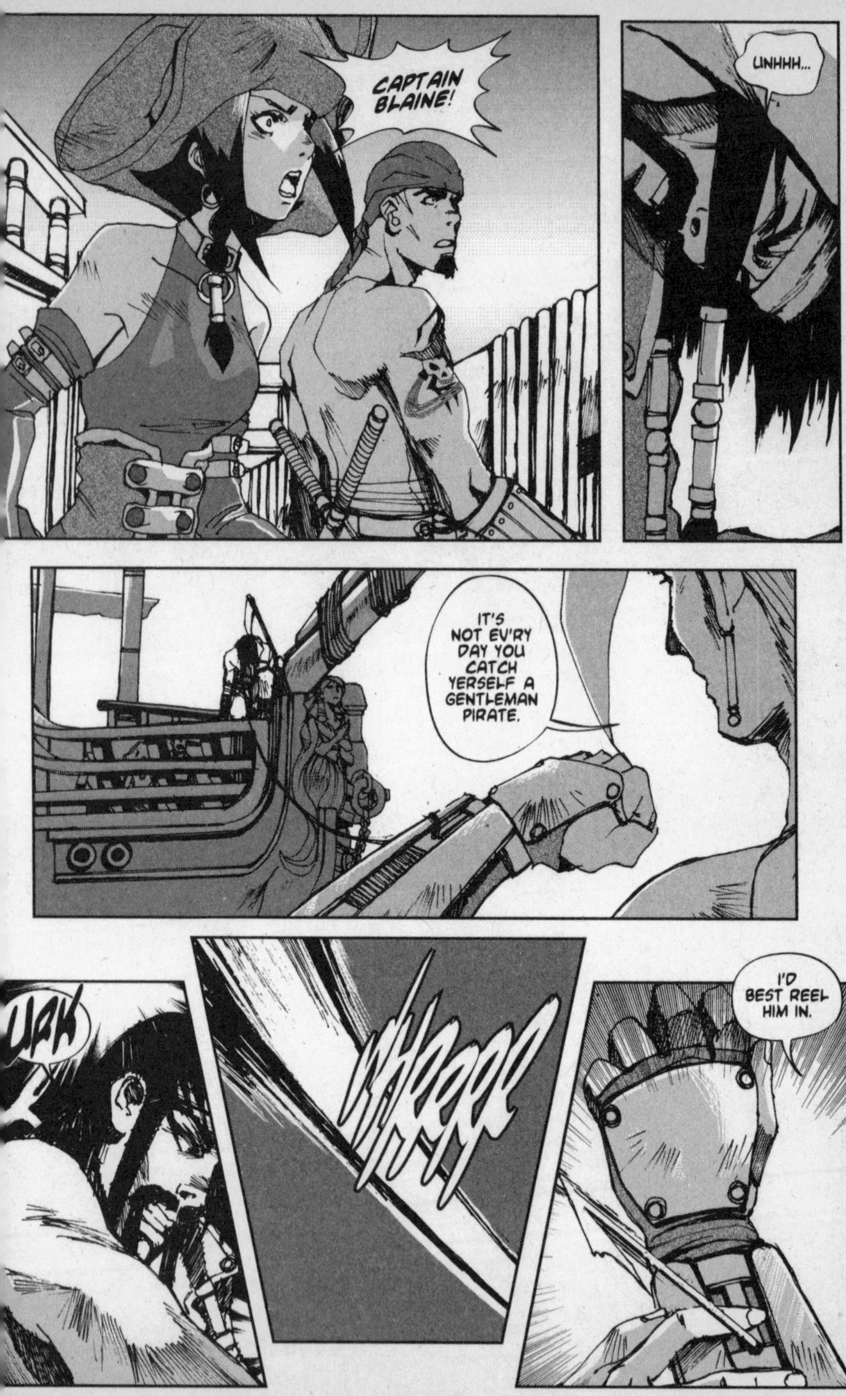
UNHHH...
CAPTAIN BLAINE!
IT'S NOT EV'RY DAY YOU CATCH YERSELF A GENTLEMAN PIRATE.
I'D BEST REEL HIM IN.
URK

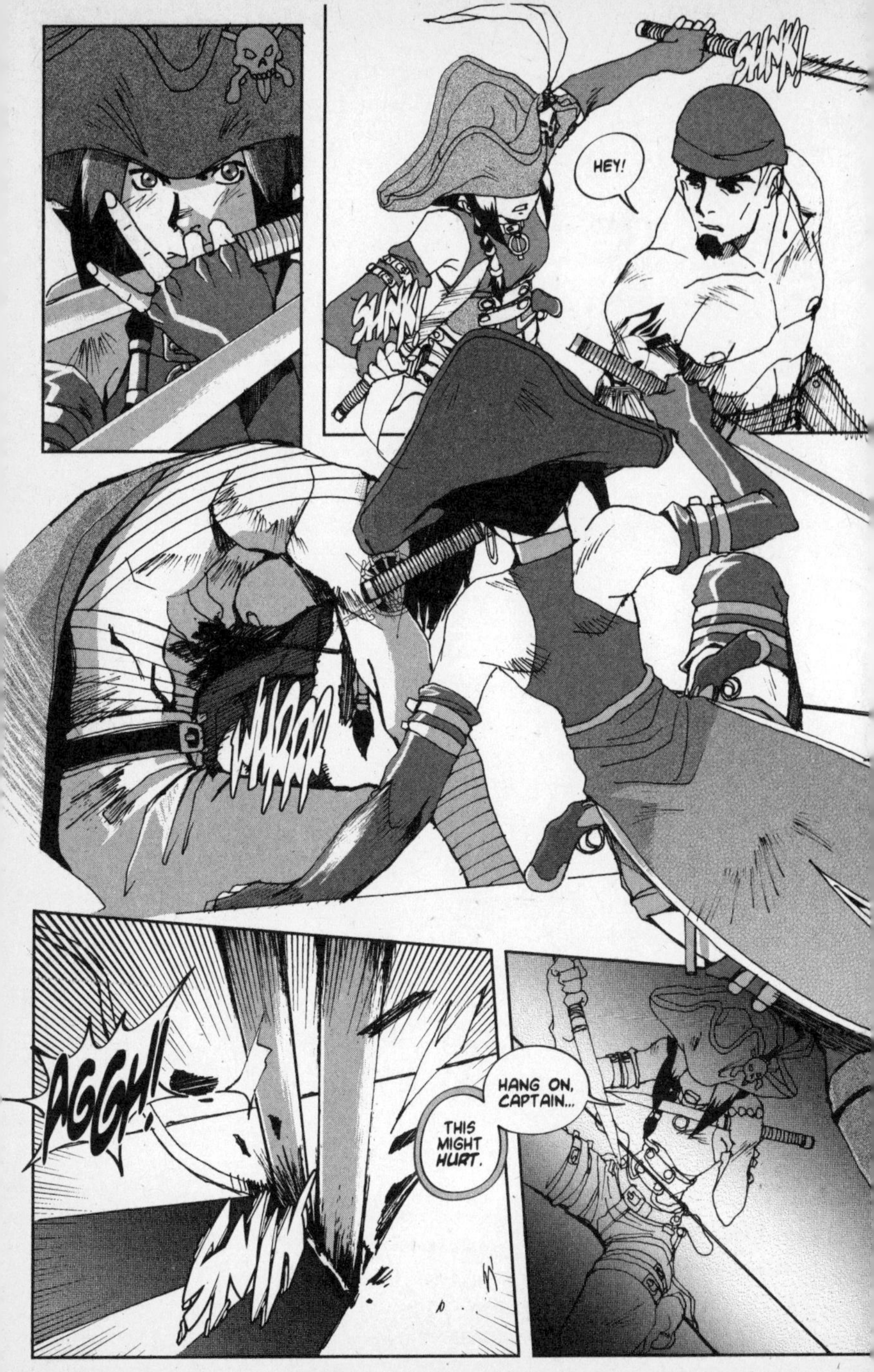
SHINK!
HEY!
SHINK!
HANG ON, CAPTAIN...
THIS MIGHT HURT.
AGGH!

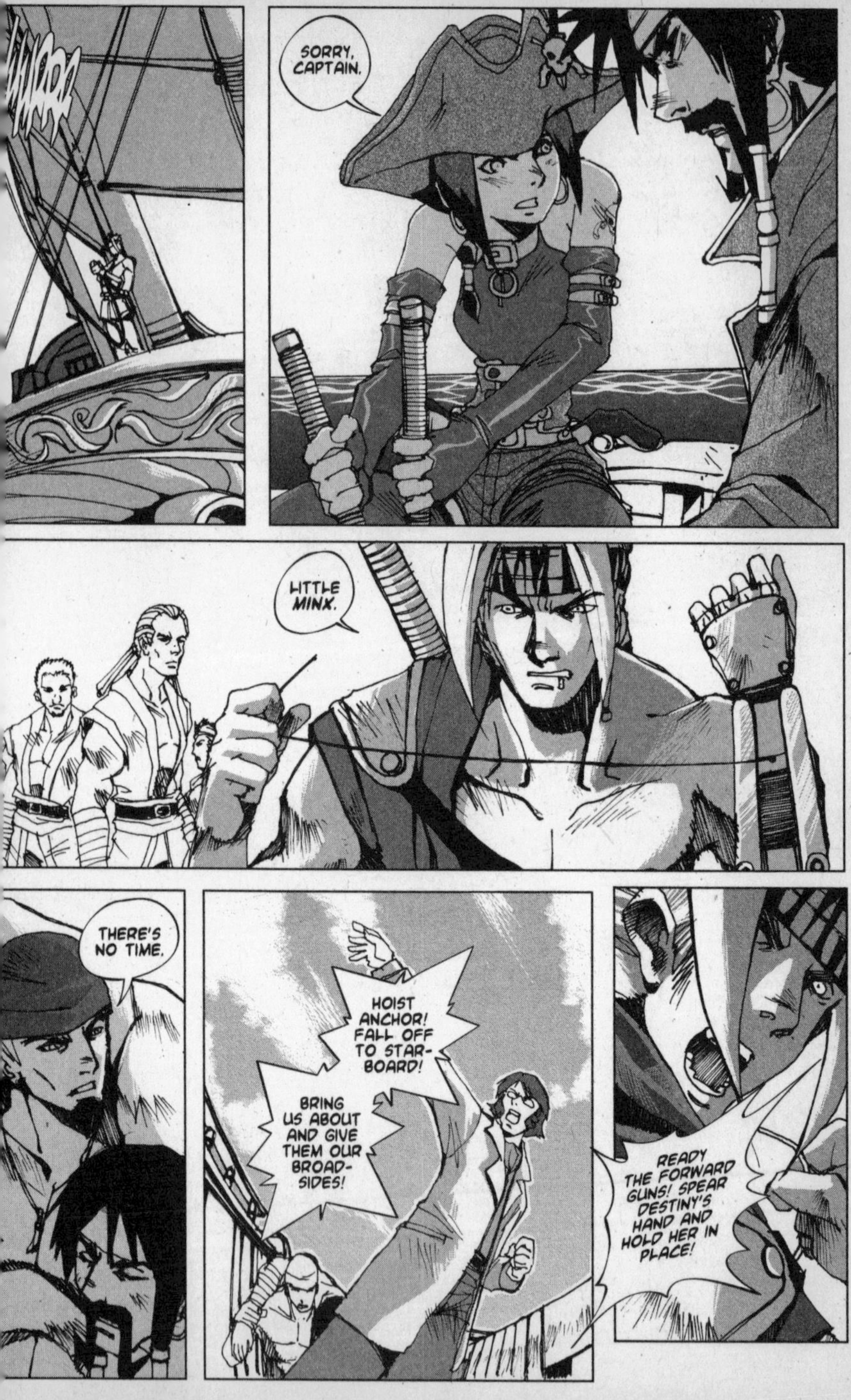
SORRY, CAPTAIN.
LITTLE MINX.
READY THE FORWARD GUNS! SPEAR DESTINY'S HAND AND HOLD HER IN PLACE!
HOIST ANCHOR! FALL OFF TO STAR-BOARD!
BRING US ABOUT AND GIVE THEM OUR BROAD-SIDES!
THERE'S NO TIME.

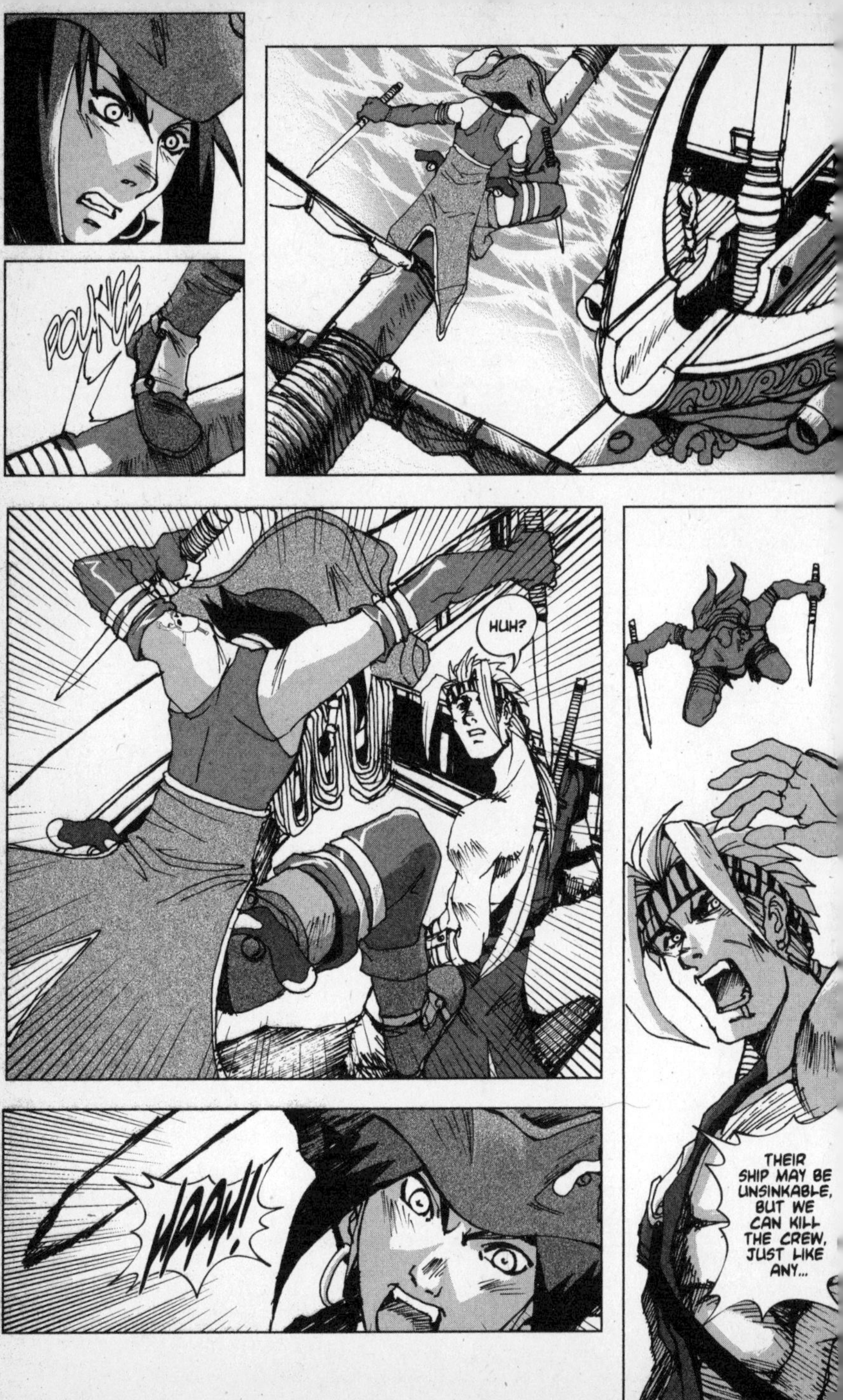
POUNCE
THEIR SHIP MAY BE UNSINKABLE, BUT WE CAN KILL THE CREW, JUST LIKE ANY...
HUH?
WAAH!

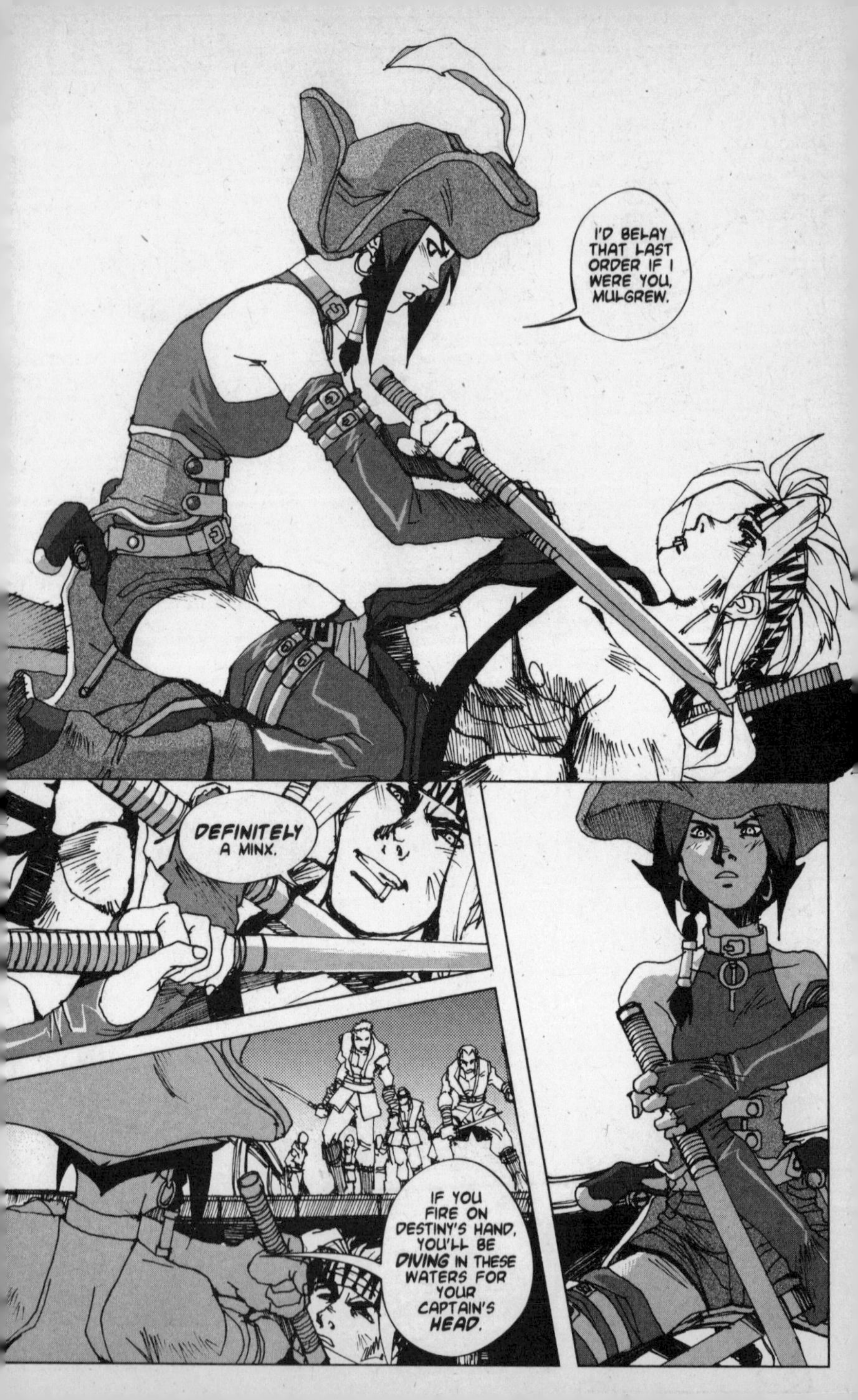
I'D BELAY THAT LAST ORDER IF I WERE YOU, MULGREW.
DEFINITELY A MINX.
IF YOU FIRE ON DESTINY'S HAND, YOU'LL BE DIVING IN THESE WATERS FOR YOUR CAPTAIN'S HEAD.

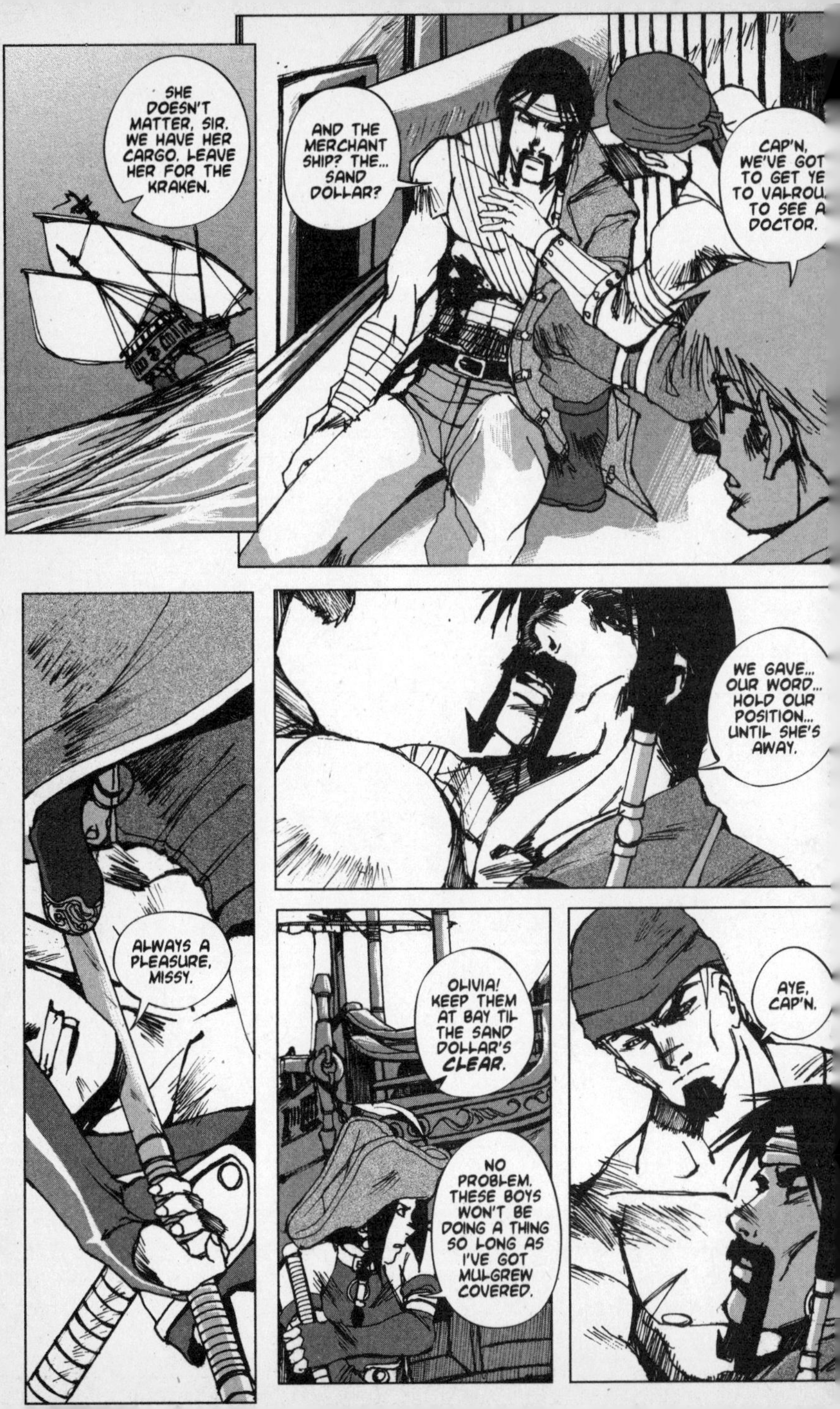
CAP'N, WE'VE GOT TO GET YE TO VALROU TO SEE A DOCTOR.
AND THE MERCHANT SHIP? THE... SAND DOLLAR?
SHE DOESN'T MATTER, SIR. WE HAVE HER CARGO. LEAVE HER FOR THE KRAKEN.
WE GAVE... OUR WORD... HOLD OUR POSITION... UNTIL SHE'S AWAY.
AYE, CAP'N.
OLIVIA! KEEP THEM AT BAY TIL THE SAND DOLLAR'S CLEAR.
NO PROBLEM. THESE BOYS WON'T BE DOING A THING SO LONG AS I'VE GOT MULGREW COVERED.
ALWAYS A PLEASURE, MISSY.

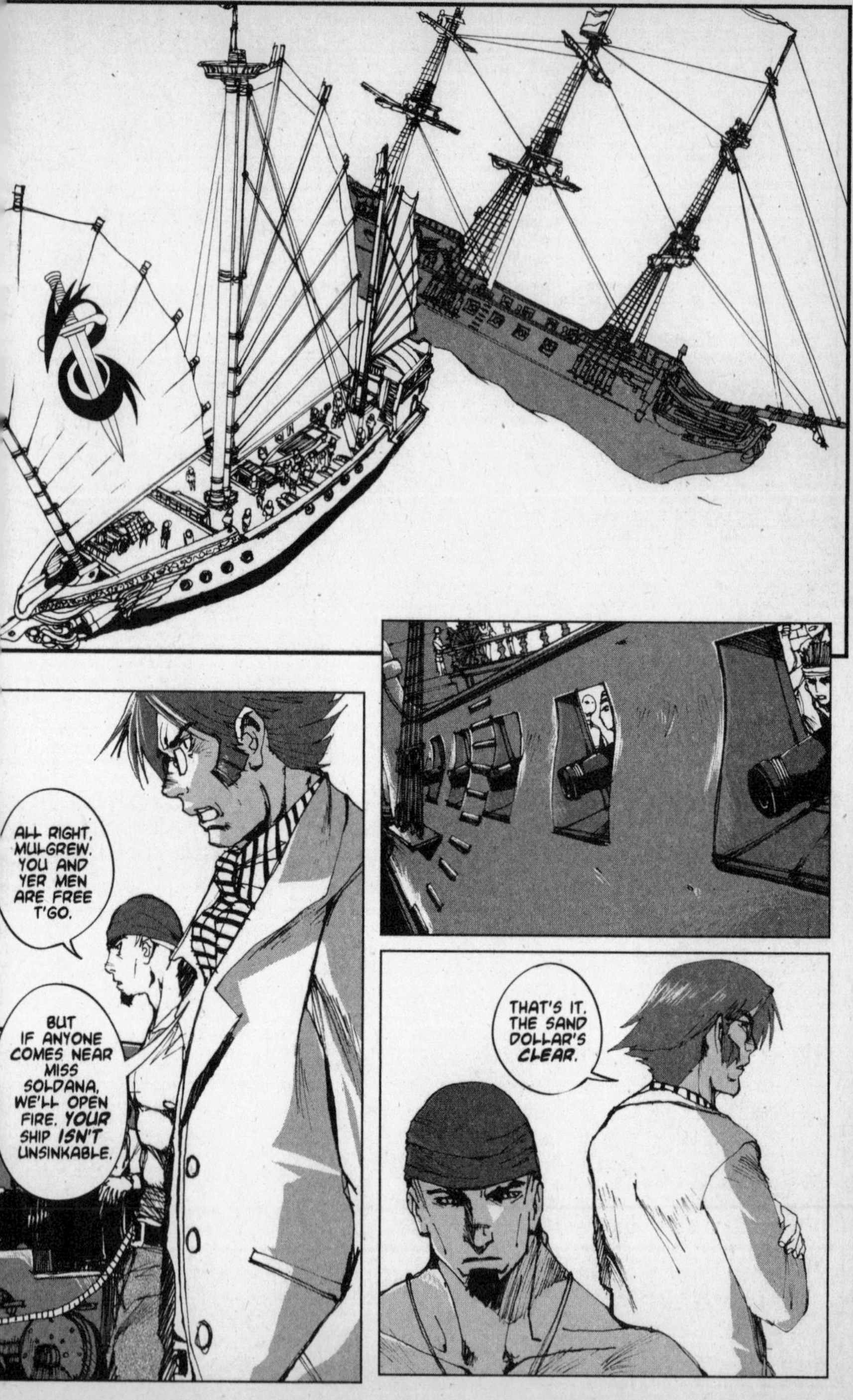
THAT'S IT. THE SAND DOLLAR'S CLEAR.
ALL RIGHT, MULGREW. YOU AND YER MEN ARE FREE T'GO.
BUT IF ANYONE COMES NEAR MISS SOLDANA, WE'LL OPEN FIRE. YOUR SHIP ISN'T UNSINKABLE.

COUNT ON IT.

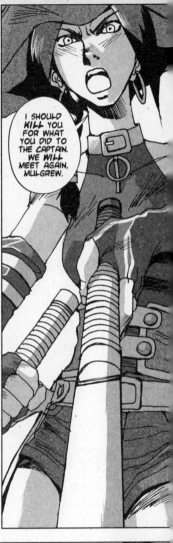

I SHOULD *KILL* YOU FOR WHAT YOU DID TO THE CAPTAIN. WE *WILL* MEET AGAIN, MULGREW.

A PLEASURE BEIN' STRADDLED BY YOU, MISSY. ONE DAY I PLAN TO RETURN THE FAVOR.

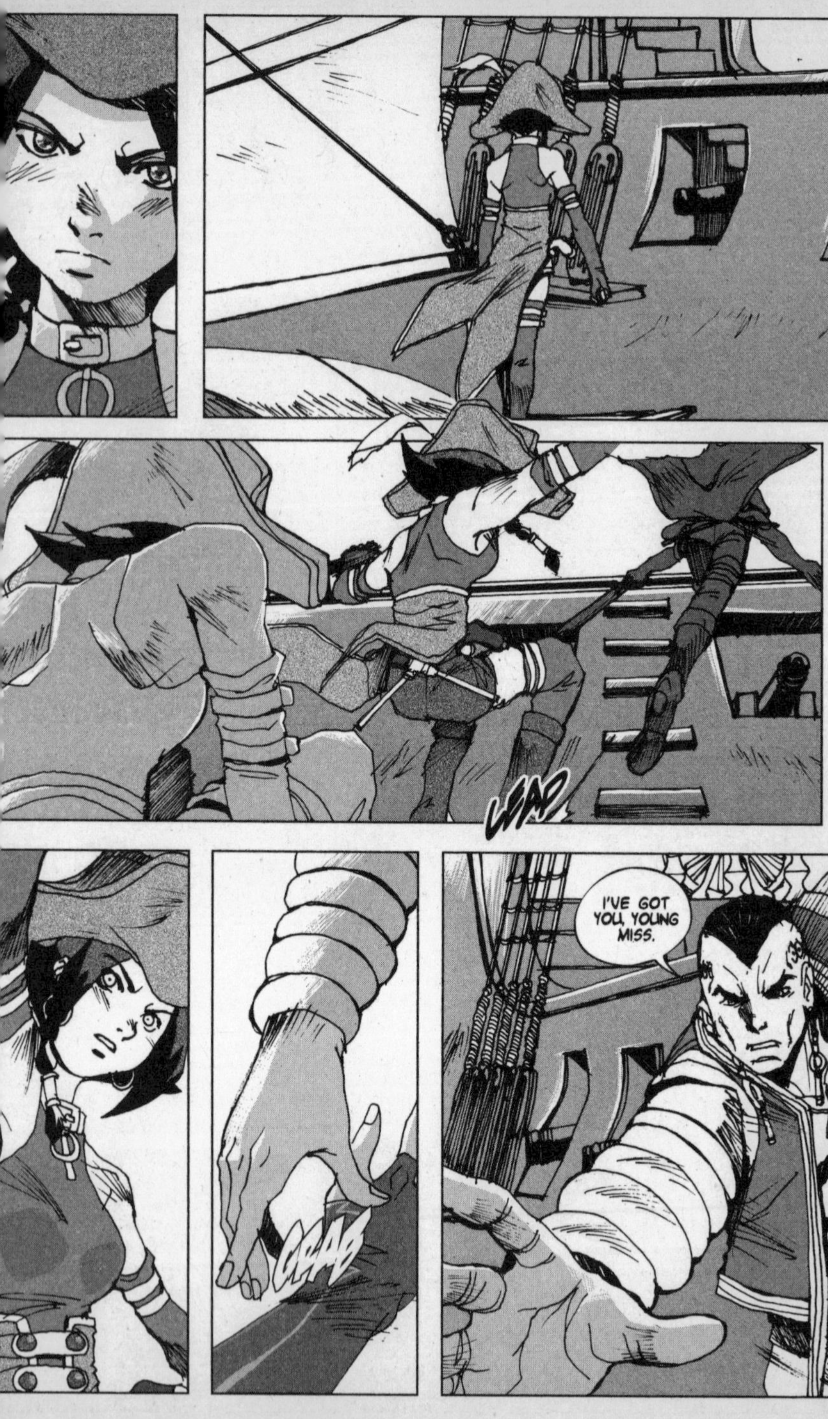
LEAP
I'VE GOT YOU, YOUNG MISS.
GRAB

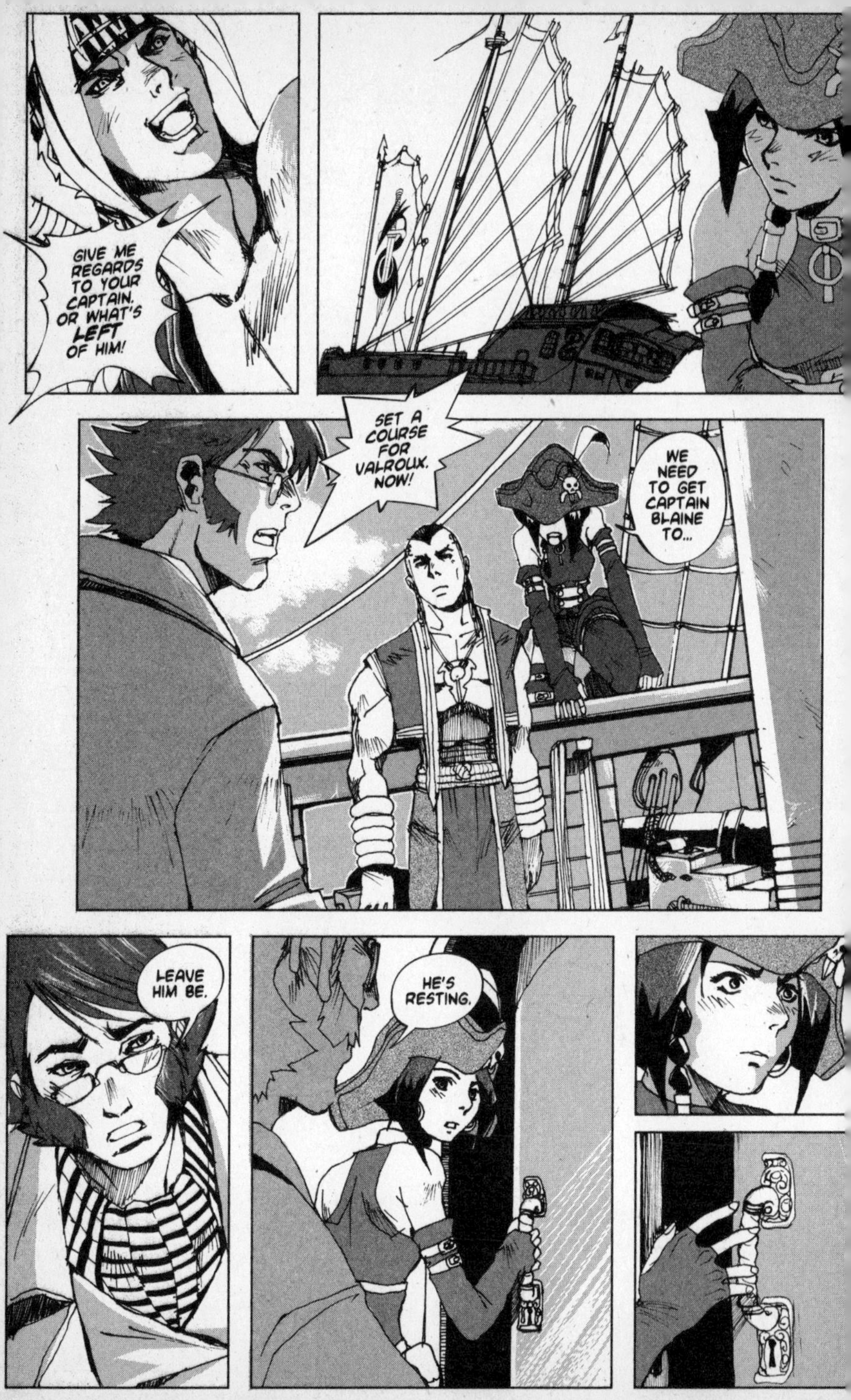
GIVE ME REGARDS TO YOUR CAPTAIN. OR WHAT'S **LEFT** OF HIM!
WE NEED TO GET CAPTAIN BLAINE TO...
SET A COURSE FOR VALROUX. NOW!
HE'S RESTING.
LEAVE HIM BE.

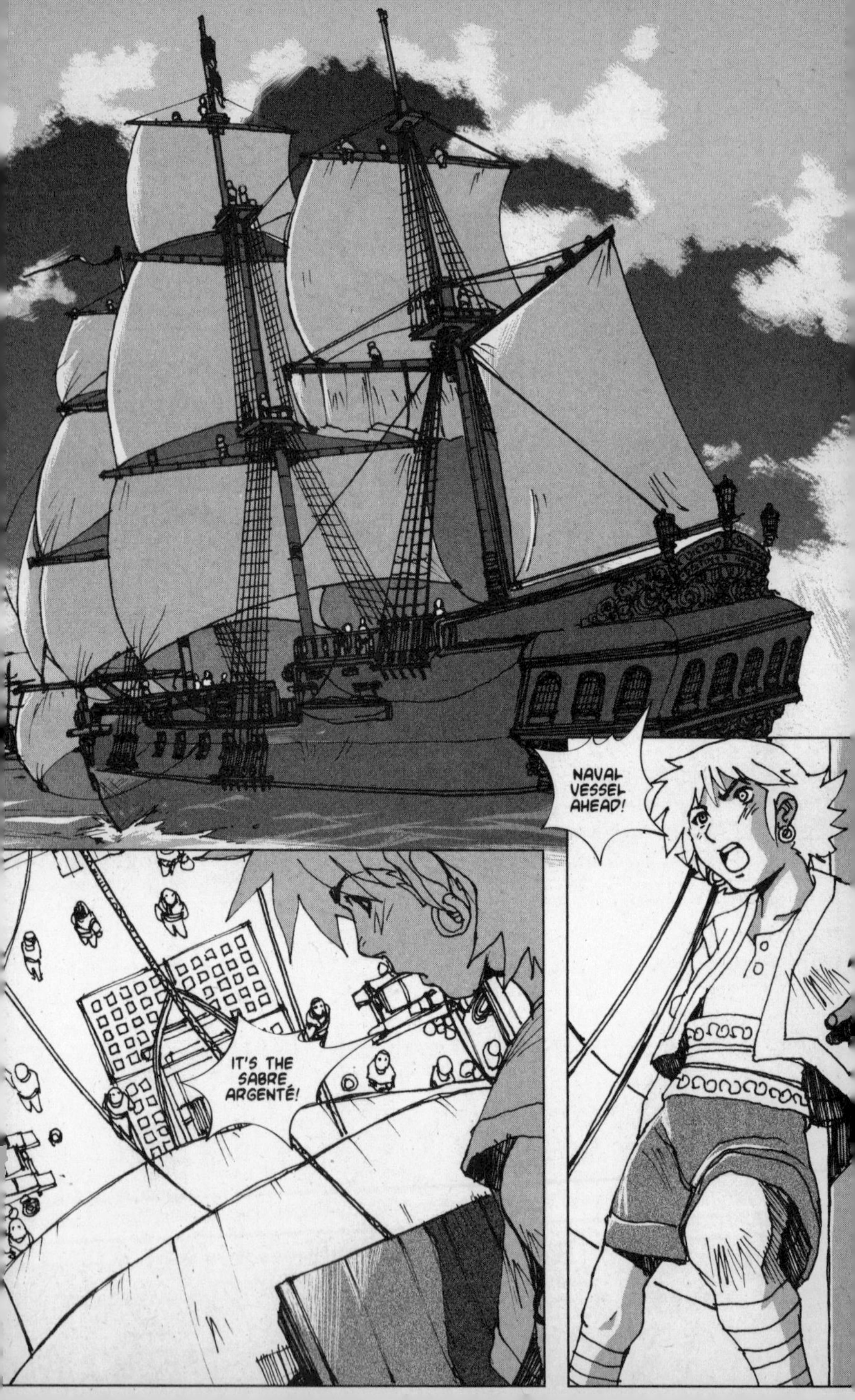
NAVAL VESSEL AHEAD!
IT'S THE SABRE ARGENTÉ!

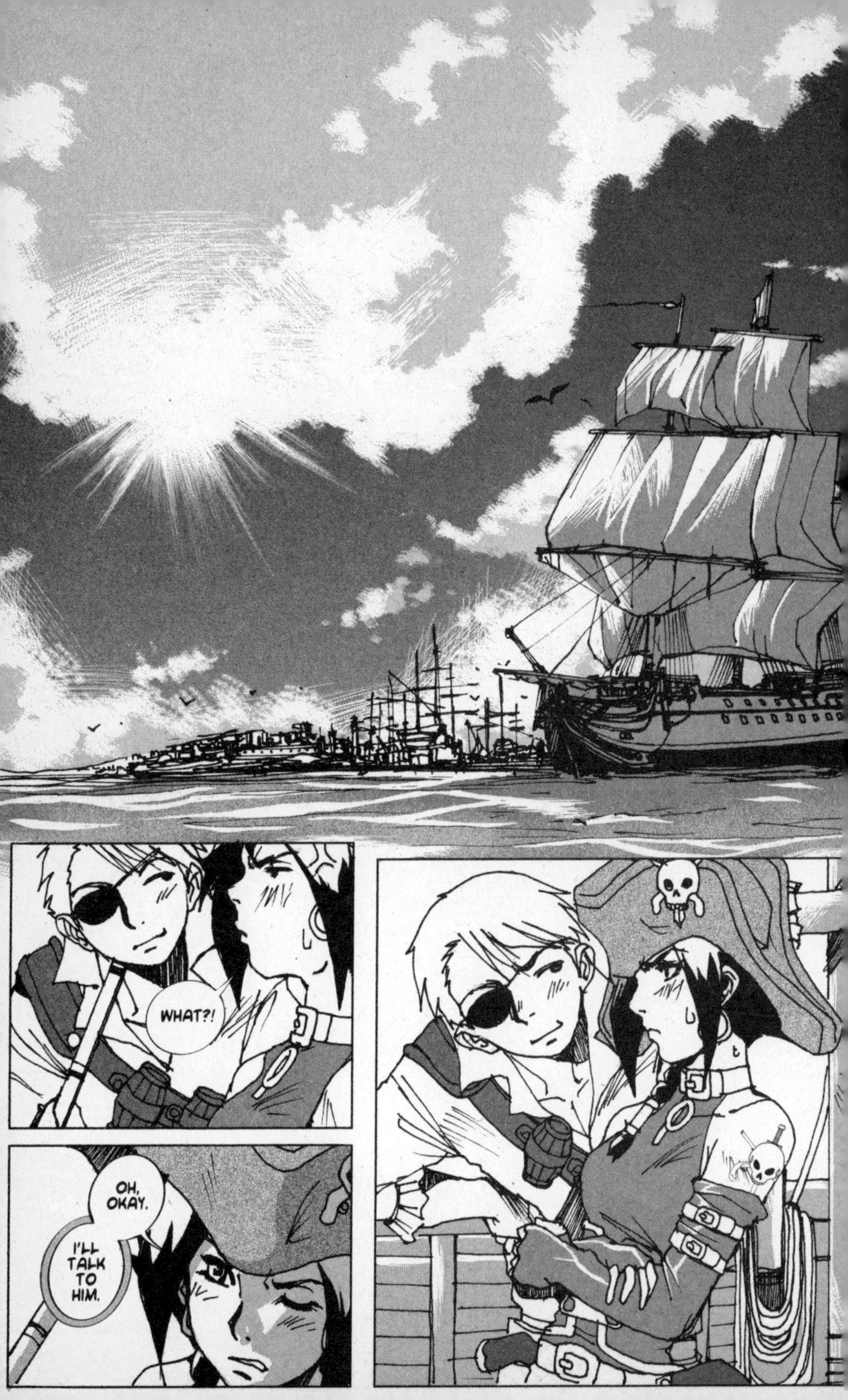
WHAT?!
OH, OKAY.
I'LL TALK TO HIM.

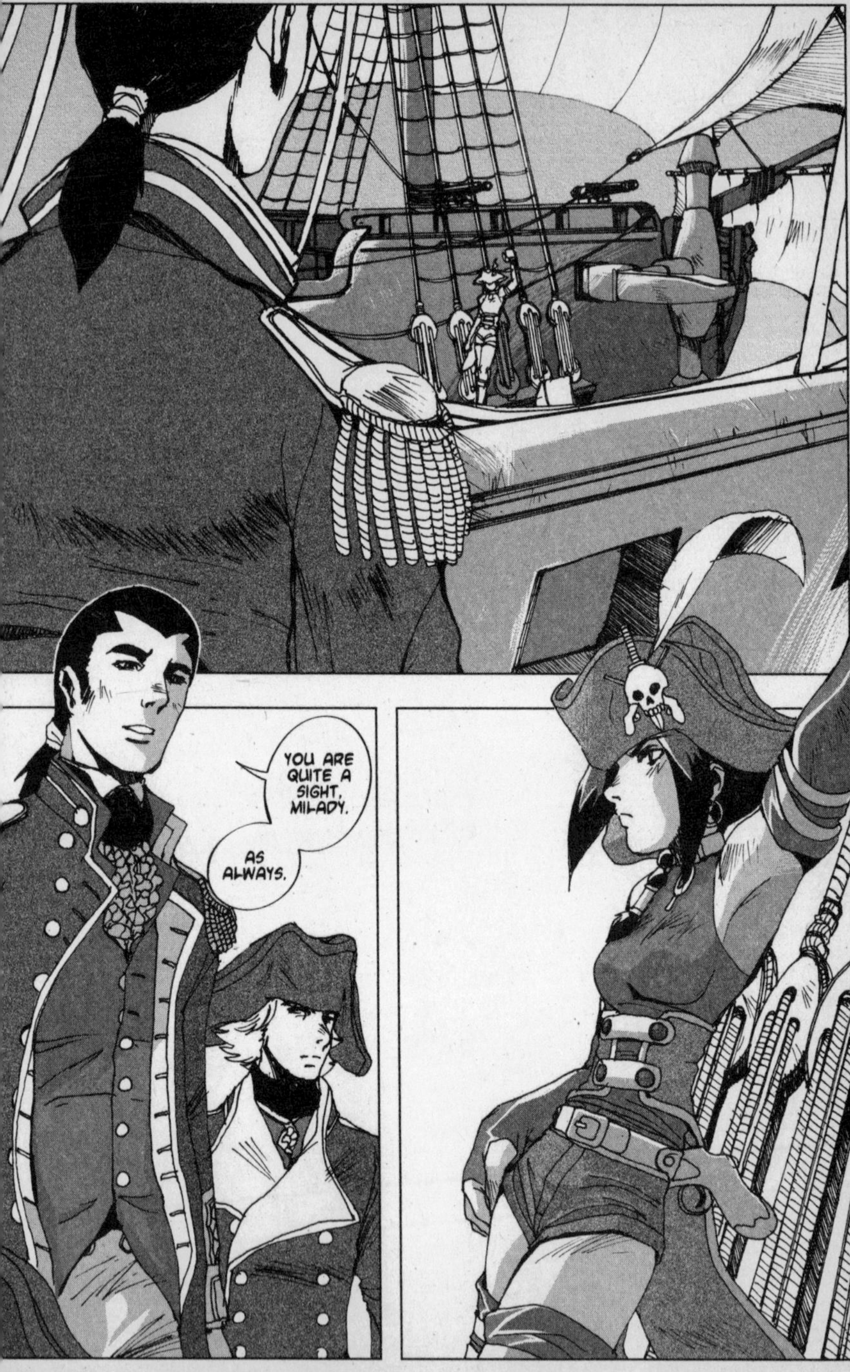
YOU ARE QUITE A SIGHT, MILADY.
AS ALWAYS.

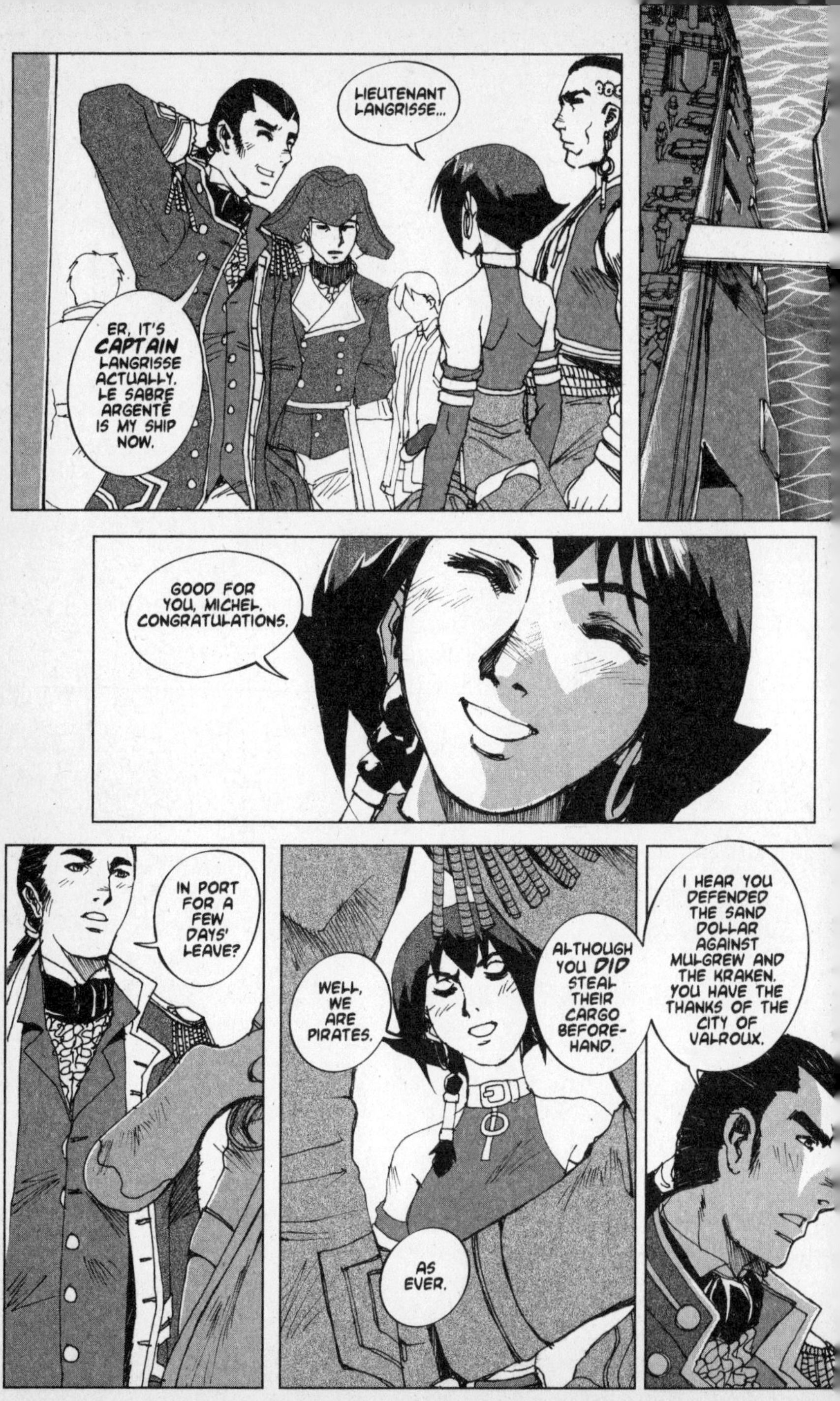

LIEUTENANT LANGRISSE...
ER, IT'S **CAPTAIN** LANGRISSE ACTUALLY. LE SABRE ARGENTÉ IS MY SHIP NOW.
GOOD FOR YOU, MICHEL. CONGRATULATIONS.
I HEAR YOU DEFENDED THE SAND DOLLAR AGAINST MULGREW AND THE KRAKEN. YOU HAVE THE THANKS OF THE CITY OF VALROUX.
ALTHOUGH YOU **DID** STEAL THEIR CARGO BEFORE-HAND.
WELL, WE ARE PIRATES.
AS EVER.
IN PORT FOR A FEW DAYS' LEAVE?

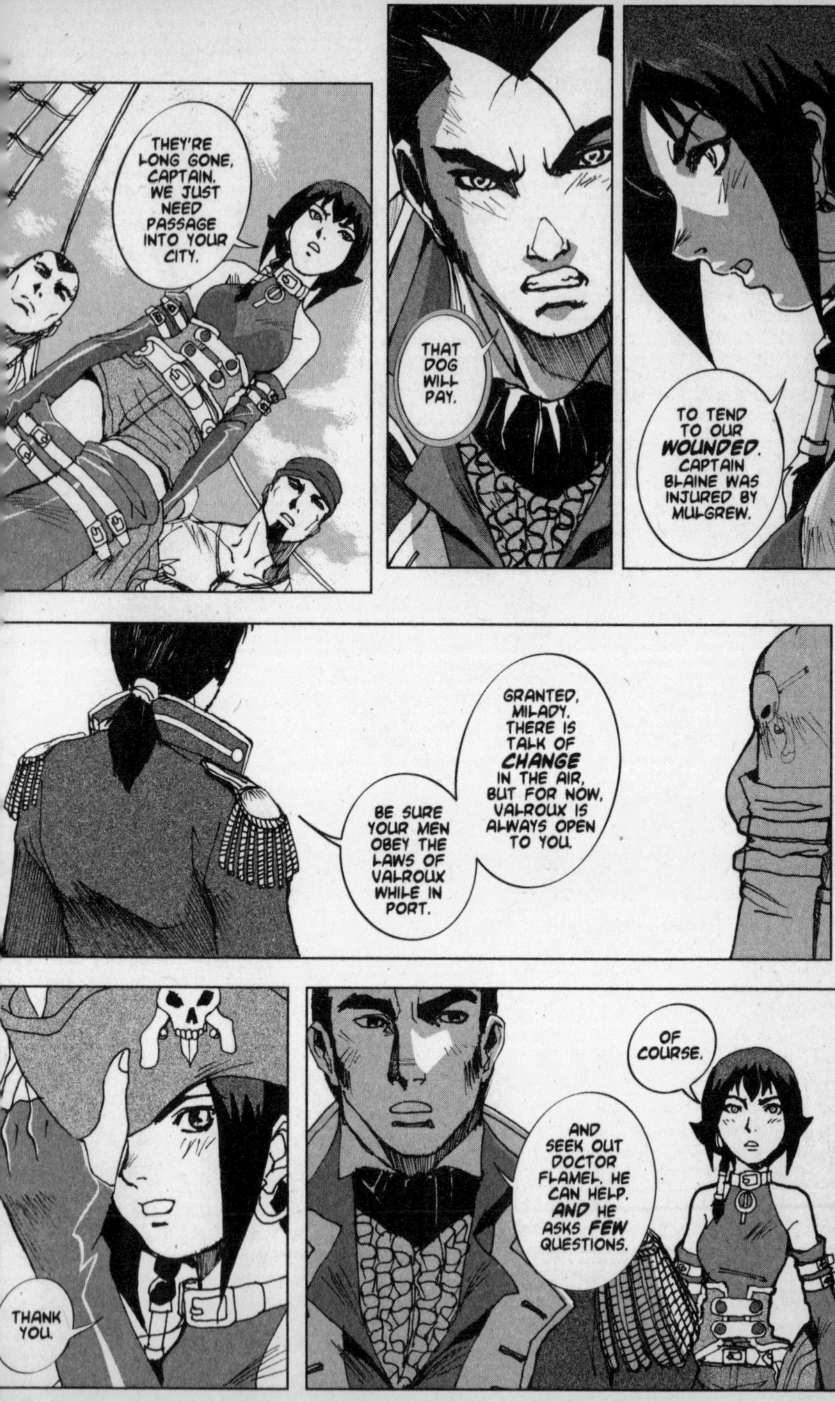
THEY'RE LONG GONE, CAPTAIN. WE JUST NEED PASSAGE INTO YOUR CITY.
THAT DOG WILL PAY.
TO TEND TO OUR **WOUNDED**. CAPTAIN BLAINE WAS INJURED BY MULGREW.
GRANTED, MILADY, THERE IS TALK OF **CHANGE** IN THE AIR, BUT FOR NOW, VALROUX IS ALWAYS OPEN TO YOU.
BE SURE YOUR MEN OBEY THE LAWS OF VALROUX WHILE IN PORT.
THANK YOU.
AND SEEK OUT DOCTOR FLAMEL. HE CAN HELP. **AND** HE ASKS **FEW** QUESTIONS.
OF COURSE.

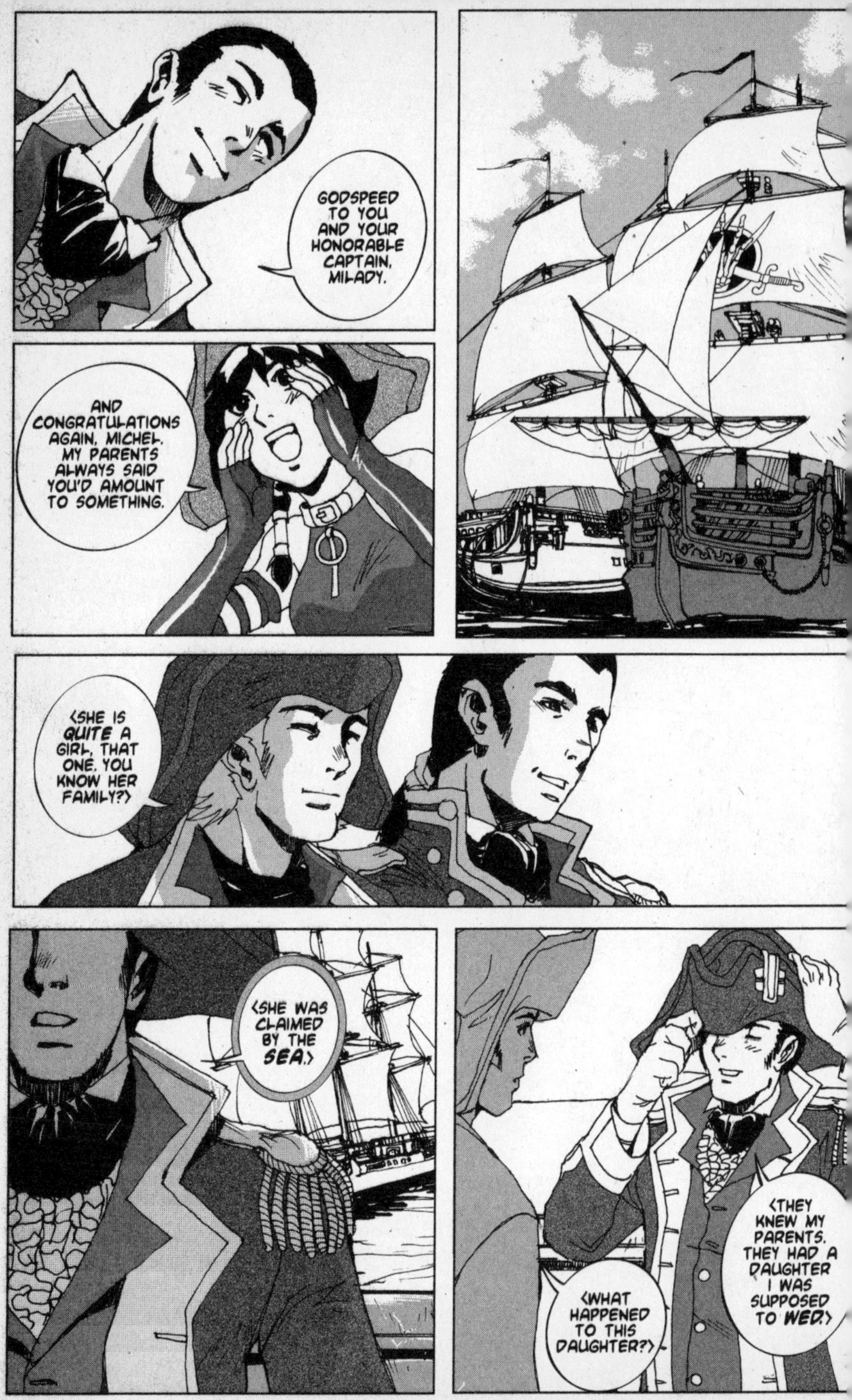
GODSPEED TO YOU AND YOUR HONORABLE CAPTAIN, MILADY.
AND CONGRATULATIONS AGAIN, MICHEL. MY PARENTS ALWAYS SAID YOU'D AMOUNT TO SOMETHING.
<SHE IS *QUITE* A GIRL, THAT ONE. YOU KNOW HER FAMILY?>
<THEY KNEW MY PARENTS. THEY HAD A DAUGHTER I WAS SUPPOSED TO *WED.*>
<WHAT HAPPENED TO THIS DAUGHTER?>
<SHE WAS CLAIMED BY THE *SEA.*>

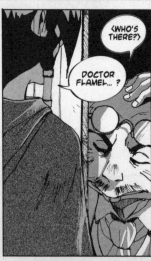

‹WHO'S THERE?›

DOCTOR FLAMEL...?

‹WELL, WELL!›

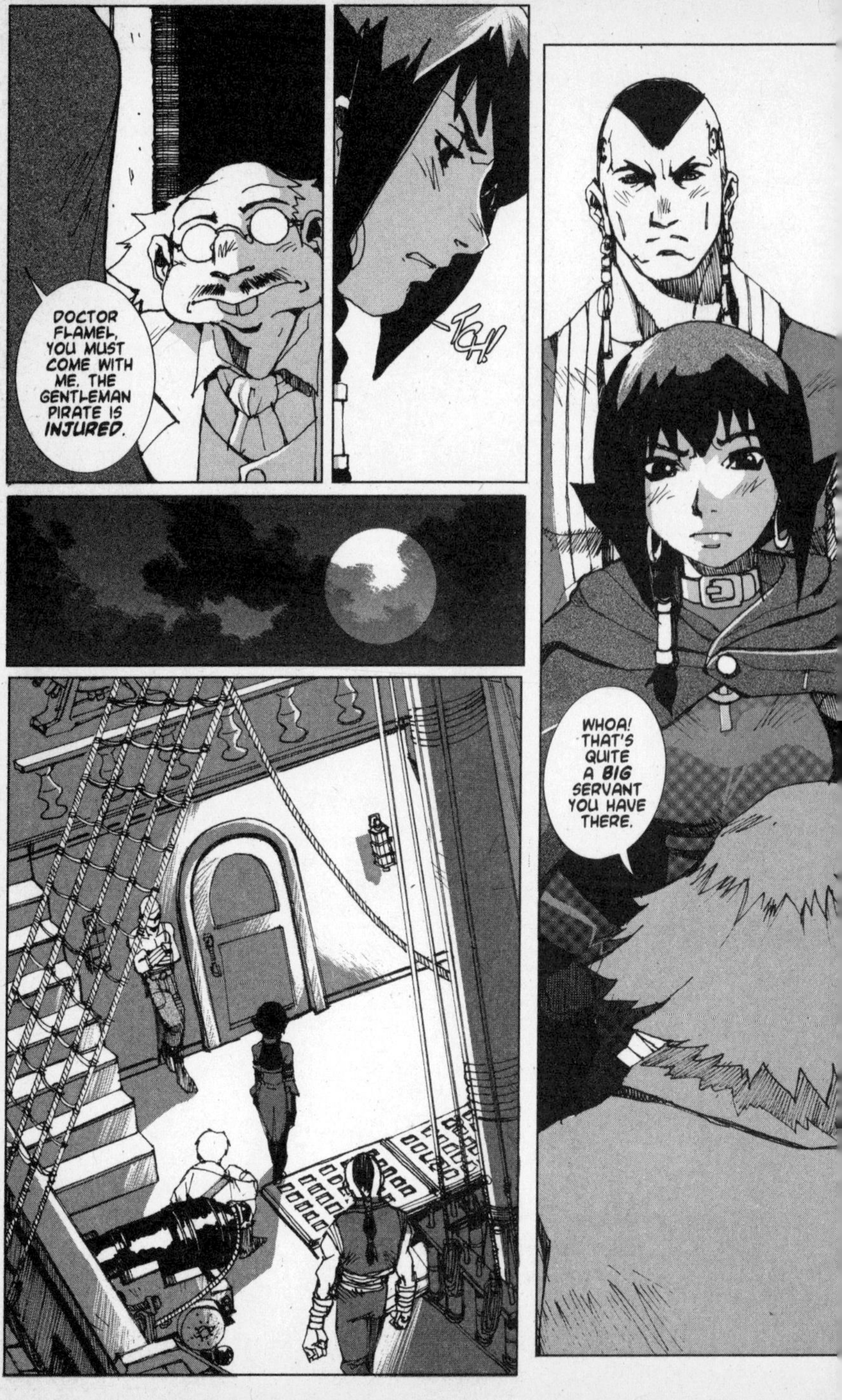
WHOA! THAT'S QUITE A BIG SERVANT YOU HAVE THERE.
TCH!
DOCTOR FLAMEL, YOU MUST COME WITH ME. THE GENTLEMAN PIRATE IS INJURED.

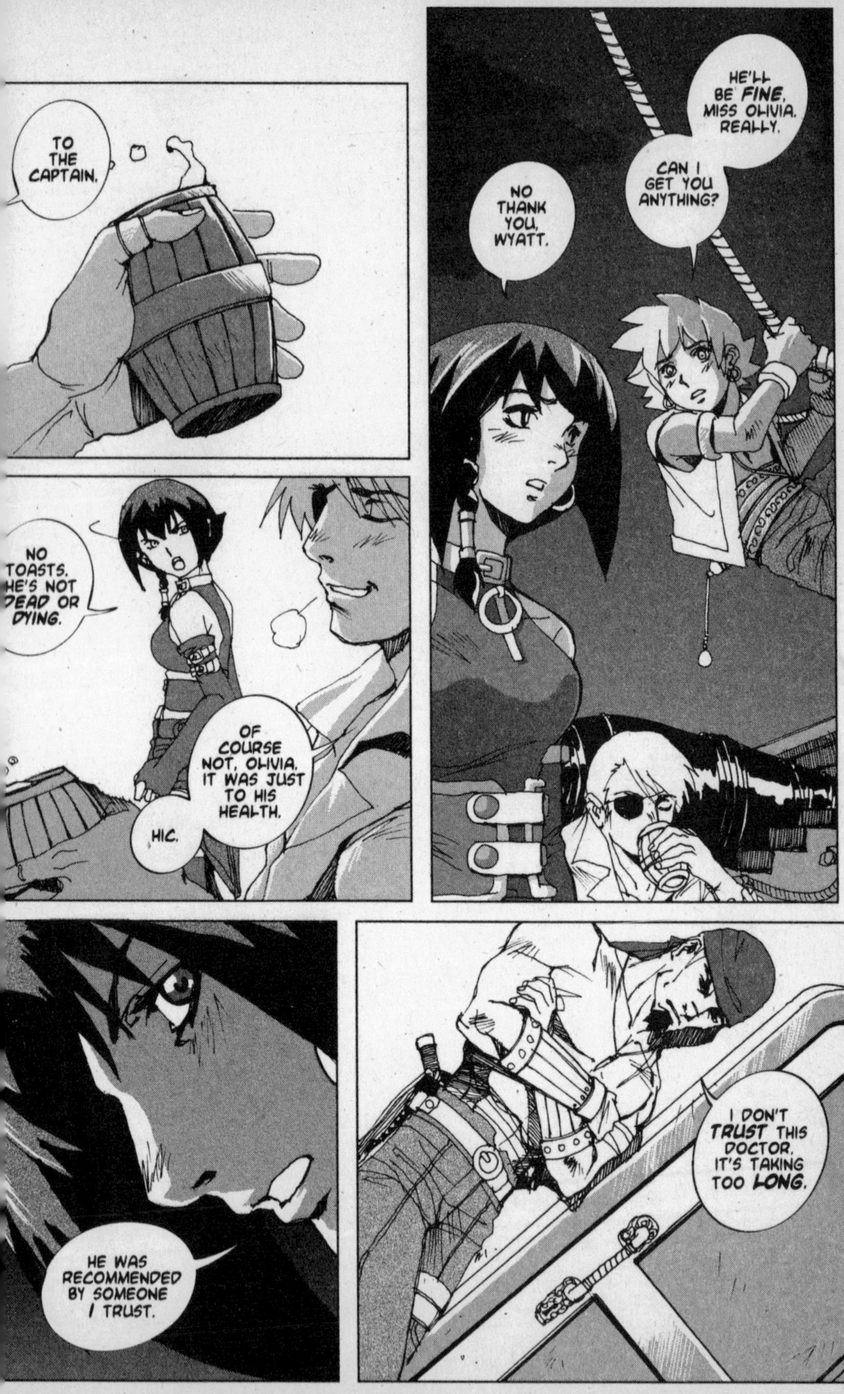
HE'LL BE FINE, MISS OLIVIA. REALLY.
CAN I GET YOU ANYTHING?
NO THANK YOU, WYATT.
TO THE CAPTAIN.
NO TOASTS. HE'S NOT DEAD OR DYING.
OF COURSE NOT, OLIVIA. IT WAS JUST TO HIS HEALTH.
HIC.
I DON'T TRUST THIS DOCTOR. IT'S TAKING TOO LONG.
HE WAS RECOMMENDED BY SOMEONE I TRUST.

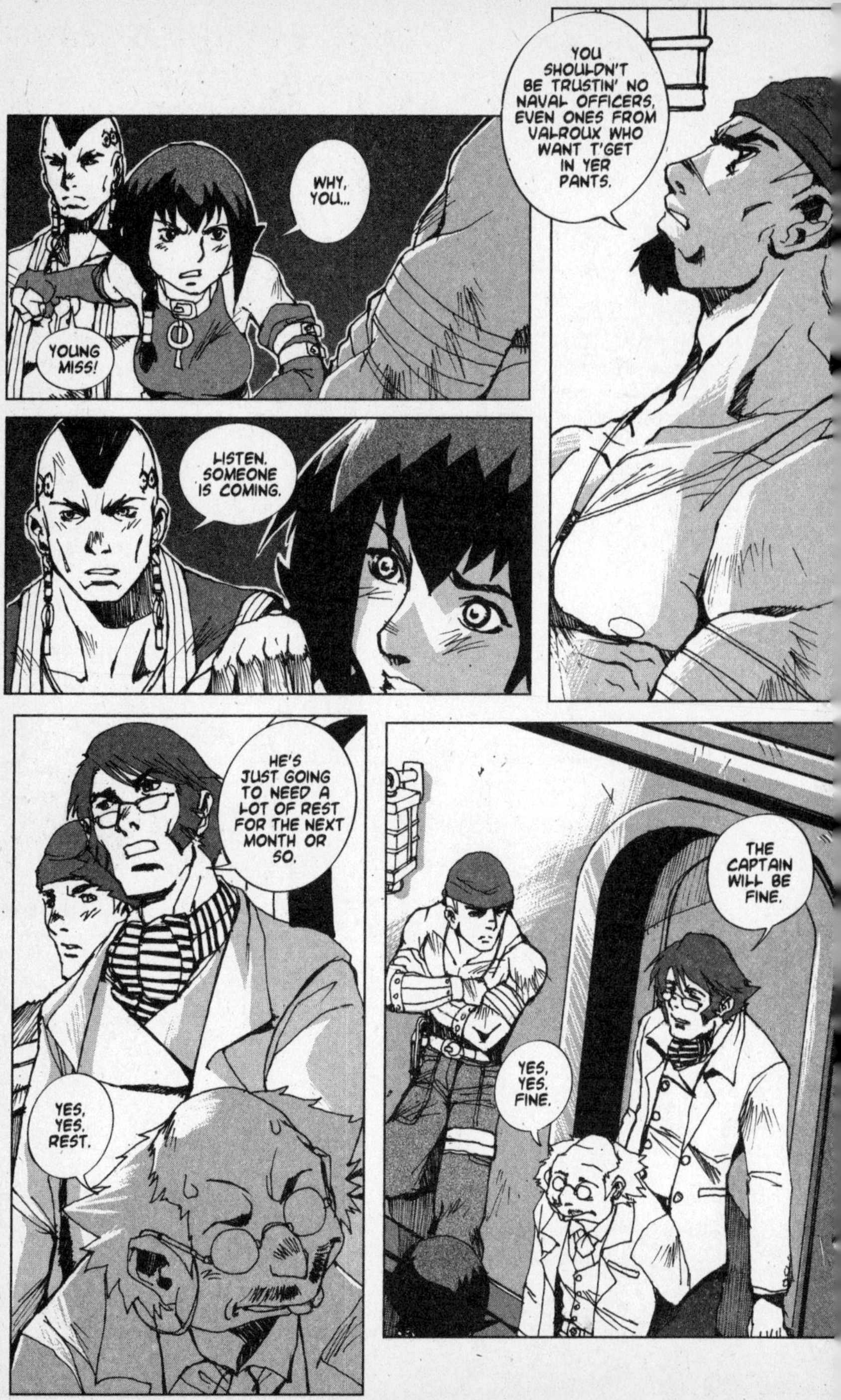
YOU SHOULDN'T BE TRUSTIN' NO NAVAL OFFICERS, EVEN ONES FROM VALROUX WHO WANT T'GET IN YER PANTS.
WHY, YOU...
YOUNG MISS!
LISTEN. SOMEONE IS COMING.
THE CAPTAIN WILL BE FINE.
YES, YES. FINE.
HE'S JUST GOING TO NEED A LOT OF REST FOR THE NEXT MONTH OR SO.
YES, YES. REST.

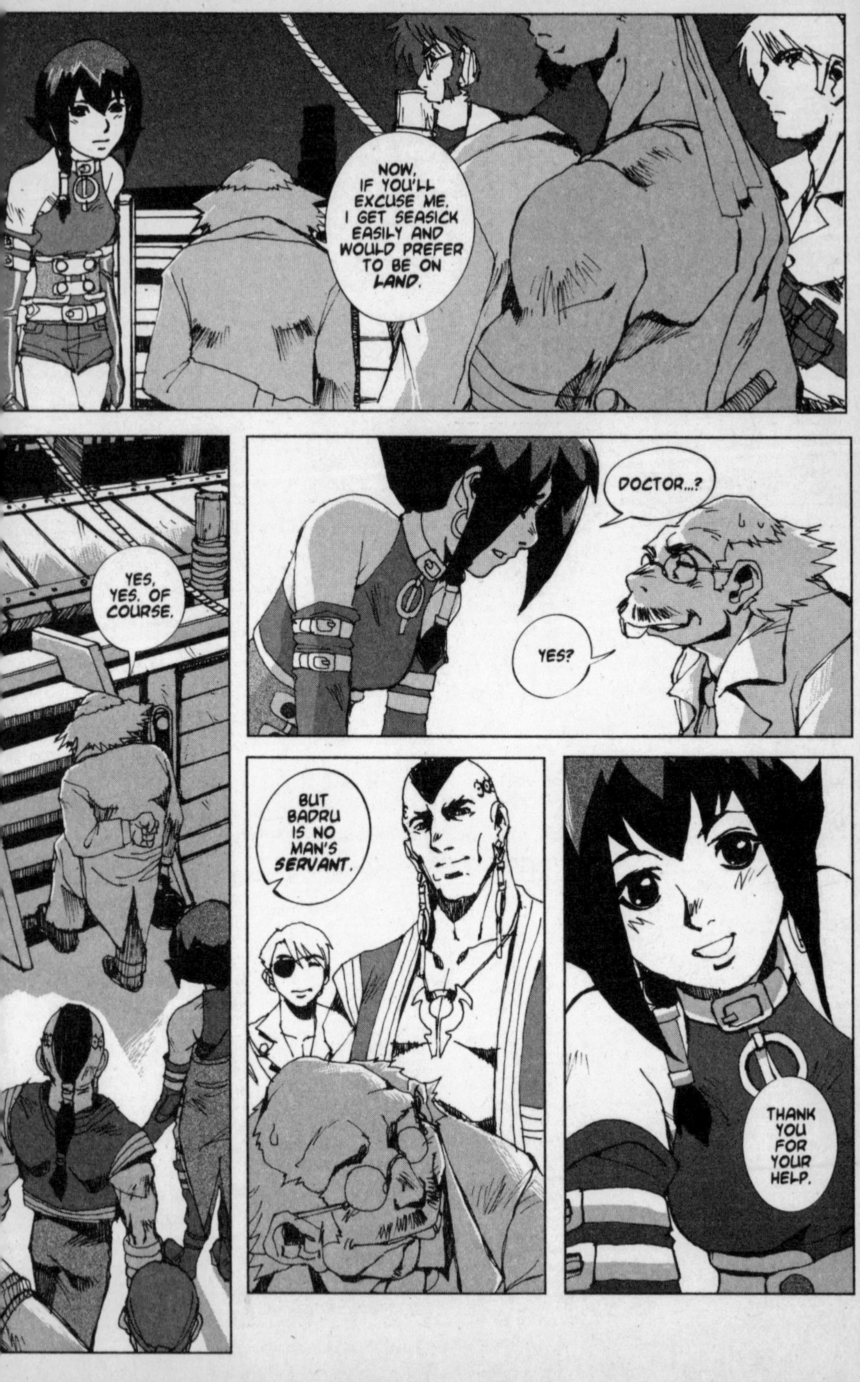
NOW, IF YOU'LL EXCUSE ME. I GET SEASICK EASILY AND WOULD PREFER TO BE ON LAND.
DOCTOR...?
YES?
THANK YOU FOR YOUR HELP.
BUT BADRU IS NO MAN'S SERVANT.
YES, YES. OF COURSE.

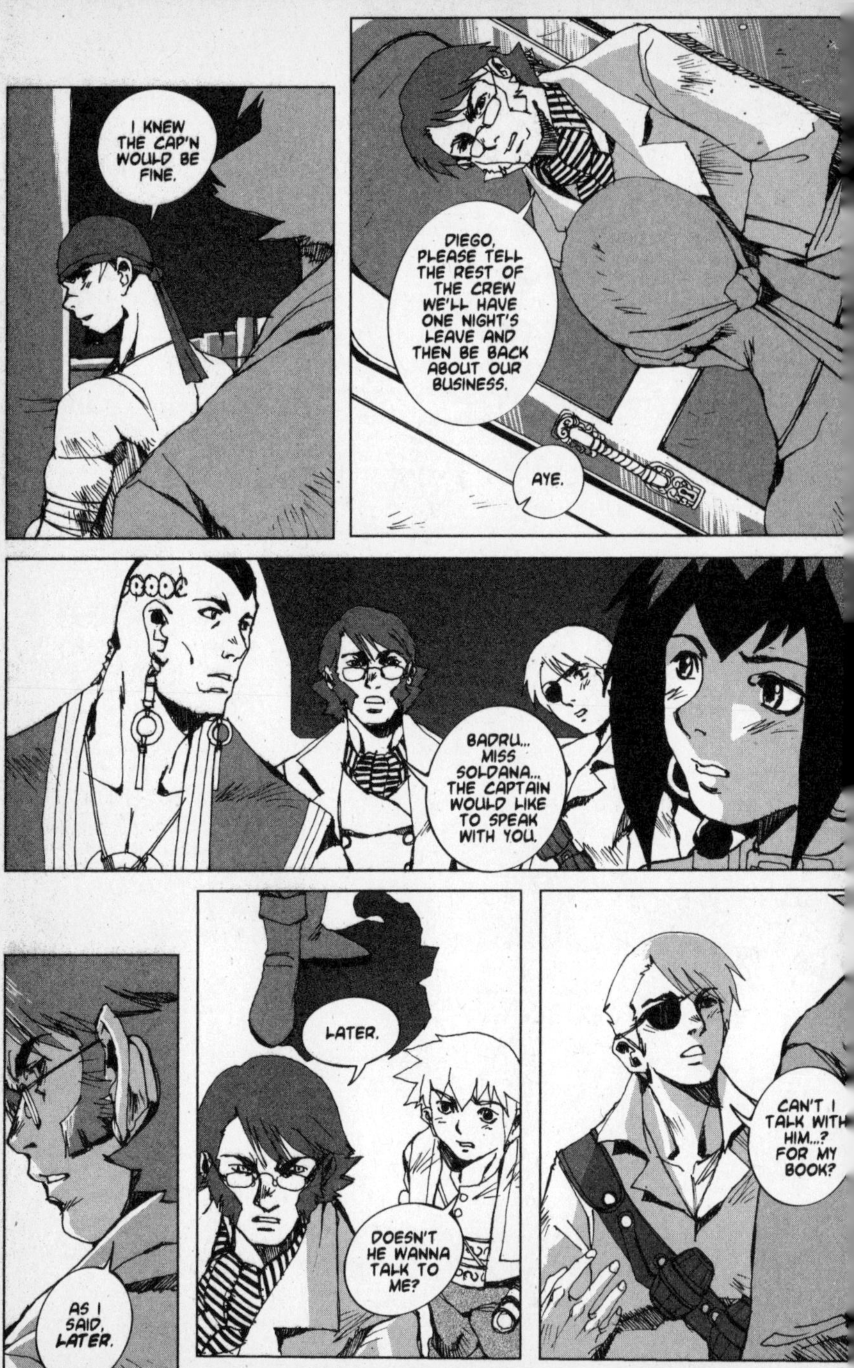
DIEGO, PLEASE TELL THE REST OF THE CREW WE'LL HAVE ONE NIGHT'S LEAVE AND THEN BE BACK ABOUT OUR BUSINESS.
AYE.
I KNEW THE CAP'N WOULD BE FINE.
BADRU... MISS SOLDANA... THE CAPTAIN WOULD LIKE TO SPEAK WITH YOU.
CAN'T I TALK WITH HIM...? FOR MY BOOK?
LATER.
DOESN'T HE WANNA TALK TO ME?
AS I SAID, LATER.

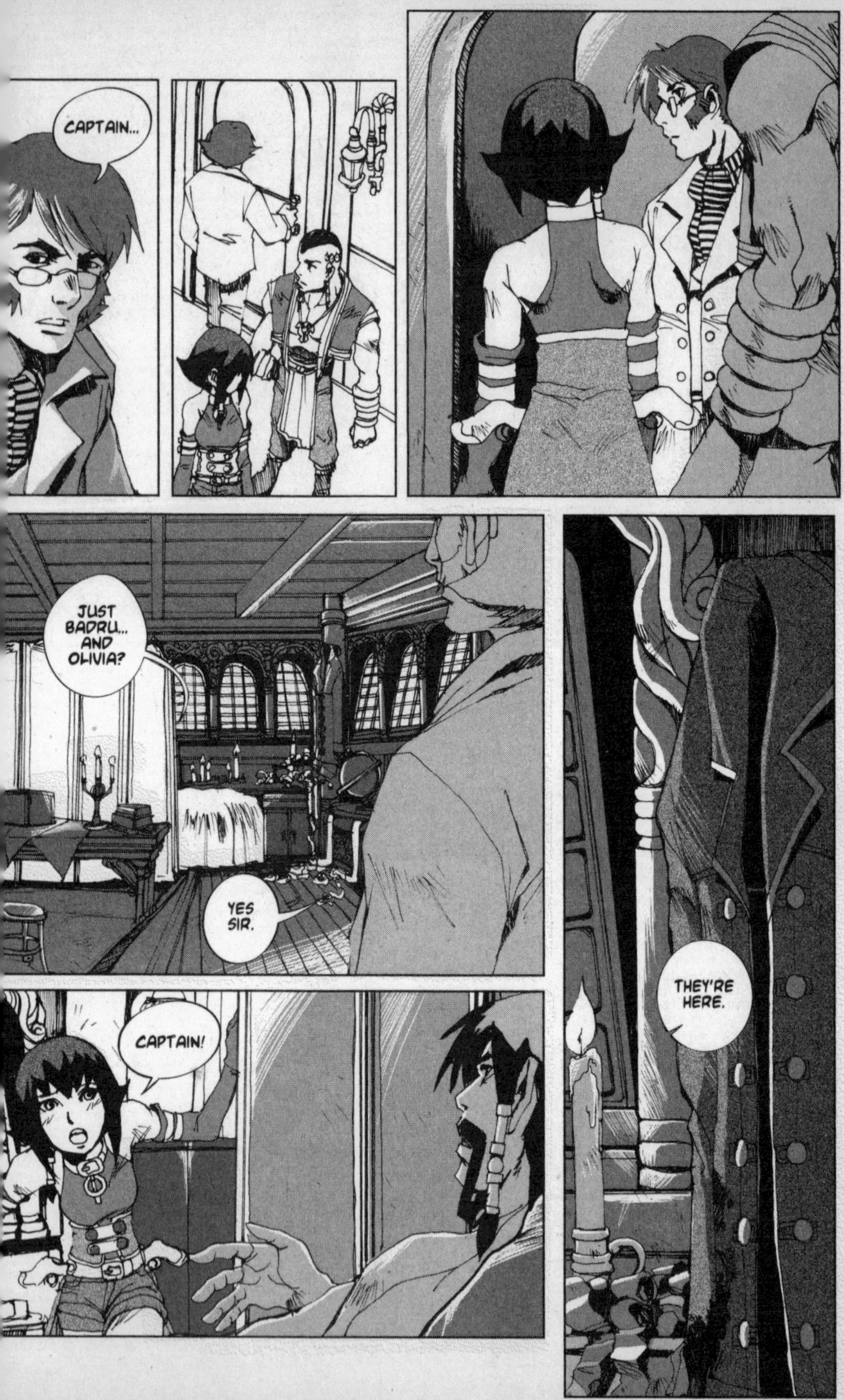
CAPTAIN...
THEY'RE HERE.
JUST BADRU... AND OLIVIA?
YES SIR.
CAPTAIN!

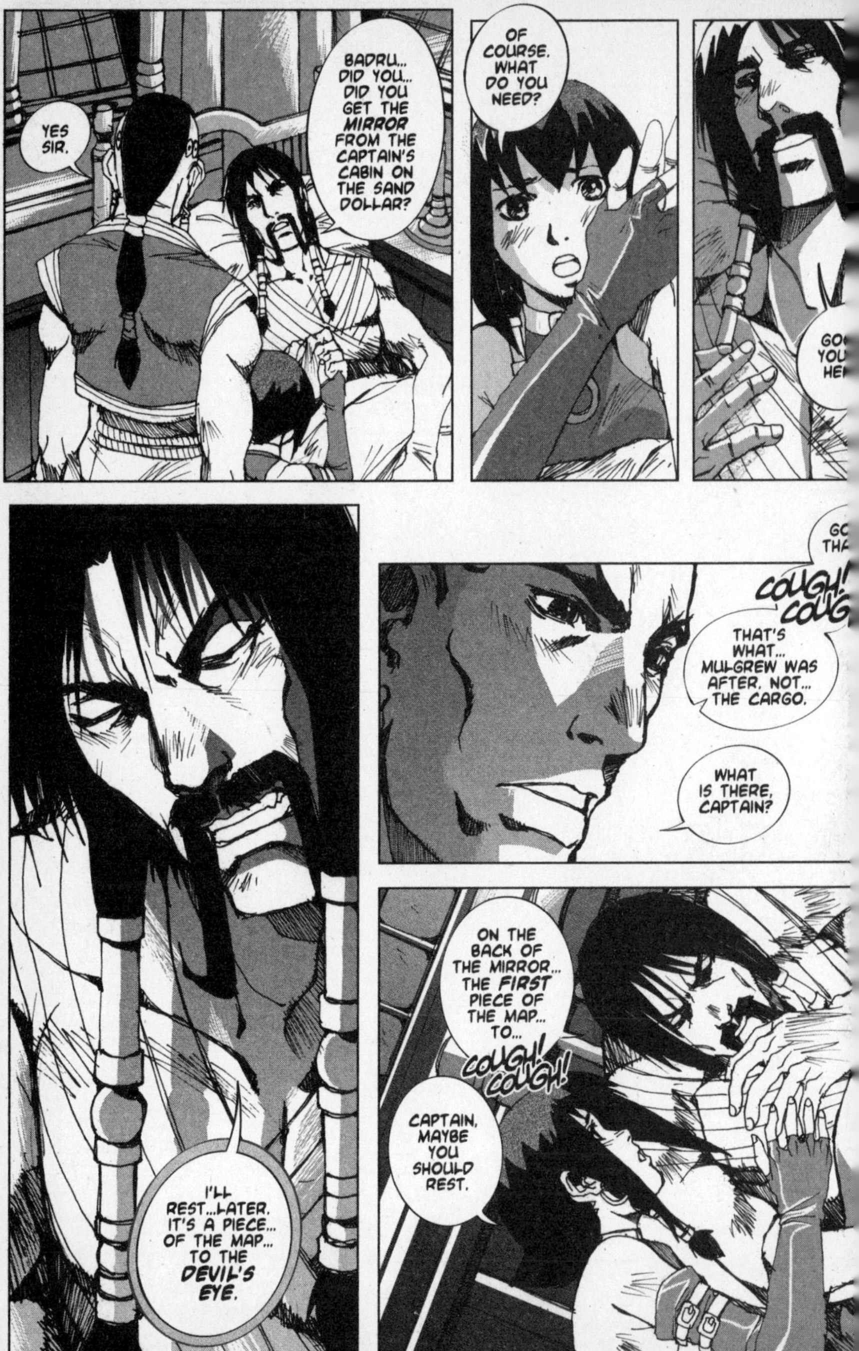
OF COURSE. WHAT DO YOU NEED?
BADRU... DID YOU... DID YOU GET THE **MIRROR** FROM THE CAPTAIN'S CABIN ON THE SAND DOLLAR?
YES SIR.
COUGH! COUGH!
THAT'S WHAT... MULGREW WAS AFTER, NOT... THE CARGO.
WHAT IS THERE, CAPTAIN?
ON THE BACK OF THE MIRROR... THE **FIRST** PIECE OF THE MAP... TO...
COUGH! COUGH!
CAPTAIN, MAYBE YOU SHOULD REST.
I'LL REST...LATER. IT'S A PIECE... OF THE MAP... TO THE **DEVIL'S EYE**.

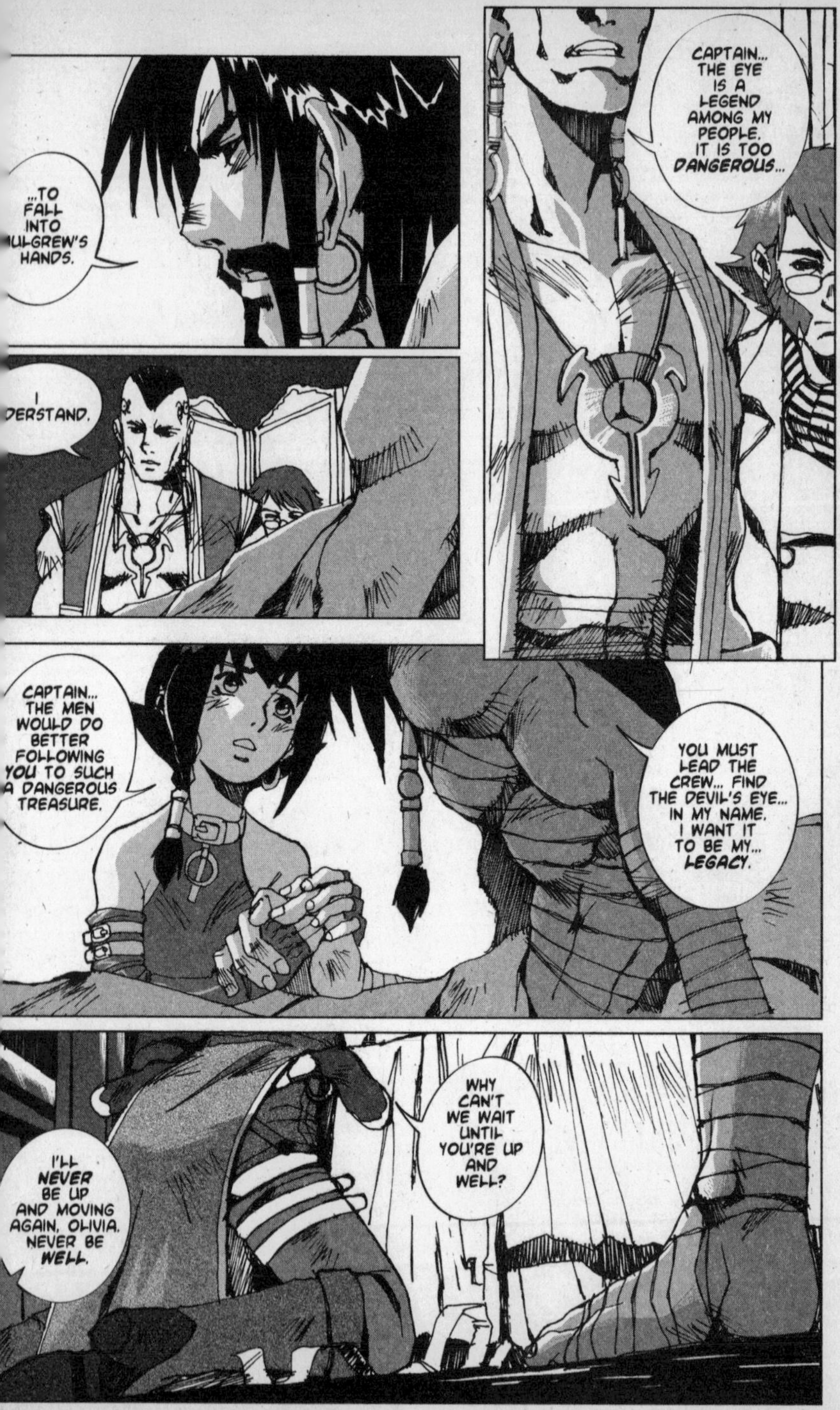
CAPTAIN... THE EYE IS A LEGEND AMONG MY PEOPLE. IT IS TOO DANGEROUS...
...TO FALL INTO ULGREW'S HANDS.
I DERSTAND.
YOU MUST LEAD THE CREW... FIND THE DEVIL'S EYE... IN MY NAME. I WANT IT TO BE MY... LEGACY.
CAPTAIN... THE MEN WOULD DO BETTER FOLLOWING YOU TO SUCH A DANGEROUS TREASURE.
WHY CAN'T WE WAIT UNTIL YOU'RE UP AND WELL?
I'LL NEVER BE UP AND MOVING AGAIN, OLIVIA. NEVER BE WELL.

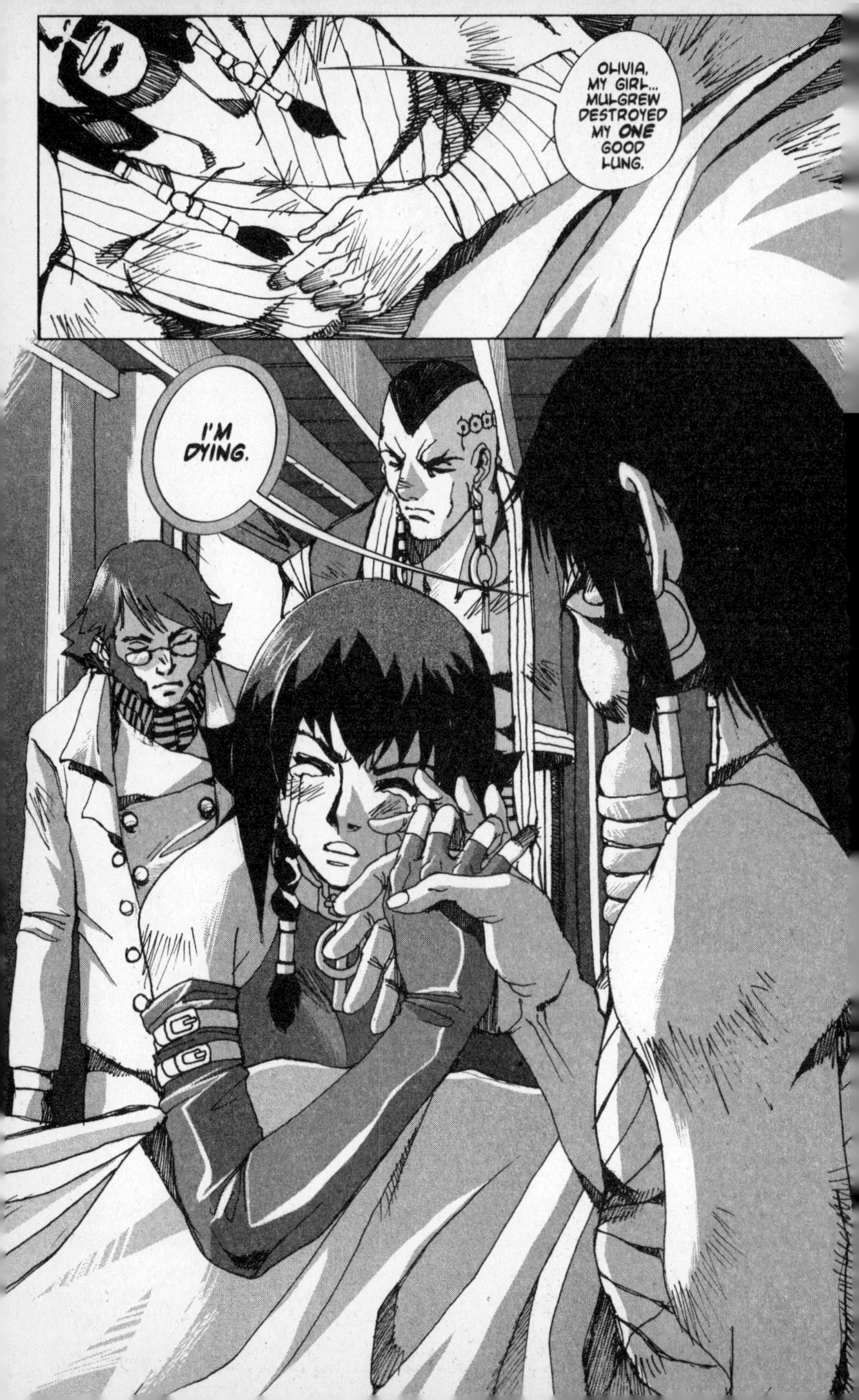
OLIVIA, MY GIRL... MULGREW DESTROYED MY ONE GOOD LUNG.
I'M DYING.

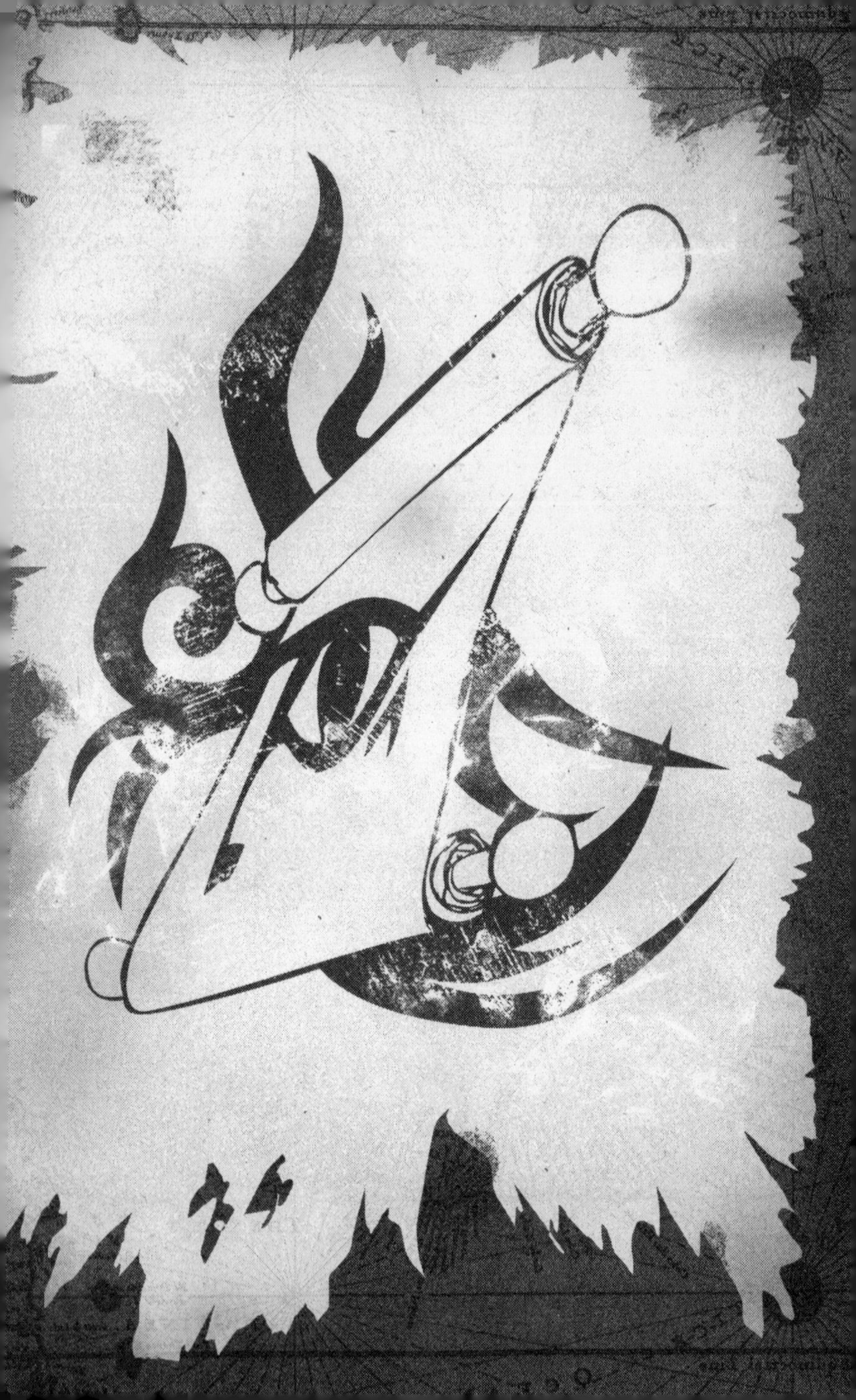

CHAPTER 4
Heir To The Sea

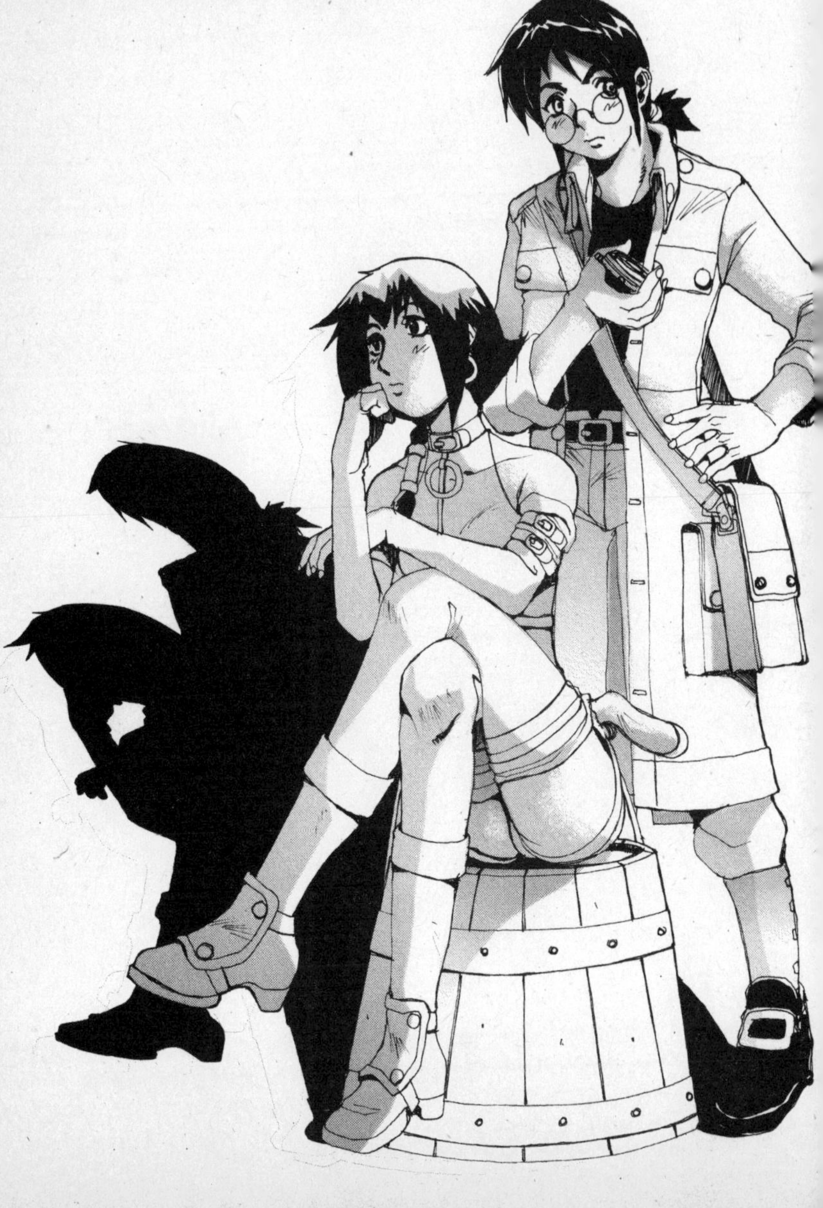

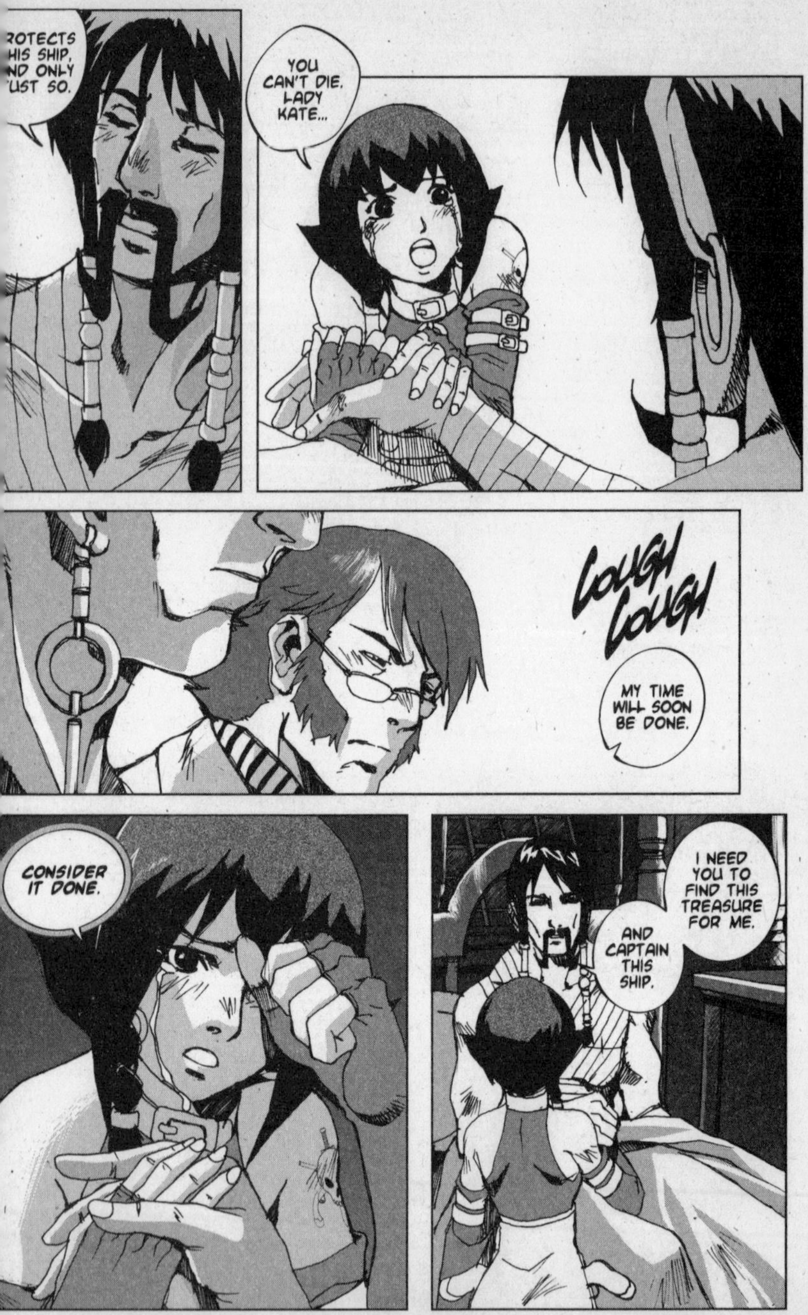
YOU CAN'T DIE. LADY KATE...
ROTECTS HIS SHIP, ND ONLY UST SO.
COUGH COUGH
MY TIME WILL SOON BE DONE.
I NEED YOU TO FIND THIS TREASURE FOR ME.
AND CAPTAIN THIS SHIP.
CONSIDER IT DONE.

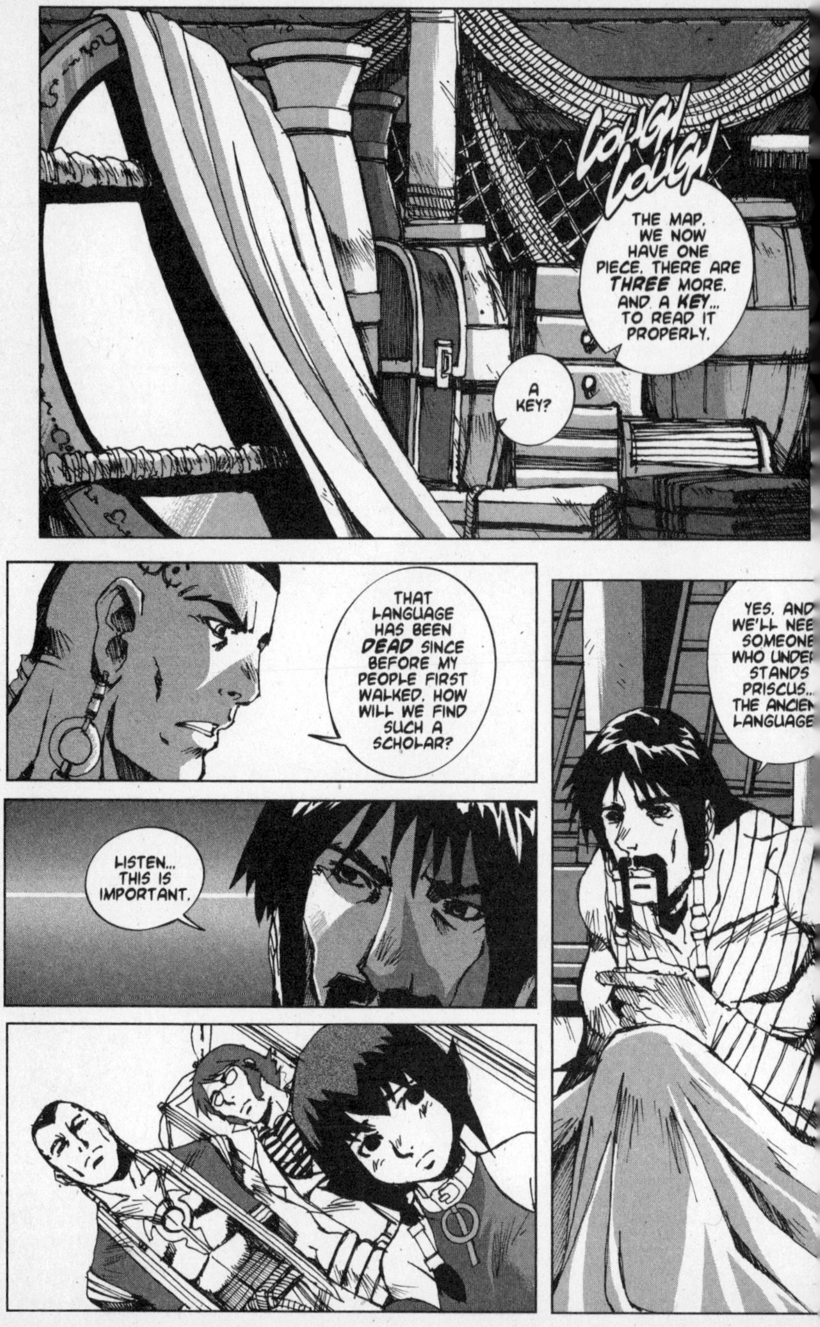
COUGH COUGH
THE MAP. WE NOW HAVE ONE PIECE. THERE ARE **THREE** MORE. AND A **KEY**... TO READ IT PROPERLY.
A KEY?
YES. AND WE'LL NEE SOMEONE WHO UNDER STANDS PRISCUS... THE ANCIEN LANGUAGE
THAT LANGUAGE HAS BEEN **DEAD** SINCE BEFORE MY PEOPLE FIRST WALKED. HOW WILL WE FIND SUCH A SCHOLAR?
LISTEN... THIS IS IMPORTANT.

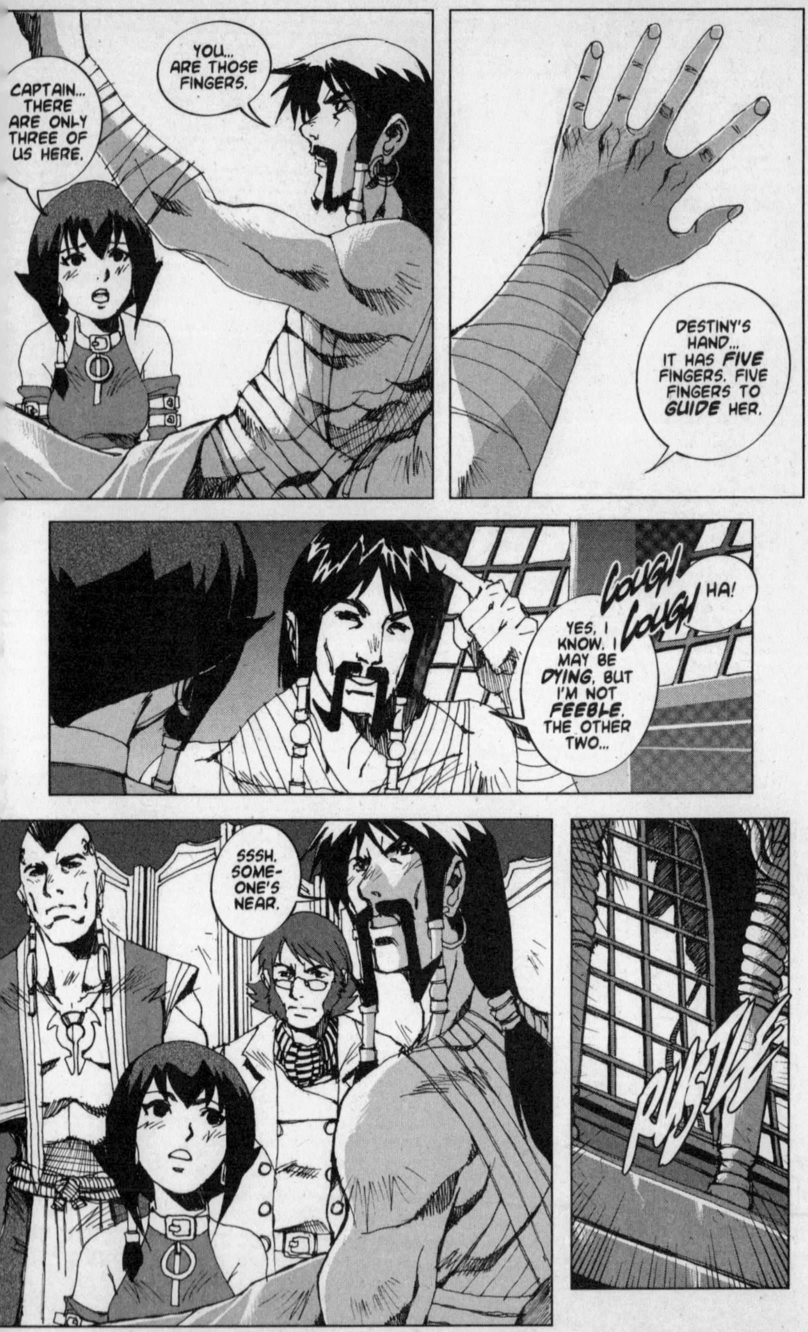
DESTINY'S HAND... IT HAS FIVE FINGERS. FIVE FINGERS TO GUIDE HER.
YOU... ARE THOSE FINGERS.
CAPTAIN... THERE ARE ONLY THREE OF US HERE.
COUGH COUGH
HA!
YES, I KNOW. I MAY BE DYING, BUT I'M NOT FEEBLE. THE OTHER TWO...
SSSH. SOME-ONE'S NEAR.

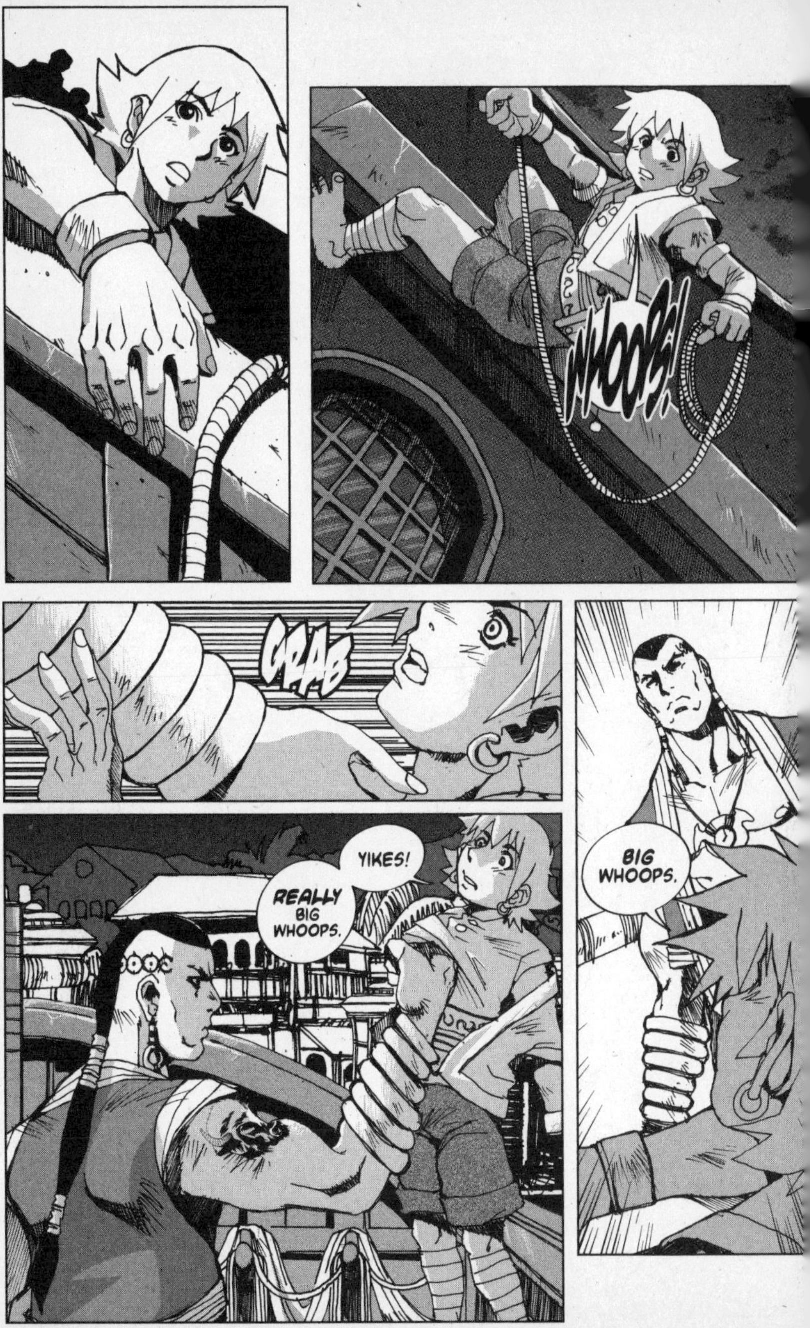
WHOOPS!
BIG WHOOPS.
GRAB
YIKES!
REALLY BIG WHOOPS.

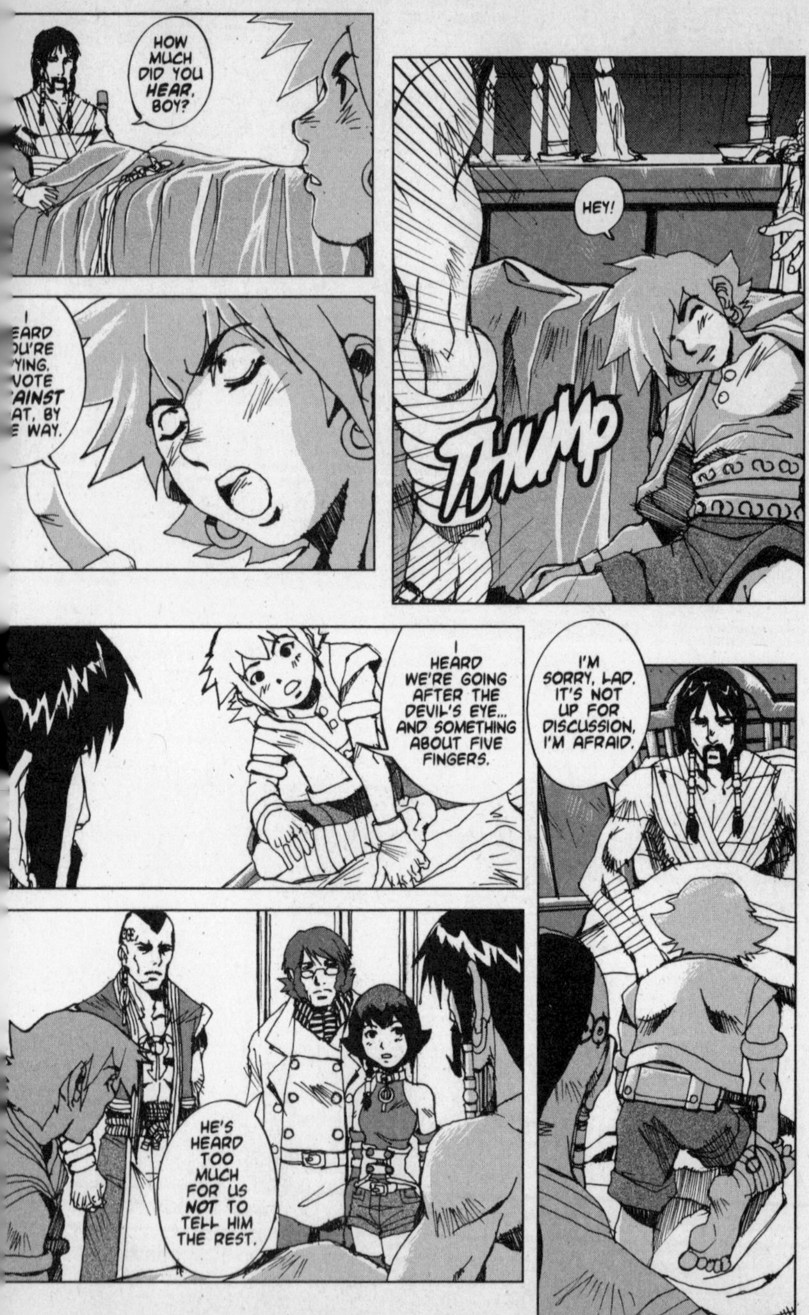
HEY!
THUMP
HOW MUCH DID YOU HEAR, BOY?
I EARD OU'RE YING. VOTE AINST AT, BY E WAY.
I'M SORRY, LAD. IT'S NOT UP FOR DISCUSSION, I'M AFRAID.
I HEARD WE'RE GOING AFTER THE DEVIL'S EYE... AND SOMETHING ABOUT FIVE FINGERS.
HE'S HEARD TOO MUCH FOR US NOT TO TELL HIM THE REST.

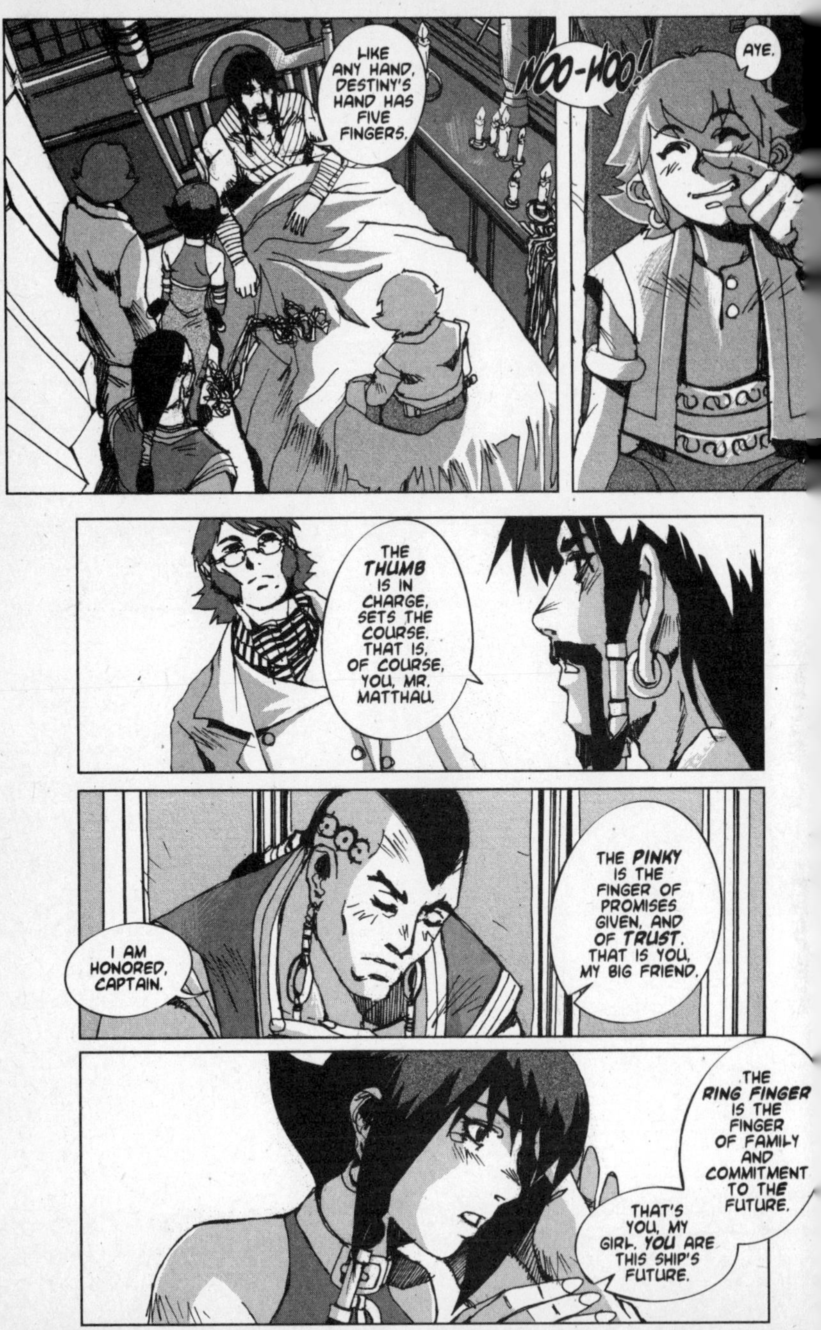
AYE.
WOO-HOO!
LIKE ANY HAND, DESTINY'S HAND HAS FIVE FINGERS.
THE THUMB IS IN CHARGE, SETS THE COURSE. THAT IS, OF COURSE, YOU, MR. MATTHAU.
THE PINKY IS THE FINGER OF PROMISES GIVEN, AND OF TRUST. THAT IS YOU, MY BIG FRIEND.
I AM HONORED, CAPTAIN.
THE RING FINGER IS THE FINGER OF FAMILY AND COMMITMENT TO THE FUTURE.
THAT'S YOU, MY GIRL. YOU ARE THIS SHIP'S FUTURE.

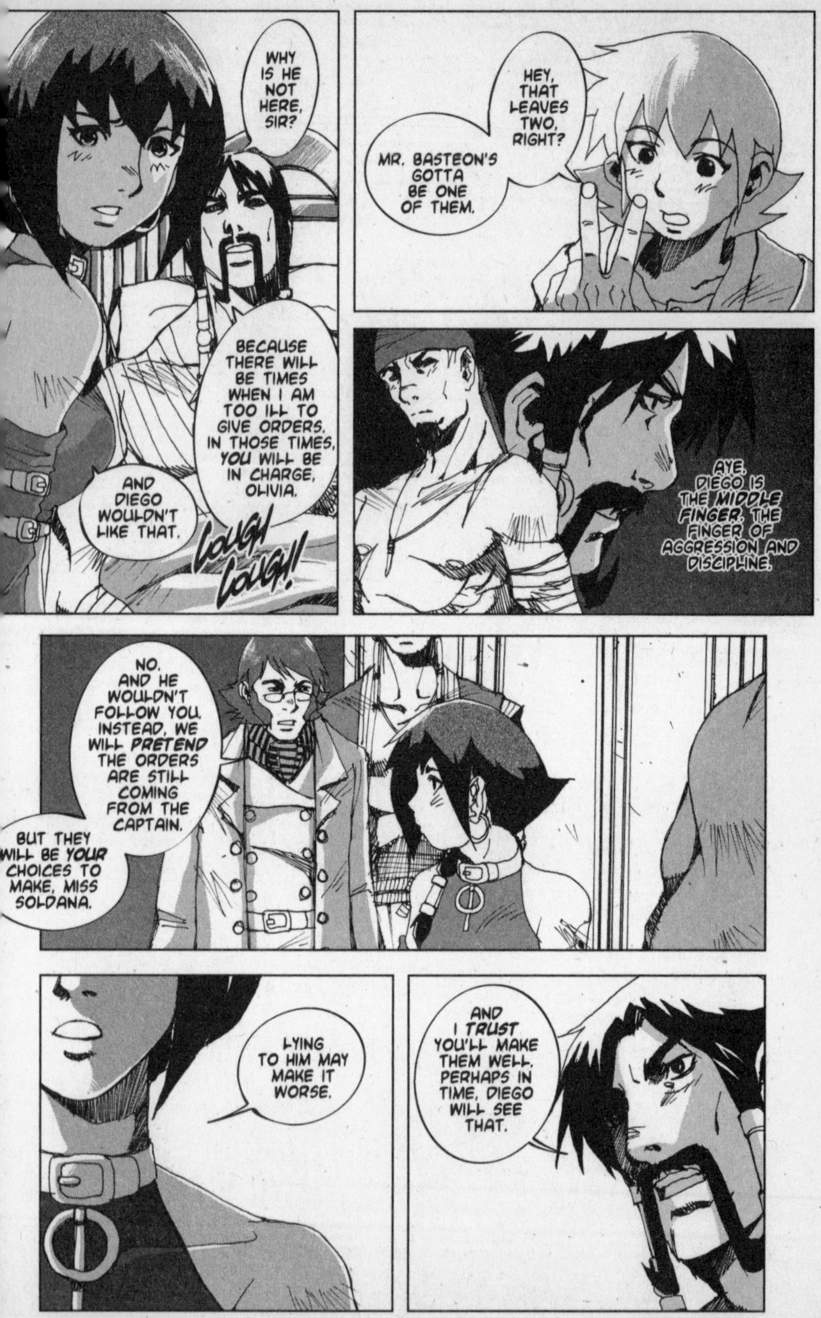
HEY, THAT LEAVES TWO, RIGHT?
MR. BASTEON'S GOTTA BE ONE OF THEM.
AYE. DIEGO IS THE MIDDLE FINGER, THE FINGER OF AGGRESSION AND DISCIPLINE.
WHY IS HE NOT HERE, SIR?
BECAUSE THERE WILL BE TIMES WHEN I AM TOO ILL TO GIVE ORDERS. IN THOSE TIMES, YOU WILL BE IN CHARGE, OLIVIA.
AND DIEGO WOULDN'T LIKE THAT.
COUGH COUGH!!
NO, AND HE WOULDN'T FOLLOW YOU. INSTEAD, WE WILL PRETEND THE ORDERS ARE STILL COMING FROM THE CAPTAIN.
BUT THEY WILL BE YOUR CHOICES TO MAKE, MISS SOLDANA.
AND I TRUST YOU'LL MAKE THEM WELL. PERHAPS IN TIME, DIEGO WILL SEE THAT.
LYING TO HIM MAY MAKE IT WORSE.

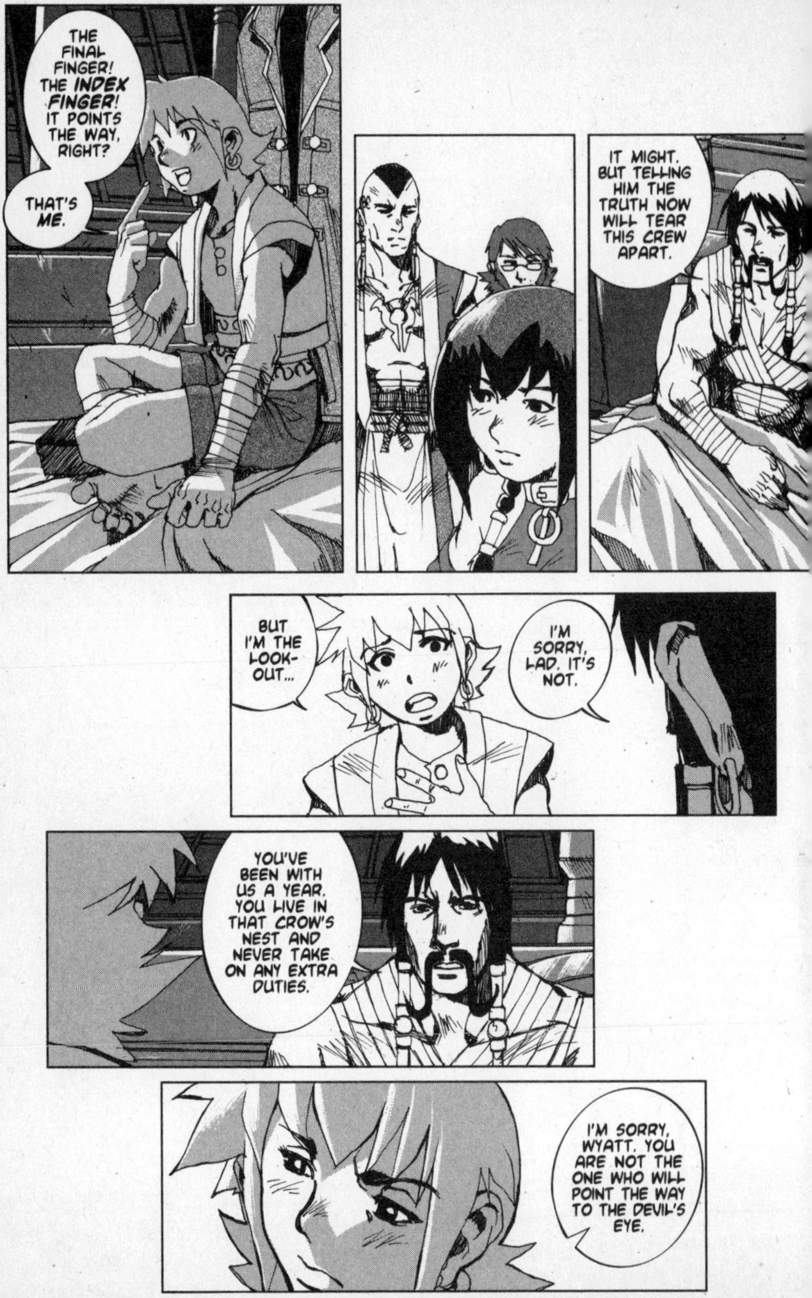
IT MIGHT. BUT TELLING HIM THE TRUTH NOW WILL TEAR THIS CREW APART.
THE FINAL FINGER! THE *INDEX FINGER!* IT POINTS THE WAY, RIGHT?
THAT'S *ME.*
I'M SORRY, LAD. IT'S NOT.
BUT I'M THE LOOK-OUT...
YOU'VE BEEN WITH US A YEAR. YOU LIVE IN THAT CROW'S NEST AND NEVER TAKE ON ANY EXTRA DUTIES.
I'M SORRY, WYATT. YOU ARE NOT THE ONE WHO WILL POINT THE WAY TO THE DEVIL'S EYE.

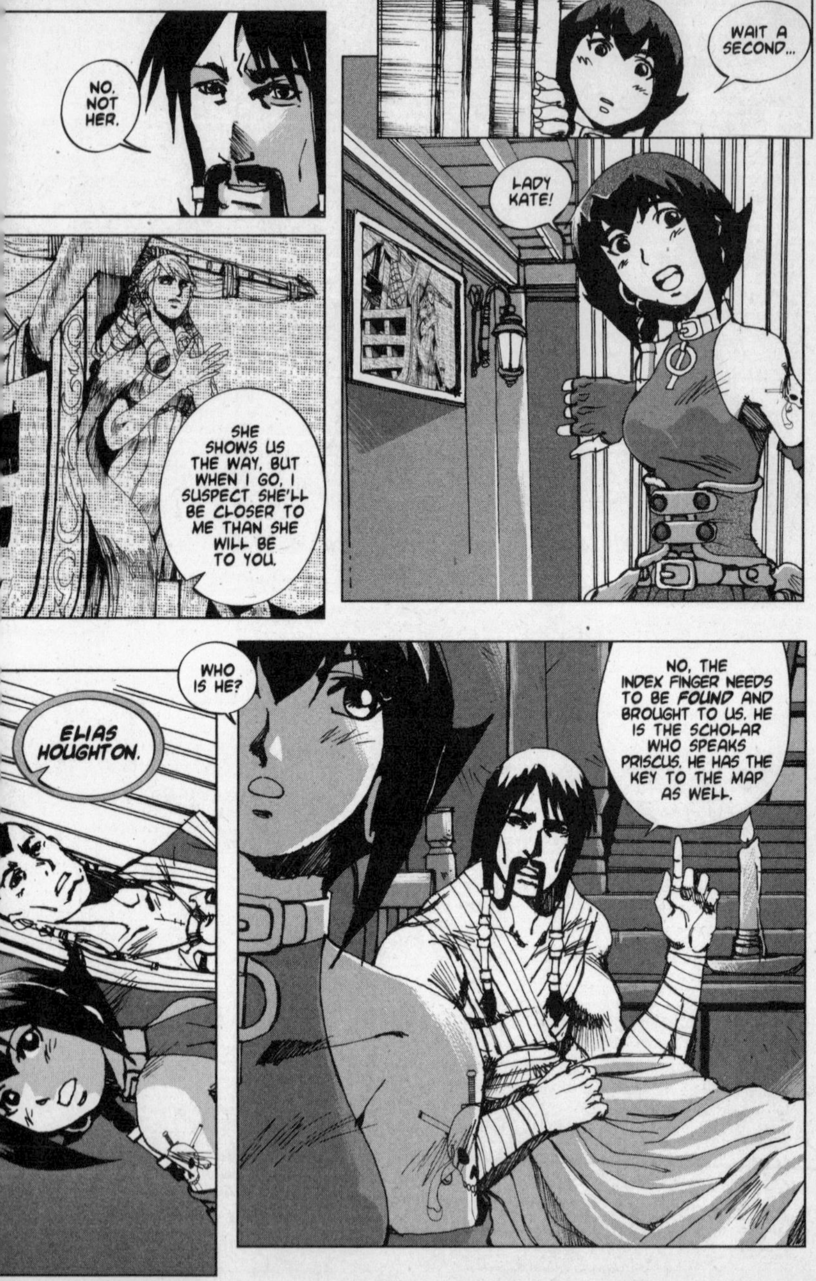
WAIT A SECOND...
LADY KATE!
NO. NOT HER.
SHE SHOWS US THE WAY, BUT WHEN I GO, I SUSPECT SHE'LL BE CLOSER TO ME THAN SHE WILL BE TO YOU.
NO, THE INDEX FINGER NEEDS TO BE *FOUND* AND BROUGHT TO US. HE IS THE SCHOLAR WHO SPEAKS PRISCUS. HE HAS THE KEY TO THE MAP AS WELL.
WHO IS HE?
ELIAS HOUGHTON.

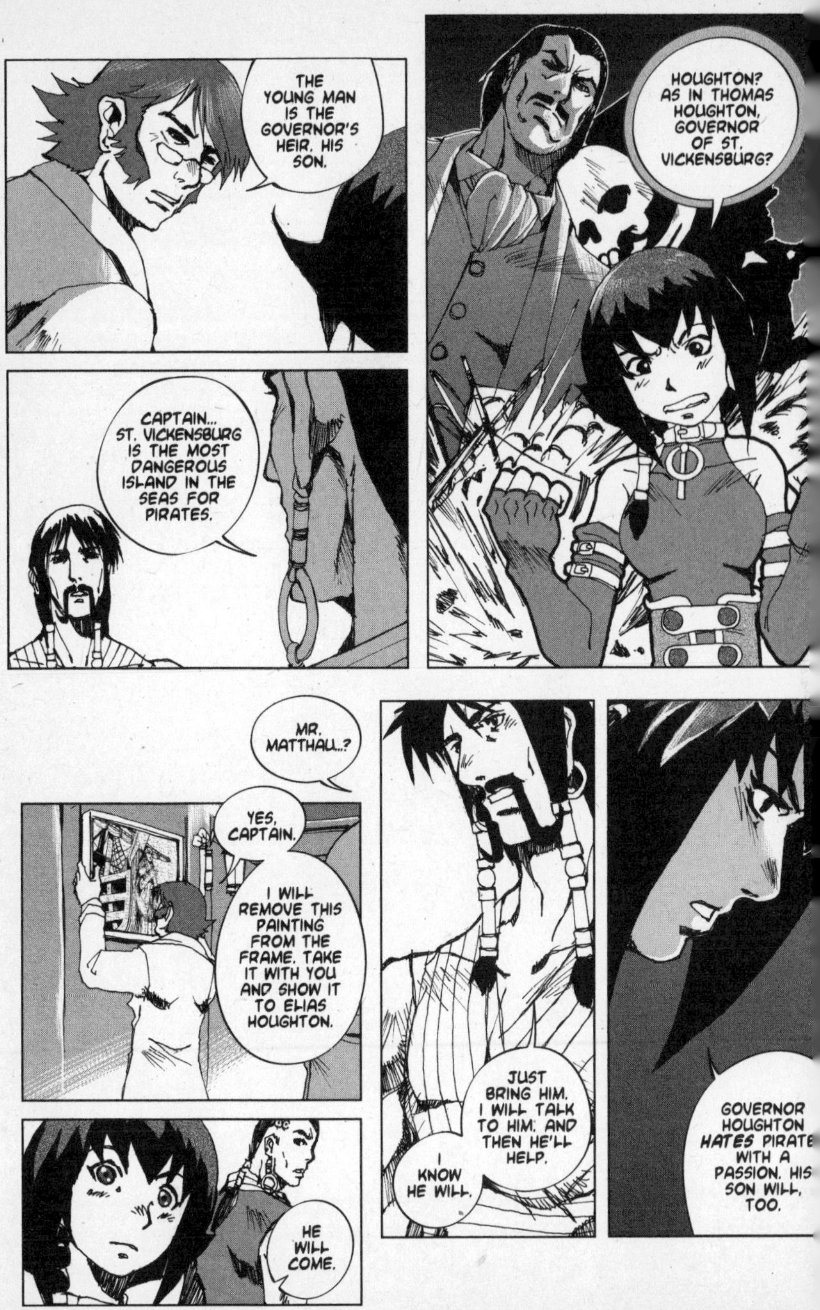
HOUGHTON? AS IN THOMAS HOUGHTON, GOVERNOR OF ST. VICKENSBURG?
THE YOUNG MAN IS THE GOVERNOR'S HEIR. HIS SON.
CAPTAIN... ST. VICKENSBURG IS THE MOST DANGEROUS ISLAND IN THE SEAS FOR PIRATES.
GOVERNOR HOUGHTON HATES PIRATE WITH A PASSION. HIS SON WILL, TOO.
JUST BRING HIM. I WILL TALK TO HIM. AND THEN HE'LL HELP.
I KNOW HE WILL.
MR. MATTHAU...?
YES, CAPTAIN.
I WILL REMOVE THIS PAINTING FROM THE FRAME. TAKE IT WITH YOU AND SHOW IT TO ELIAS HOUGHTON.
HE WILL COME.

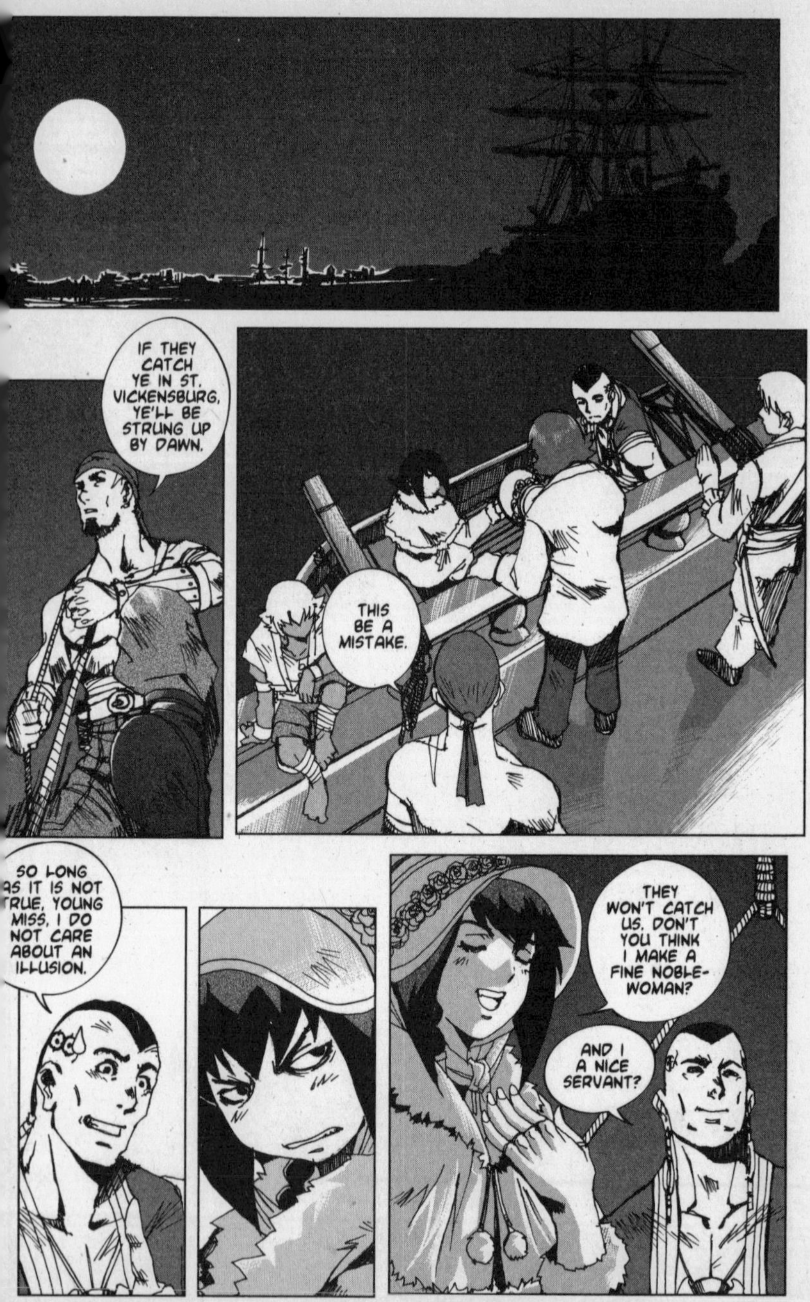
THIS BE A MISTAKE.
IF THEY CATCH YE IN ST. VICKENSBURG, YE'LL BE STRUNG UP BY DAWN.
THEY WON'T CATCH US. DON'T YOU THINK I MAKE A FINE NOBLE-WOMAN?
AND I A NICE SERVANT?
SO LONG AS IT IS NOT TRUE, YOUNG MISS, I DO NOT CARE ABOUT AN ILLUSION.

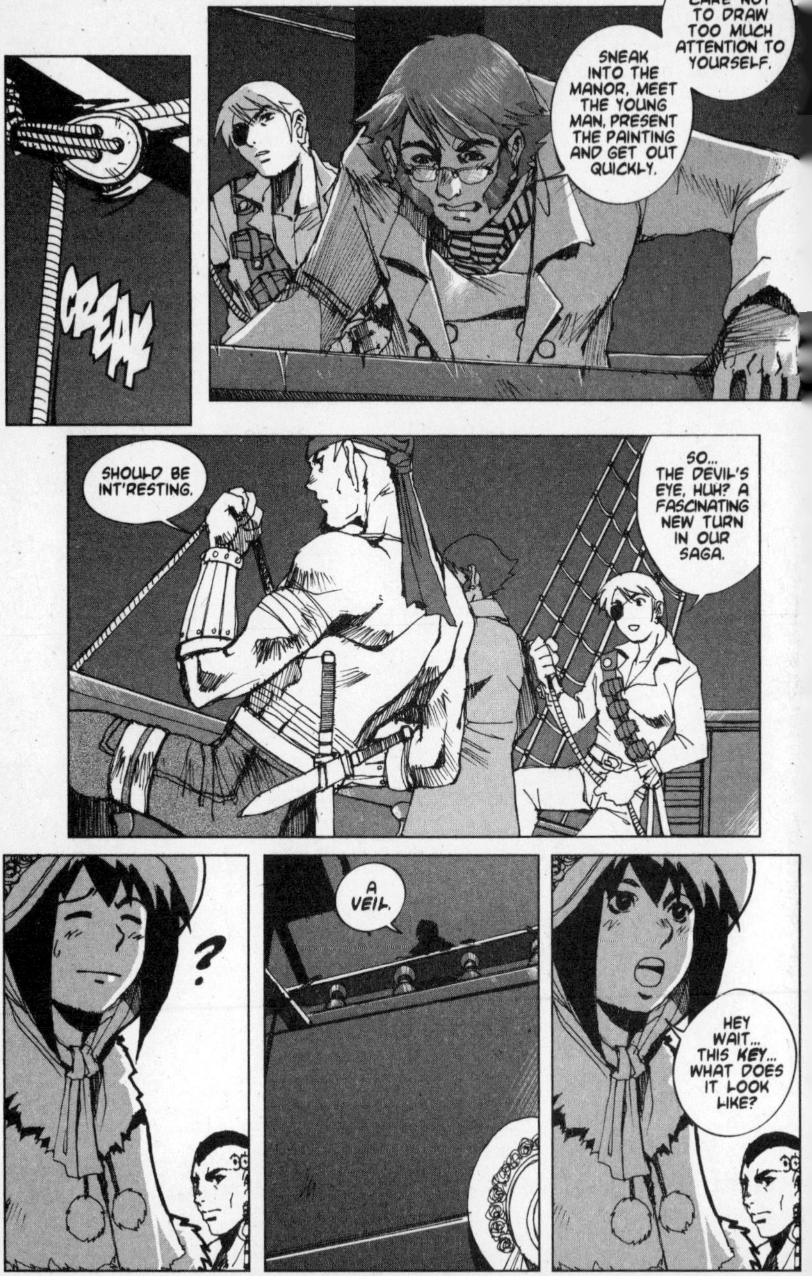
TAKE CARE NOT TO DRAW TOO MUCH ATTENTION TO YOURSELF.
SNEAK INTO THE MANOR, MEET THE YOUNG MAN, PRESENT THE PAINTING AND GET OUT QUICKLY.
CREAK
SO... THE DEVIL'S EYE, HUH? A FASCINATING NEW TURN IN OUR SAGA.
SHOULD BE INT'RESTING.
HEY WAIT... THIS KEY... WHAT DOES IT LOOK LIKE?
A VEIL.
?

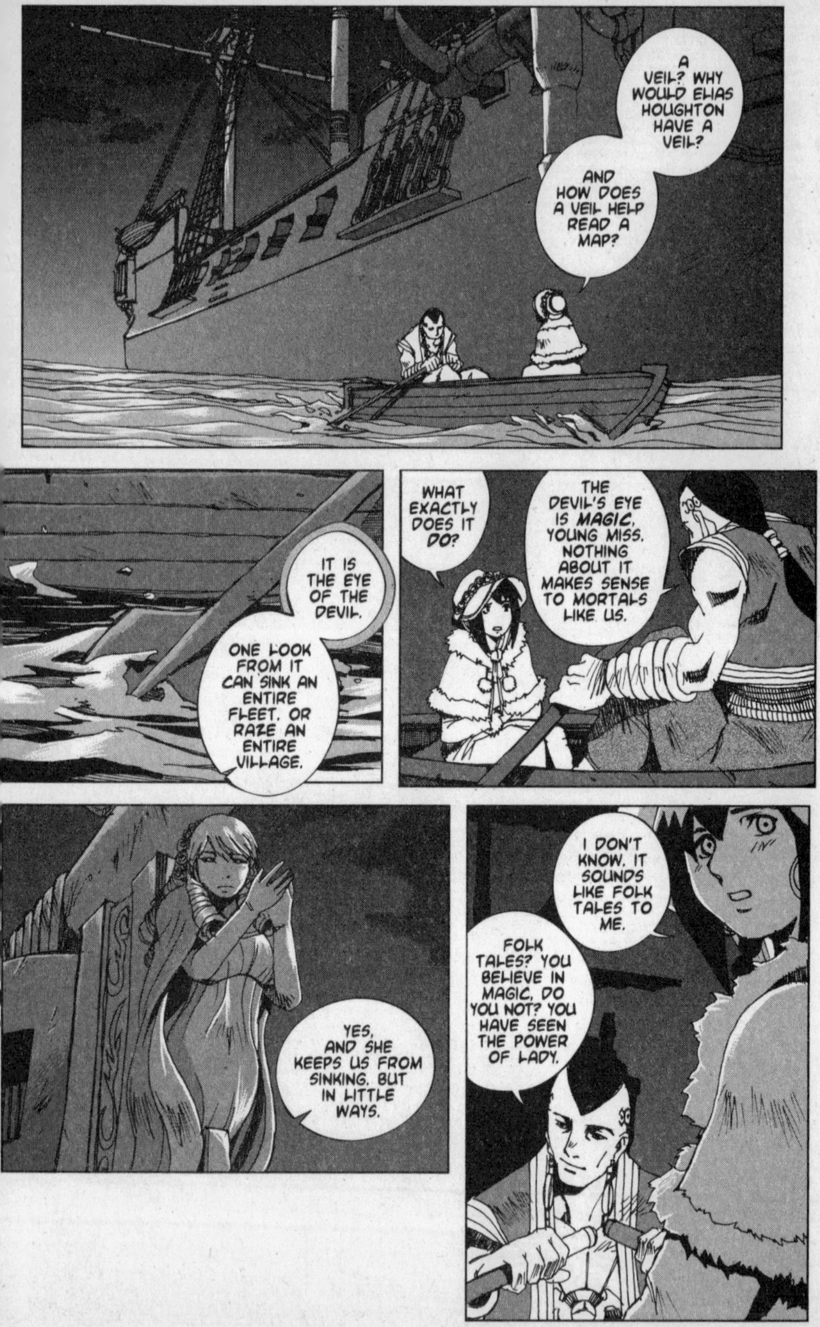
A VEIL? WHY WOULD ELIAS HOUGHTON HAVE A VEIL?
AND HOW DOES A VEIL HELP READ A MAP?
WHAT EXACTLY DOES IT DO?
THE DEVIL'S EYE IS MAGIC, YOUNG MISS. NOTHING ABOUT IT MAKES SENSE TO MORTALS LIKE US.
IT IS THE EYE OF THE DEVIL.
ONE LOOK FROM IT CAN SINK AN ENTIRE FLEET, OR RAZE AN ENTIRE VILLAGE.
I DON'T KNOW. IT SOUNDS LIKE FOLK TALES TO ME.
FOLK TALES? YOU BELIEVE IN MAGIC, DO YOU NOT? YOU HAVE SEEN THE POWER OF LADY.
YES, AND SHE KEEPS US FROM SINKING. BUT IN LITTLE WAYS.

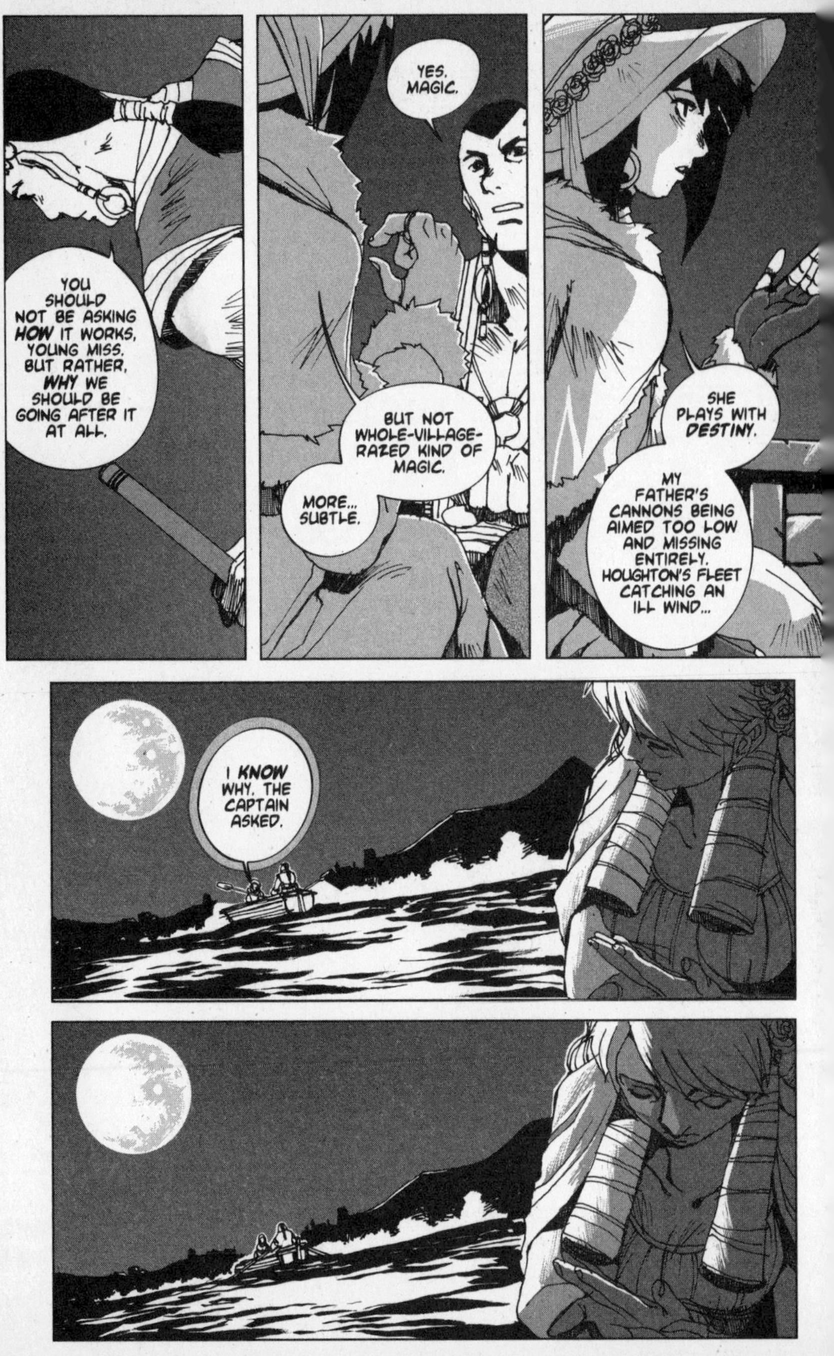
SHE PLAYS WITH DESTINY.
MY FATHER'S CANNONS BEING AIMED TOO LOW AND MISSING ENTIRELY. HOUGHTON'S FLEET CATCHING AN ILL WIND...
YES. MAGIC.
BUT NOT WHOLE-VILLAGE-RAZED KIND OF MAGIC.
MORE... SUBTLE.
YOU SHOULD NOT BE ASKING HOW IT WORKS, YOUNG MISS. BUT RATHER, WHY WE SHOULD BE GOING AFTER IT AT ALL.
I KNOW WHY. THE CAPTAIN ASKED.

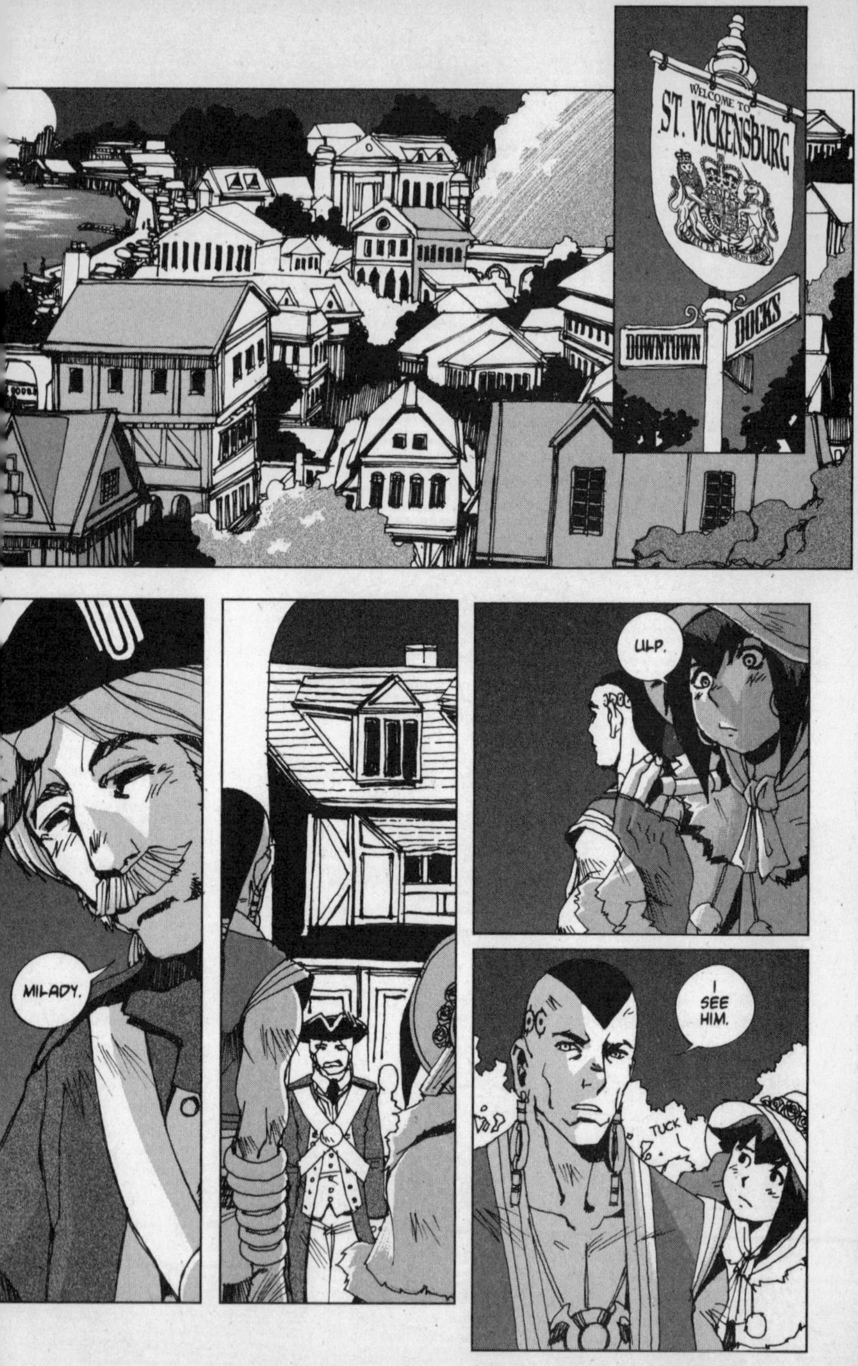
WELCOME TO
ST. VICKENSBURG
DOWNTOWN
DOCKS
ULP.
I SEE HIM.
TUCK
MILADY.

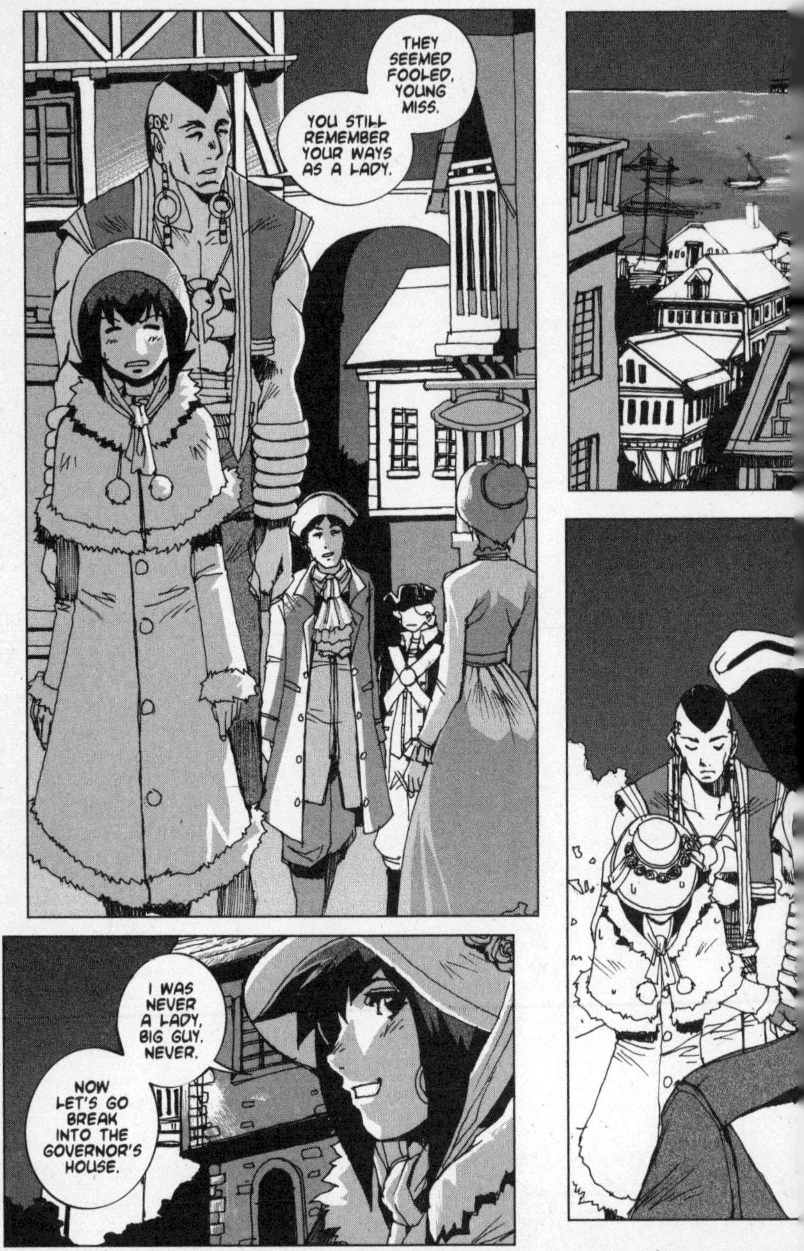
THEY SEEMED FOOLED, YOUNG MISS.
YOU STILL REMEMBER YOUR WAYS AS A LADY.
I WAS NEVER A LADY, BIG GUY. NEVER.
NOW LET'S GO BREAK INTO THE GOVERNOR'S HOUSE.

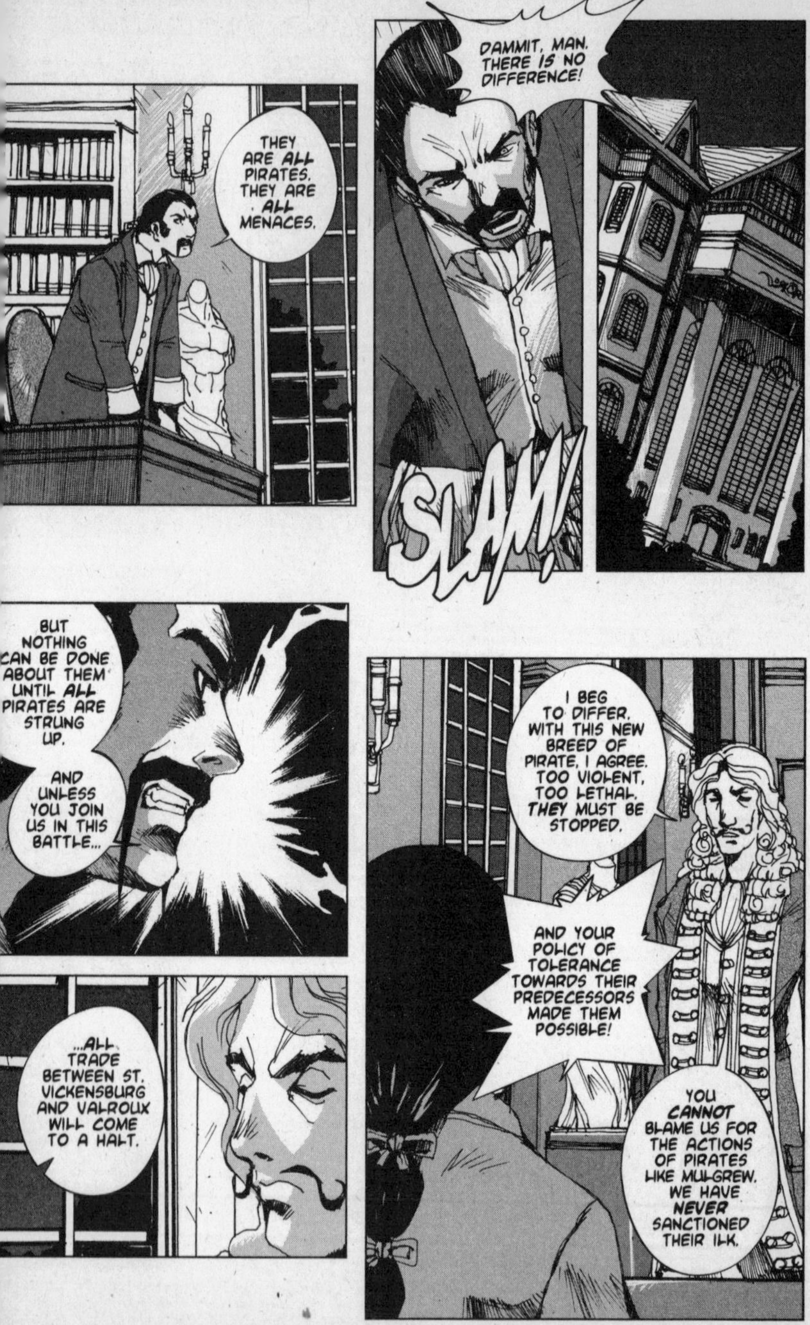

DAMMIT, MAN. THERE IS NO DIFFERENCE!
SLAM!
THEY ARE ALL PIRATES. THEY ARE ALL MENACES.
I BEG TO DIFFER. WITH THIS NEW BREED OF PIRATE, I AGREE. TOO VIOLENT, TOO LETHAL. THEY MUST BE STOPPED.
AND YOUR POLICY OF TOLERANCE TOWARDS THEIR PREDECESSORS MADE THEM POSSIBLE!
YOU CANNOT BLAME US FOR THE ACTIONS OF PIRATES LIKE MULGREW. WE HAVE NEVER SANCTIONED THEIR ILK.
BUT NOTHING CAN BE DONE ABOUT THEM UNTIL ALL PIRATES ARE STRUNG UP.
AND UNLESS YOU JOIN US IN THIS BATTLE...
...ALL TRADE BETWEEN ST. VICKENSBURG AND VALROUX WILL COME TO A HALT.

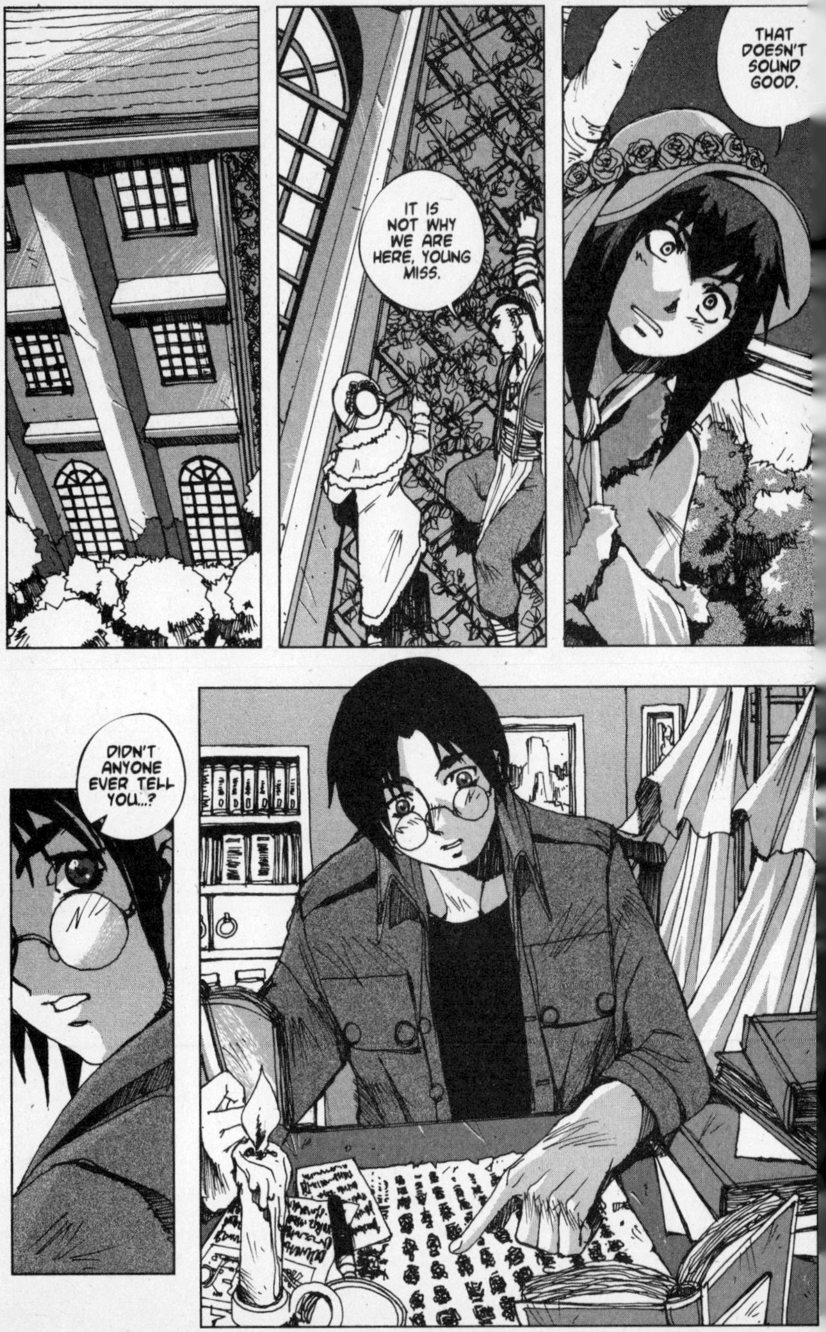
THAT DOESN'T SOUND GOOD.
IT IS NOT WHY WE ARE HERE, YOUNG MISS.
DIDN'T ANYONE EVER TELL YOU...?

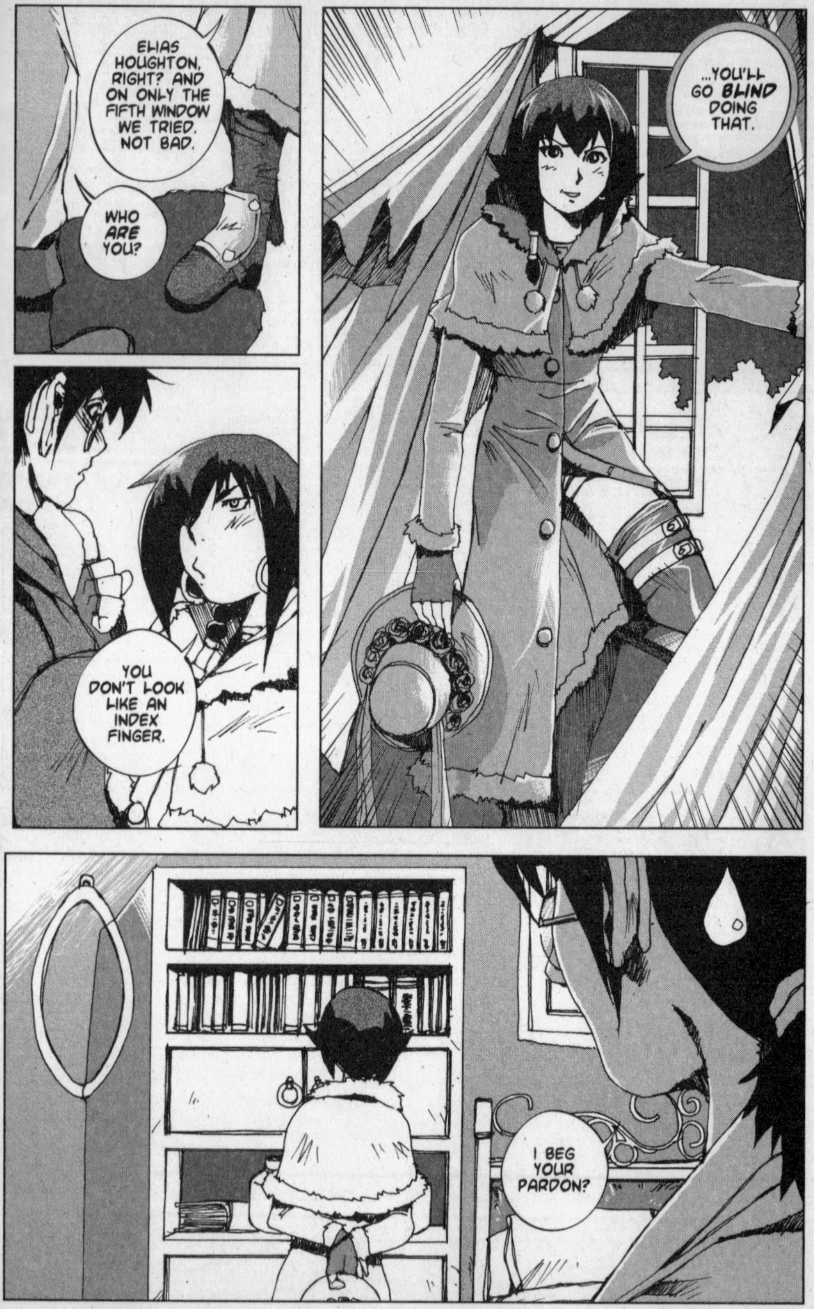
...YOU'LL GO BLIND DOING THAT.
ELIAS HOUGHTON, RIGHT? AND ON ONLY THE FIFTH WINDOW WE TRIED. NOT BAD.
WHO ARE YOU?
YOU DON'T LOOK LIKE AN INDEX FINGER.
I BEG YOUR PARDON?

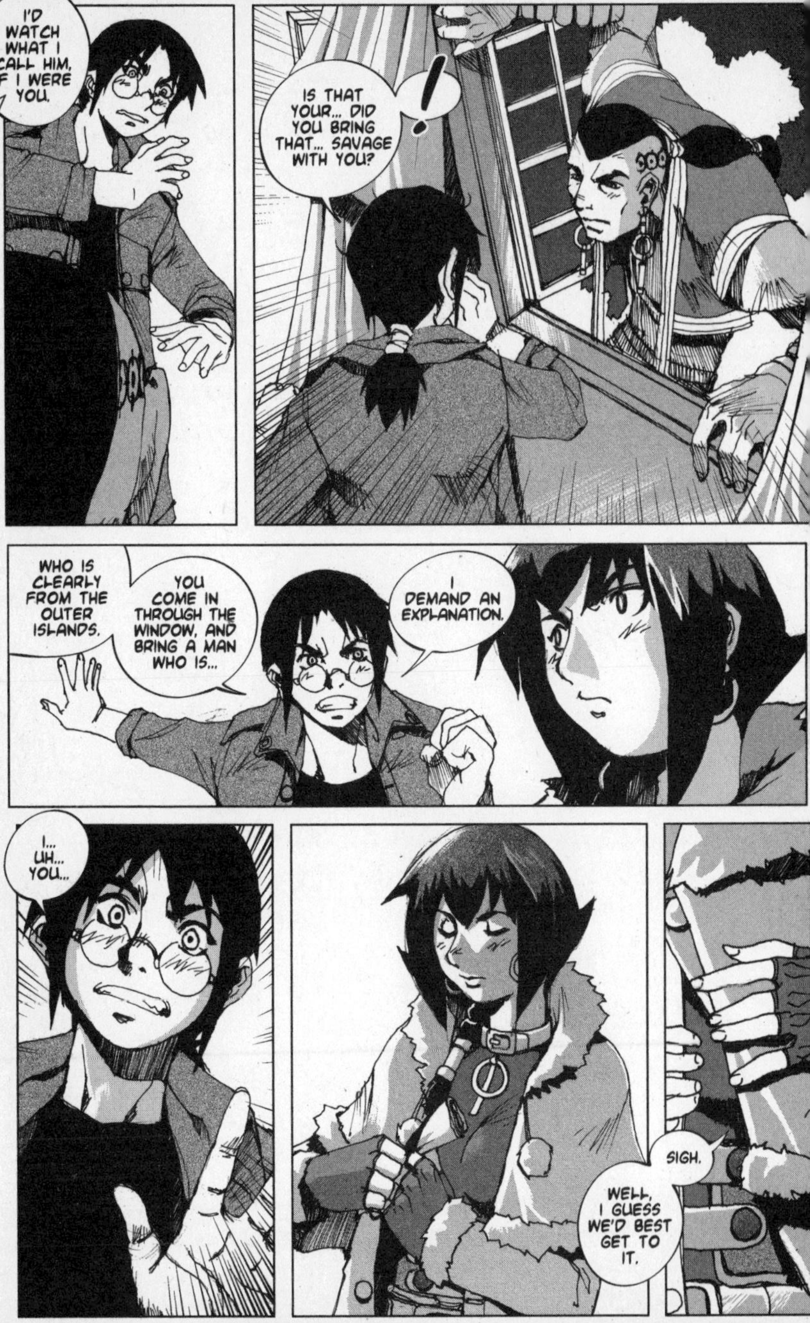
!
IS THAT YOUR... DID YOU BRING THAT... SAVAGE WITH YOU?
I'D WATCH WHAT I CALL HIM, IF I WERE YOU.
I DEMAND AN EXPLANATION.
YOU COME IN THROUGH THE WINDOW, AND BRING A MAN WHO IS...
WHO IS CLEARLY FROM THE OUTER ISLANDS.
SIGH.
WELL, I GUESS WE'D BEST GET TO IT.
I... UH... YOU...

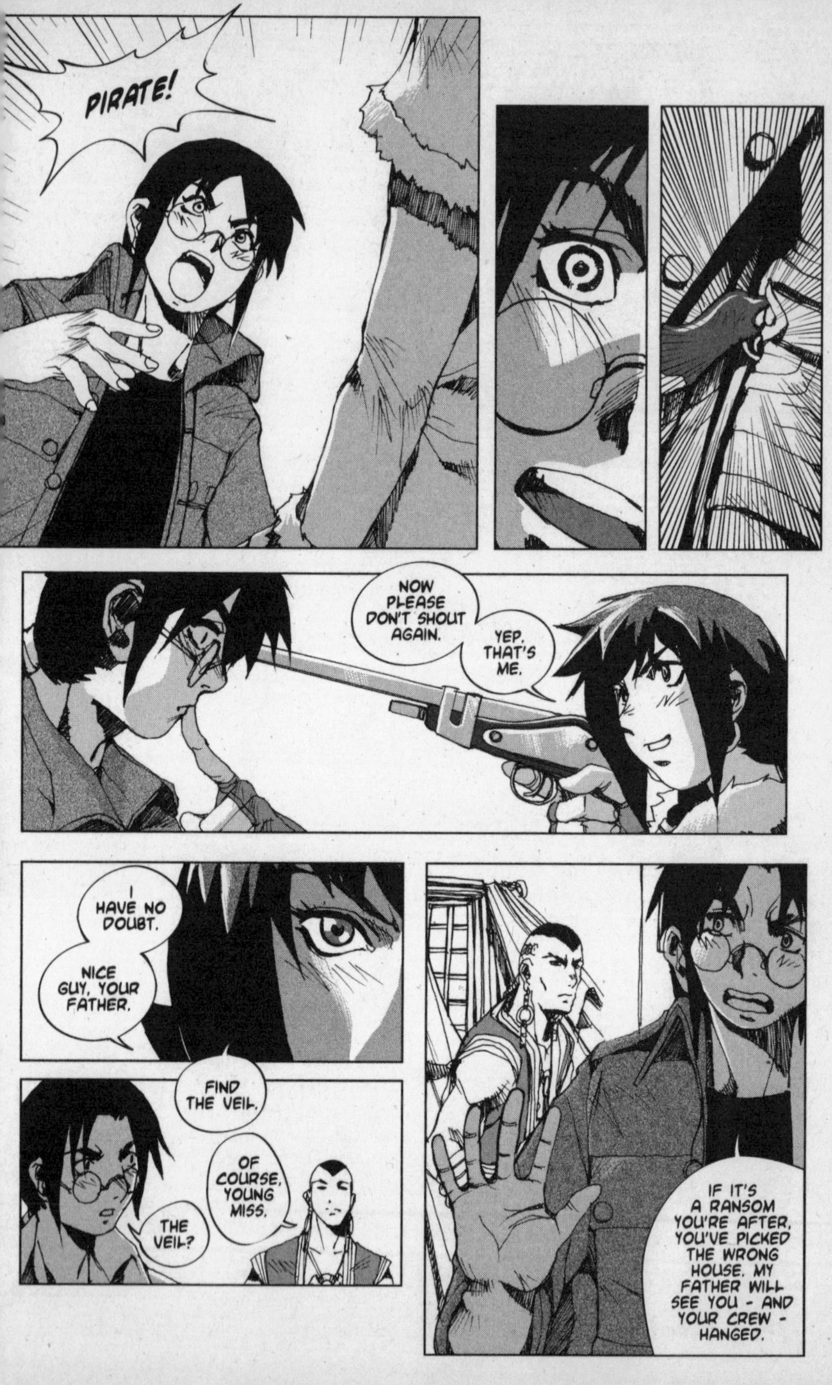
PIRATE!
YEP. THAT'S ME.
NOW PLEASE DON'T SHOUT AGAIN.
IF IT'S A RANSOM YOU'RE AFTER, YOU'VE PICKED THE WRONG HOUSE. MY FATHER WILL SEE YOU - AND YOUR CREW - HANGED.
I HAVE NO DOUBT.
NICE GUY, YOUR FATHER.
FIND THE VEIL.
OF COURSE, YOUNG MISS.
THE VEIL?

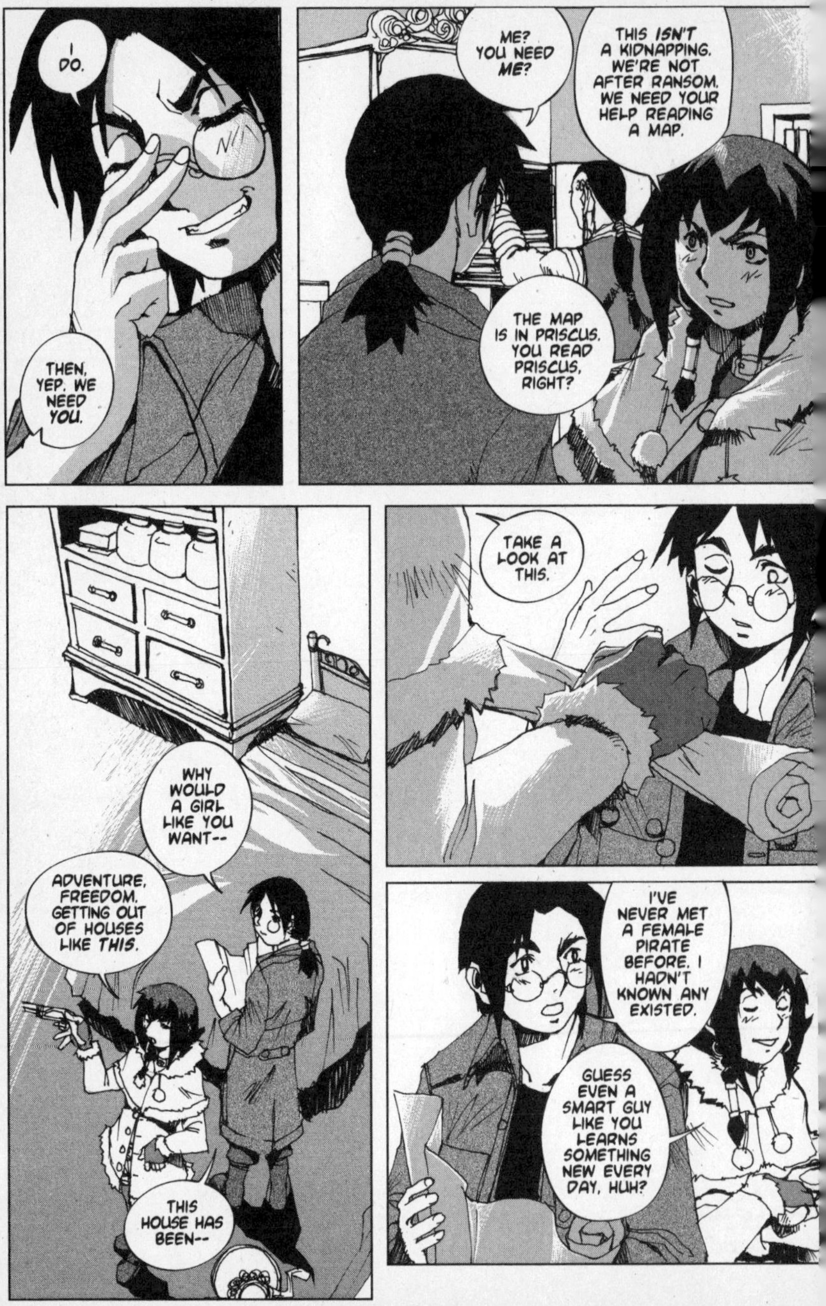
I DO.
THEN, YEP. WE NEED *YOU*.
ME? YOU NEED *ME*?
THIS *ISN'T* A KIDNAPPING. WE'RE NOT AFTER RANSOM. WE NEED YOUR HELP READING A MAP.
THE MAP IS IN PRISCUS. YOU READ PRISCUS, RIGHT?
WHY WOULD A GIRL LIKE YOU WANT--
ADVENTURE, FREEDOM. GETTING OUT OF HOUSES LIKE *THIS*.
THIS HOUSE HAS BEEN--
TAKE A LOOK AT THIS.
I'VE NEVER MET A FEMALE PIRATE BEFORE. I HADN'T KNOWN ANY EXISTED.
GUESS EVEN A SMART GUY LIKE YOU LEARNS SOMETHING NEW EVERY DAY, HUH?

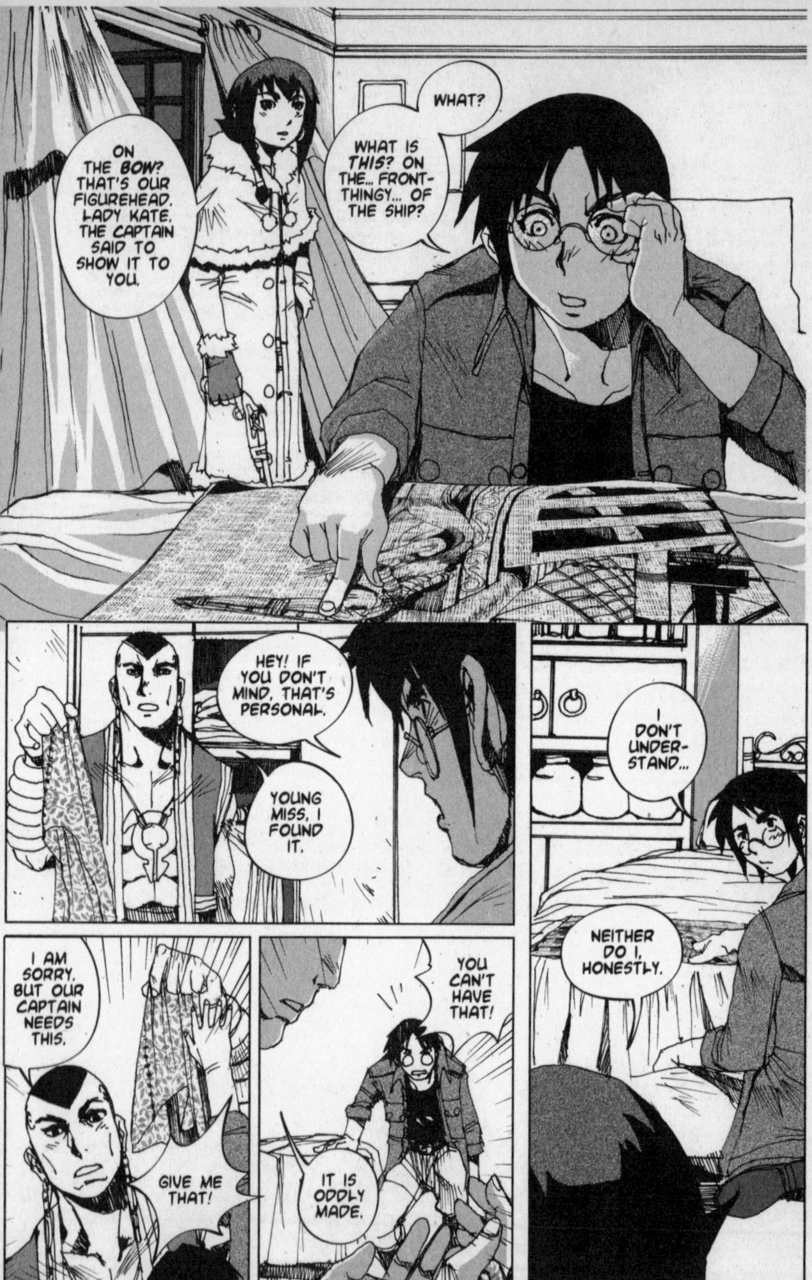
WHAT?
WHAT IS THIS? ON THE... FRONT-THINGY... OF THE SHIP?
ON THE BOW? THAT'S OUR FIGUREHEAD, LADY KATE. THE CAPTAIN SAID TO SHOW IT TO YOU.
I DON'T UNDER-STAND...
NEITHER DO I, HONESTLY.
HEY! IF YOU DON'T MIND, THAT'S PERSONAL.
YOUNG MISS, I FOUND IT.
YOU CAN'T HAVE THAT!
IT IS ODDLY MADE.
I AM SORRY, BUT OUR CAPTAIN NEEDS THIS.
GIVE ME THAT!

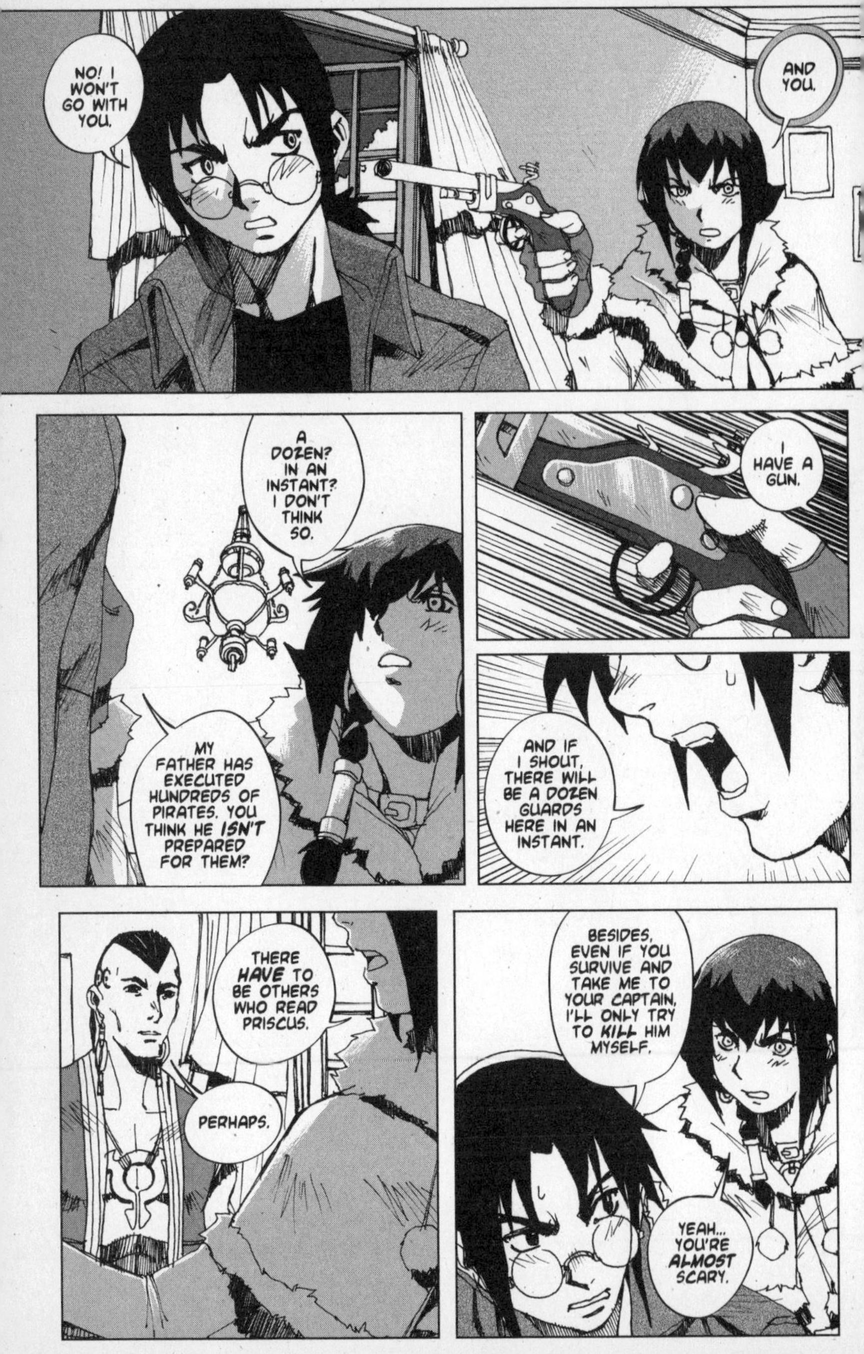
AND YOU.
NO! I WON'T GO WITH YOU.
I HAVE A GUN.
AND IF I SHOUT, THERE WILL BE A DOZEN GUARDS HERE IN AN INSTANT.
A DOZEN? IN AN INSTANT? I DON'T THINK SO.
MY FATHER HAS EXECUTED HUNDREDS OF PIRATES. YOU THINK HE **ISN'T** PREPARED FOR THEM?
BESIDES, EVEN IF YOU SURVIVE AND TAKE ME TO YOUR CAPTAIN, I'LL ONLY TRY TO **KILL** HIM MYSELF.
YEAH... YOU'RE **ALMOST** SCARY.
THERE **HAVE** TO BE OTHERS WHO READ PRISCUS.
PERHAPS.

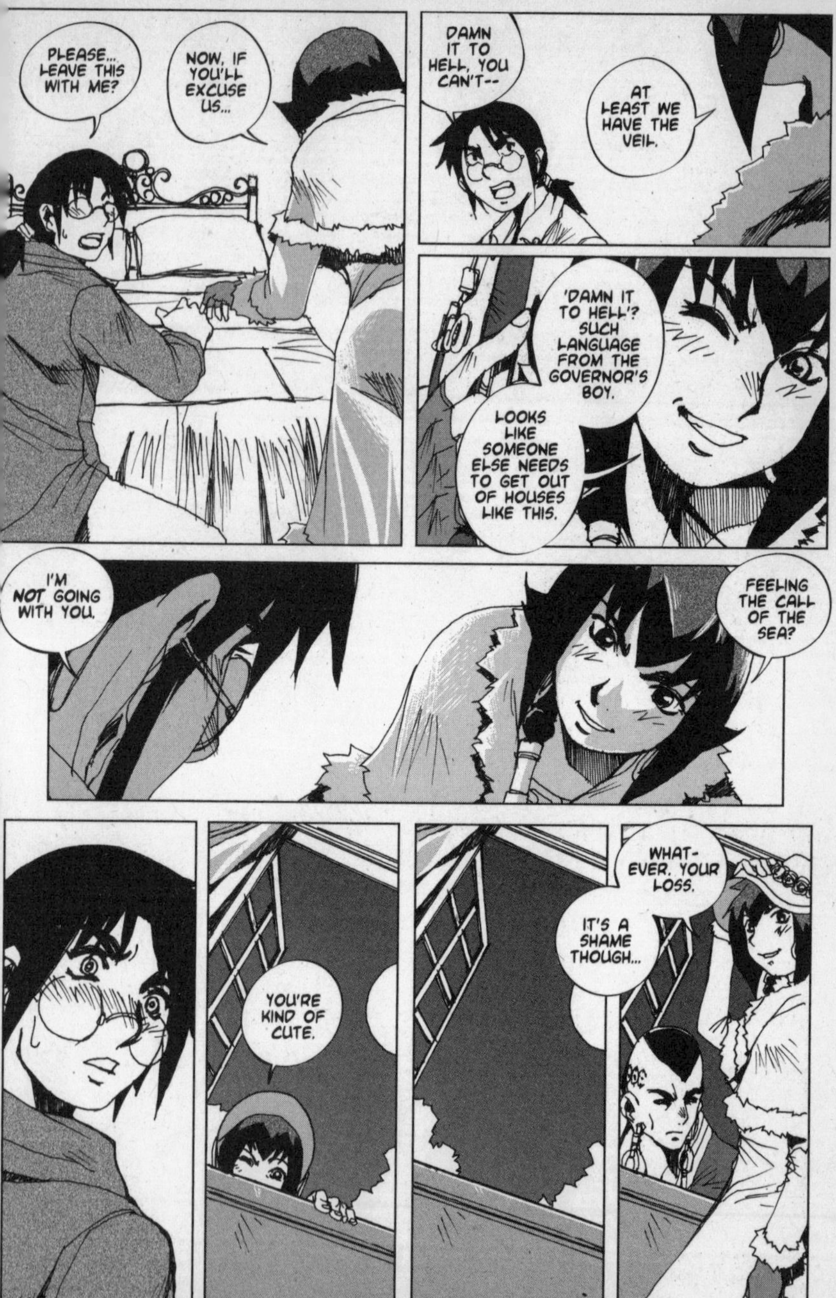
DAMN IT TO HELL, YOU CAN'T--
AT LEAST WE HAVE THE VEIL.
'DAMN IT TO HELL'? SUCH LANGUAGE FROM THE GOVERNOR'S BOY.
LOOKS LIKE SOMEONE ELSE NEEDS TO GET OUT OF HOUSES LIKE THIS.
NOW, IF YOU'LL EXCUSE US...
PLEASE... LEAVE THIS WITH ME?
FEELING THE CALL OF THE SEA?
I'M **NOT** GOING WITH YOU.
WHAT-EVER. YOUR LOSS.
IT'S A SHAME THOUGH...
YOU'RE KIND OF CUTE.

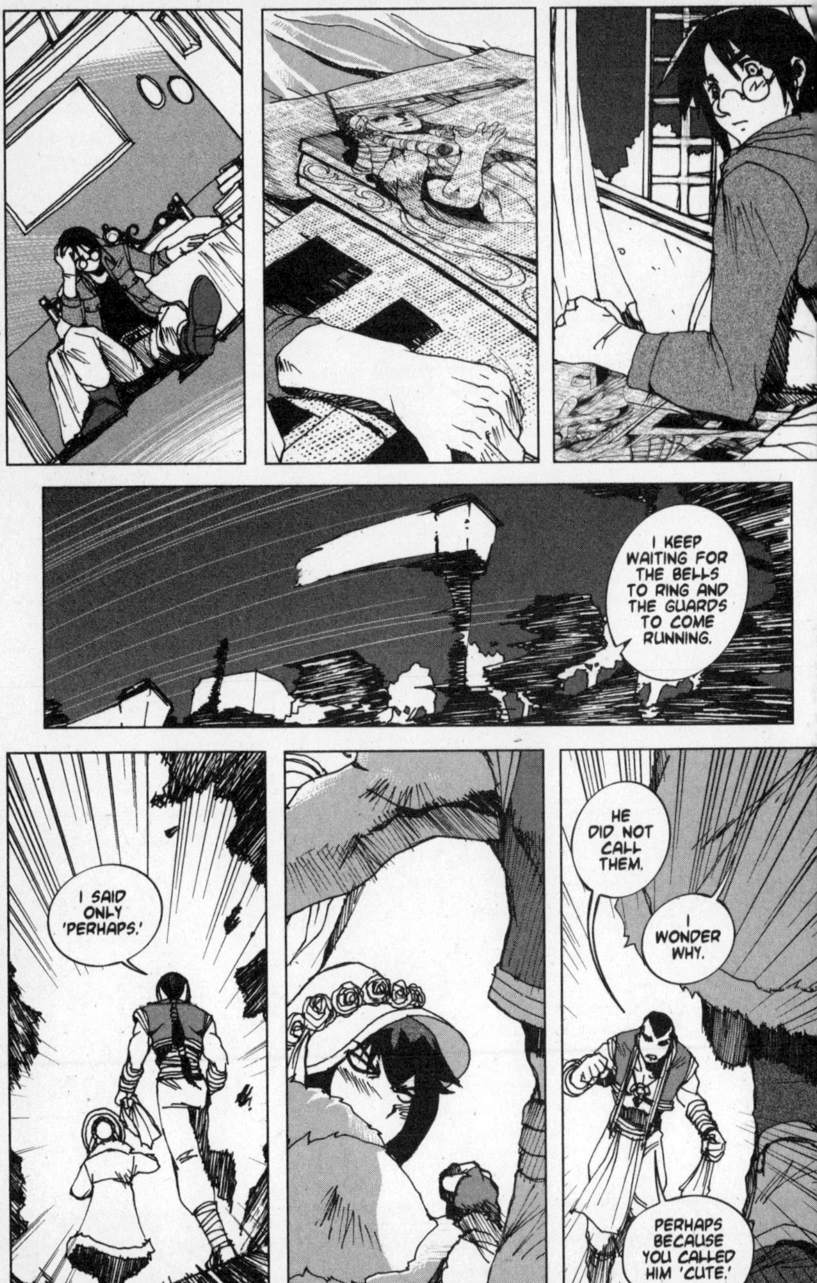
I KEEP WAITING FOR THE BELLS TO RING AND THE GUARDS TO COME RUNNING.
HE DID NOT CALL THEM.
I WONDER WHY.
PERHAPS BECAUSE YOU CALLED HIM 'CUTE.'
I SAID ONLY 'PERHAPS.'

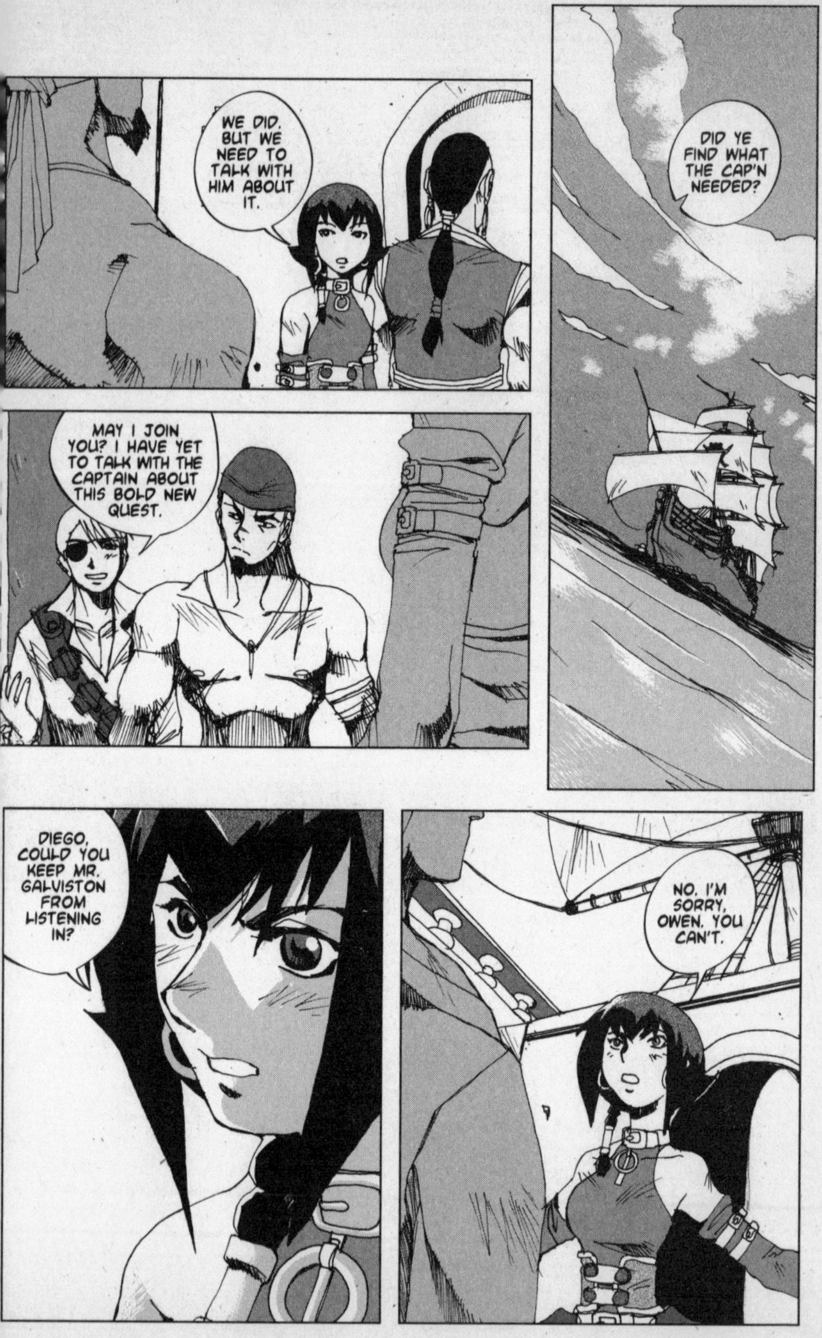
DID YE FIND WHAT THE CAP'N NEEDED?
WE DID. BUT WE NEED TO TALK WITH HIM ABOUT IT.
MAY I JOIN YOU? I HAVE YET TO TALK WITH THE CAPTAIN ABOUT THIS BOLD NEW QUEST.
NO. I'M SORRY, OWEN. YOU CAN'T.
DIEGO, COULD YOU KEEP MR. GALVISTON FROM LISTENING IN?

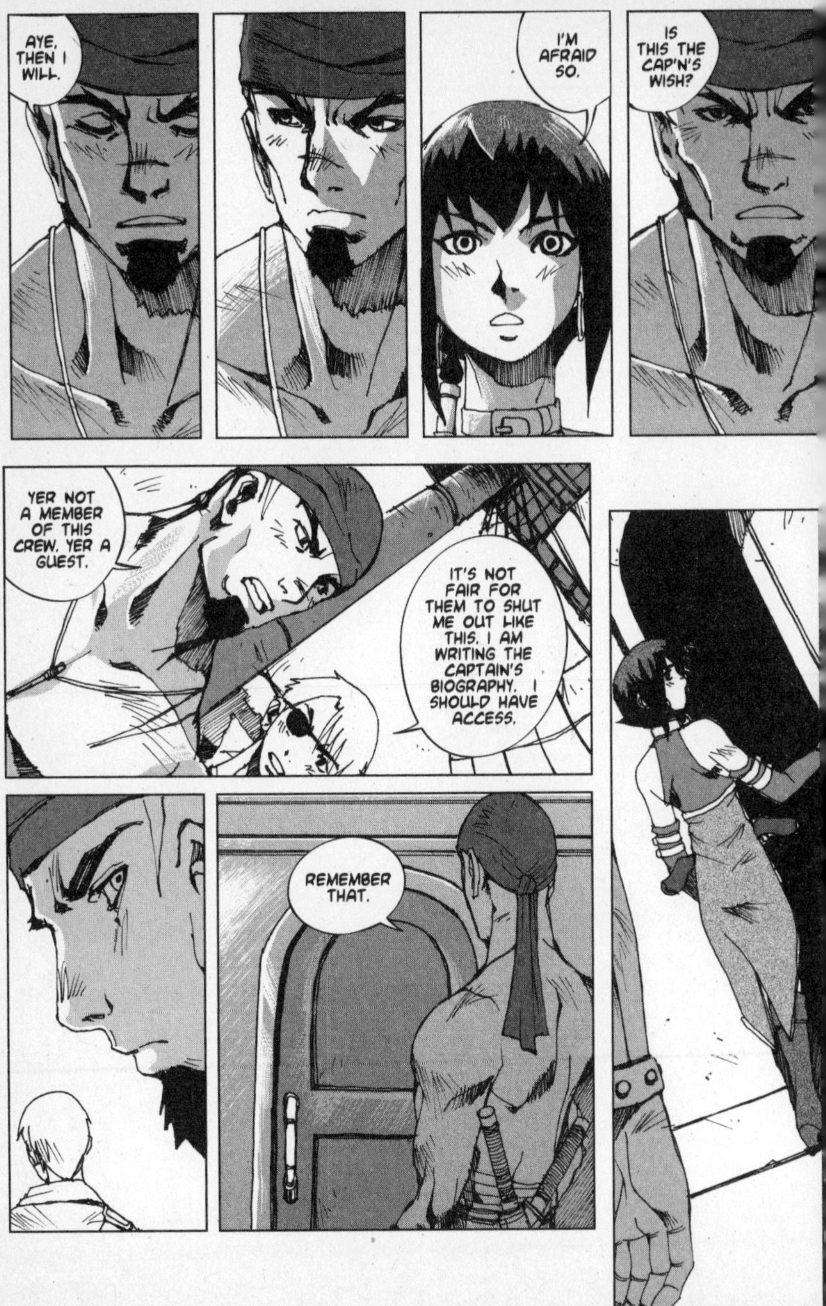
IS THIS THE CAP'N'S WISH?
I'M AFRAID SO.
AYE, THEN I WILL.
IT'S NOT FAIR FOR THEM TO SHUT ME OUT LIKE THIS. I AM WRITING THE CAPTAIN'S BIOGRAPHY. I SHOULD HAVE ACCESS.
YER NOT A MEMBER OF THIS CREW. YER A GUEST.
REMEMBER THAT.

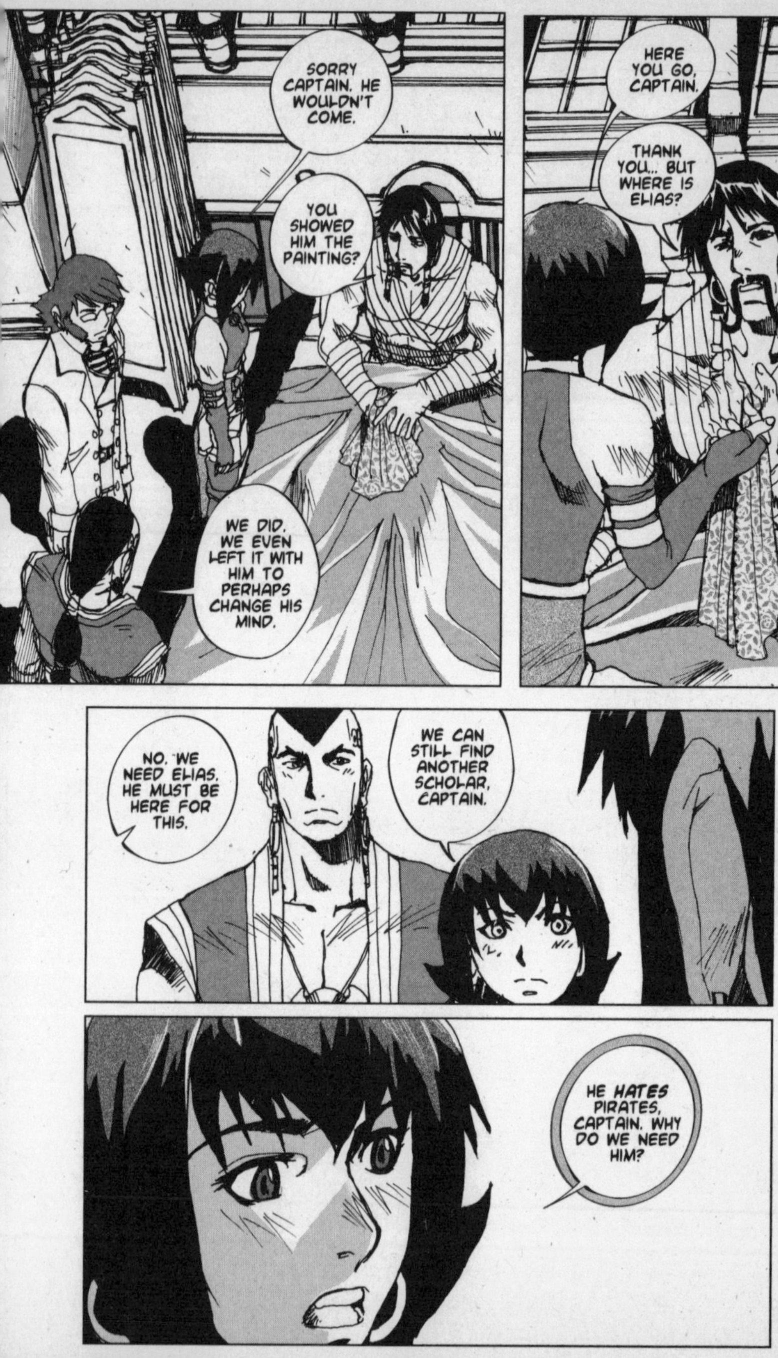
HERE YOU GO, CAPTAIN.
THANK YOU... BUT WHERE IS ELIAS?
SORRY CAPTAIN. HE WOULDN'T COME.
YOU SHOWED HIM THE PAINTING?
WE DID, WE EVEN LEFT IT WITH HIM TO PERHAPS CHANGE HIS MIND.
WE CAN STILL FIND ANOTHER SCHOLAR, CAPTAIN.
NO. WE NEED ELIAS. HE MUST BE HERE FOR THIS.
HE *HATES* PIRATES, CAPTAIN. WHY DO WE NEED HIM?

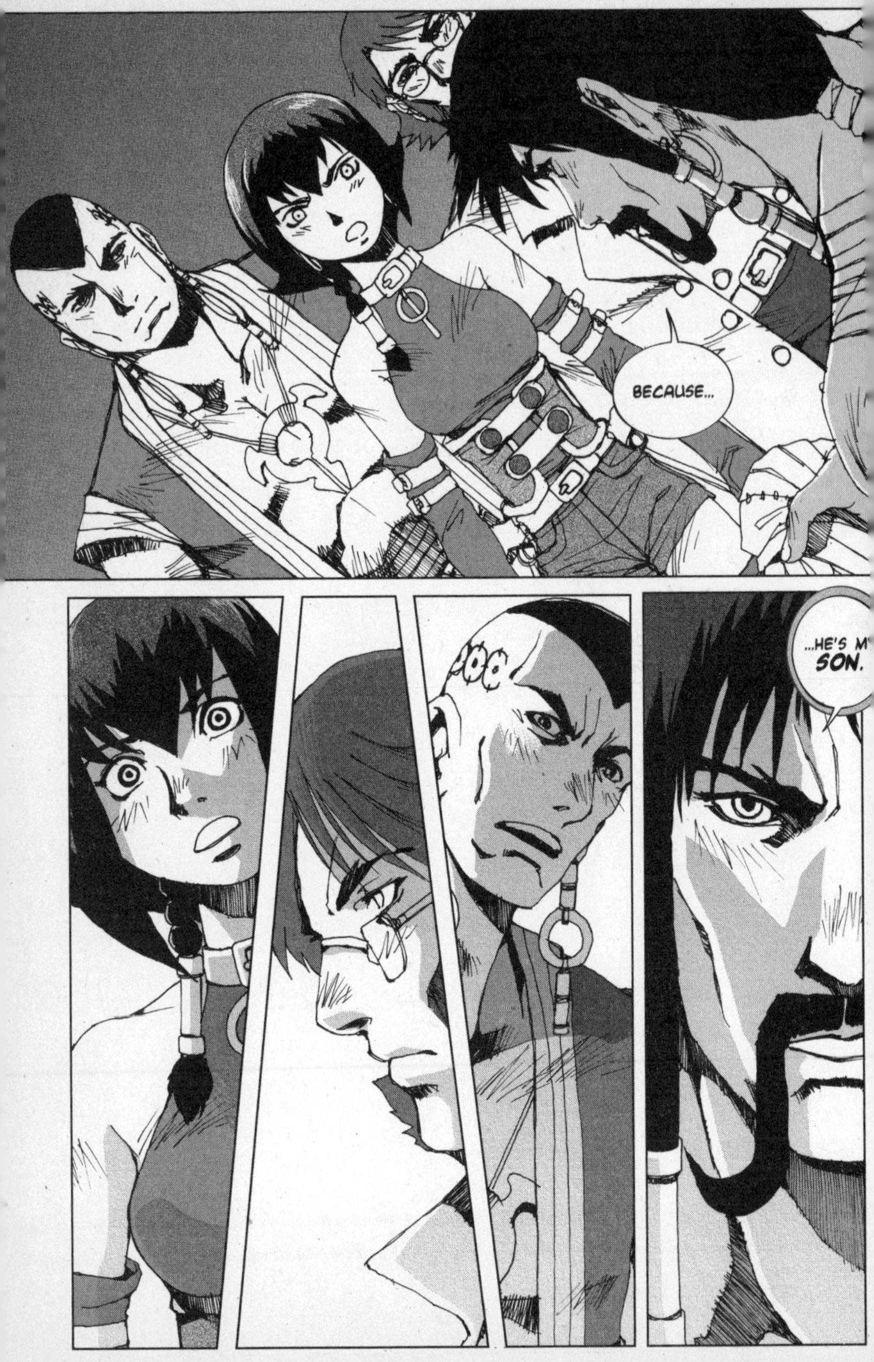
BECAUSE...
...HE'S MY SON.

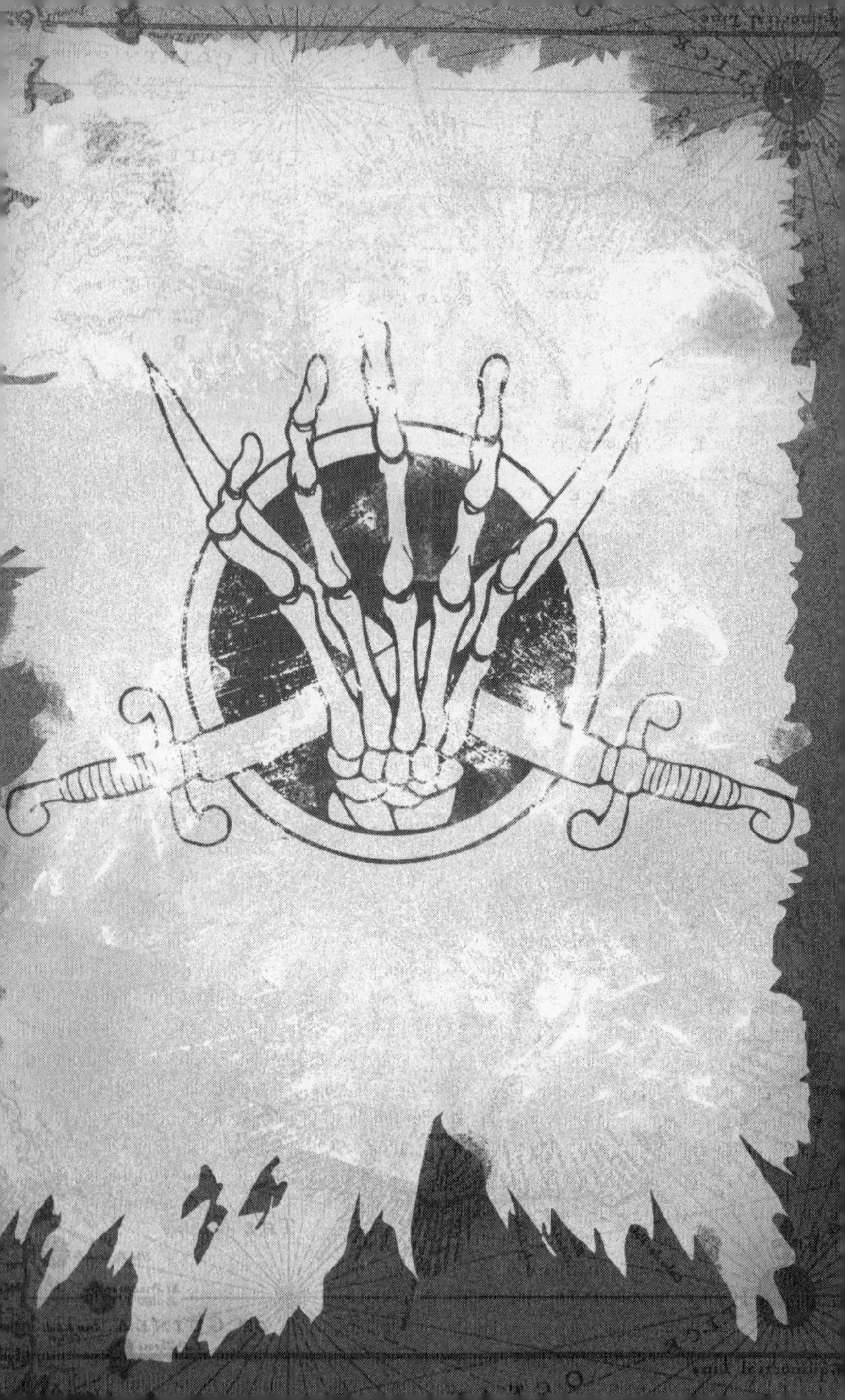

CHAPTER 5
Reunion

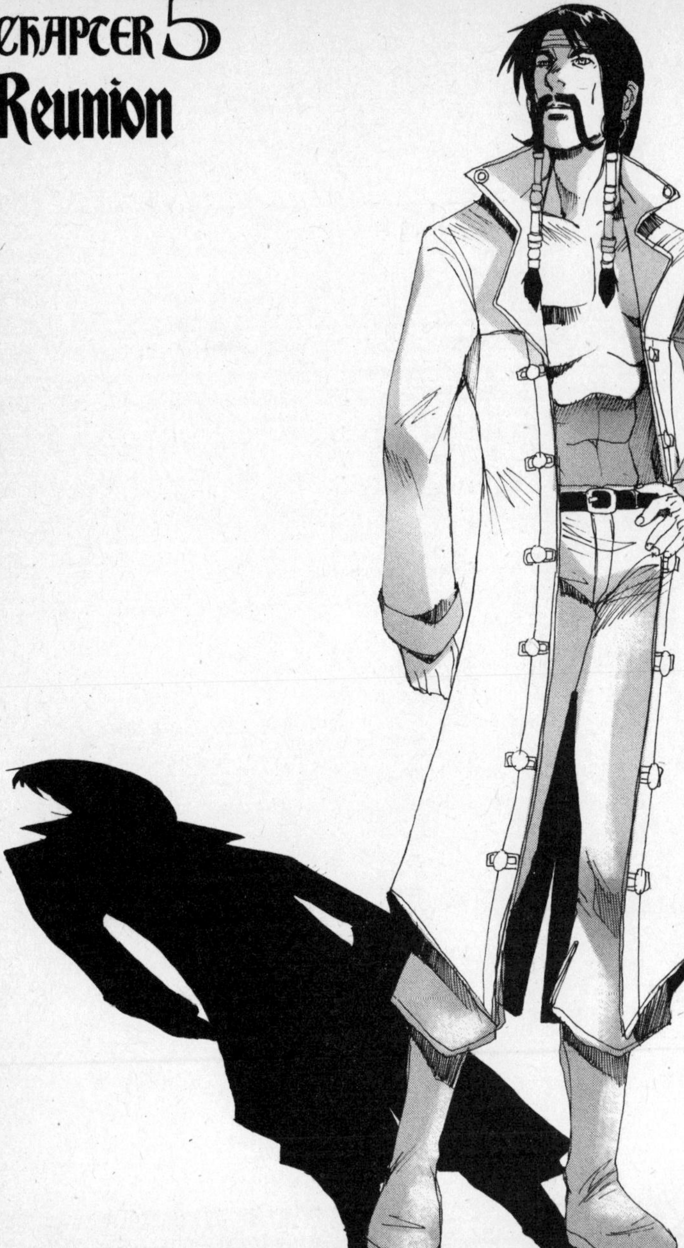

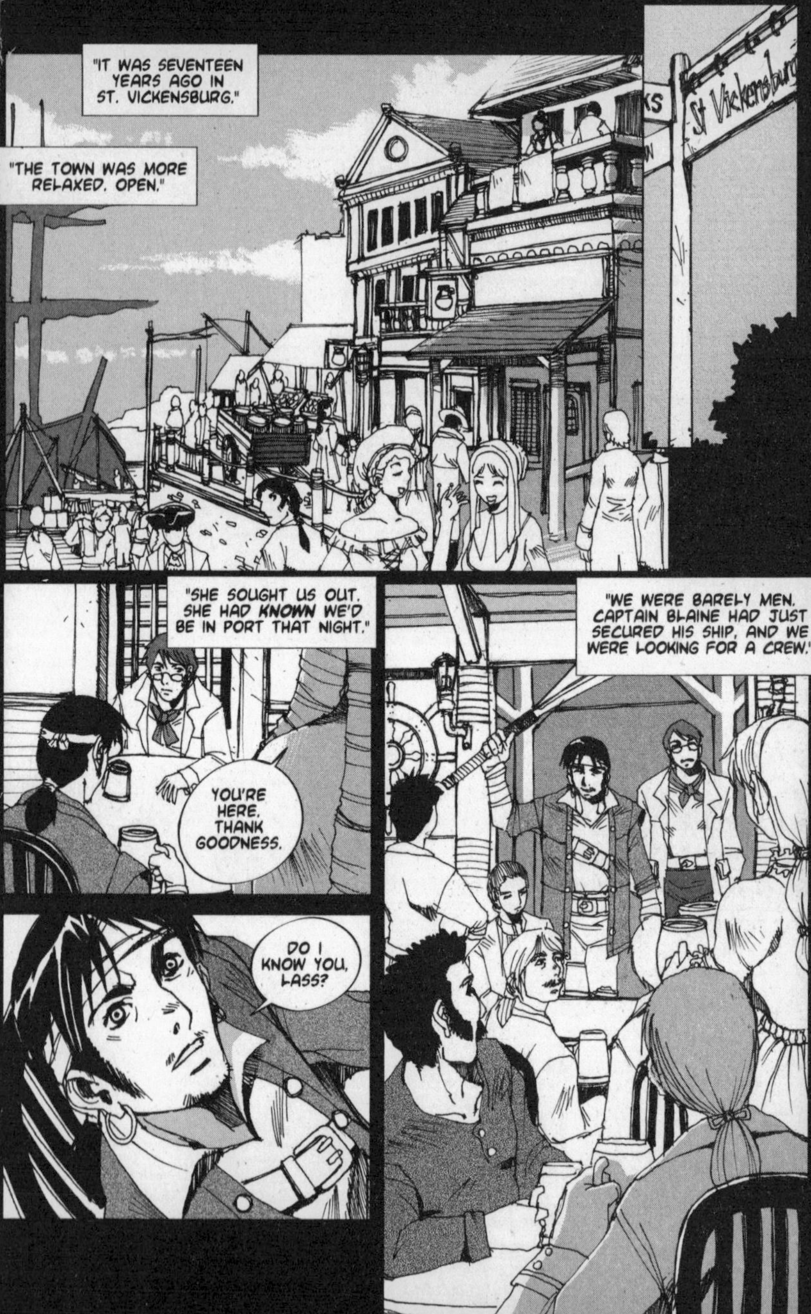
"IT WAS SEVENTEEN YEARS AGO IN ST. VICKENSBURG."
"THE TOWN WAS MORE RELAXED. OPEN."
"WE WERE BARELY MEN. CAPTAIN BLAINE HAD JUST SECURED HIS SHIP, AND WE WERE LOOKING FOR A CREW."
"SHE SOUGHT US OUT. SHE HAD *KNOWN* WE'D BE IN PORT THAT NIGHT."
YOU'RE HERE. THANK GOODNESS.
DO I KNOW YOU, LASS?

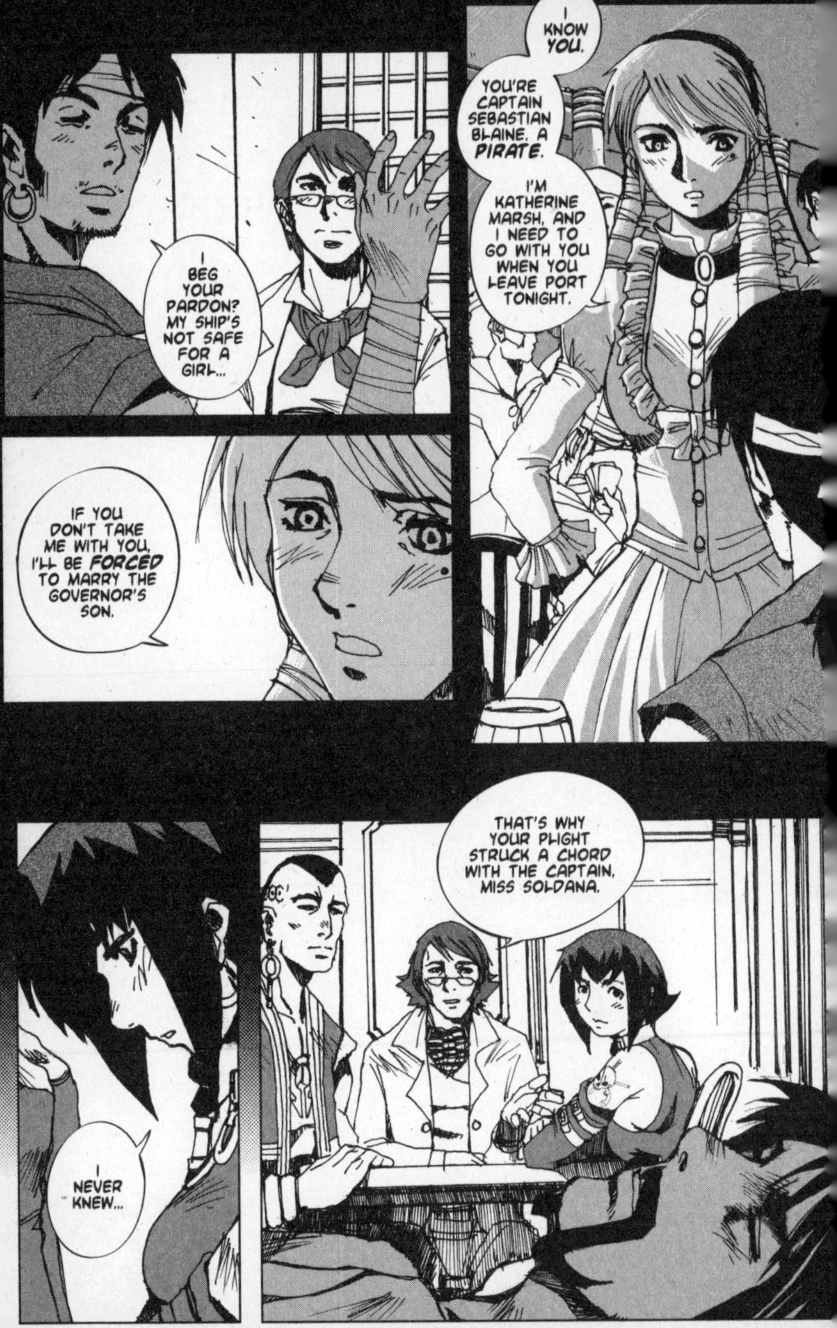
I KNOW *YOU*.
YOU'RE CAPTAIN SEBASTIAN BLAINE. A *PIRATE*.
I'M KATHERINE MARSH, AND I NEED TO GO WITH YOU WHEN YOU LEAVE PORT TONIGHT.
I BEG YOUR PARDON? MY SHIP'S NOT SAFE FOR A GIRL...
IF YOU DON'T TAKE ME WITH YOU, I'LL BE *FORCED* TO MARRY THE GOVERNOR'S SON.
THAT'S WHY YOUR PLIGHT STRUCK A CHORD WITH THE CAPTAIN, MISS SOLDANA.
I NEVER KNEW...

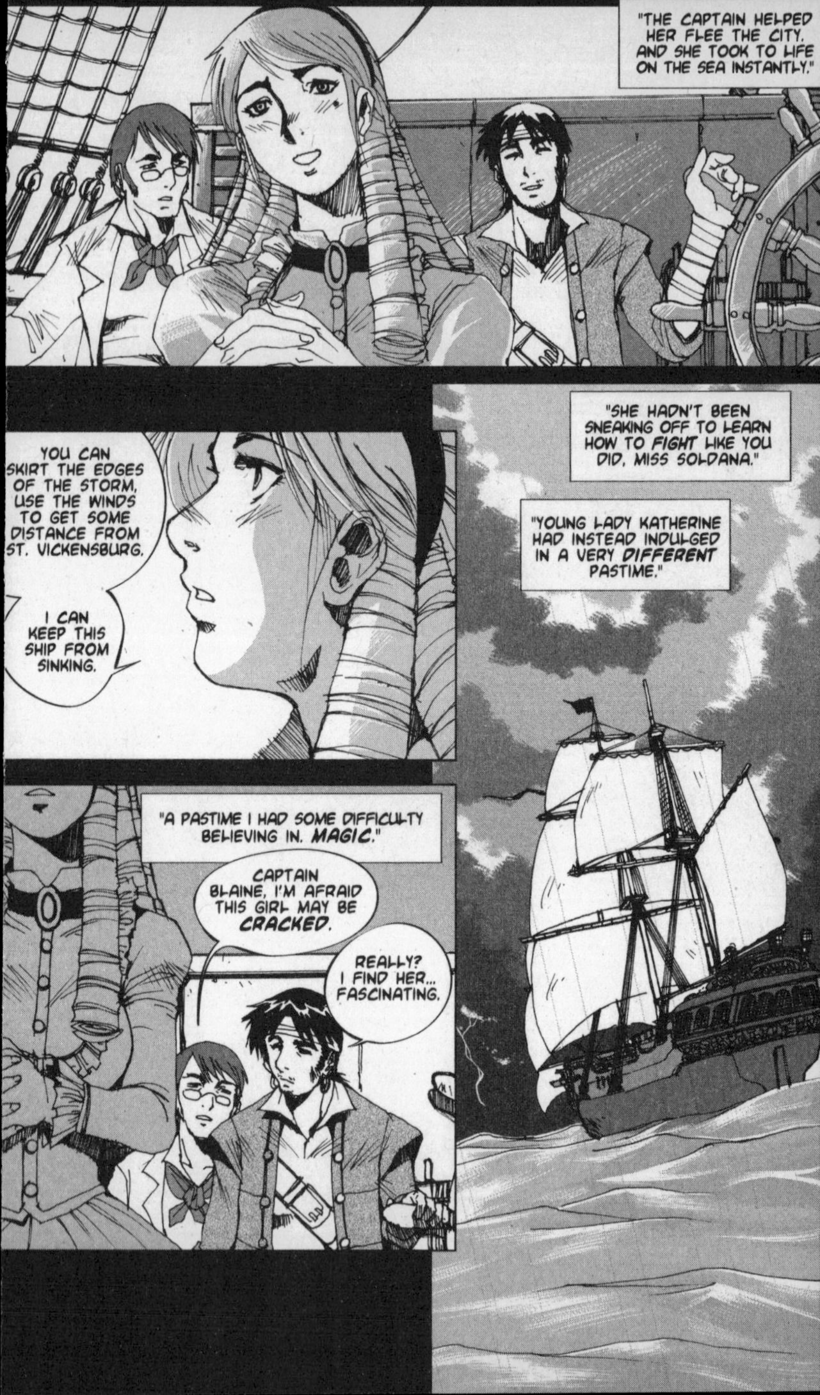
"THE CAPTAIN HELPED HER FLEE THE CITY. AND SHE TOOK TO LIFE ON THE SEA INSTANTLY."
"SHE HADN'T BEEN SNEAKING OFF TO LEARN HOW TO *FIGHT* LIKE YOU DID, MISS SOLDANA."
"YOUNG LADY KATHERINE HAD INSTEAD INDULGED IN A VERY *DIFFERENT* PASTIME."
YOU CAN SKIRT THE EDGES OF THE STORM, USE THE WINDS TO GET SOME DISTANCE FROM ST. VICKENSBURG.
I CAN KEEP THIS SHIP FROM SINKING.
"A PASTIME I HAD SOME DIFFICULTY BELIEVING IN. *MAGIC*."
CAPTAIN BLAINE, I'M AFRAID THIS GIRL MAY BE *CRACKED*.
REALLY? I FIND HER... FASCINATING.

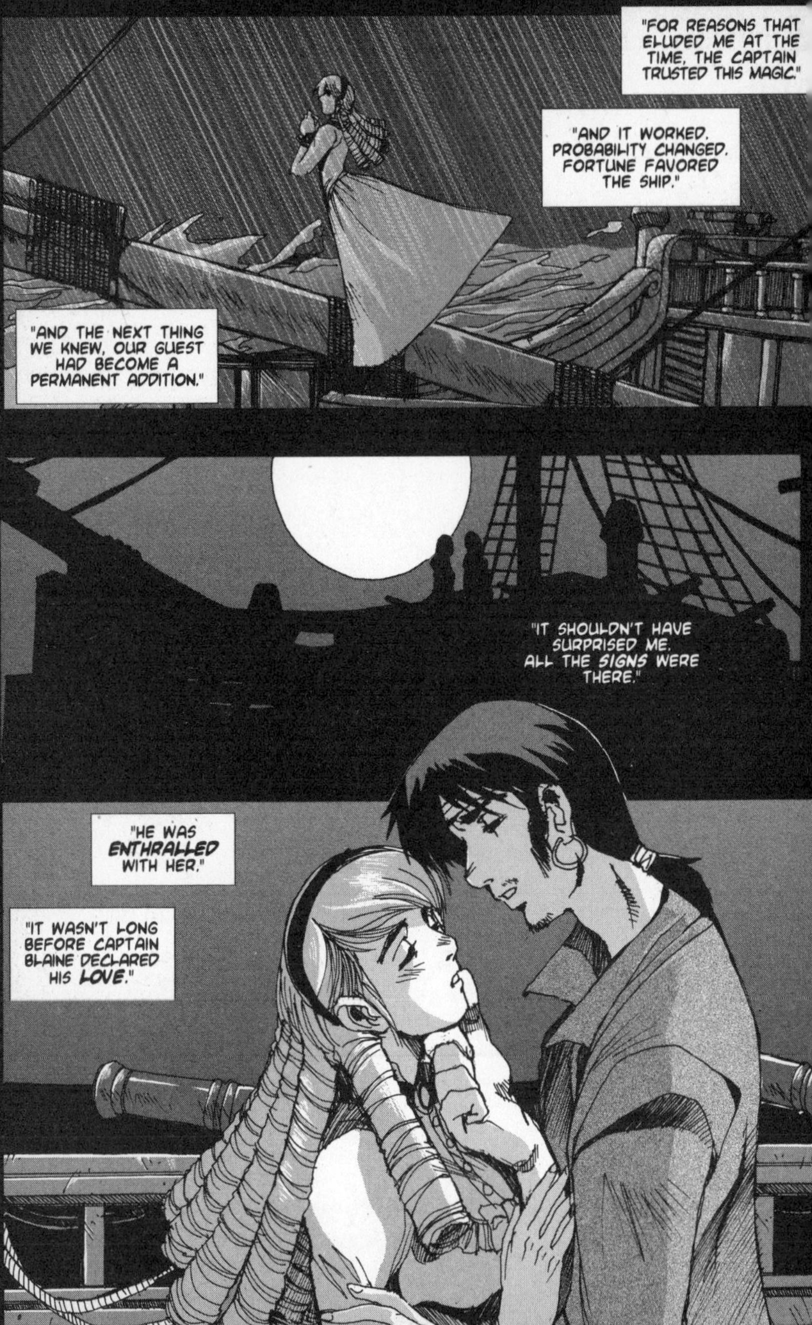
"FOR REASONS THAT ELUDED ME AT THE TIME, THE CAPTAIN TRUSTED THIS MAGIC."
"AND IT WORKED. PROBABILITY CHANGED. FORTUNE FAVORED THE SHIP."
"AND THE NEXT THING WE KNEW, OUR GUEST HAD BECOME A PERMANENT ADDITION."
"IT SHOULDN'T HAVE SURPRISED ME. ALL THE SIGNS WERE THERE."
"HE WAS ENTHRALLED WITH HER."
"IT WASN'T LONG BEFORE CAPTAIN BLAINE DECLARED HIS LOVE."

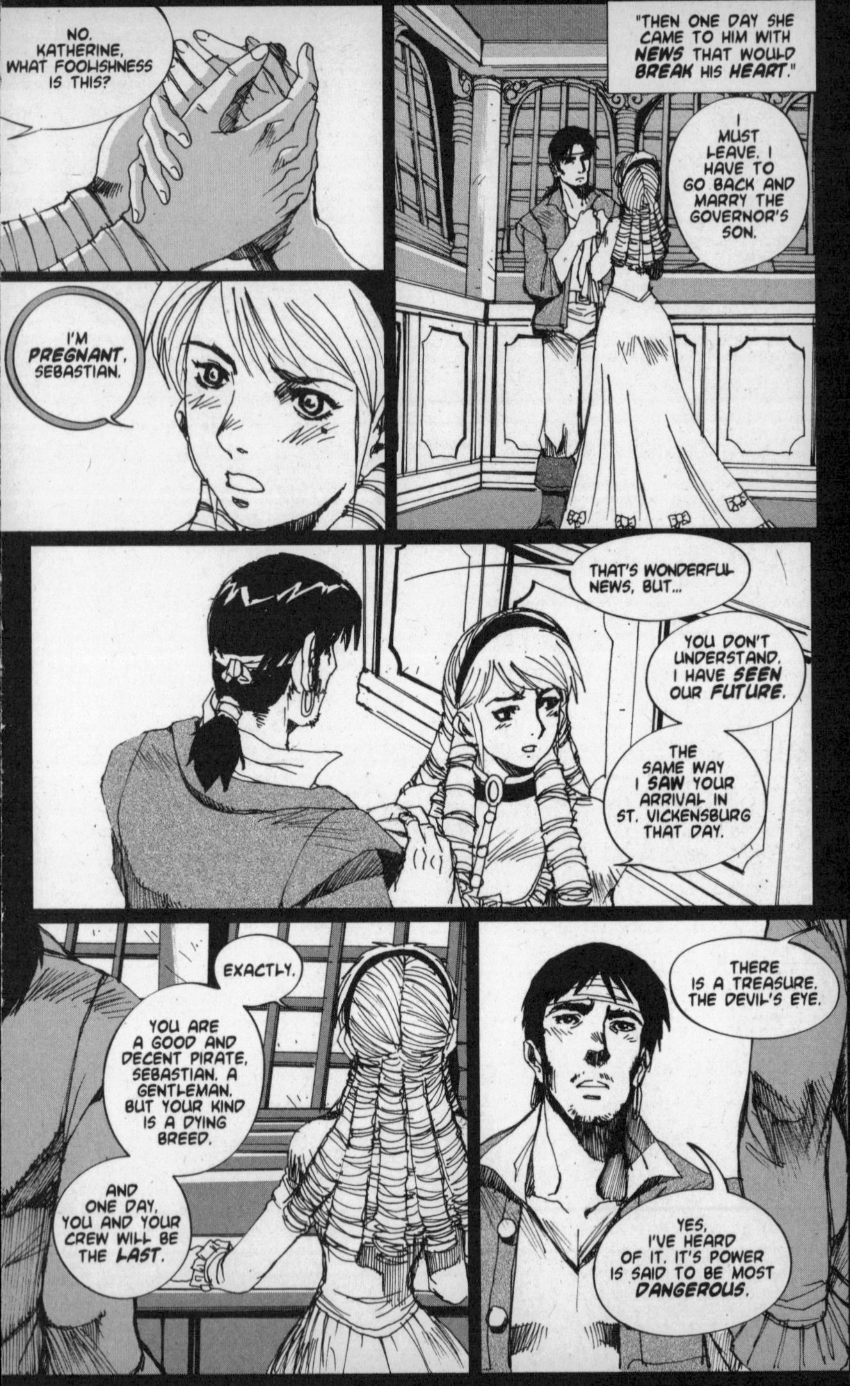
"THEN ONE DAY SHE CAME TO HIM WITH NEWS THAT WOULD BREAK HIS HEART."
I MUST LEAVE. I HAVE TO GO BACK AND MARRY THE GOVERNOR'S SON.
NO. KATHERINE, WHAT FOOLISHNESS IS THIS?
I'M PREGNANT, SEBASTIAN.
THAT'S WONDERFUL NEWS, BUT...
YOU DON'T UNDERSTAND. I HAVE SEEN OUR FUTURE.
THE SAME WAY I SAW YOUR ARRIVAL IN ST. VICKENSBURG THAT DAY.
THERE IS A TREASURE. THE DEVIL'S EYE.
YES, I'VE HEARD OF IT. IT'S POWER IS SAID TO BE MOST DANGEROUS.
EXACTLY.
YOU ARE A GOOD AND DECENT PIRATE, SEBASTIAN. A GENTLEMAN. BUT YOUR KIND IS A DYING BREED.
AND ONE DAY, YOU AND YOUR CREW WILL BE THE LAST.

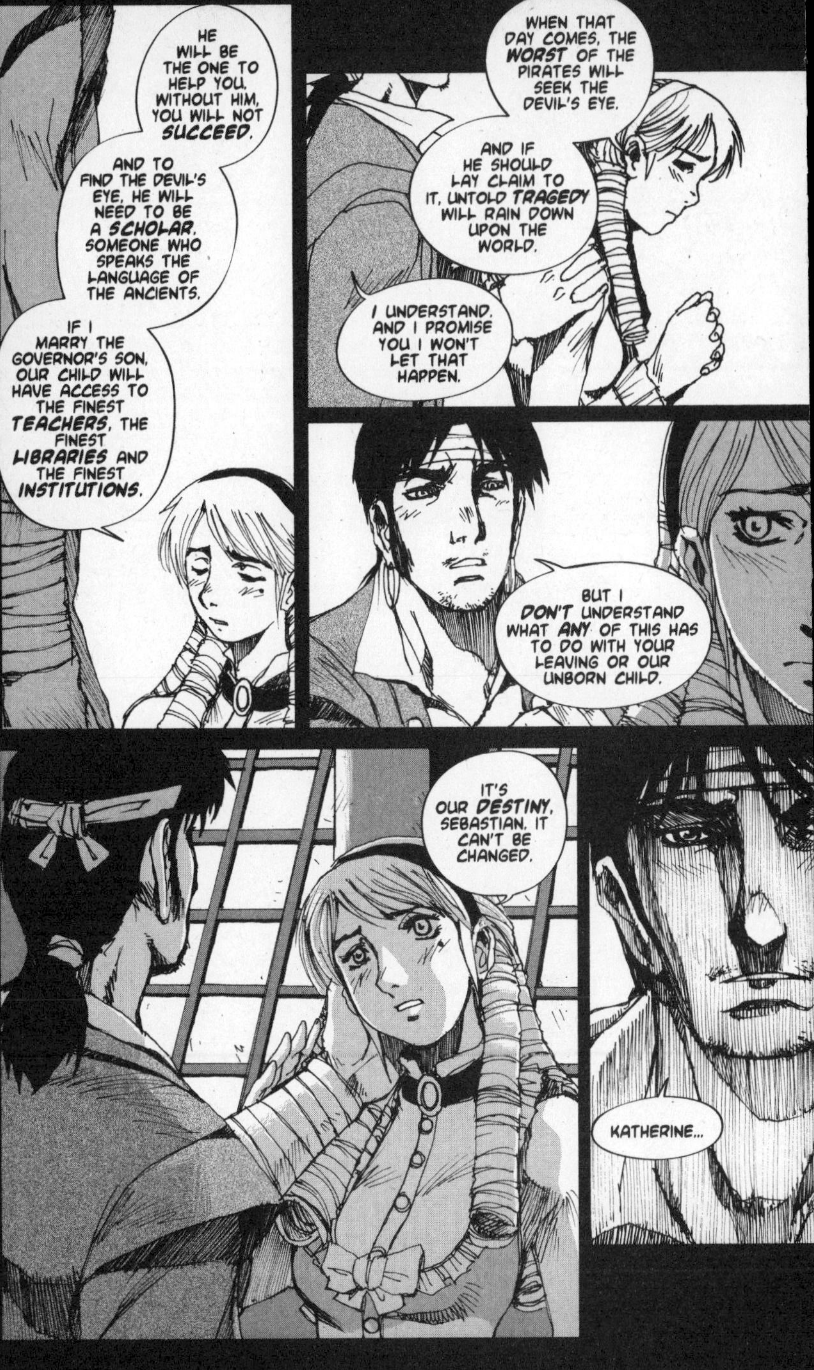
WHEN THAT DAY COMES, THE WORST OF THE PIRATES WILL SEEK THE DEVIL'S EYE.
AND IF HE SHOULD LAY CLAIM TO IT, UNTOLD TRAGEDY WILL RAIN DOWN UPON THE WORLD.
I UNDERSTAND. AND I PROMISE YOU I WON'T LET THAT HAPPEN.
BUT I DON'T UNDERSTAND WHAT ANY OF THIS HAS TO DO WITH YOUR LEAVING OR OUR UNBORN CHILD.
HE WILL BE THE ONE TO HELP YOU. WITHOUT HIM, YOU WILL NOT SUCCEED.
AND TO FIND THE DEVIL'S EYE, HE WILL NEED TO BE A SCHOLAR. SOMEONE WHO SPEAKS THE LANGUAGE OF THE ANCIENTS.
IF I MARRY THE GOVERNOR'S SON, OUR CHILD WILL HAVE ACCESS TO THE FINEST TEACHERS, THE FINEST LIBRARIES AND THE FINEST INSTITUTIONS.
KATHERINE...
IT'S OUR DESTINY, SEBASTIAN. IT CAN'T BE CHANGED.

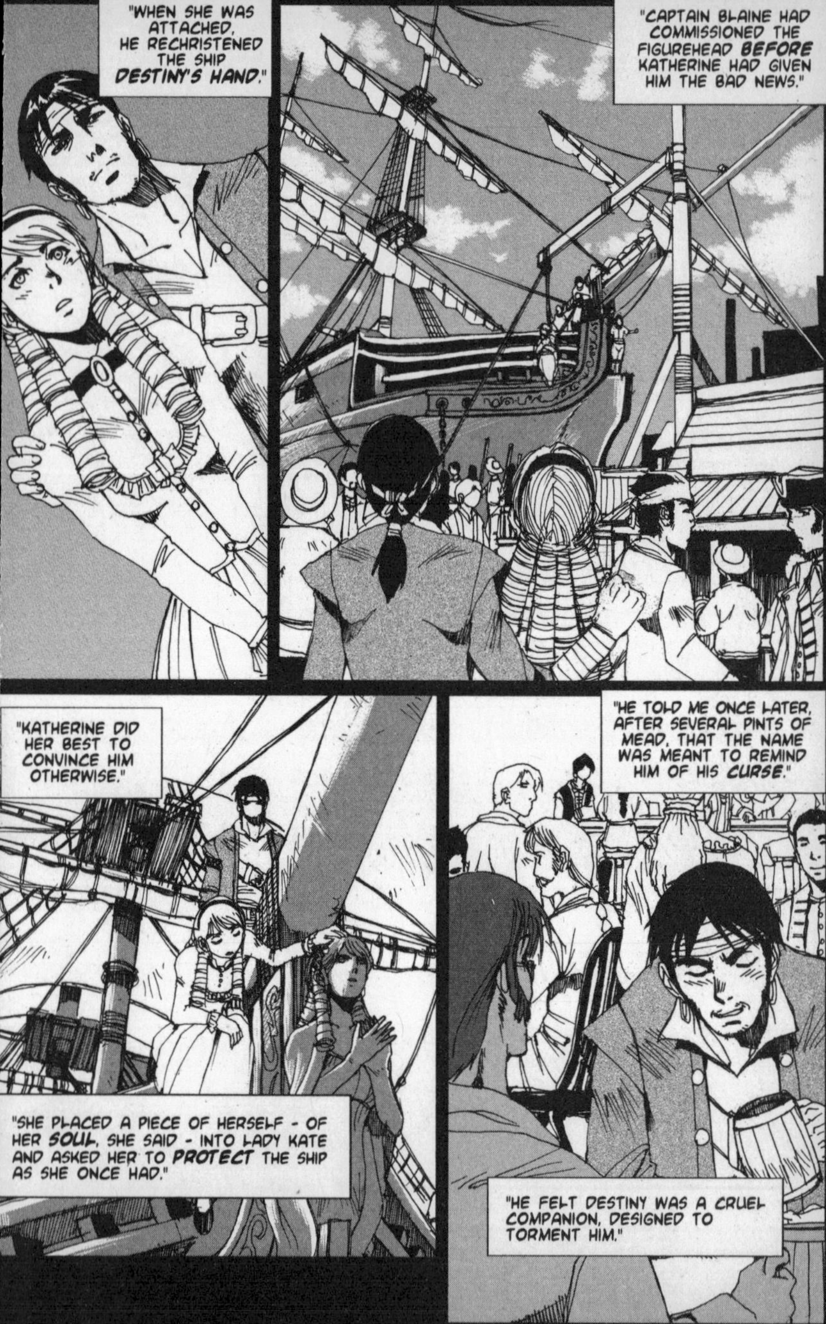
"CAPTAIN BLAINE HAD COMMISSIONED THE FIGUREHEAD BEFORE KATHERINE HAD GIVEN HIM THE BAD NEWS."
"WHEN SHE WAS ATTACHED, HE RECHRISTENED THE SHIP DESTINY'S HAND."
"HE TOLD ME ONCE LATER, AFTER SEVERAL PINTS OF MEAD, THAT THE NAME WAS MEANT TO REMIND HIM OF HIS CURSE."
"HE FELT DESTINY WAS A CRUEL COMPANION, DESIGNED TO TORMENT HIM."
"KATHERINE DID HER BEST TO CONVINCE HIM OTHERWISE."
"SHE PLACED A PIECE OF HERSELF - OF HER SOUL, SHE SAID - INTO LADY KATE AND ASKED HER TO PROTECT THE SHIP AS SHE ONCE HAD."

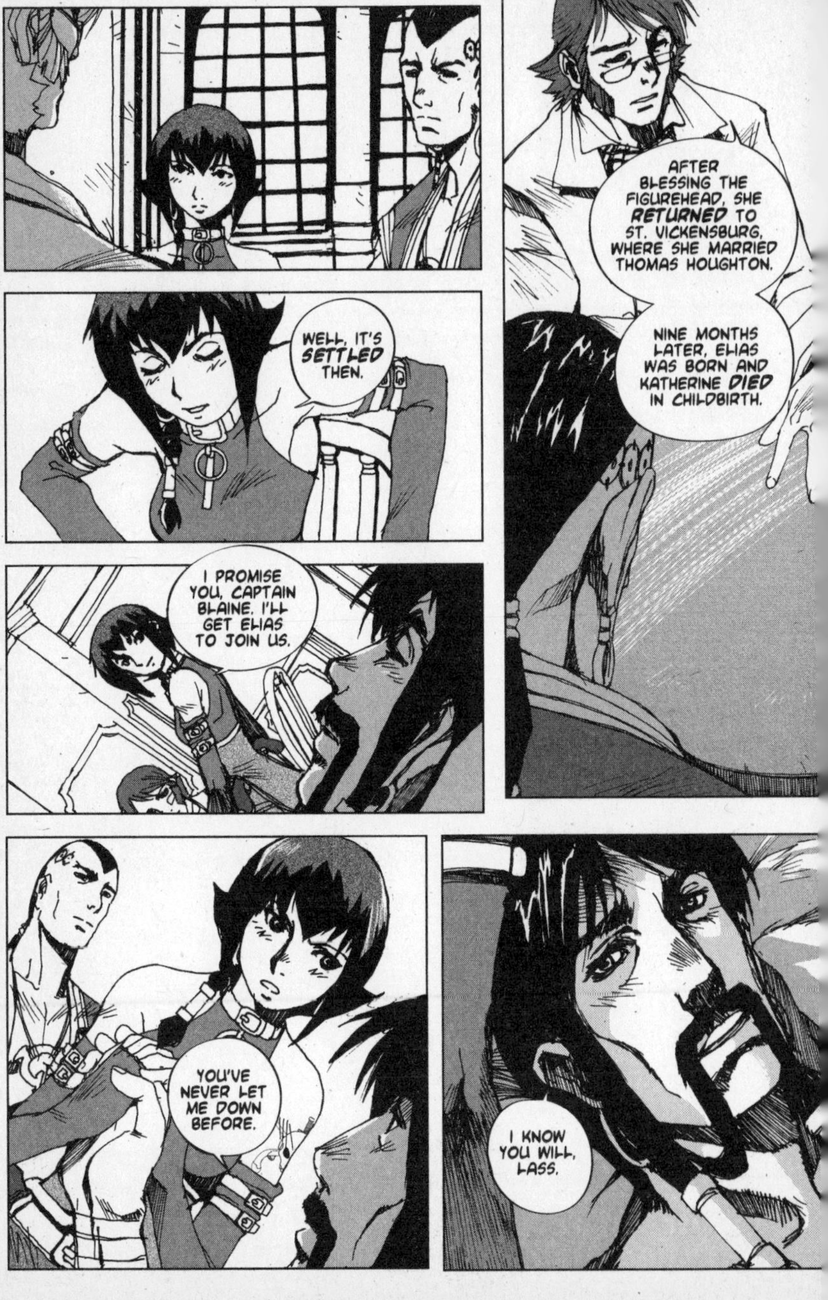
AFTER BLESSING THE FIGUREHEAD, SHE **RETURNED** TO ST. VICKENSBURG, WHERE SHE MARRIED THOMAS HOUGHTON.
NINE MONTHS LATER, ELIAS WAS BORN AND KATHERINE **DIED** IN CHILDBIRTH.
WELL, IT'S **SETTLED** THEN.
I PROMISE YOU, CAPTAIN BLAINE. I'LL GET ELIAS TO JOIN US.
I KNOW YOU WILL, LASS.
YOU'VE NEVER LET ME DOWN BEFORE.

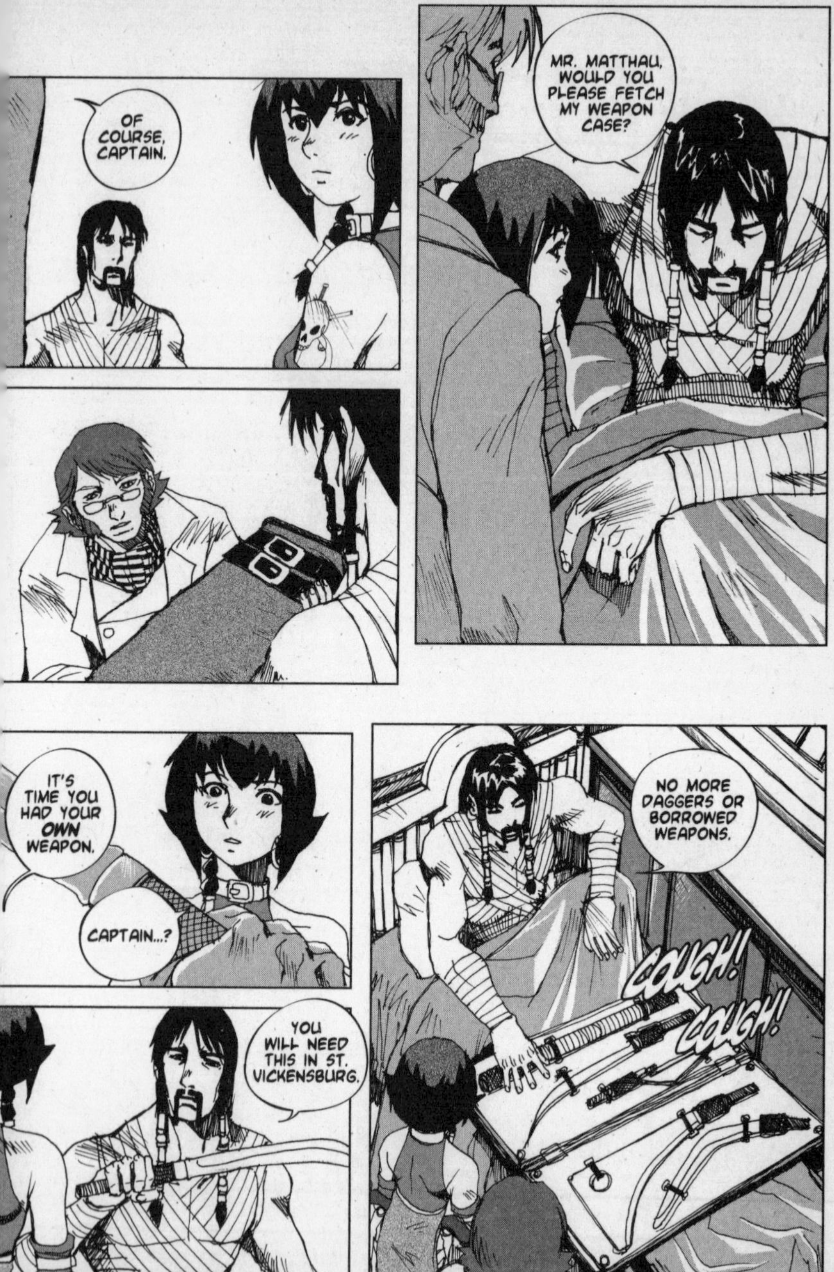
MR. MATTHAU, WOULD YOU PLEASE FETCH MY WEAPON CASE?
OF COURSE, CAPTAIN.
NO MORE DAGGERS OR BORROWED WEAPONS.
COUGH!
COUGH!
IT'S TIME YOU HAD YOUR *OWN* WEAPON.
CAPTAIN...?
YOU WILL NEED THIS IN ST. VICKENSBURG.

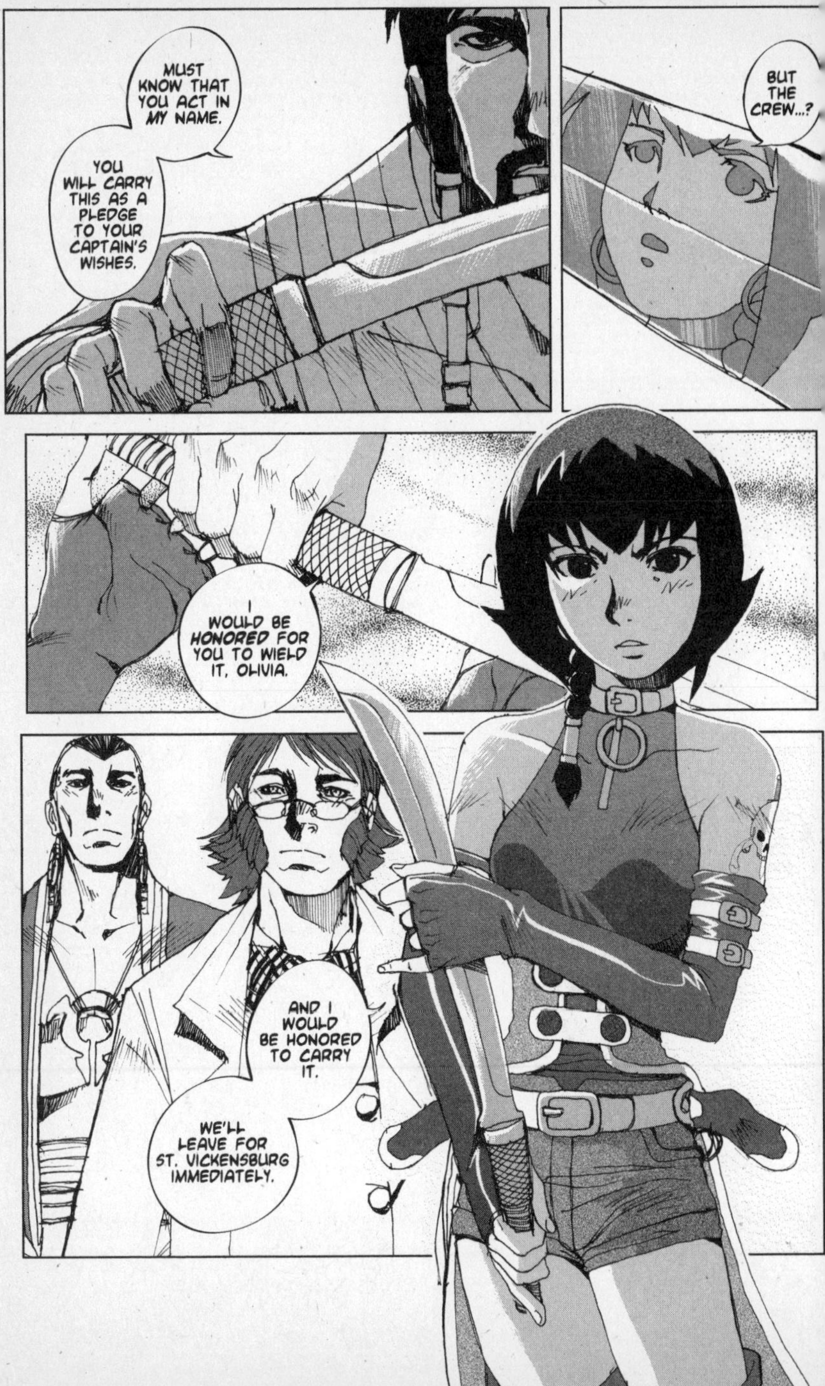
MUST KNOW THAT YOU ACT IN MY NAME.
YOU WILL CARRY THIS AS A PLEDGE TO YOUR CAPTAIN'S WISHES.
BUT THE CREW...?
I WOULD BE HONORED FOR YOU TO WIELD IT, OLIVIA.
AND I WOULD BE HONORED TO CARRY IT.
WE'LL LEAVE FOR ST. VICKENSBURG IMMEDIATELY.

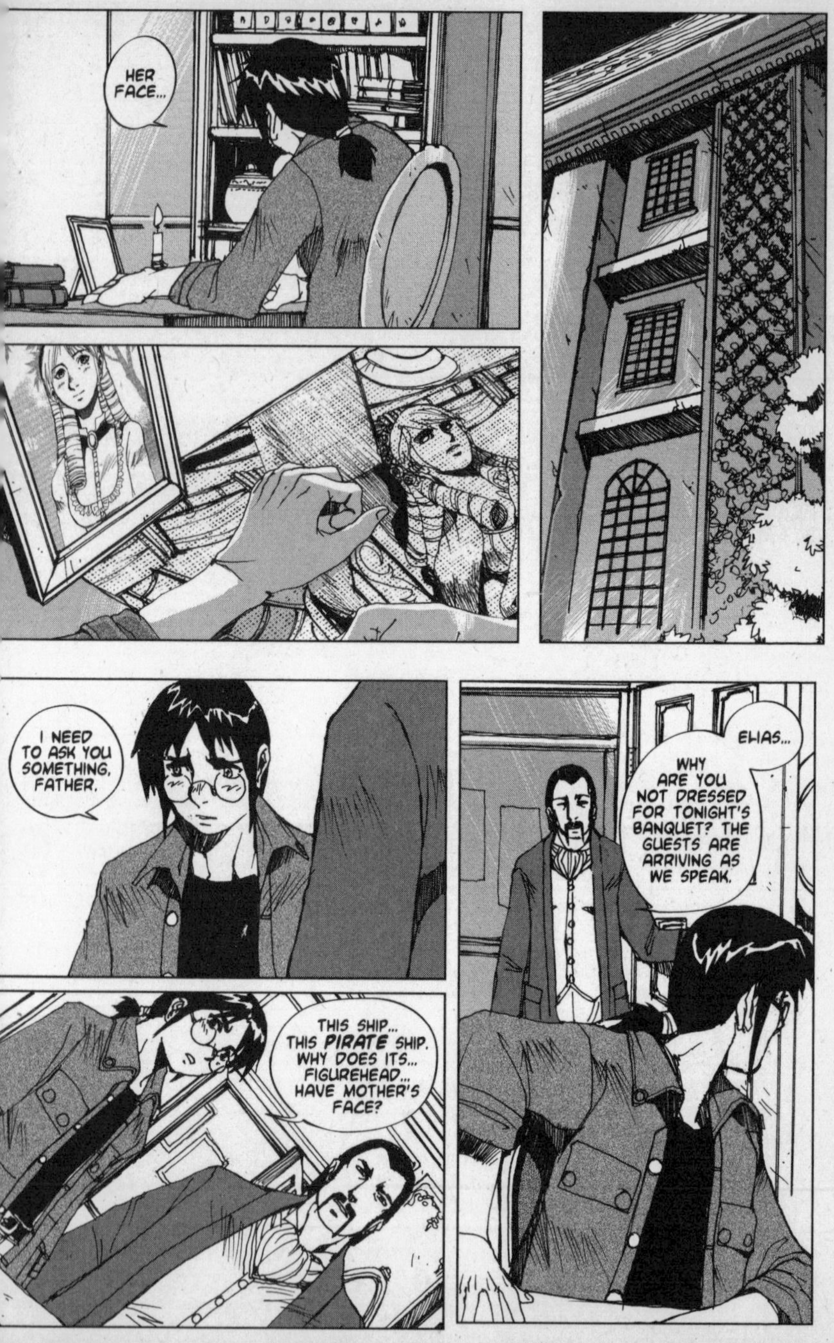
HER FACE...
ELIAS...
WHY ARE YOU NOT DRESSED FOR TONIGHT'S BANQUET? THE GUESTS ARE ARRIVING AS WE SPEAK.
I NEED TO ASK YOU SOMETHING, FATHER.
THIS SHIP... THIS PIRATE SHIP. WHY DOES ITS... FIGUREHEAD... HAVE MOTHER'S FACE?

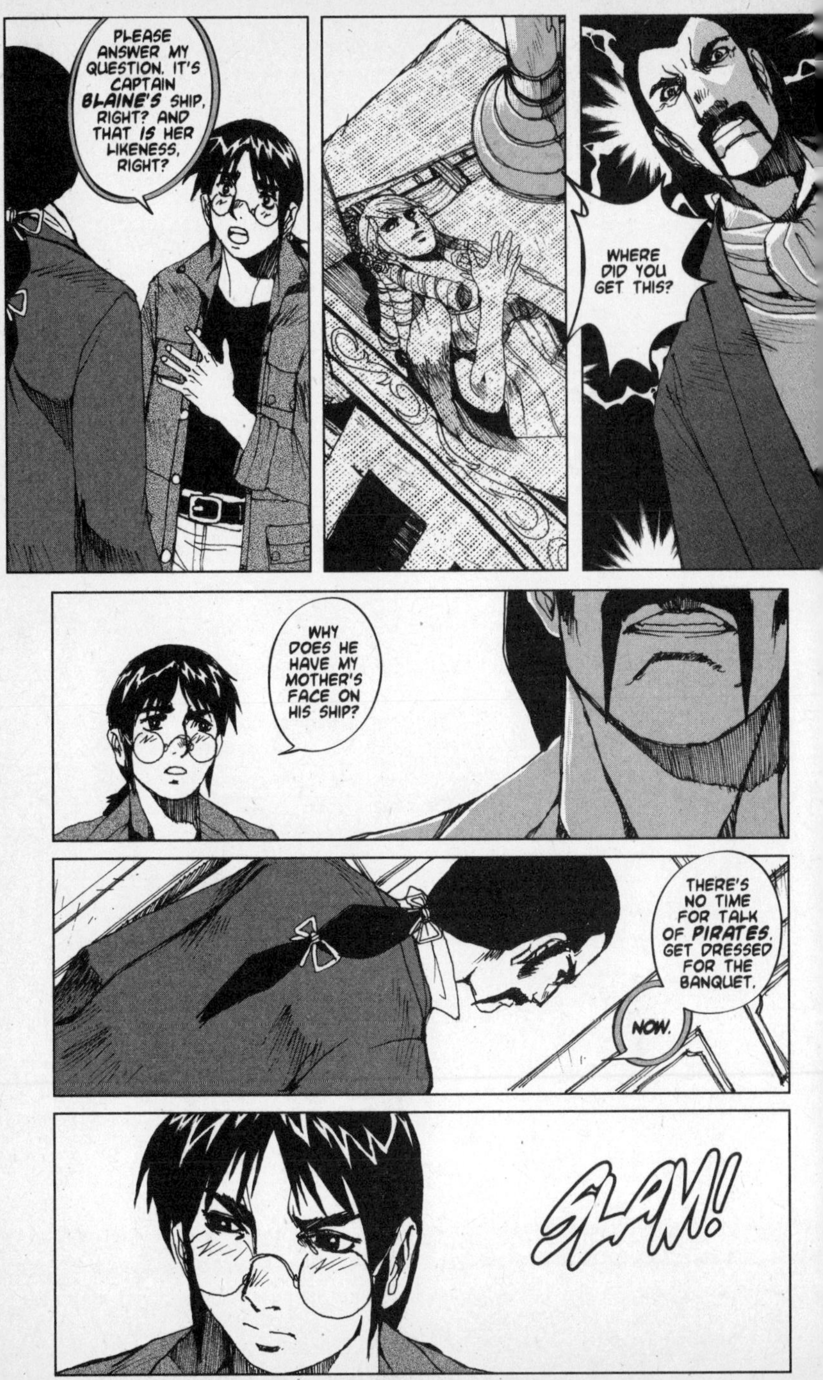
WHERE DID YOU GET THIS?
PLEASE ANSWER MY QUESTION. IT'S CAPTAIN BLAINE'S SHIP, RIGHT? AND THAT IS HER LIKENESS, RIGHT?
WHY DOES HE HAVE MY MOTHER'S FACE ON HIS SHIP?
THERE'S NO TIME FOR TALK OF PIRATES. GET DRESSED FOR THE BANQUET.
NOW.
SLAM!

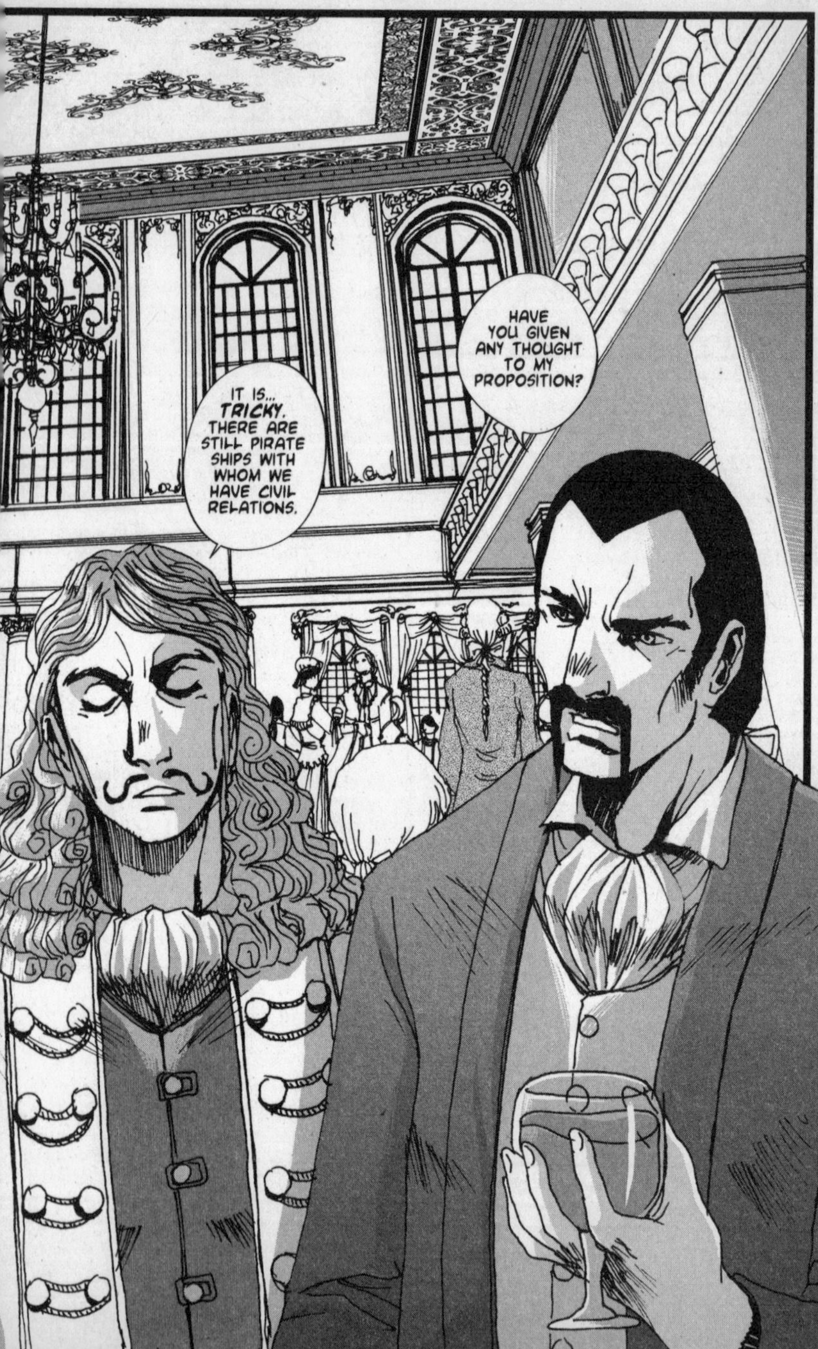
HAVE YOU GIVEN ANY THOUGHT TO MY PROPOSITION?
IT IS... TRICKY. THERE ARE STILL PIRATE SHIPS WITH WHOM WE HAVE CIVIL RELATIONS.

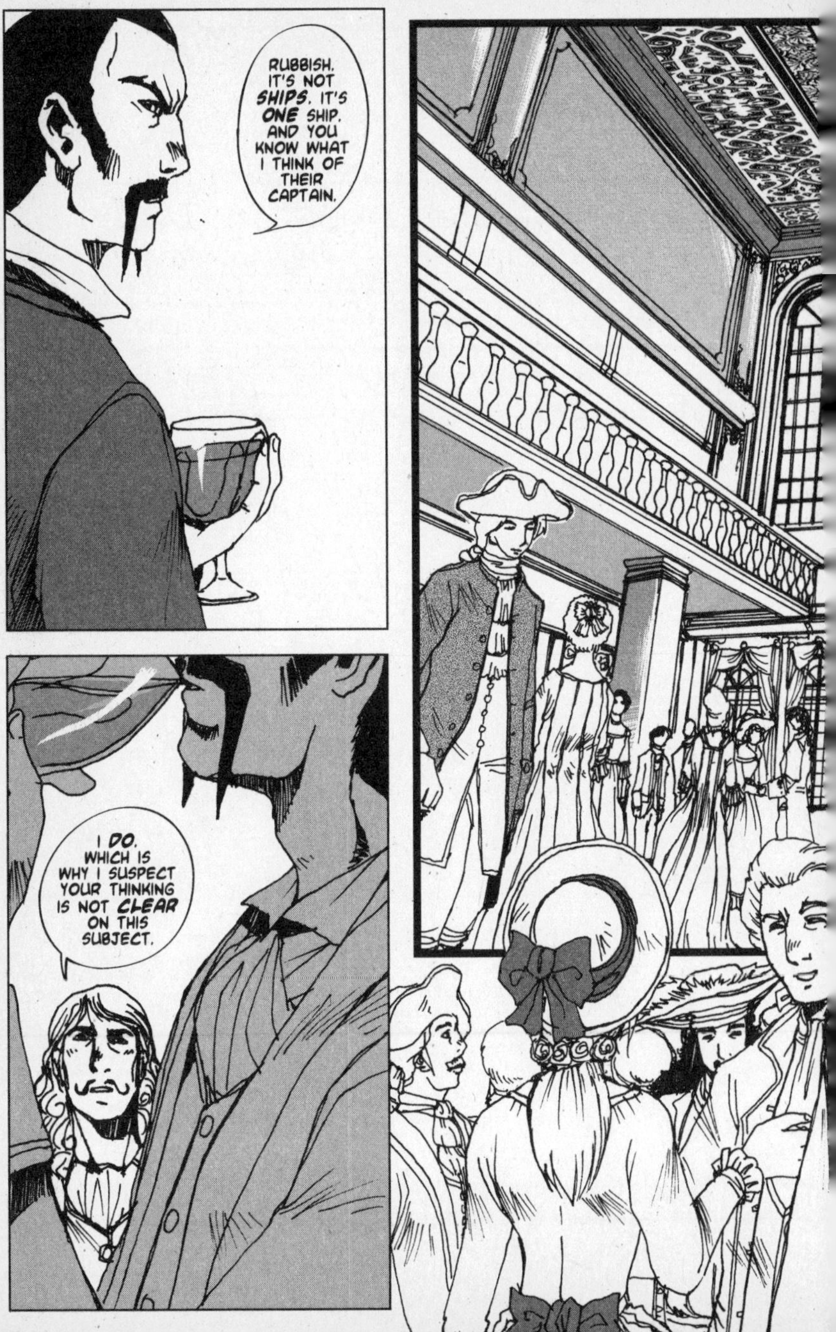
RUBBISH. IT'S NOT SHIPS. IT'S ONE SHIP. AND YOU KNOW WHAT I THINK OF THEIR CAPTAIN.
I DO. WHICH IS WHY I SUSPECT YOUR THINKING IS NOT CLEAR ON THIS SUBJECT.

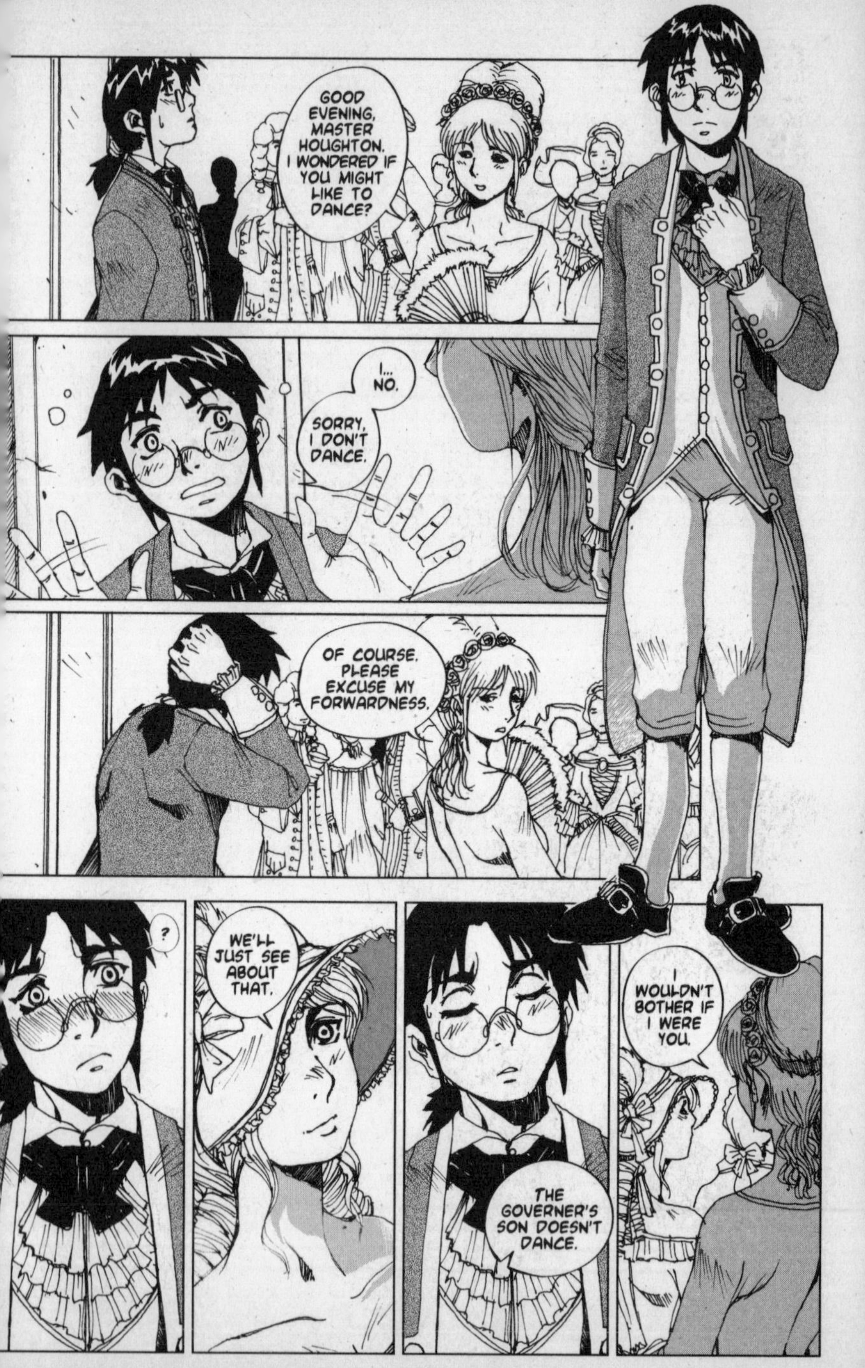
GOOD EVENING, MASTER HOUGHTON. I WONDERED IF YOU MIGHT LIKE TO DANCE?
I... NO.
SORRY, I DON'T DANCE.
OF COURSE. PLEASE EXCUSE MY FORWARDNESS.
I WOULDN'T BOTHER IF I WERE YOU.
THE GOVERNER'S SON DOESN'T DANCE.
WE'LL JUST SEE ABOUT THAT.
?

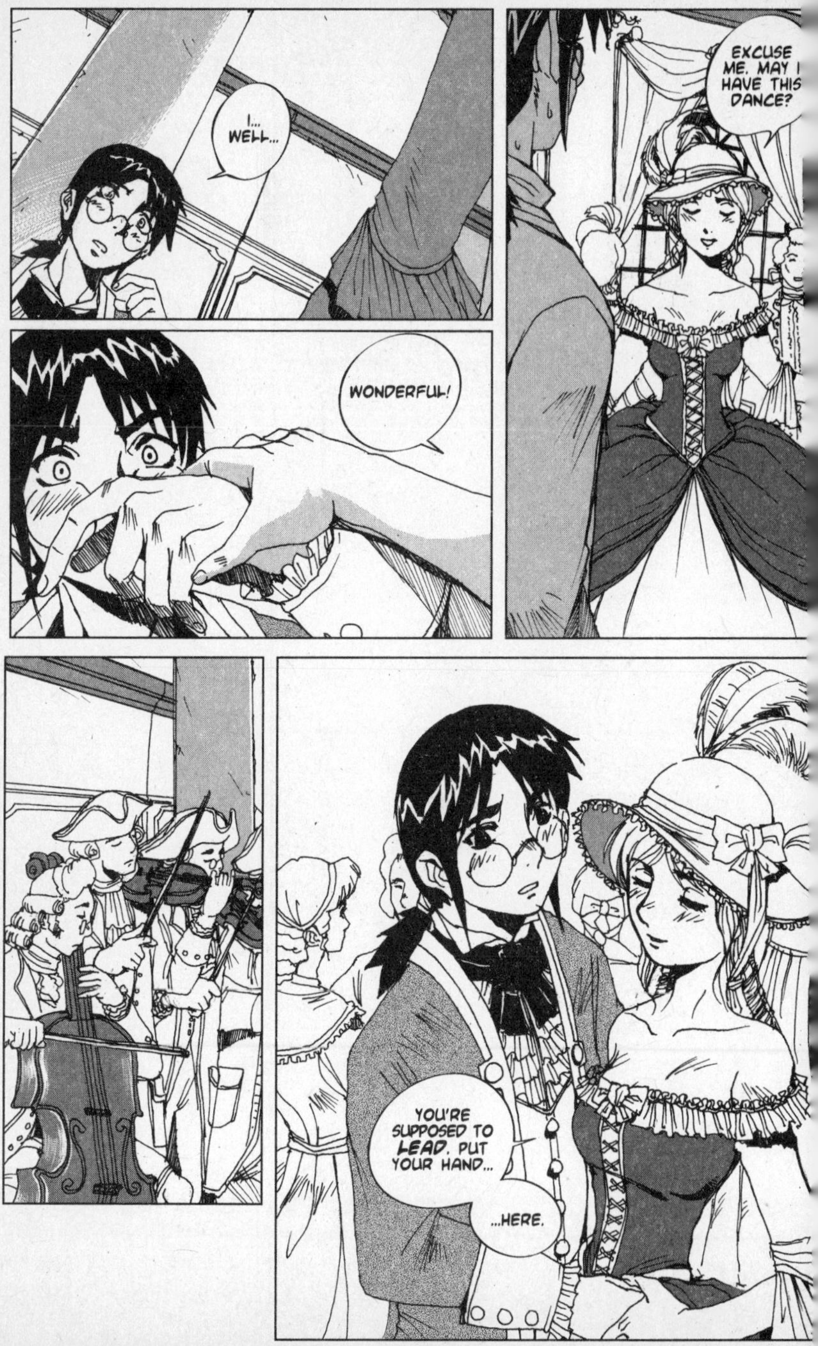
EXCUSE ME. MAY I HAVE THIS DANCE?
I... WELL...
WONDERFUL!
YOU'RE SUPPOSED TO LEAD. PUT YOUR HAND...
...HERE.

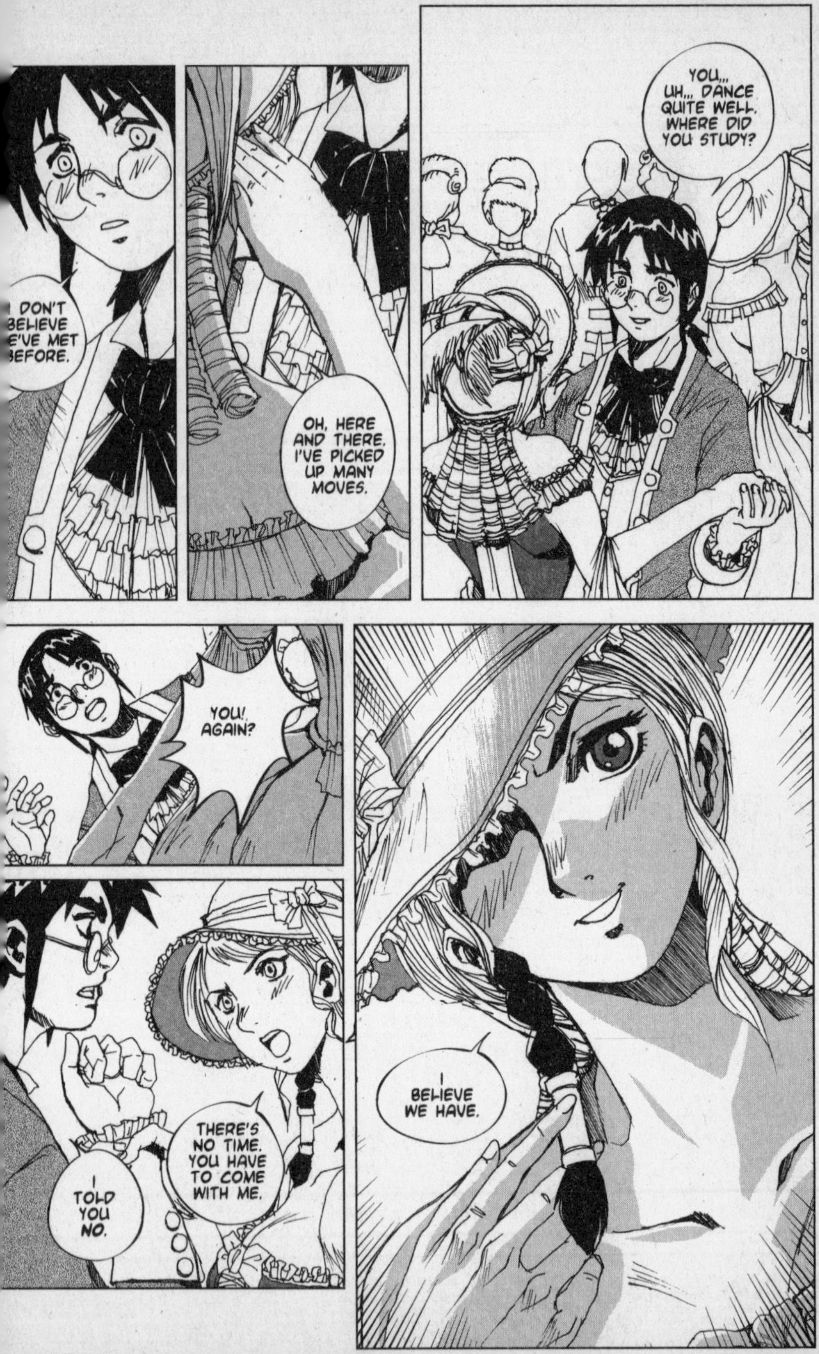
YOU,,, UH,,, DANCE QUITE WELL. WHERE DID YOU STUDY?
OH, HERE AND THERE. I'VE PICKED UP MANY MOVES.
I DON'T BELIEVE E'VE MET BEFORE.
I BELIEVE WE HAVE.
YOU! AGAIN?
THERE'S NO TIME. YOU HAVE TO COME WITH ME.
I TOLD YOU NO.

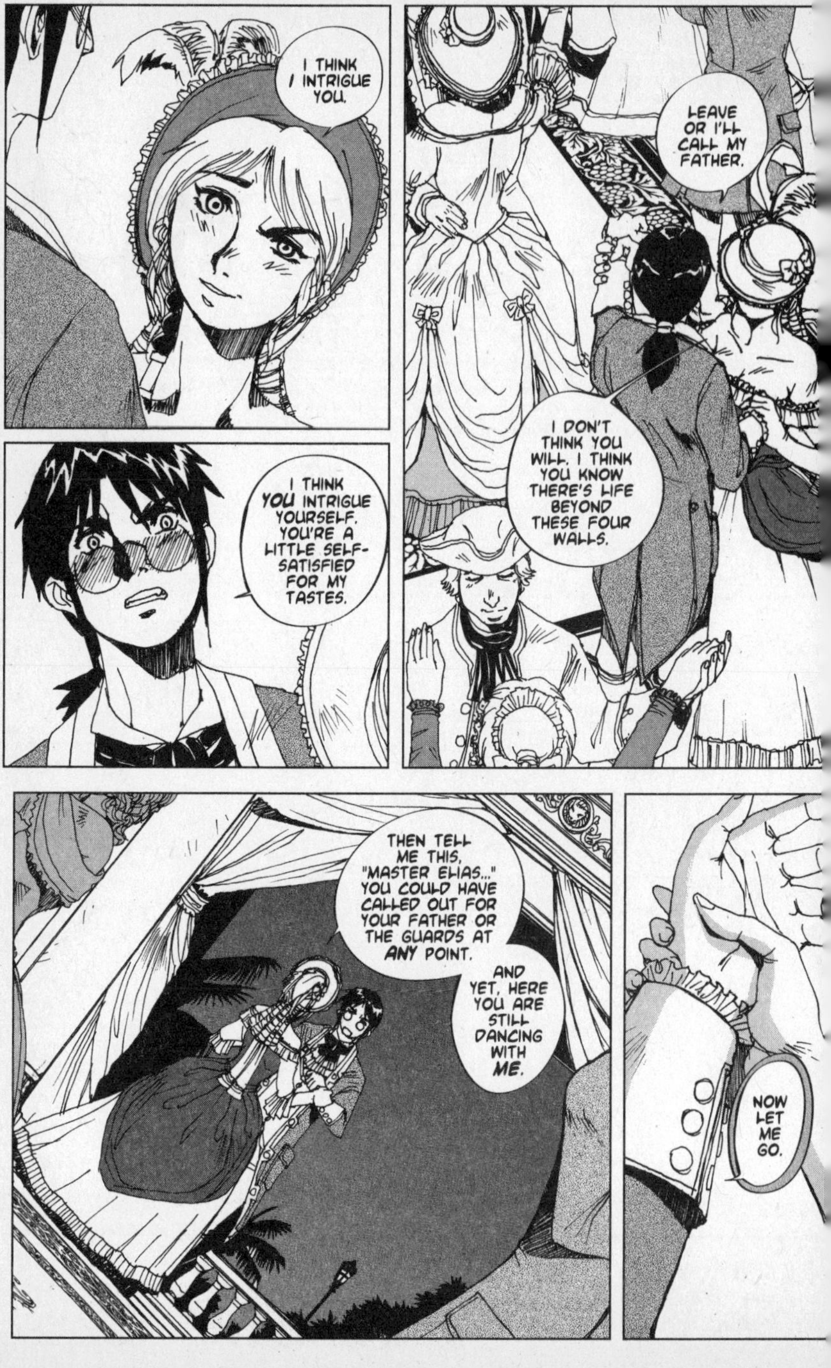
LEAVE OR I'LL CALL MY FATHER.
I DON'T THINK YOU WILL. I THINK YOU KNOW THERE'S LIFE BEYOND THESE FOUR WALLS.
I THINK I INTRIGUE YOU.
I THINK *YOU* INTRIGUE YOURSELF. YOU'RE A LITTLE SELF-SATISFIED FOR MY TASTES.
NOW LET ME GO.
THEN TELL ME THIS, "MASTER ELIAS..." YOU COULD HAVE CALLED OUT FOR YOUR FATHER OR THE GUARDS AT *ANY* POINT.
AND YET, HERE YOU ARE STILL DANCING WITH *ME*.

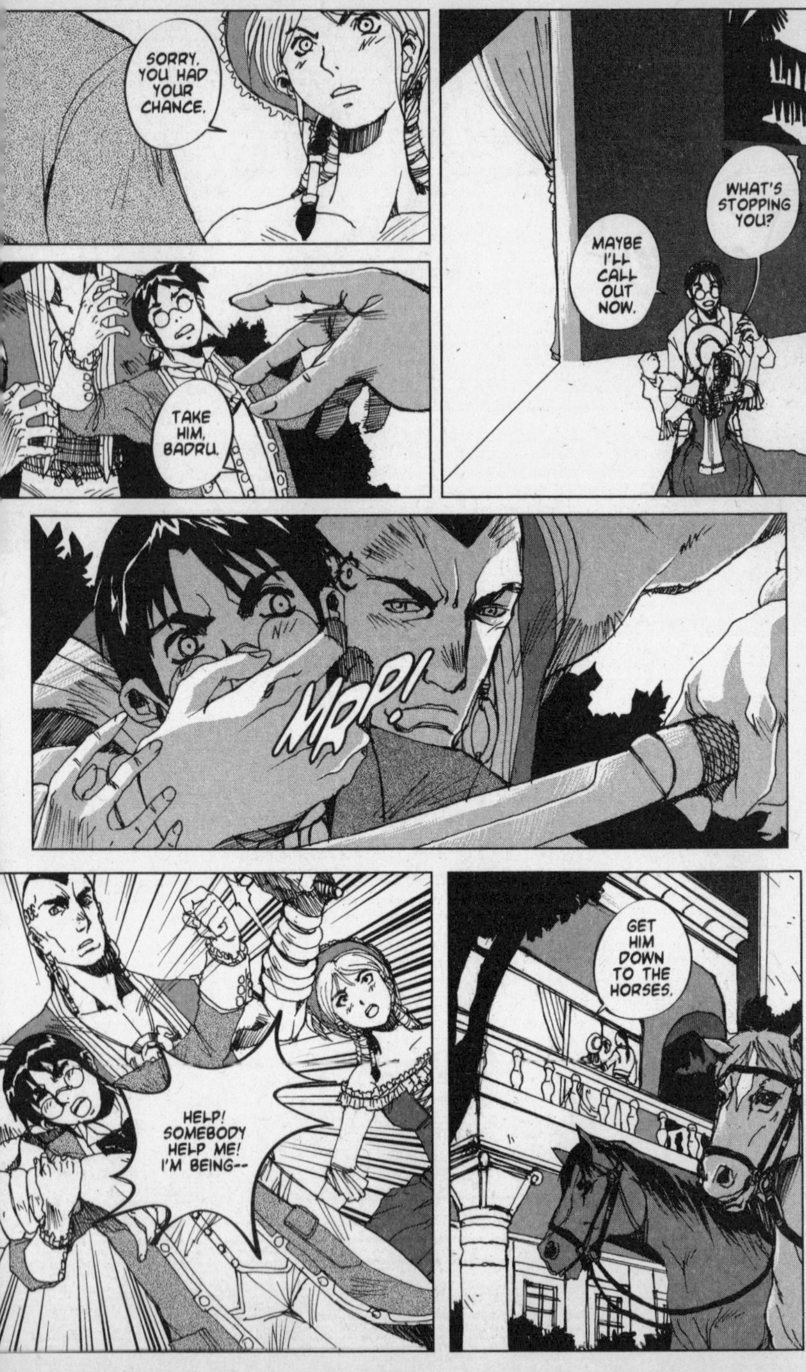
WHAT'S STOPPING YOU?
MAYBE I'LL CALL OUT NOW.
SORRY. YOU HAD YOUR CHANCE.
TAKE HIM, BADRU.
MMP!
GET HIM DOWN TO THE HORSES.
HELP! SOMEBODY HELP ME! I'M BEING--

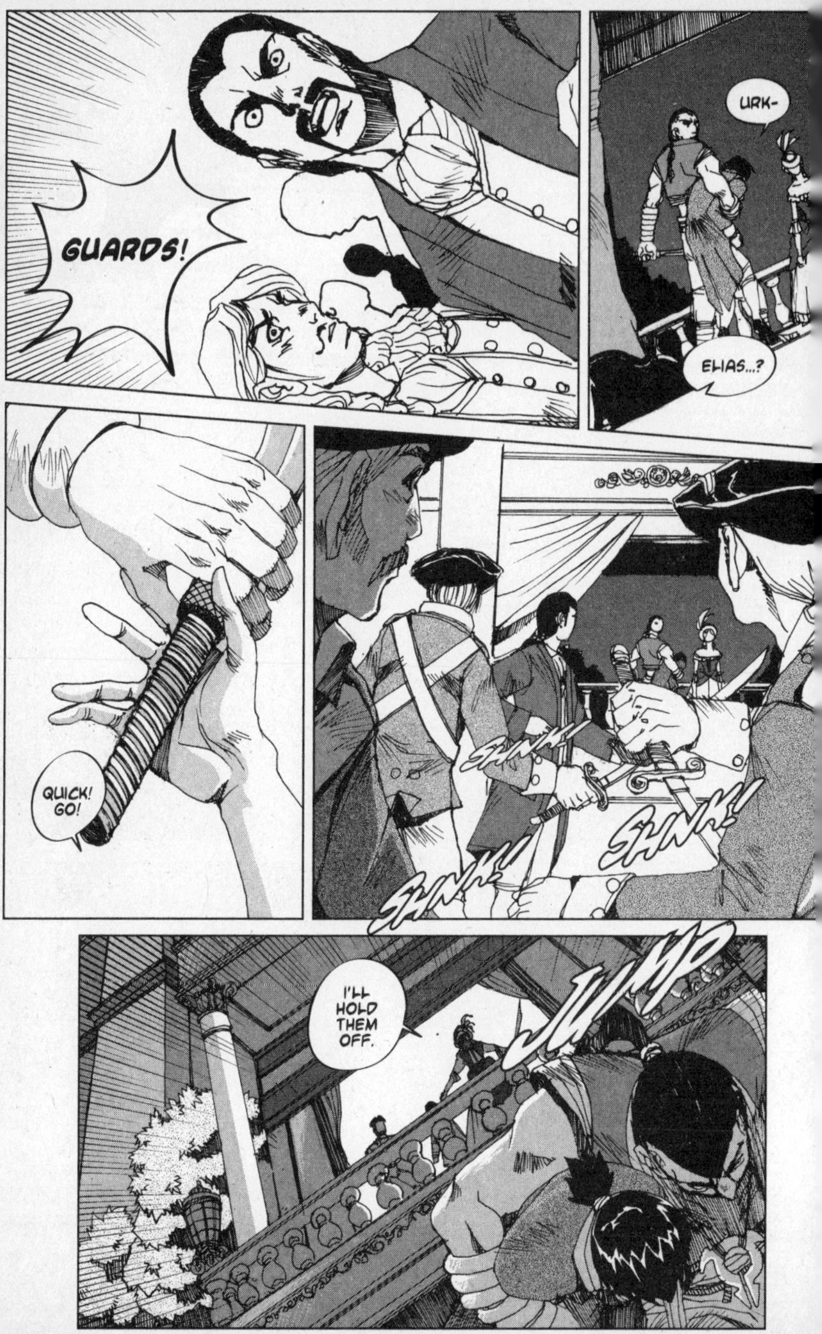
URK-
ELIAS...?
GUARDS!
SHINK!
SHINK!
SHINK!
QUICK! GO!
I'LL HOLD THEM OFF.
JUMP

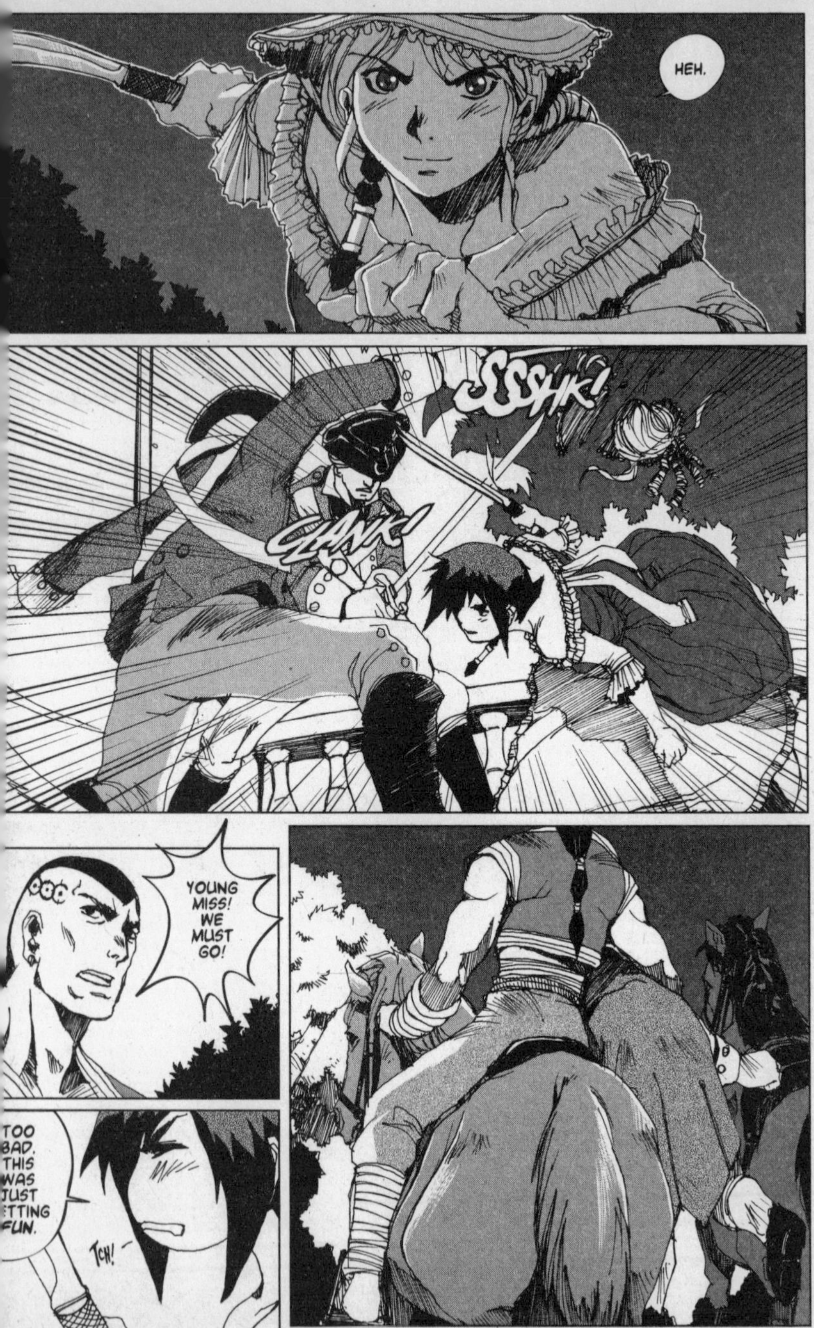
HEH.
SSSHK!
CLANK!
YOUNG MISS! WE MUST GO!
TOO BAD. THIS WAS JUST ETTING FUN.
TCH!

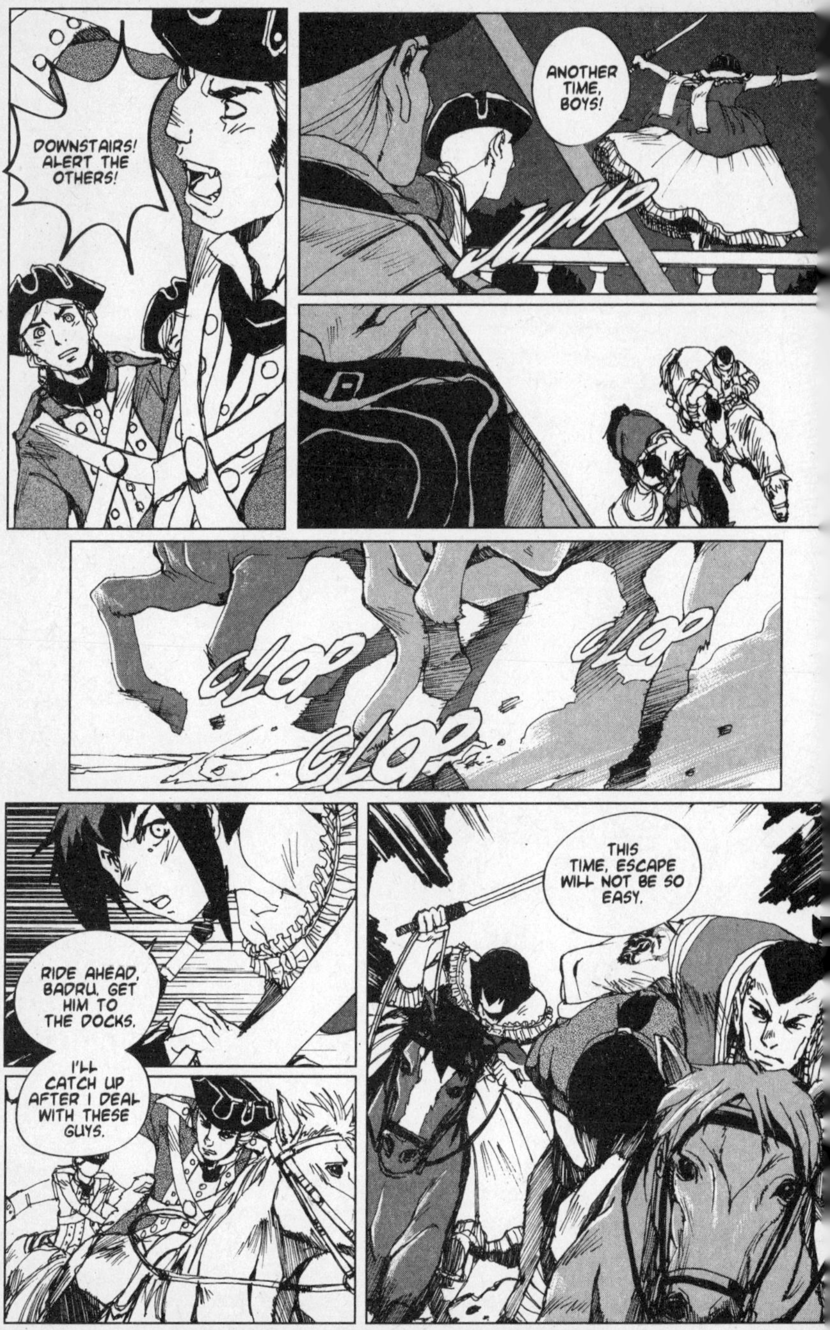
ANOTHER TIME, BOYS!
JUMP
DOWNSTAIRS! ALERT THE OTHERS!
CLOP
CLOP
CLOP
THIS TIME, ESCAPE WILL NOT BE SO EASY.
RIDE AHEAD, BADRU, GET HIM TO THE DOCKS.
I'LL CATCH UP AFTER I DEAL WITH THESE GUYS.

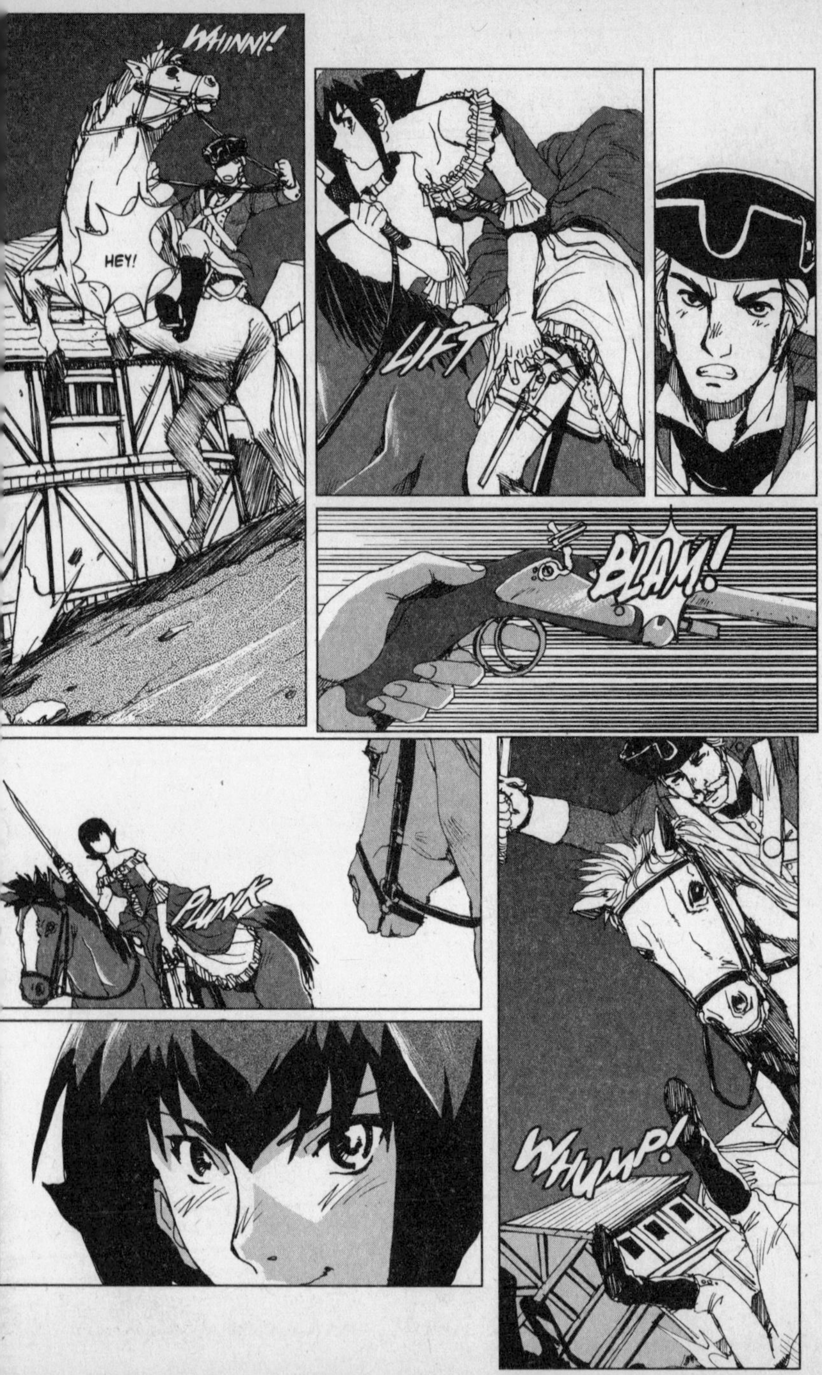
LIFT
BLAM!
WHINNY!
HEY!
WHUMP!
PLUNK

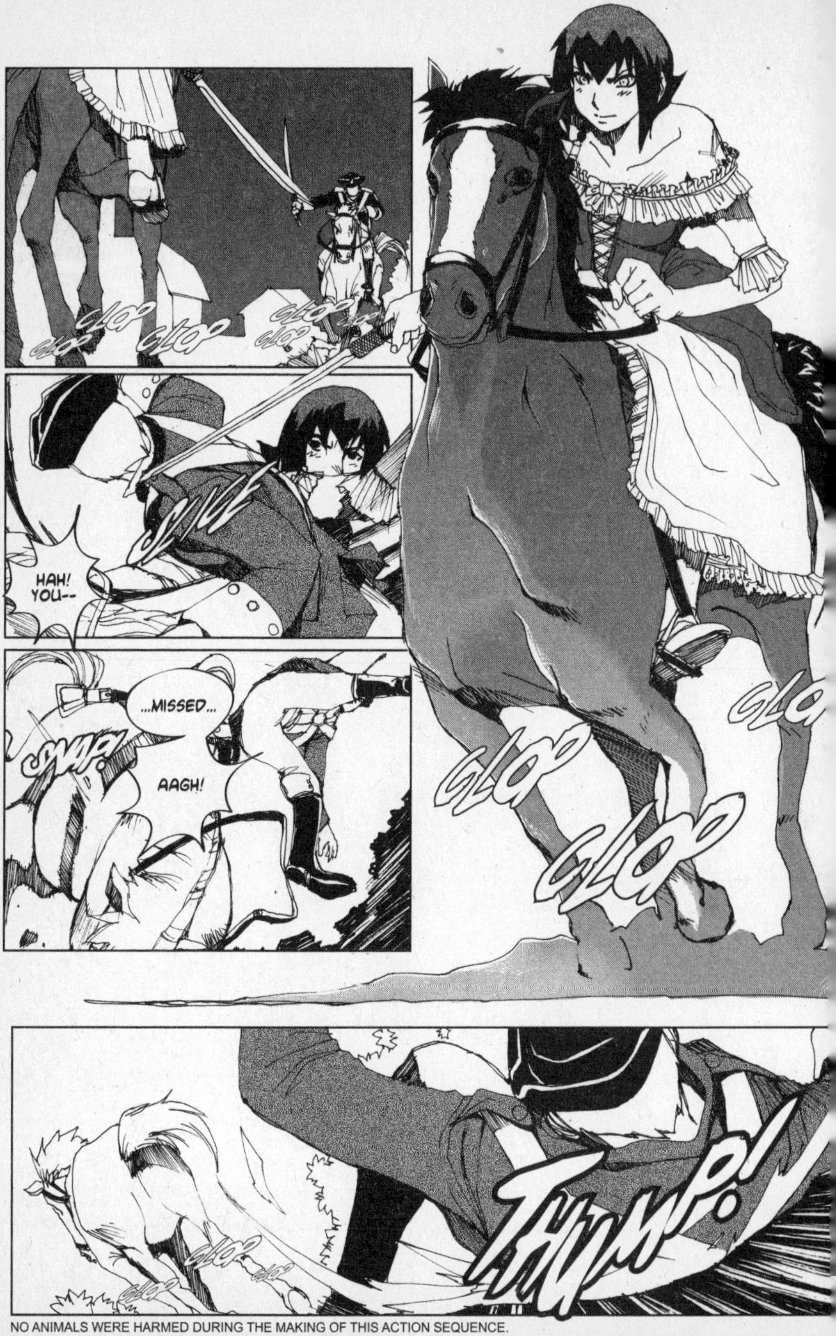
GLOP
GLOP
GLOP
GLOP GLOP GLOP
HAH! YOU--
...MISSED...
SNAP!
AAGH!
THUMP!
GLOP GLOP

NO ANIMALS WERE HARMED DURING THE MAKING OF THIS ACTION SEQUENCE.

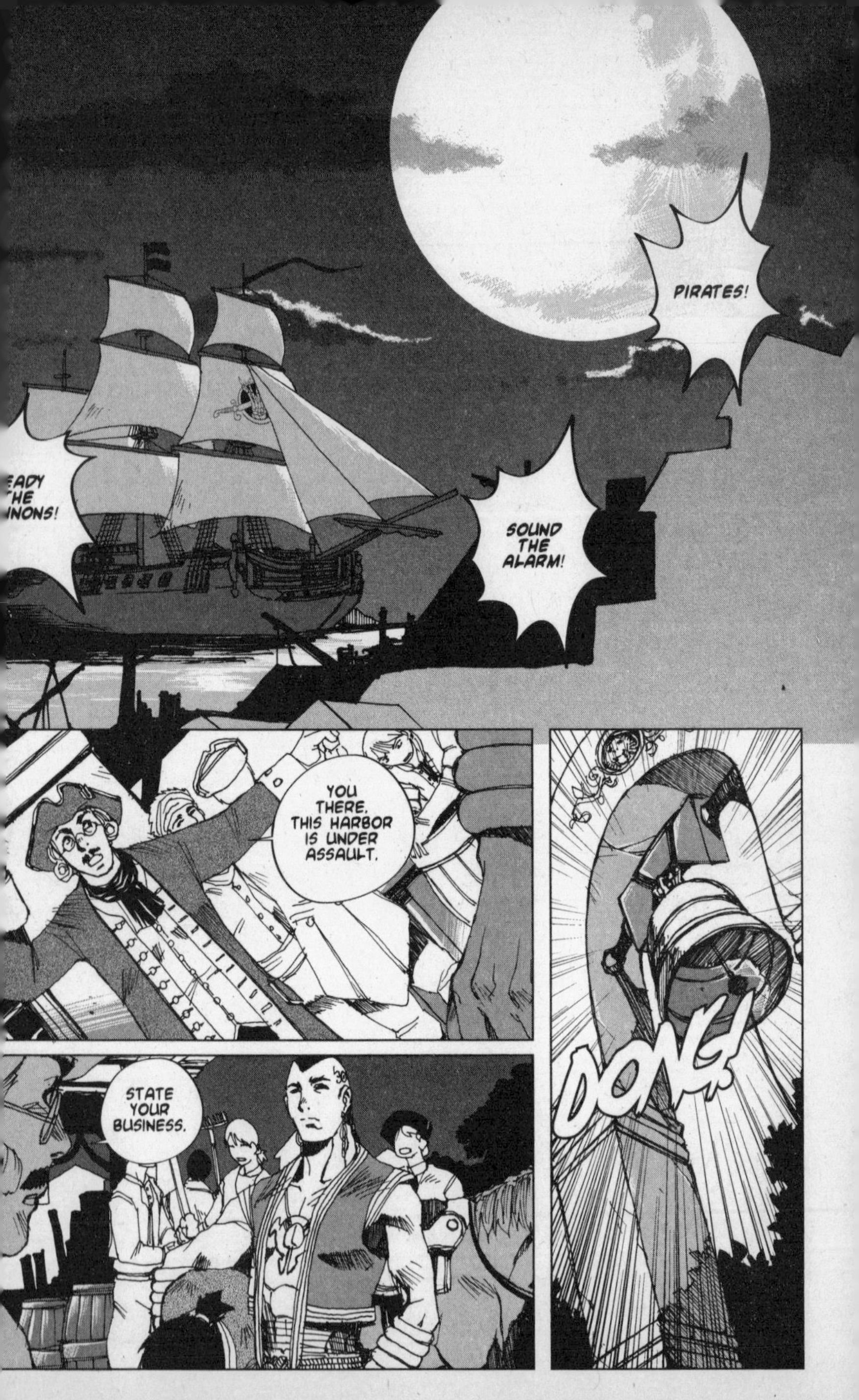
PIRATES!
SOUND THE ALARM!
EADY THE NNONS!
DONG!
YOU THERE. THIS HARBOR IS UNDER ASSAULT.
STATE YOUR BUSINESS.

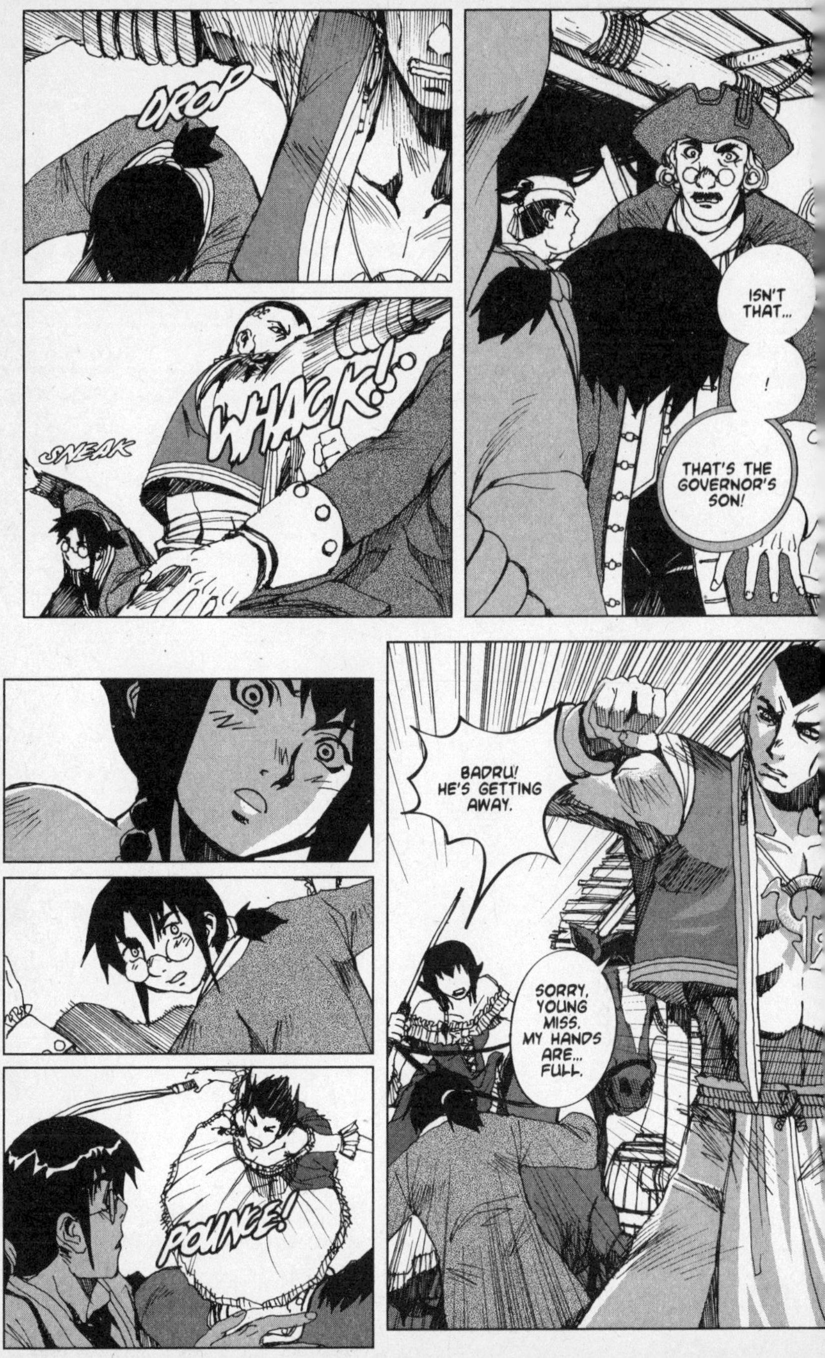
ISN'T THAT...
!
THAT'S THE GOVERNOR'S SON!
DROP
WHACK!!
SNEAK
BADRU! HE'S GETTING AWAY.
SORRY, YOUNG MISS. MY HANDS ARE... FULL.
POUNCE!

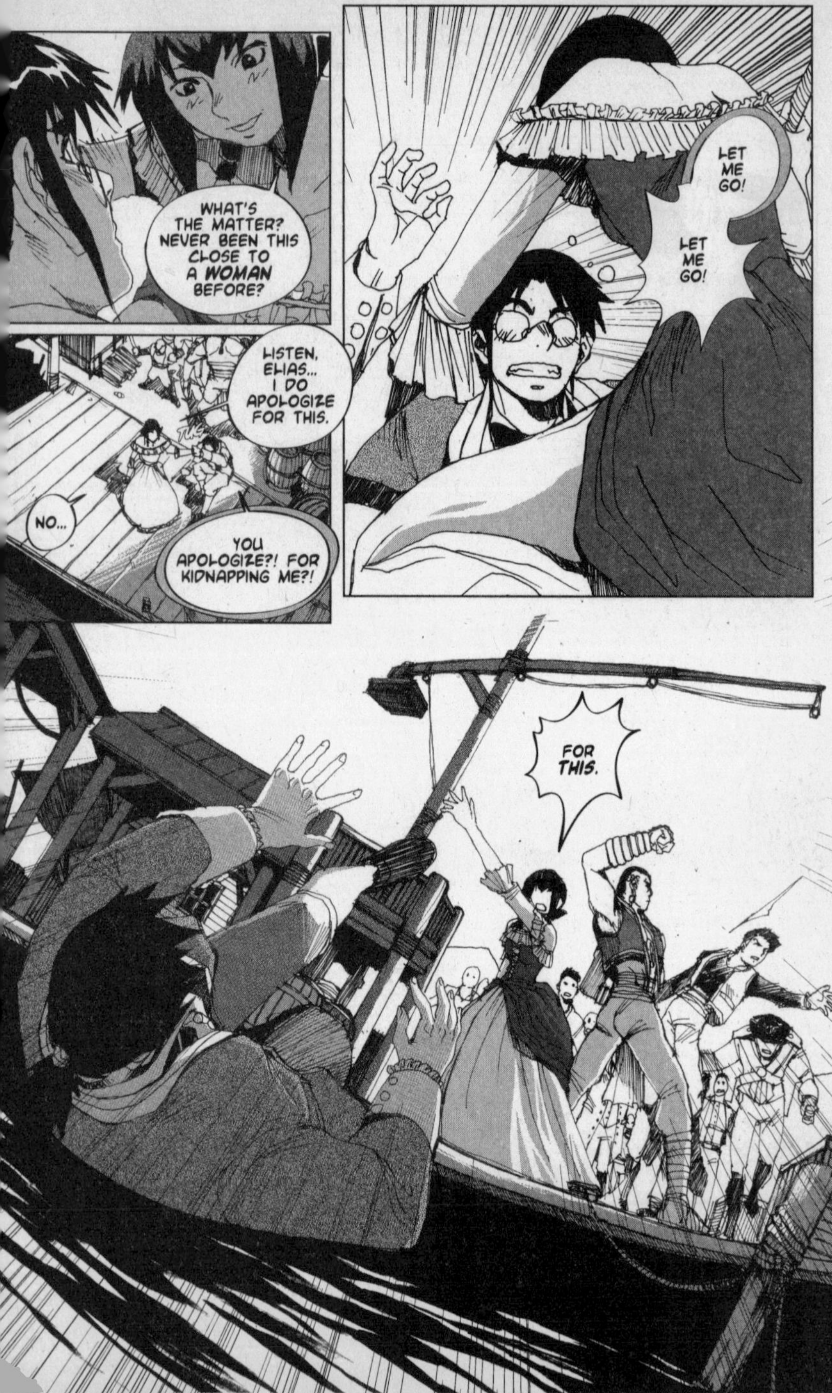
LET ME GO!
LET ME GO!
WHAT'S THE MATTER? NEVER BEEN THIS CLOSE TO A **WOMAN** BEFORE?
LISTEN, ELIAS... I DO APOLOGIZE FOR THIS.
NO...
YOU APOLOGIZE?! FOR KIDNAPPING ME?!
FOR **THIS.**

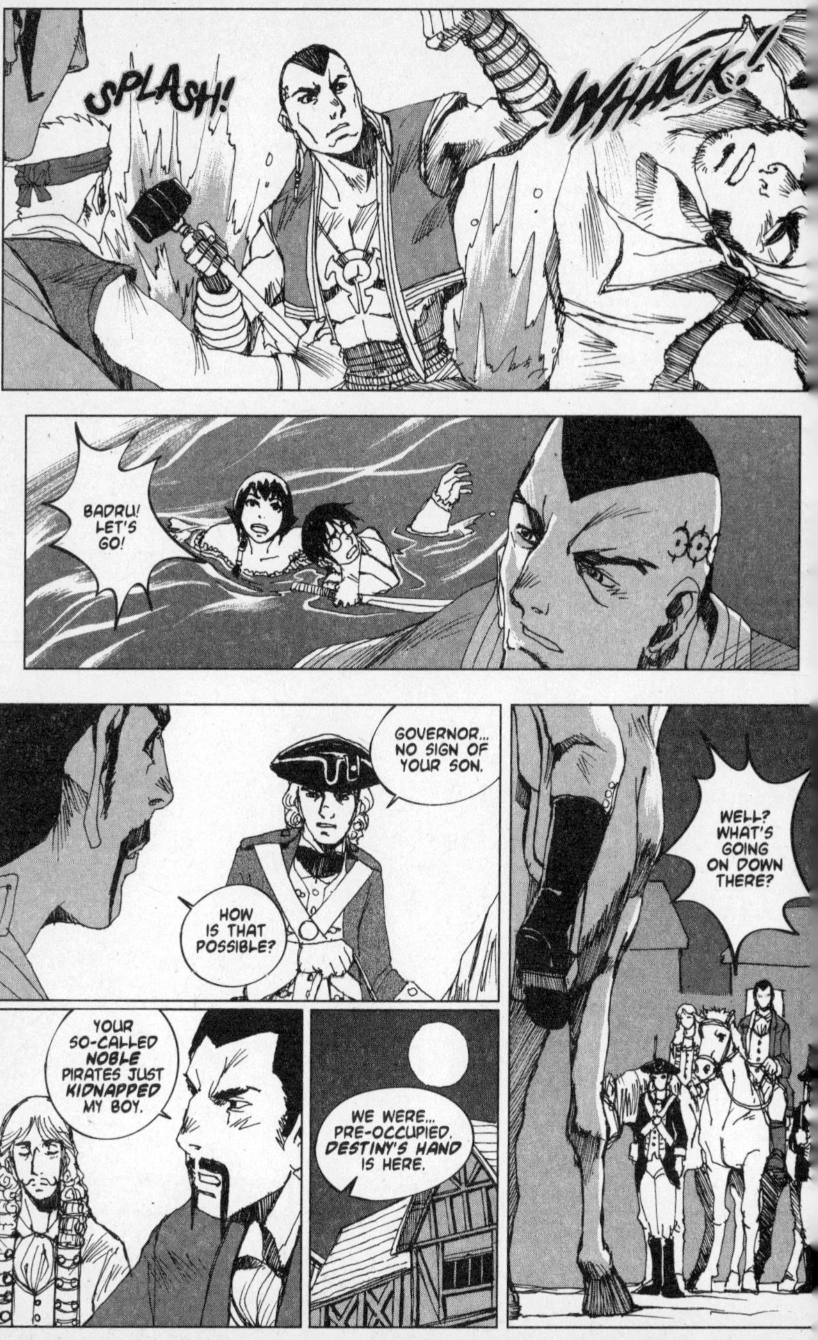
WHACK!
SPLASH!
BADRU! LET'S GO!
WELL? WHAT'S GOING ON DOWN THERE?
GOVERNOR... NO SIGN OF YOUR SON.
HOW IS THAT POSSIBLE?
WE WERE... PRE-OCCUPIED. DESTINY'S HAND IS HERE.
YOUR SO-CALLED NOBLE PIRATES JUST KIDNAPPED MY BOY.

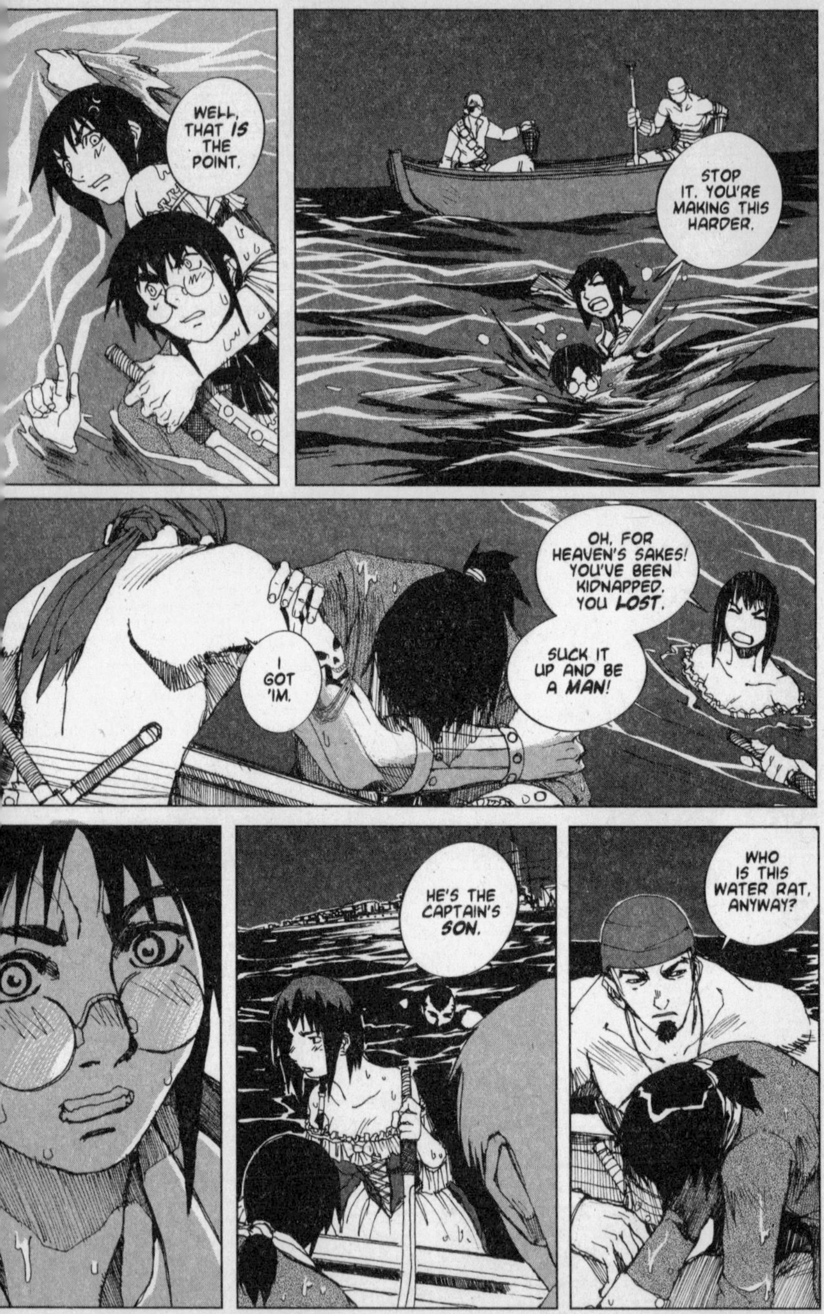
STOP IT. YOU'RE MAKING THIS HARDER.
WELL, THAT *IS* THE POINT.
OH, FOR HEAVEN'S SAKES! YOU'VE BEEN KIDNAPPED. YOU **LOST**.
SUCK IT UP AND BE A **MAN**!
I GOT 'IM.
WHO IS THIS WATER RAT, ANYWAY?
HE'S THE CAPTAIN'S **SON**.

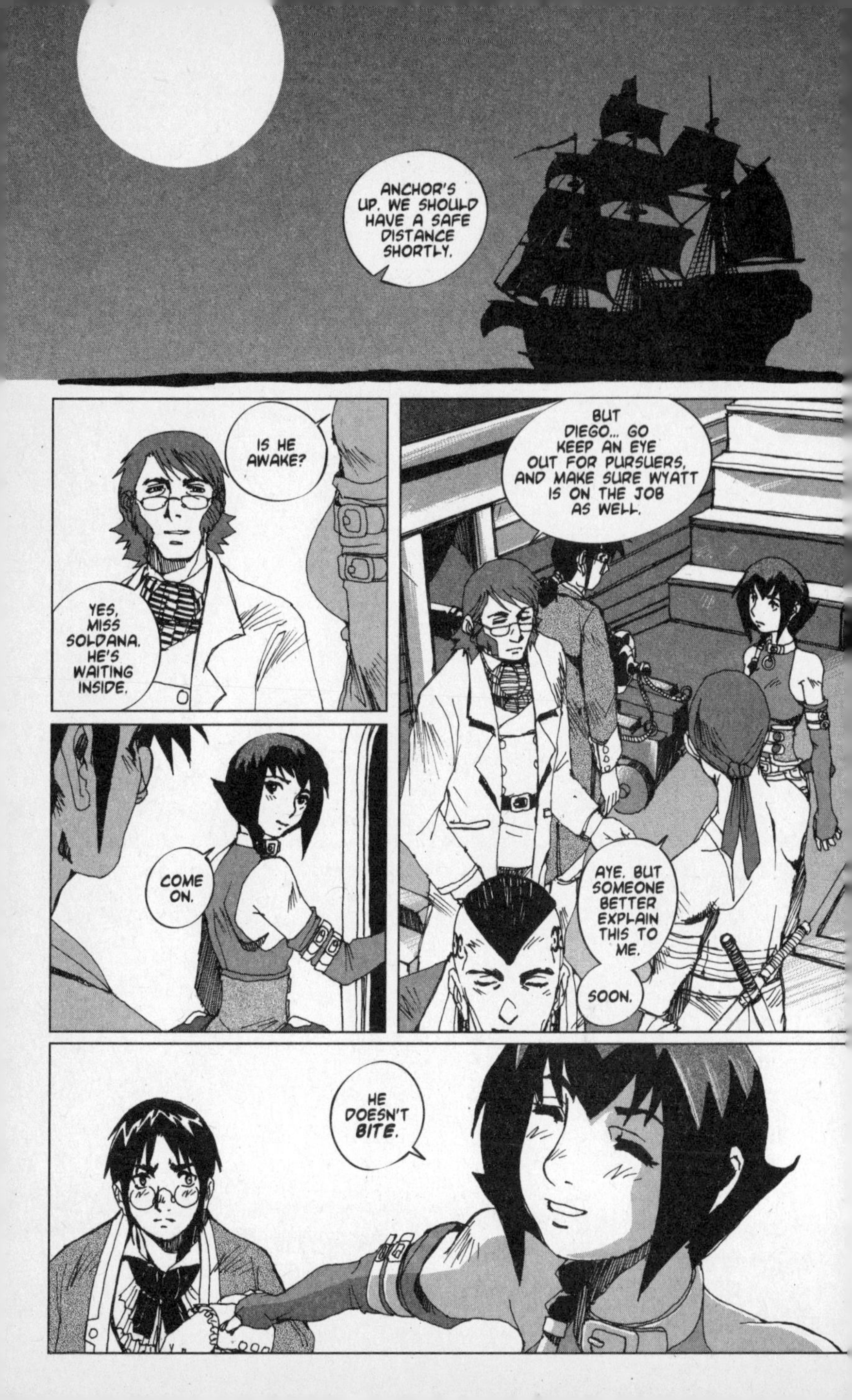
ANCHOR'S UP. WE SHOULD HAVE A SAFE DISTANCE SHORTLY.
BUT DIEGO... GO KEEP AN EYE OUT FOR PURSUERS, AND MAKE SURE WYATT IS ON THE JOB AS WELL.
AYE. BUT SOMEONE BETTER EXPLAIN THIS TO ME.
SOON.
IS HE AWAKE?
YES, MISS SOLDANA. HE'S WAITING INSIDE.
COME ON.
HE DOESN'T BITE.

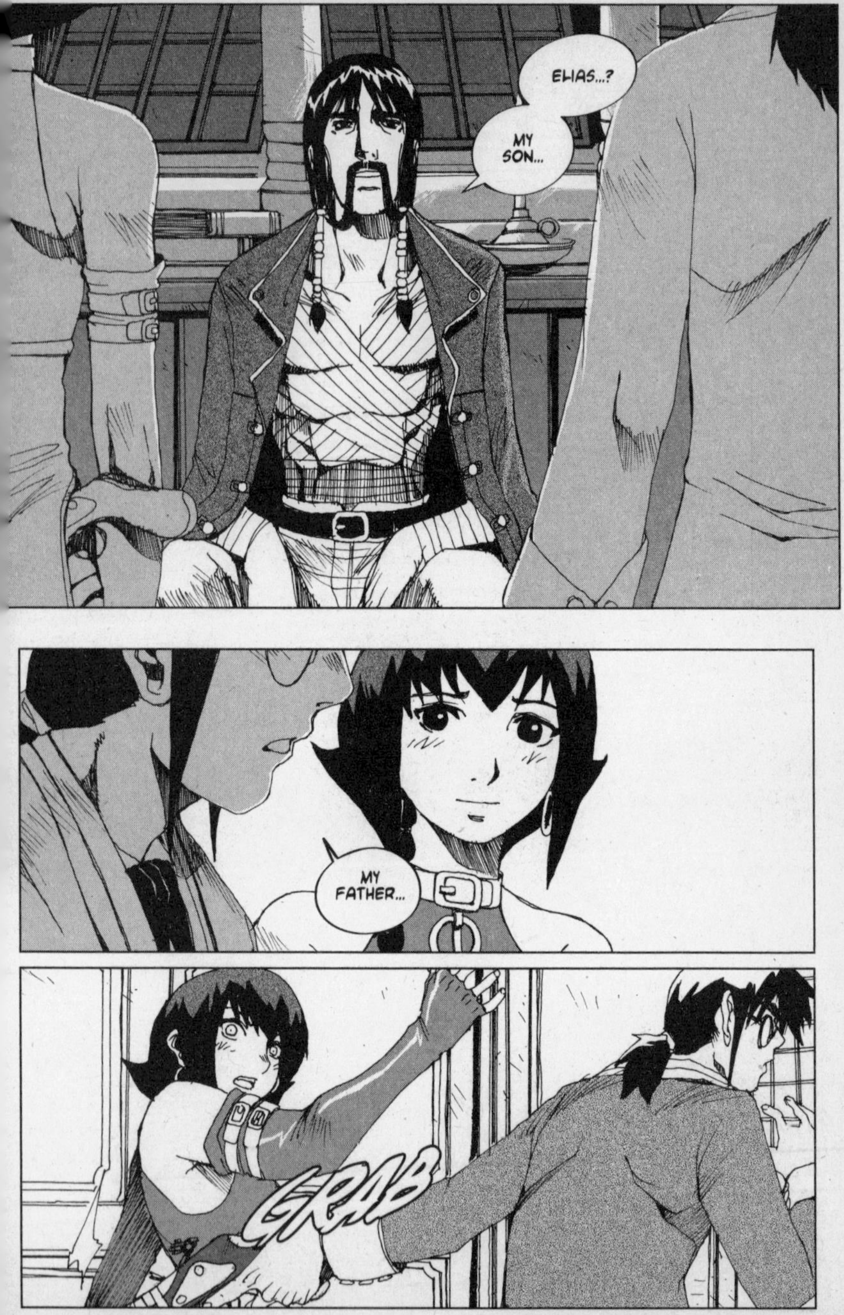
ELIAS...?
MY SON...
MY FATHER...
GRAB

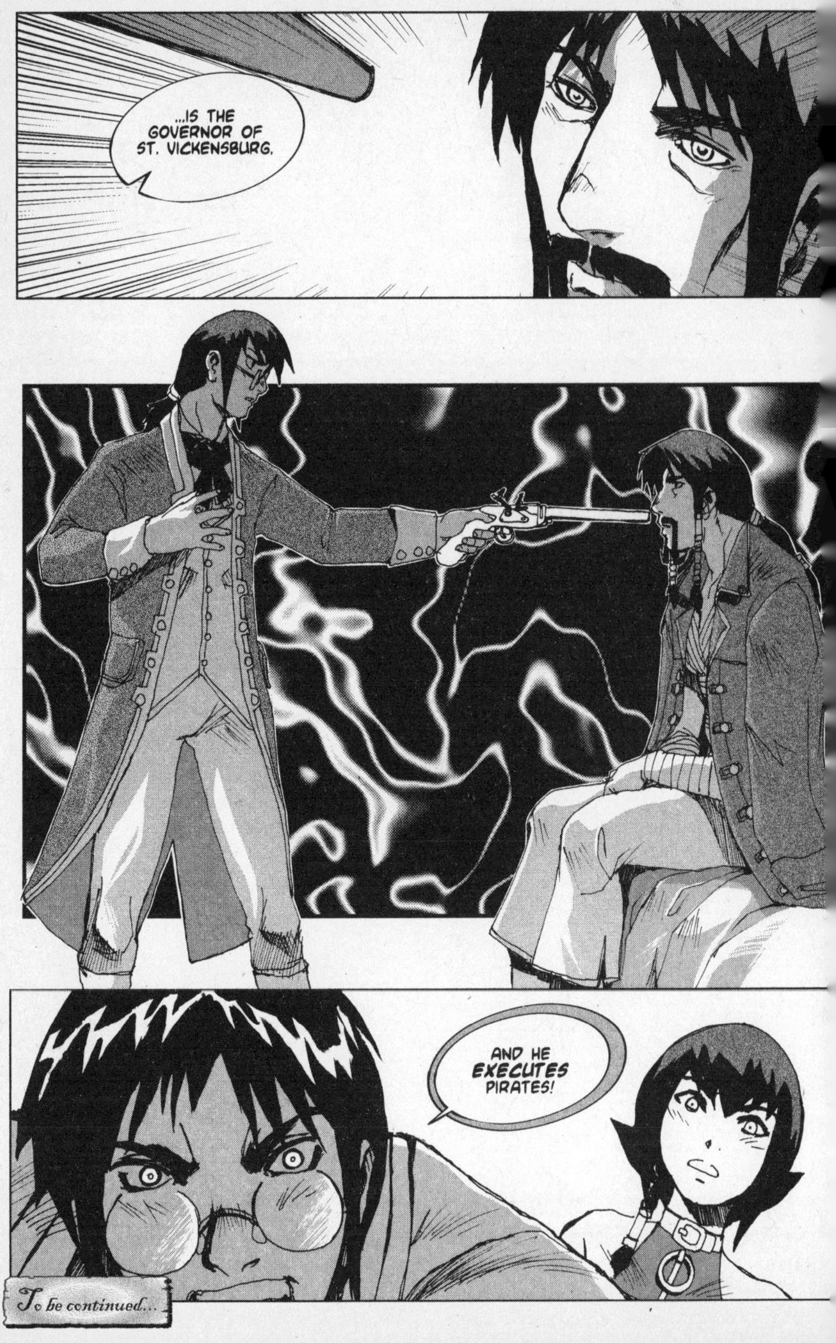
...IS THE GOVERNOR OF ST. VICKENSBURG.
AND HE EXECUTES PIRATES!
To be continued...

About the Creators

WRITERS

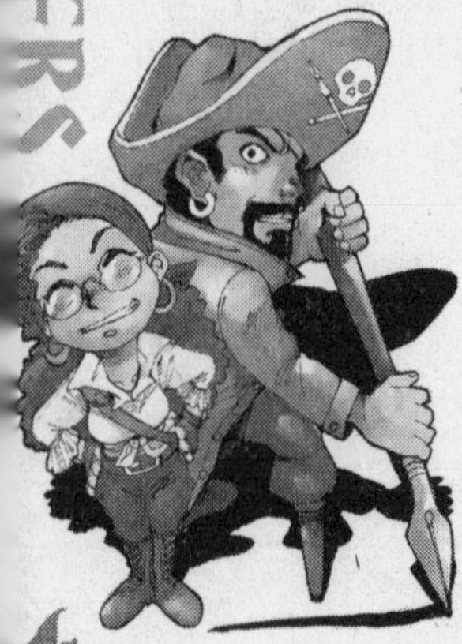

Nunzio DeFilippis & Christina Weir

Are a writing team who have worked in comics, television, video games and film. Trained as screenwriters (DeFilippis at USCs Screenwriting Program and Weir at Emerson's Television Program), they began writing together as a team on HBO's ARLISS, where they worked for two seasons. They've also contributed two stories for Disney's KIM POSSIBLE. They joined the Seven Seas crew right from the start, creating one of the company's four launch titles, AMAZING AGENT LUNA. DESTINY'S HAND is their second book with Seven Seas. They've also worked in adapting manga from Japan, working with Del Rey on SUGAR SUGAR RUNE, GURU GURU PON CHAN and KAGETORA. In American comics, they have written SKINWALKER, THREE STRIKES, MARIA'S WEDDING, ONCE IN A BLUE MOON, THE TOMB and PAST LIES for Oni Press, and spent 3 years in the world of Marvel's mutants writing NEW MUTANTS, HELLIONS and NEW X-MEN. They have also written for WONDER WOMAN, ADVENTURES OF SUPERMAN and DETECTIVE COMICS. Their first video game project is awaiting a title and release date.

Melvin Calingo

ARTIST

Is the artist of Destiny's Hand. He earned a Bachelor of Fine Arts degree in the University of the Philippines where he took up Visual Communications. Straight out of college, he took a job as a comic book artist for a local publication. Under the pseudonym Taga-ilog, he worked for Culture Crash Comics for four years where he penned and drew his own title, "Pasig" -- a post-apocalyptic action drama. He also drew artworks for a local magazine and character designs for a Japanese animation company.

Throughout his career, he has held several comic book/animationrelated talks and symposiums in various schools and universities in the Philippines.

Destiny's Hand is his US debut work.

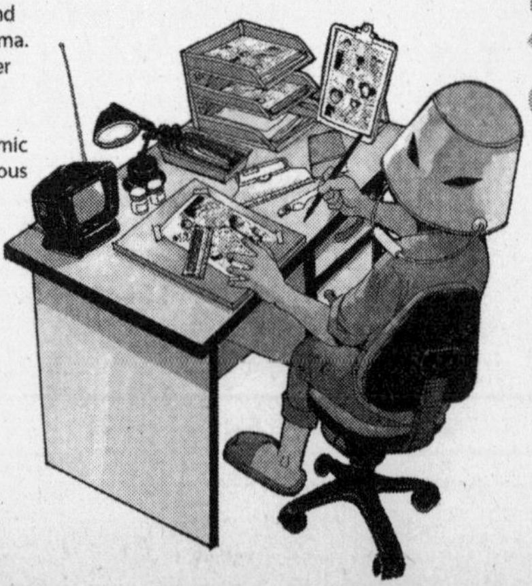

THE
CREASURE CHEST

The Making of
Destiny's Hand

Notes by Nunzio DeFilippis and Christina Weir
with the art of Melvin Calingo

Olivia Soldana is the 16 year old lead character of Destiny's Hand. She's the right hand woman to the Captain of the ship, and when he needs his crew to go on one last adventure in his name, she's the one he puts in charge. But the crew has difficulties following a girl, no matter how tough she might be. So in order to lead the crew to the Destiny's Hand and honor her Captain's request, Olivia's going to have to get creative.

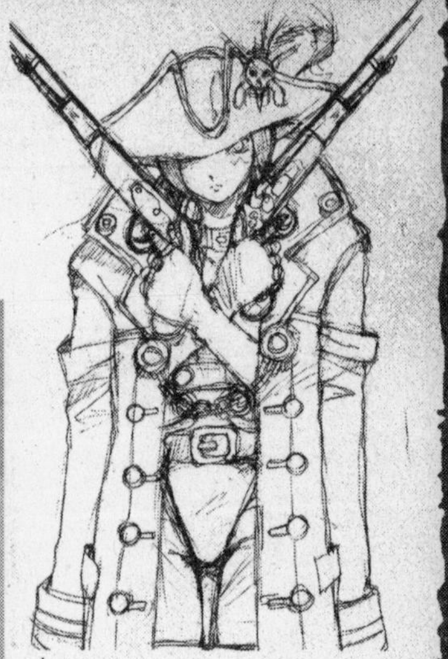

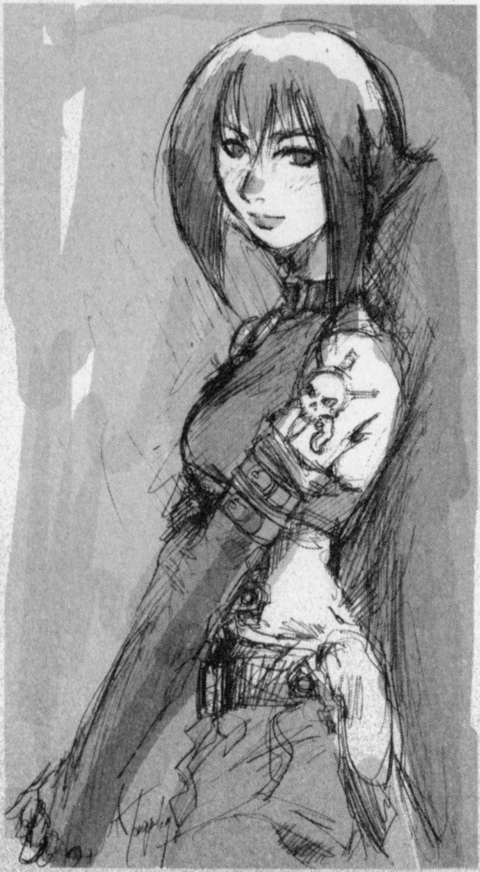

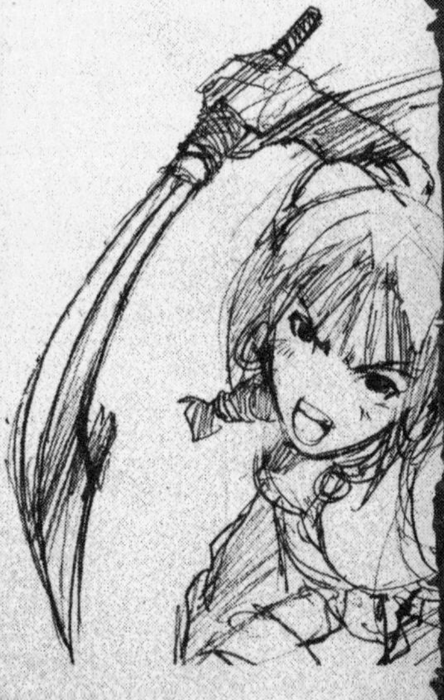

Olivia Soldana

TREASURE CHEST

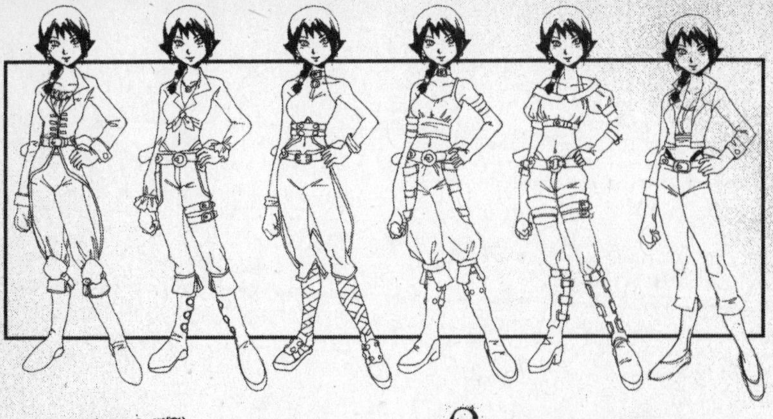

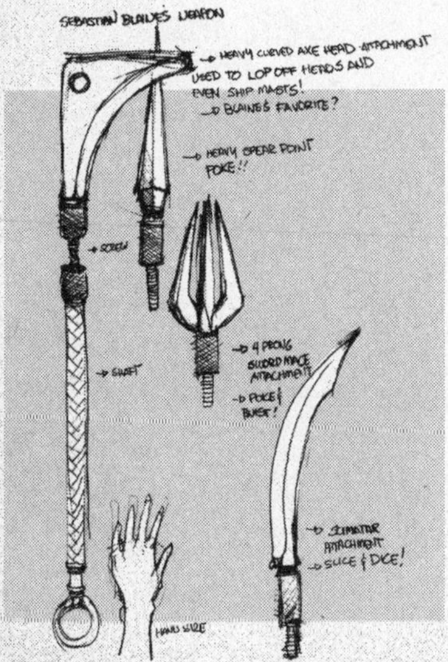
SEBASTIAN BLAINE'S WEAPON
HEAVY CURVED AXE HEAD ATTACHMENT USED TO LOP OFF HEADS AND EVEN SHIP MASTS!
BLAINE'S FAVORITE?
HEAVY SPEAR POINT POKE!!
SCREW
SHAFT
4 PRONG SWORD MACE ATTACHMENT
SCIMITAR ATTACHMENT
SLICE & DICE!
HAND SIZE

Olivia's design was the subject of a LOT of debate. Our original proposal called for something more traditionally pirate. We wanted pants (of the tight, pirate variety) and maybe an oversized shirt.

Melvin's design was far less authentic pirate, but much more what one might expect of a manga female. Jason loved it. There was a lot of back and forth, and we decided that so long as Olivia wasn't someone who conformed to how anyone expects her to dress (not her parents, and not the other pirates), it worked for us.

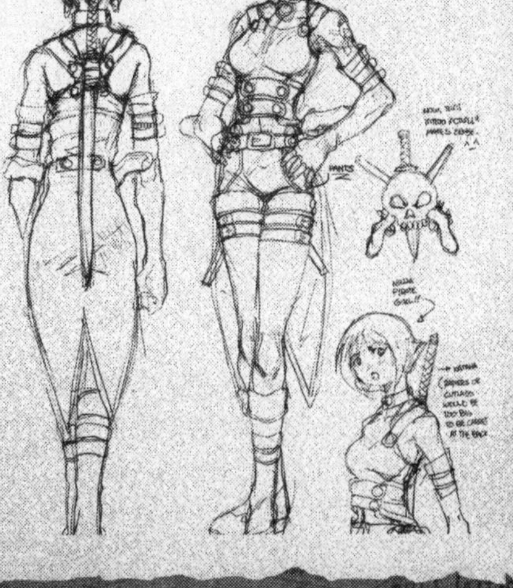

Melvin initially gave her two pistols, which we loved. But we also wanted her to have a blade, as the genre calls for knife and sword fighting. It was his idea to give her a blade that was essentially an attachment to Captain Blaine's own weapon. It cements the bond between the two characters and gives her a weapon that looks cool.

It was this sort of storytelling instinct that Melvin started bringing to the character design work that told us he was the right guy to tell this story with us.

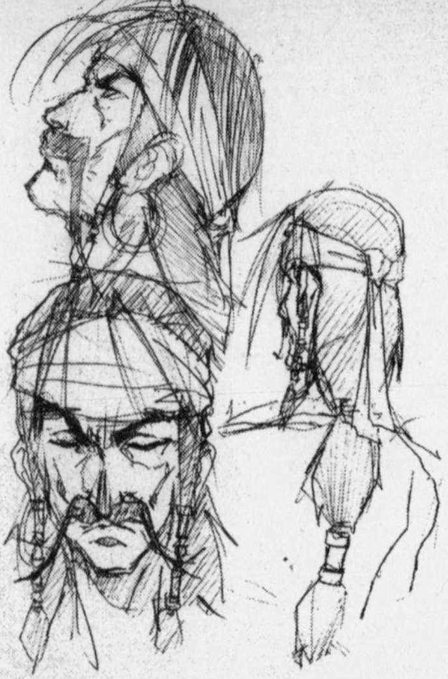

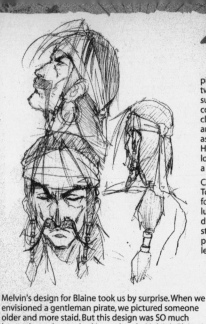

Captain Sebastian Blaine is the gentleman pirate. When he comes after your vessel, you know two things. First, his ship, Destiny's Hand, cannot be sunk. The second is, if you surrender, no harm will come to you or your crew. His men will hurt no-one, claim your cargo, escort your ship safely to a port, and even tell you cool pirate stories on the way. So, as you can guess, most ships surrender to Destiny's Hand and Captain Blaine immediately. Sure, they lose cargo. But no one gets hurt and everyone gets a memorable experience.

Captain Blaine is the last of a dying breed, though. Today's pirates are meaner, more savage. They live for the fight and the thrill of the kill as much as the lure of treasure. Blaine sees the new breed as dishonorable, and wants his crew to carry on in his style of piracy. But he knows that without him to push them, they may disband and seek jobs with less honorable crews.

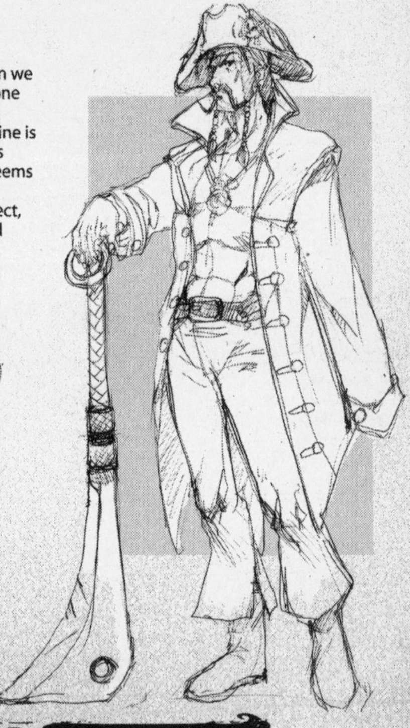

Melvin's design for Blaine took us by surprise. When we envisioned a gentleman pirate, we pictured someone older and more staid. But this design was SO much better than what we had in our heads. Melvin's Blaine is young, sexy, shirtless, but also very gentlemanly. It's hard to describe what it is about the design that seems so gentlemanly, but we think it jumps out at you without being definable in quick phrases. It's perfect, and our only note to Melvin was that Blaine should wear the cool coat pretty often.

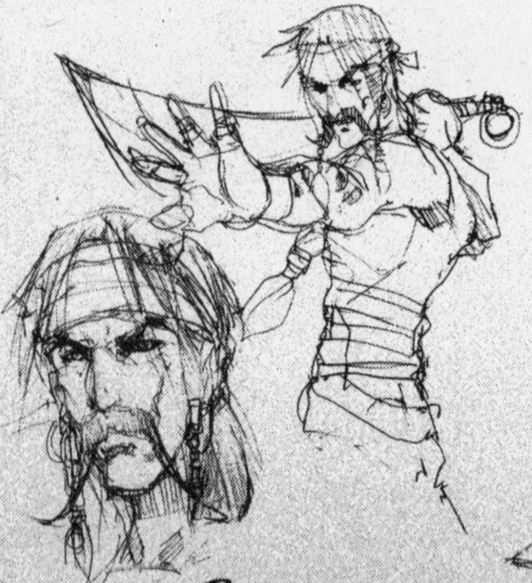

Sebastian Blaine

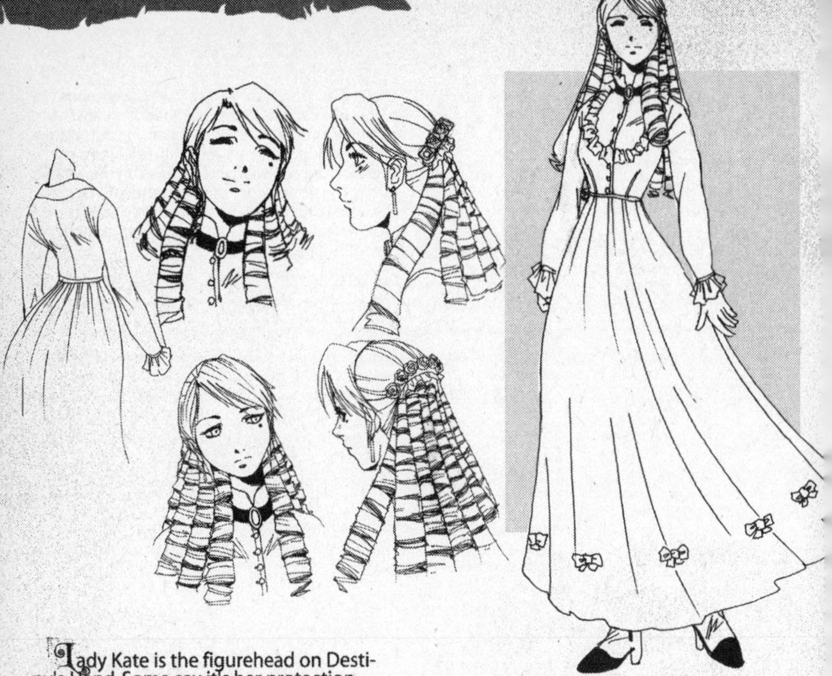

Lady Kate is the figurehead on Destiny's Hand. Some say it's her protection that makes the ship unsinkable. Who is she? That's a question that will be explored in the story itself, so we won't give too much away. But as the designs make clear, Lady Kate is inspired by a real woman, someone who meant a lot to Captain Blaine.

Like Blaine, Melvin got Lady Kate right on the first try. The woman has a gentle charm and a beauty that we'll need - though we can't tell you why just yet.

And the figurehead has a sadness that is absolutely vital. She also looks like a beautiful figurehead, one that would look gorgeous on a real ship.

The orb in the figurehead's hands was so striking to us, we worked it into the story! When the story starts, Lady Kate's hands are empty. If the crew wants to find The Devil's Eye, that will have to change.

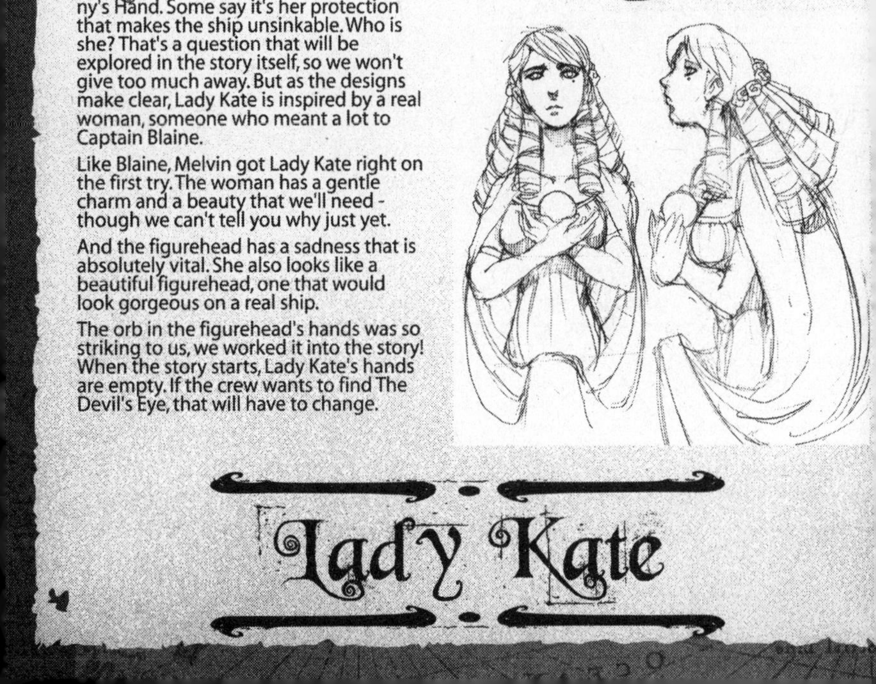

Lady Kate

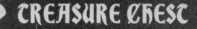

Diego Basteon is an the ship's boatswain (pronounced bosun). Discipline is his domain on Destiny's Hand. Of Blaine's key lieutennants, he's the one who least fits the 'gentlemanly' motif. He longs for more battle, and is a bit tired of the surrenders and the entertaining of the surrendering crew. To him, this is a dog and pony show. And he'd rather face a good battle. But Diego owes his life to Blaine, and will follow his orders no matter what he thinks of them.

Diego's weapon of choice is a Cat O'Nine Tails. He uses it to maintain discipline on the ship and ensure that the crew follows Blaine's orders. Some worry he enjoys flogging disobedient sailors too much, that it's where he finds his battle since so many ships surrender to Destiny's Hand. But the crew is well-disciplined and generally he doesn't need to flog anyone, so if this is his release, Diego must be very frustrated.

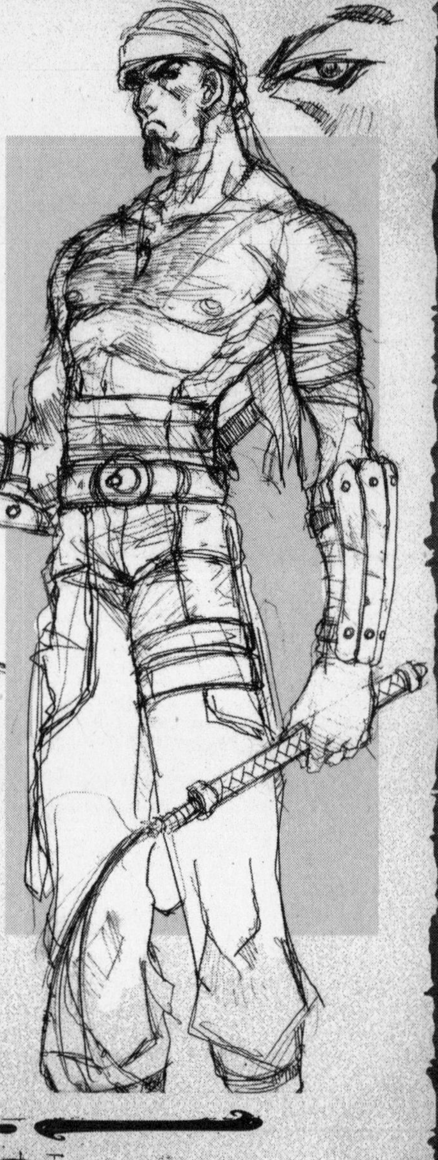

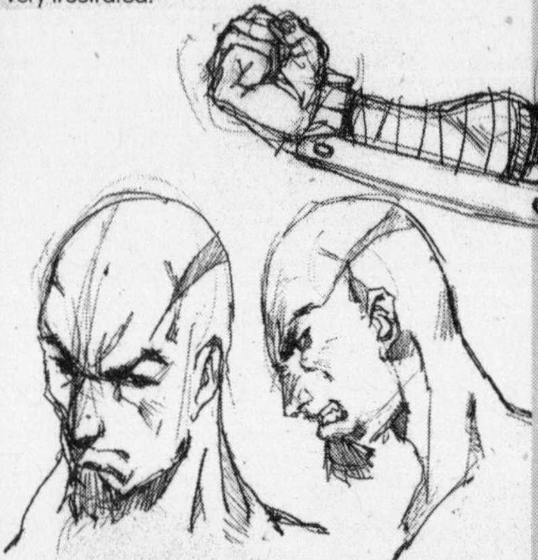

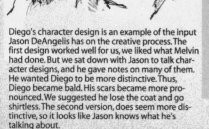

Diego's character design is an example of the input Jason DeAngelis has on the creative process. The first design worked well for us, we liked what Melvin had done. But we sat down with Jason to talk character designs, and he gave notes on many of them. He wanted Diego to be more distinctive. Thus, Diego became bald. His scars became more pronounced. We suggested he lose the coat and go shirtless. The second version, does seem more distinctive, so it looks like Jason knows what he's talking about.

Lastly, Diego's last name was once Fortuna, but Jason worried that this was a pretty happy sounding name for such a grim guy. We decided Basteon would reflect his strength and dour-ness.

Diego Basteon

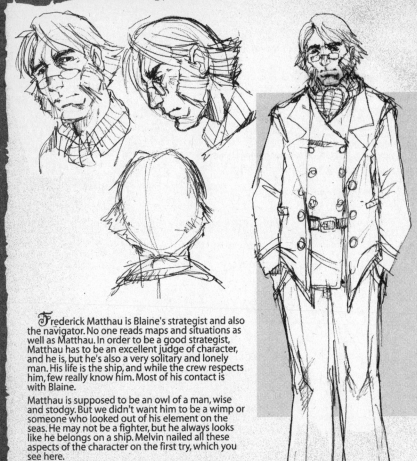

Frederick Matthau is Blaine's strategist and also the navigator. No one reads maps and situations as well as Matthau. In order to be a good strategist, Matthau has to be an excellent judge of character, and he is, but he's also a very solitary and lonely man. His life is the ship, and while the crew respects him, few really know him. Most of his contact is with Blaine.

Matthau is supposed to be an owl of a man, wise and stodgy. But we didn't want him to be a wimp or someone who looked out of his element on the seas. He may not be a fighter, but he always looks like he belongs on a ship. Melvin nailed all these aspects of the character on the first try, which you see here.

Melvin also succeeded in depicting a certain inner decency, which we really wanted for Matthau. In making him a little withdrawn from the crew and also a strategist, there was a chance he could have come off as manipulative. That's not in this design, and we're glad. Matthau may be the one who guides things on the ship behind the scenes, but in the end, he is 100% loyal to Blaine.

Frederik Matthau

Badru is a native from one of the local islands. He is viewed by many in the crew as a primitive, maybe even a bit savage. But he's one of the few crewmembers who can read, and despite his massive frame and skill in fighting, he doesn't tend towards violence. He admires Blaine's gentlemanly way with piracy.

Badru was completely redesigned before the sketch you see here. The first design for Badru wasn't in a design sketch. It was in a 5 page sequence done by Melvin at the very early stages of character and story breakdowns. Melvin was, we think, trying to make certain he had the job (in our minds he already had it by then, so maybe he was just flexing his sequential muscles) and he put together five pages of Olivia (then named Andrea) and Badru coming ashore to look for medicine for Blaine. It was unscripted, just stuff Melvin came up with. It was very cute stuff, and a good test drive on Olivia's look.

But Badru at the time didn't look very different, ethnically, from the rest of the crew. So when we sat down with Jason to talk designs (see our notes on Diego for more on that), one of the things we discussed was Badru. We wanted him to be an islander, with traces of Native American to his design. While Destiny's Hand is set in a fictional world with fictional ports, the feel is very Caribbean. So if you look at the setting as vaguely Caribbean, then think of Badru as a native of one of the islands like Hispaniola. Given the cues to redraw him, Melvin, as usual, hit the design out of the park. As you can see.

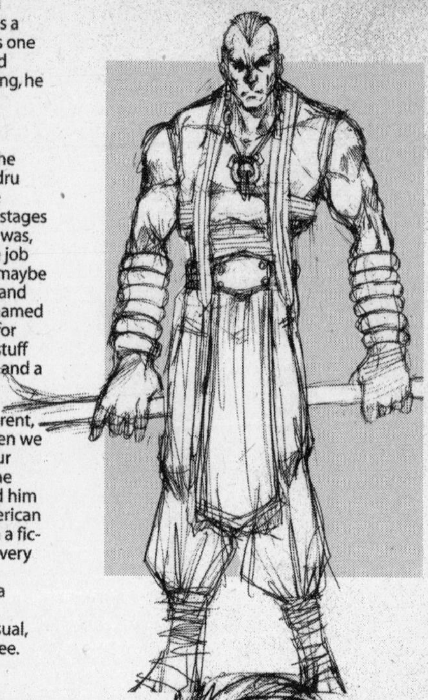

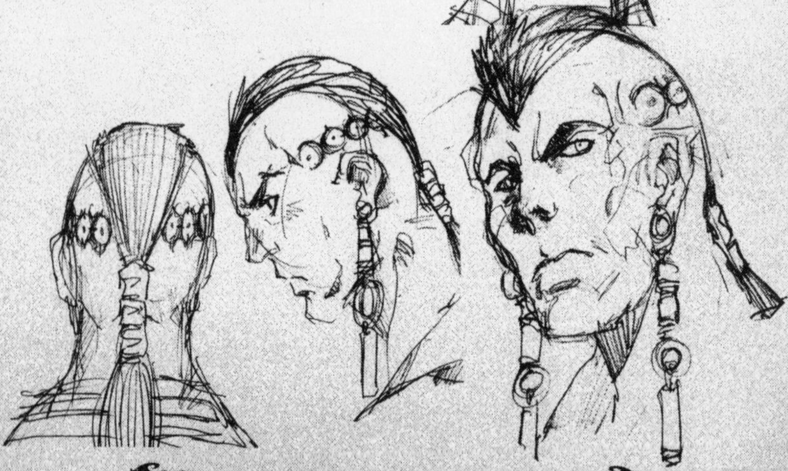

Badru

TREASURE CHEST

Ah, Owen. Owen is a bard... a scribe... a mooch. He came aboard Destiny's Hand to write a biography of the gentleman pirate. That was six years ago. He hasn't left since. He has been the 'guest' of the crew ever since. Diego has insisted that Owen pull his own weight, so he works alongside the crew on raids, and takes point in entertaining surrendered sailors.

Owen has a weakness for alcohol, and has become fascinated with the life of piracy his subject leads. He says he's still there because his story is 'ongoing.' But it's possible he's just staying because he's become one of the crew. He likes the respect he gets in the ports and especially the attention he gets from the ladies for being a pirate.

The full body design on Owen was Melvin's first try. It looked great to us. The bandolier of mini-kegs was perfect and we suddenly envisioned him drinking from them mid battle. But we also see him lighting a wick on one and tossing it at an enemy. Explosive stuff, that booze. The closeup gives you a better view of Owen's eyepatch. Some among the crew think it's fake. But no one has ever just pulled it off to check. Because if you're wrong... gross. Plus, Blaine has told the crew not to harass Owen, and that means Diego will punish anyone who does. And no one wants that.

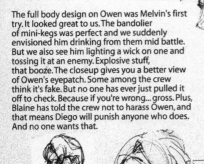

Owen Galviston

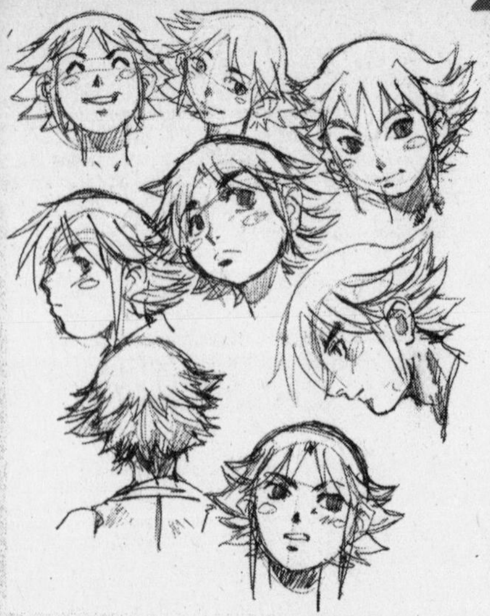

As you can see, Melvin's designs ran with the urchin notion. He's drawn Wyatt as pretty 'Oliver Twist.' Which works for us. We also like his spiky hair which manages to be both boy-tough and androgynous at the same time. That's hard to pull off. But Melvin strikes again.

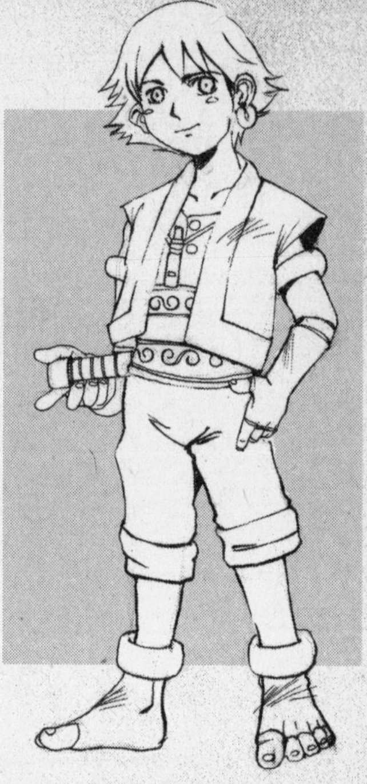

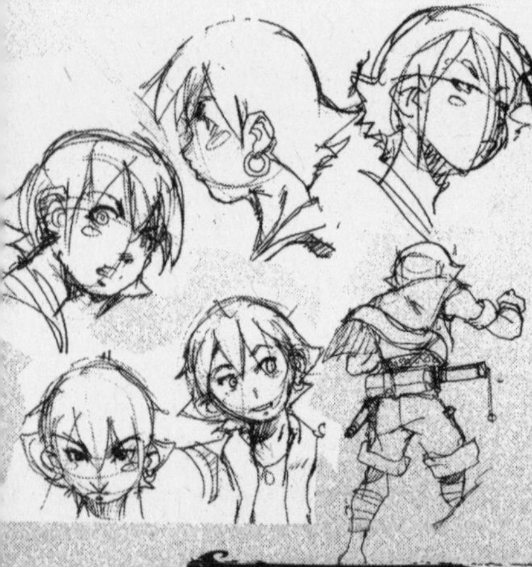

Wyatt is the lookout on Destiny's Hand. He hopes to be accepted as a topman (a crewman assigned to work on the sails) at some point, but he's not super-skilled with the sails yet. But that's where he loves to be. He loves climbing the masts and he sometimes even sleeps in the crow's nest. He's the kind of kid who always sees what he's not supposed to, not just because of his keen eyesight (which serves him well as lookout) but also because he's nosy.

Wyatt joined the crew only last year, stowing away when they were in port one day. No one knows how he got on board, and no one knows whether he was from that port or somewhere else entirely. He's never given anyone his last name. He's a runaway, a street urchin, a kid with no place to go back to, and a strong desire to be an important crewman on Destiny's Hand. Right now, he's more of a pest than anything else. But he's a useful pest.

Wyatt

TREASURE CHEST

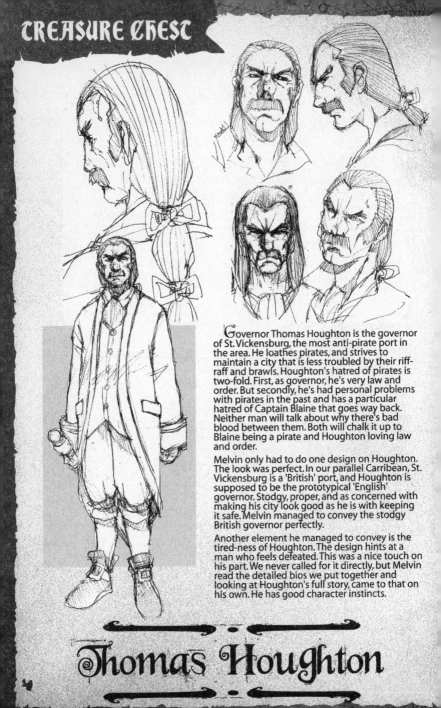

Governor Thomas Houghton is the governor of St. Vickensburg, the most anti-pirate port in the area. He loathes pirates, and strives to maintain a city that is less troubled by their riff-raff and brawls. Houghton's hatred of pirates is two-fold. First, as governor, he's very law and order. But secondly, he's had personal problems with pirates in the past and has a particular hatred of Captain Blaine that goes way back. Neither man will talk about why there's bad blood between them. Both will chalk it up to Blaine being a pirate and Houghton loving law and order.

Melvin only had to do one design on Houghton. The look was perfect. In our parallel Carribean, St. Vickensburg is a 'British' port, and Houghton is supposed to be the prototypical 'English' governor. Stodgy, proper, and as concerned with making his city look good as he is with keeping it safe. Melvin managed to convey the stodgy British governor perfectly.

Another element he managed to convey is the tired-ness of Houghton. The design hints at a man who feels defeated. This was a nice touch on his part. We never called for it directly, but Melvin read the detailed bios we put together and looking at Houghton's full story, came to that on his own. He has good character instincts.

Thomas Houghton

4

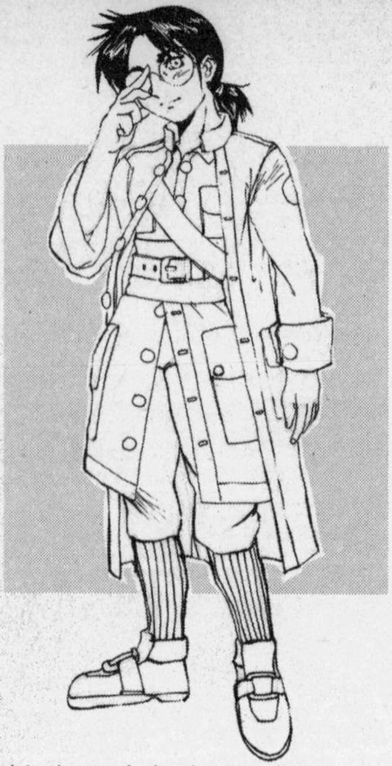

Elias Houghton is the son of Governor Houghton and has inherited his father's distaste for pirates. But that's a problem, because Elias is the one guy who will be able to lead Destiny's Hand to the Devil's Eye. Elias is a scholar, a linguist. He's the only one Blaine knows of who is fully fluent in a now-dead tongue. Every map piece, every artifact, every clue leading to the treasure is in that tongue, so if Olivia's going to lead the crew to the treasure that Blaine wants, she's going to have to get Elias' help - whether he wants to give it or not.

Elias is a romantic interest for Olivia, and is also a dramatic and comedic foil for her. He had to be her opposite number - the complete opposite of everything she is - but in a way that generates sparks as much as it generates tension.

So Elias needed to be the anti-Olivia. She wants nothing more than to be a great pirate. He wants nothing to do with piracy. She is educated and articulate but would rather be cussing and brawling. He thinks the life of piracy is the life of illiterate degenerates. She acts first, thinks later. He thinks always. Melvin captures a sort of nebbishy cuteness with Elias that works perfectly. He looks like someone who'd look down his nose at pirates. But he's cute enough to be worthy of romantic tensions with our lead.

But Melvin also got the last, key ingredient. He also looks like someone who has a bit of pirate buried within him, doesn't he?

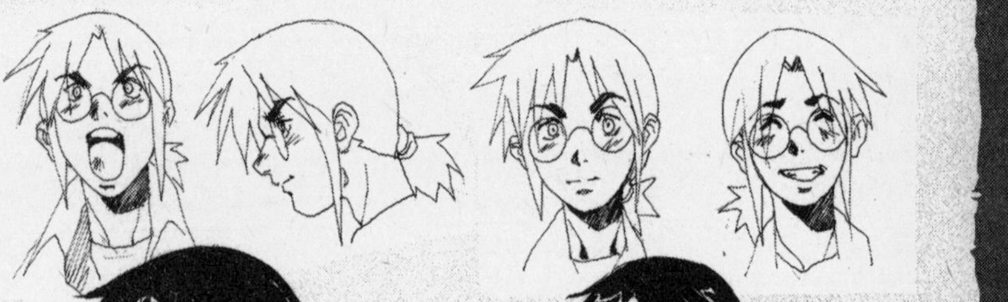

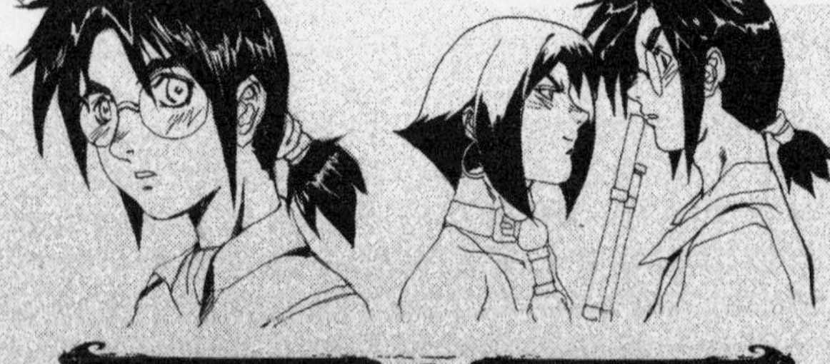

Elias Houghton

CREASURE CHEST

We all know, deep down inside that real pirates were probably not like Blaine. We pretend they were. In reality, too many were like this guy. Lars Mulgrew. A raping, pillaging, town-sacking, brutalizing kind of pirate who uses his crew's prowess and the freedom of the waves to do whatever he likes no matter who gets hurt or dies.

Lars Mulgrew is the new breed of pirate. He's everything that Blaine hates. Too many young pirates follow his way, the way of blood and anger. Blaine knows that Mulgrew is after the Devil's Eye, and that's at least part of the reason why he wants his crew to go after it. The Devil's Eye in Mulgrew's hand would be a disaster.

Melvin's design was not what we were expecting for Mulgrew. He drew him far sexier than we imagined. He's so sexy, in fact, that we now have to wonder about putting some sexual tension between Mulgrew and Olivia down the line. The design was so very different from what we pictured. Yet it was perfect.

In discussions with Jason, we took a good look at the full Mulgrew design and focused on the one shot of him holding up his fist. You can see there, he has an odd wrist brace. Just looking at that art spun the three of us off in random speculation. And from that was born the notion that Mulgrew has a special weapon attached to his wrist. We talked about it a lot, and what we came up with is a spring loaded grapple launcher. This can spear an enemy and then the coils will retract into the launcher, pulling that enemy towards you on the barbed end.

Melvin did a new design for the weapon. His design looks more handcuff/capture-y than spear-y. But we figure the ends of that cuff are barbed and can stick into the target. Nasty weapon, huh?

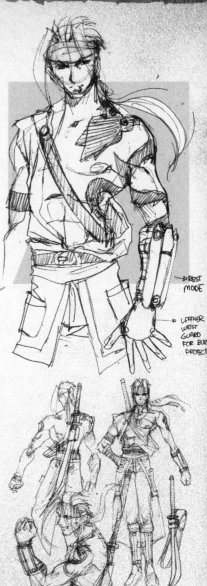

PRIEST MODE

LEATHER WRIST GUARD FOR BUR PROTECT

Lars Mulgrew

If you look back at Lars Mulgrew's design, you'll see a cool tattoo that works across his left shoulder. That's a Kraken. Mulgrew's ship is called The Kraken, named after one of the most feared mythical creatures of the deep. Since Destiny's Hand has Lady Kate, the Kraken has its own figurehead. This figurehead inspires terror in all who behold it.

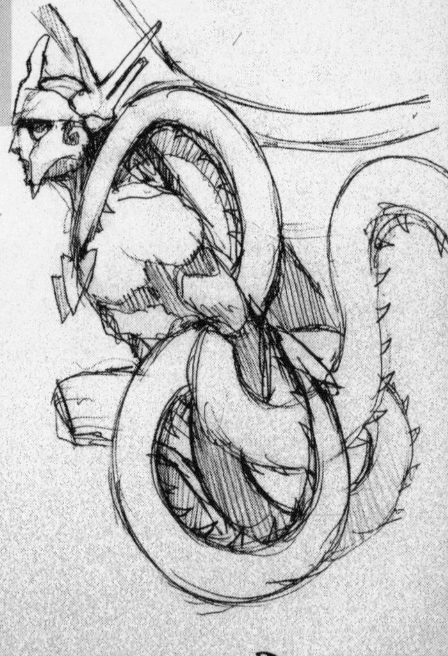

Melvin did this one based on the notion that the ship was called the Kraken, but we didn't ask for a specific figurehead design. He just decided he needed to design it in advance. And he did a fine job. It looks like a real figurehead. That's an important part of what Melvin is bringing to this book. Everything piratey - the ships, the coats, the figureheads. He gives them an authenticity that says he's either really familiar with ships and the sea, or he loves pirate stories or both. He's the perfect man for the job.

The Kraken

TREASURE CHEST

The last character is Michel Langrisse. He is Captain of the defense fleet of the port of Valroux. Unlike St. Vickensberg, Valroux is a very pirate-friendly port. Pirates who respect laws while in port can come and go freely. Blaine's crew is particularly welcome because they never hurt innocents and try to avoid killing anyone.

Valroux is our "French" port. It has a more fun-loving side than the "British" port of St. Vickensburg, and anything goes there. Langrisse is well groomed and respectable, so he doesn't typify that aspect of the city. But he has a certain flexibility that allows such a port to exist and not fall into chaos. He respects the people's rights to do what they like, but knows when to put his foot down and restore order.

Langrisse cuts Destiny's Hand a lot of slack for a couple of reasons. One, as we said, they are the decent side of piracy, and he wants their ways to have rewards. The other is Olivia. Michel has a history with Olivia that will be explored. He can offer her a certain respectability to her life, if ever she wanted to settle down. Unfortunately for him, settling down is hardly on Olivia's agenda.

Our only concern with Langrisse's original design (the full design) was that he seemed a bit older than we wanted. We envisioned him just having become Captain, at maybe 20 years old or so. it was vital he not be too much older than Olivia because he needed to be a viable romantic option and not just a creepy older guy who was into teenage girls. The face designs were Melvin's second go, and all make him seem younger. We particularly like the one in the upper right and also the laughing one in the bottom left.

Michel Langrisse

The Tattoos of Destiny's Hand:

When we first came up with the characters for Destiny's Hand, we gave short descriptions and let Melvin have a go at designs. He drew basic designs for the many characters, and central to a couple of them (most importantly Olivia) were some cool tattoo designs.

We sat down with Jason DeAngelis to go over the designs, to see what we thought of them. Jason wanted everything to be as iconic as possible, and among other ideas we came up with that day (including the five fingers idea) was the idea that the key members of the crew of Destiny's Hand should have personalized tattoos.

This notion did not work its way into dialogue or plot just yet, but the tattoos are there, on the crew, an unspoken piece of detail. One day, it'll come up in plot. But for now, we'll discuss the tattoos here.

Sebastian Blaine

The choice for Blaine's tattoo was already made for us. We had asked for a skeletal hand in front of crossbones to serve as Destiny's Hand's colors. Melvin instead gave us a skeletal hand in front of crossed swords. It looked great, and the flag for the ship was one of the first designs that came in.

So when we decided each member of the crew had their own tattoo, it made perfect sense that Blaine, the ship's Captain, had the flag itself.

Even though the flag was decided upon quickly, there were still minor revisions. One of Melvin's early designs had an Ouroboros (the symbol of the snake consuming its own tail) instead of the circle behind the ship's logo. It looked really cool, but while the Ouroboros is usually a positive symbol, it still seemed to imply the crew would consume itself in some way, and we wanted Blaine's crew to not have such an ill omen.

Olivia Soldana

As we mentioned earlier, the tattoo for Olivia was part of Melvin's original design. There was some back and forth about Olivia's outfit that went into the character design discussions (we eventually went with an early Melvin design and shelved our reservations, and we have to say, she looks pretty cool). But during those discussions, one thing that never changed was the tattoo. We loved it on the first artwork he did for Olivia, and we still love it.

The crossed pistols behind the skull made such a strong impression on us, we decided that Olivia carries the pistols. So Melvin started drawing them crossed and tucked in at the back of her belt.

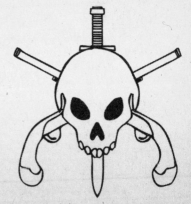

Diego Basteon

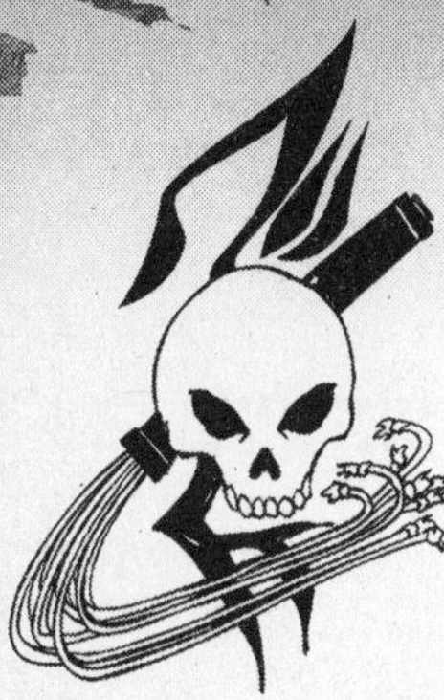

When we decided to create tattoos for the whole crew, we sent a 'character bible' to Melvin. It was a short list of details. It included character weapon, character tattoo, and design notes from our meeting with Jason.

On Diego, the first two categories were the same. Weapon: Cat O'Nine Tails. Tattoo: Cat O'Nine Tails

What you see is Melvin's final design. His first was as basic as our request – a simple drawing of the weapon. But this newer design has more flair to it. When the initial one came in, we heard from Jason that Melvin was tweaking it. The final version came about during the pages of Diego's fight with Olivia. We saw the art on those pages, and suddenly, Diego had a killer tattoo. The last question was size – Buckethead did two versions of the page where Diego stands ready to fight Olivia. One had the tattoo you see in the final product, the other had it way bigger. Jason suggested the final size, and Diego's tattoo was complete.

Frederick Matthau

Our tattoo note on Matthau was, as most of them were, vague, leaving some room for Melvin to get creative. We simply asked for "a map. Or maybe a compass."

What we got instead was what you see here. That was all Melvin, and his first take on the tattoo was the only one he needed, because it looks perfect.

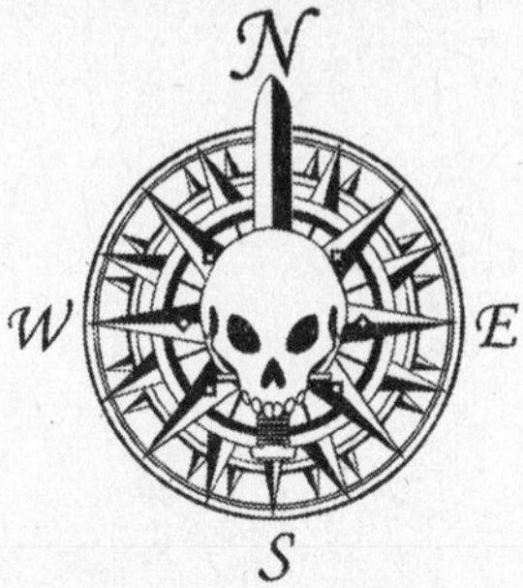
N
W
E
S

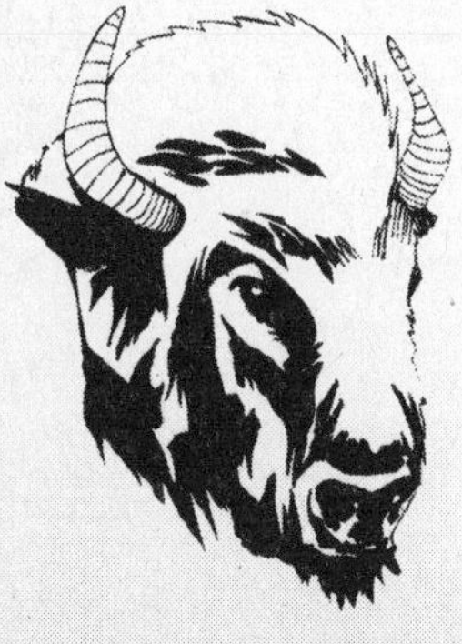

Badru

We asked for something completely different on Badru, something that ultimately didn't work. Our initial notes called for "a skeletal arm except bones are bent to simulate a bulging muscle."

We never saw Melvin's attempts at this, but we imagine that this design proved impossible to draw as a realistic tattoo, particularly one that would show up well on the pages of a black and white manga.

Instead, Melvin went another way entirely, using our call for Native American imagery on Badru to give the big man a tattoo of another life that was nearly wiped out when white people came West – the buffalo. It symbolizes the size, strength and grace of Badru perfectly.

Owen Galviston

When we talked about Owen's design, we got very enamored of the little kegs Melvin drew on the bard's bandolier. We talked with Jason for a long time about how they could explode in battle, about comic bits of him drinking from them. We got a little obsessed with the damn things.

So when it came time for Owen's tattoo, we asked for a drawing of the mini-keg. As an afterthought, we mentioned another possible design, the Quill.

Fortunately, Melvin was not at our meeting, so he wasn't swept up in the keg hysteria and was able to see that the Quill was really the right symbol for Owen. If he'd been there with us, Owen's tattoo would probably have been a keg, which wouldn't have shown him as a writer at all, just as a lush. Nice save, Melvin.

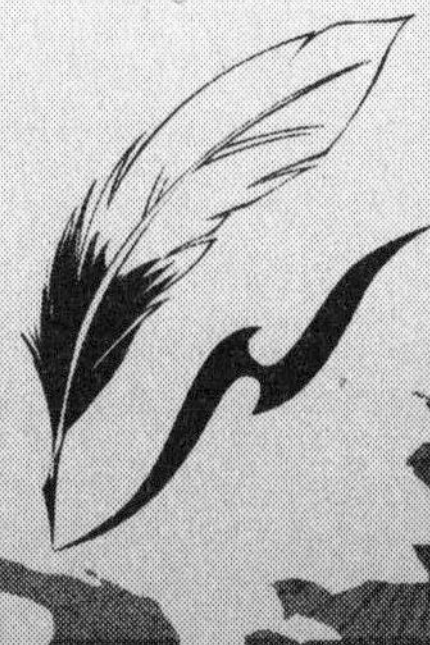

Wyatt

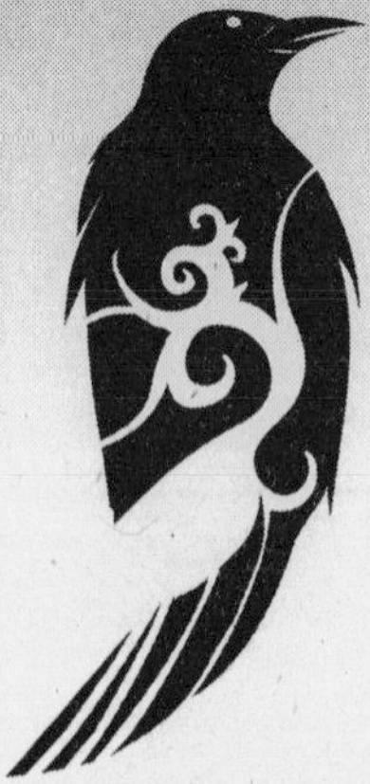

In most cases, we're showing you only the final design and discussing its evolution. But this is one case where we think showing both designs will be more fun.

In our character bible, we asked for Wyatt's tattoo to be either a "crow in a nest" or an "eye." The crow in the nest proved too clunky an image, so Melvin tried the eye. This is what we got:

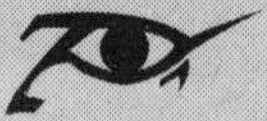

This is an absolutely gorgeous tattoo. We loved it. However, it is, as Jason pointed out, almost too mystical for the very simple character of Wyatt. He's a kid, and not steeped in any supernatural elements. The Egyptian motif on this eye didn't quite work with that. So Jason sent Melvin back to the drawing board, and the final result called back to the image of the crow. But it's got some flair to it, as well.

Still, we wanted Wyatt's earlier tattoo design to be shown here, because it was such a nice image for a tattoo, just ultimately not one that fit the character.

Lars Mulgrew

We know, we know, Lars Mulgrew's not a member of the crew. But still, a guy like him just demands a tattoo, you know? Mulgrew's original designs featured a tattoo on his shoulder, and even a small design by Melvin. We loved it.

So when we decided to give tattoos to the whole crew, we didn't want that to mean Mulgrew lost his. He is a pirate, after all, and it's not like Destiny's Hand invented the idea of tattoos on pirates.

Mulgrew's tattoo has since evolved a tiny bit, but this was not the result of any notes on our part. Like any talented artist, Melvin is always tweaking his stuff, looking for ways to improve it. He added the dagger to the tattoo. Looks great to us.

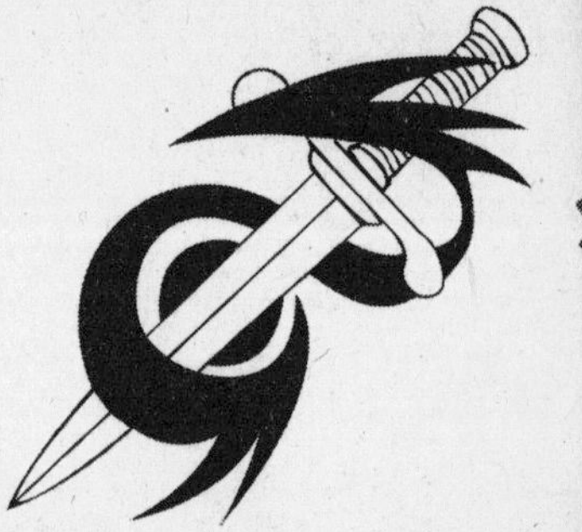

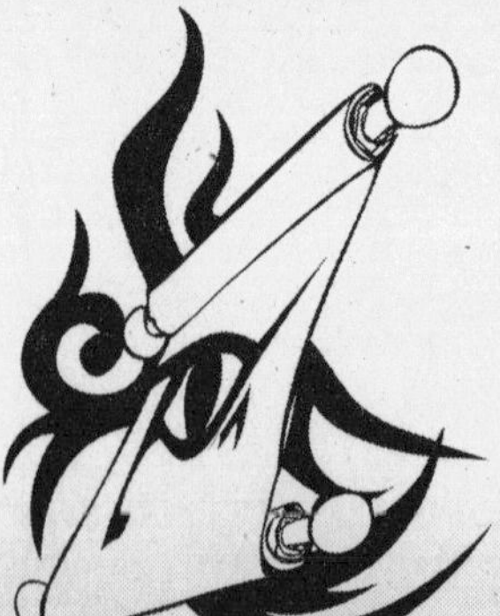

Elias Houghton

Elias doesn't have a tattoo when we meet him. In fact, he would shudder at the thought of getting one.

But if and when he makes any peace with the role the crew has in mind for him, they're going to insist he get one (in fact, that will probably be the point when the crew's tattoos get explained in story). So we asked for a design from Melvin to cover what tattoo the crew would force him to get.

The first design was a book with a pirate skull and crossbones on the cover. It looked good to us, but Melvin went ahead and completely redesigned. As you can see, he worked the rejected Wyatt tattoo into Elias' final design. A good artist never lets his good stuff go to waste. It works much better on Elias, given his mother's legacy.

But man is that a lot of ink! The crew may really have it in for Elias if they give him that detailed a tattoo. Perhaps Owen can give him a shot from a mini keg first.

In Volume 2 of

Destiny's HAND

Written by Nunzio DeFilippis and Christina Weir
Illustrated by Melvin Calingo

The crew of Destiny's Hand sets a course for the legendary
Isle du Diablo, home of the Devil's Eye. But will their newly found scholar
help them in their quest? Or will he finish off the dying Captain Blaine?
And what happens when Governor Houghton comes after his son, and
forces the Island of Valroux to join his anti-pirate campaign? With the
governor on their heels, and a potential traitor in their midst, the crew
starts a race with the Kraken for the ultimate treasure, and the winner will
determine the fate of everyone on the seas!

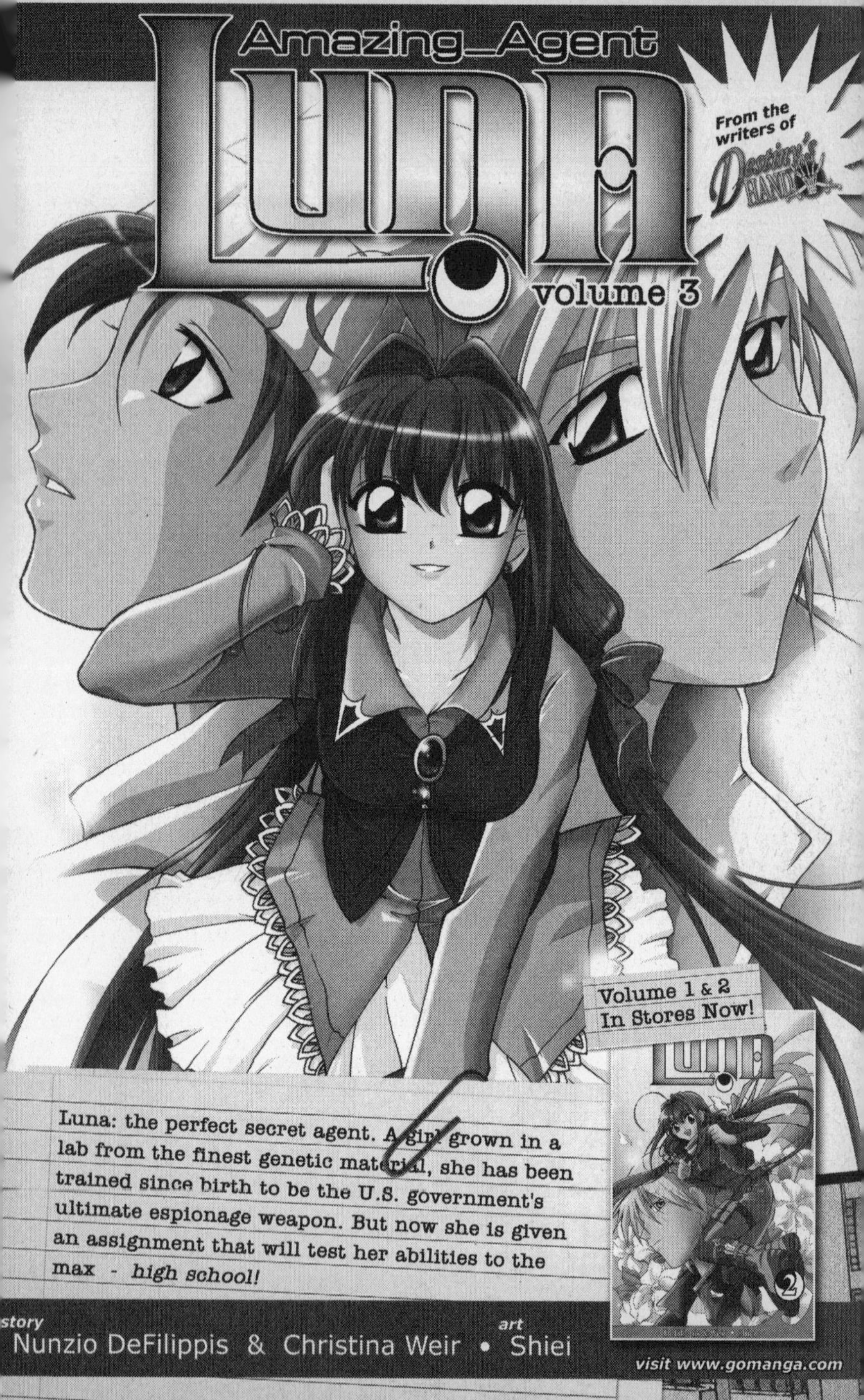
Amazing_Agent
LUNA
volume 3
From the writers of
Destiny's Hand
Volume 1 & 2
In Stores Now!
LUNA
2
Luna: the perfect secret agent. A girl grown in a lab from the finest genetic material, she has been trained since birth to be the U.S. government's ultimate espionage weapon. But now she is given an assignment that will test her abilities to the max - *high school!*
story
Nunzio DeFilippis & Christina Weir
art
Shiei
visit www.gomanga.com

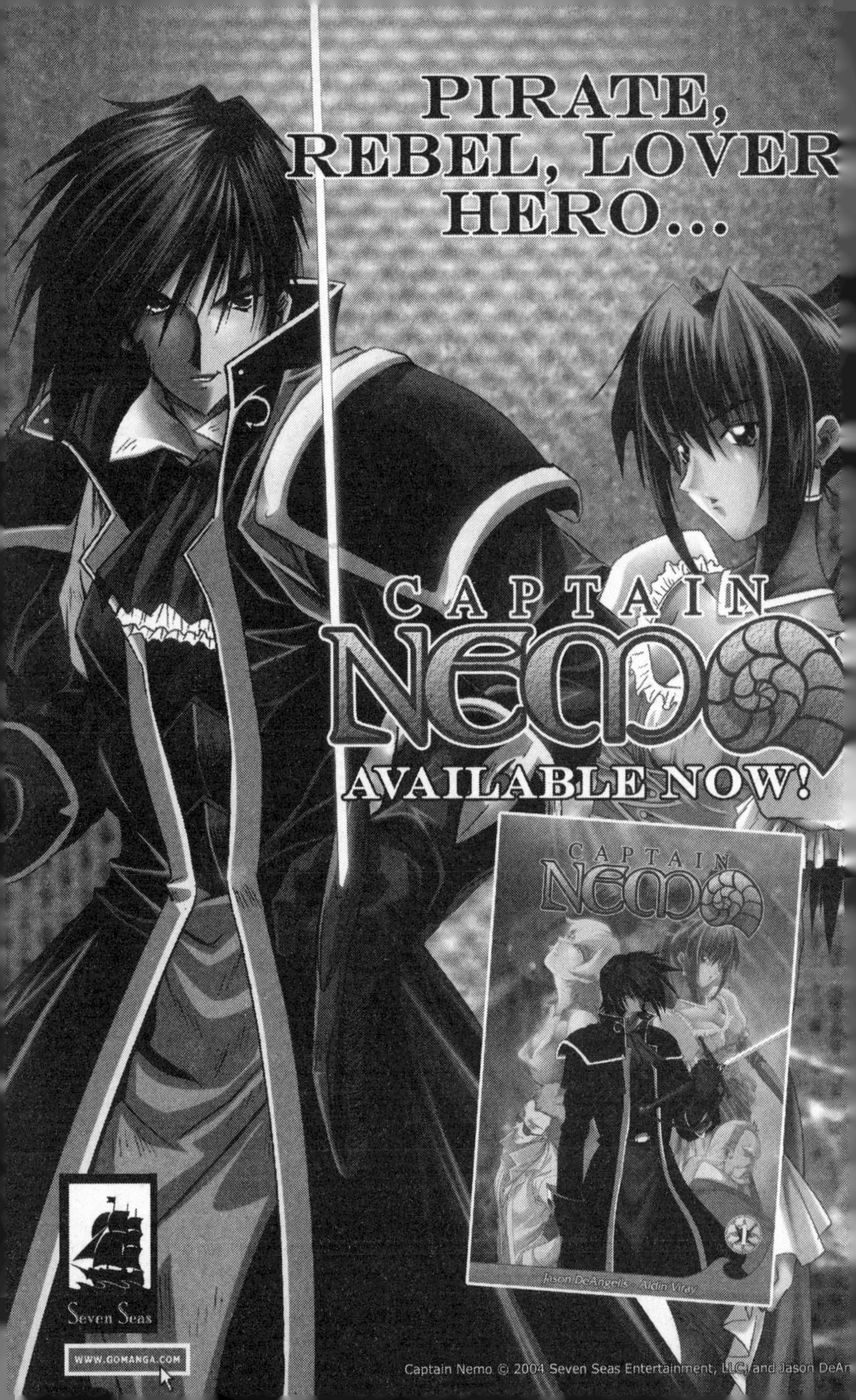
PIRATE, REBEL, LOVER HERO...
CAPTAIN NEMO
AVAILABLE NOW!
CAPTAIN NEMO
1
Jason DeAngelis · Aldin Viray
Seven Seas
WWW.GOMANGA.COM
Captain Nemo © 2004 Seven Seas Entertainment, LLC, and Jason DeAn

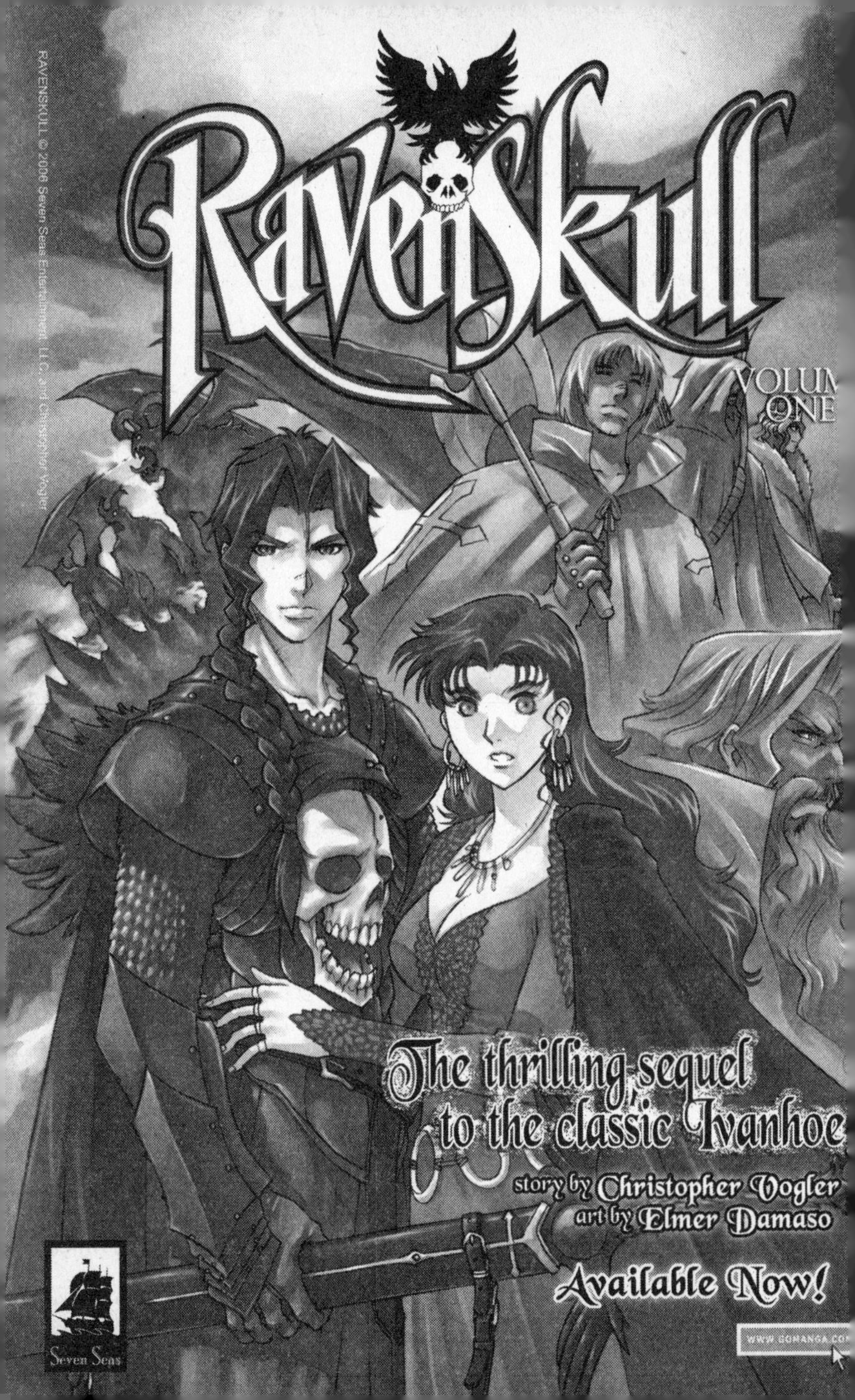
RavenSkull
VOLUM
ONE
The thrilling sequel to the classic Ivanhoe
story by Christopher Vogler
art by Elmer Damaso
Available Now!
WWW.GOMANGA.CO
Seven Seas
RAVENSKULL © 2006 Seven Seas Entertainment, LLC and Christopher Vogler

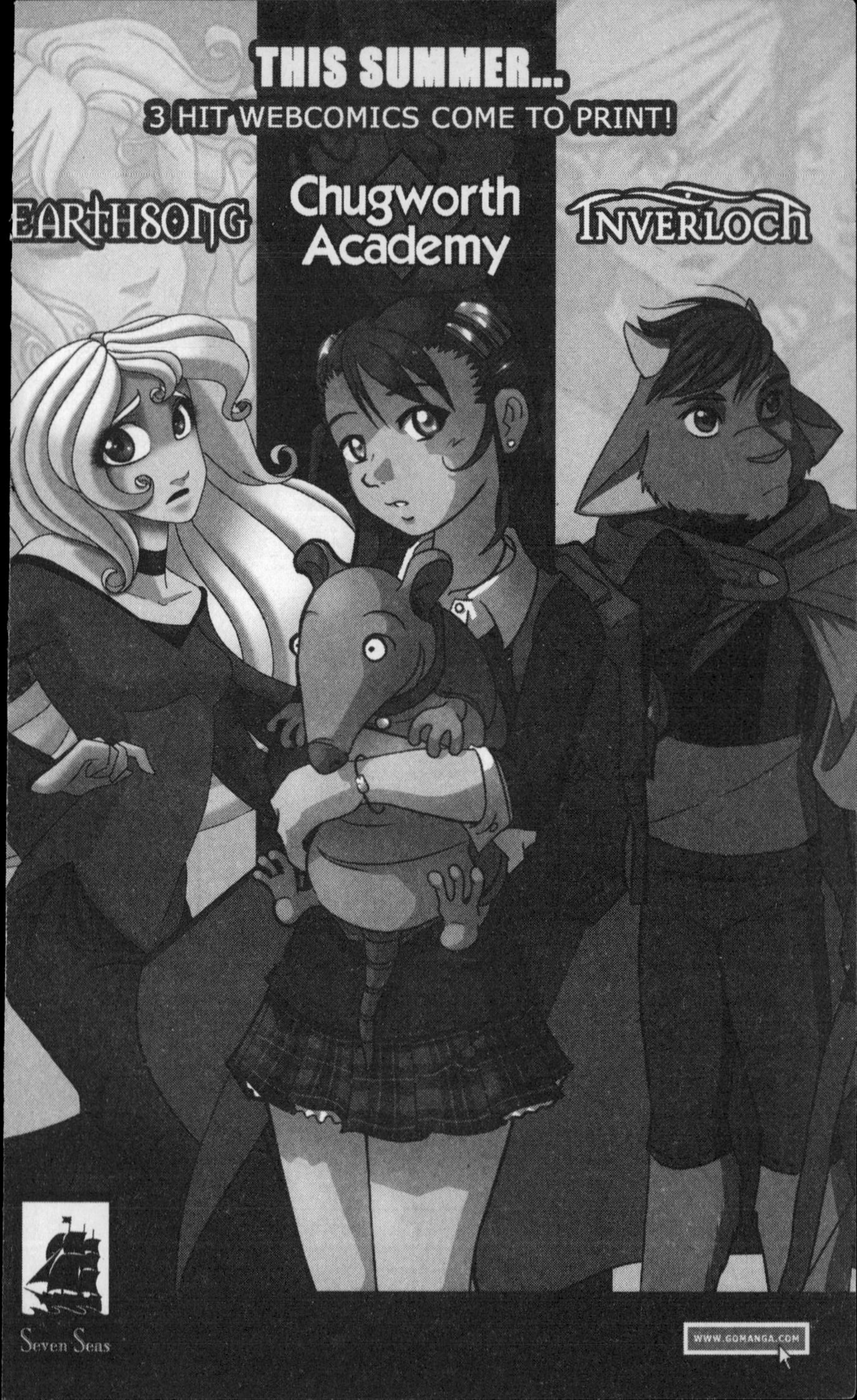

THIS SUMMER...
3 HIT WEBCOMICS COME TO PRINT!
EARTHSONG
Chugworth Academy
INVERLOCH
Seven Seas
WWW.GOMANGA.COM

TWO STRAIGHT GUYS + FIVE YAOI FANGIRLS =
AOI HOUSE
AS SEEN IN
NEWTYPE
USA
Seven Sea
NOW AVAILABLE!!!
WWW.GOMANGA.C

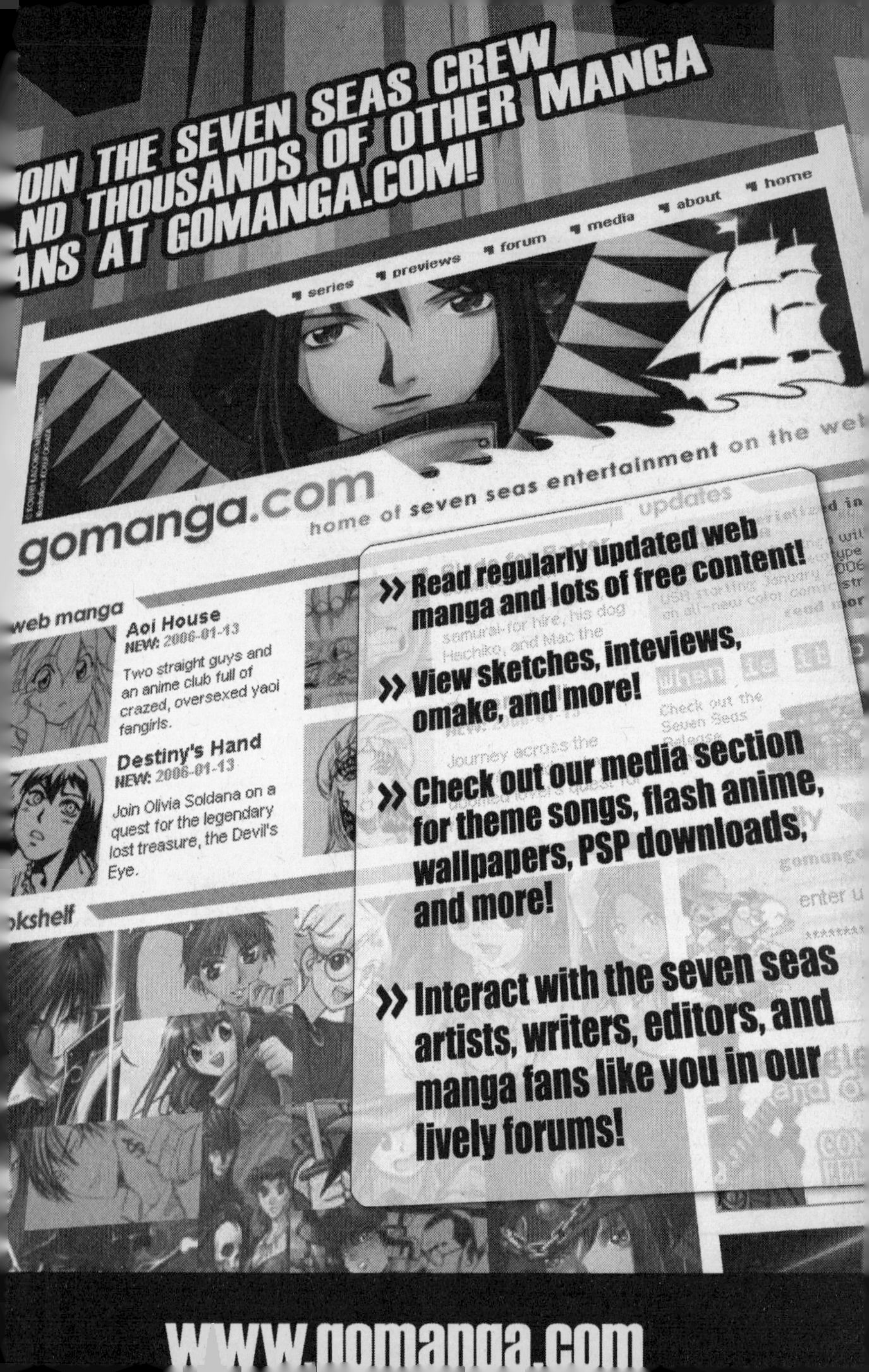
JOIN THE SEVEN SEAS CREW AND THOUSANDS OF OTHER MANGA FANS AT GOMANGA.COM!
series
previews
forum
media
about
home
gomanga.com
home of seven seas entertainment on the web
updates
web manga
Aoi House
NEW: 2006-01-13
Two straight guys and an anime club full of crazed, oversexed yaoi fangirls.
Destiny's Hand
NEW: 2006-01-13
Join Olivia Soldana on a quest for the legendary lost treasure, the Devil's Eye.
» Read regularly updated web manga and lots of free content!
» View sketches, inteviews, omake, and more!
» Check out our media section for theme songs, flash anime, wallpapers, PSP downloads, and more!
» Interact with the seven seas artists, writers, editors, and manga fans like you in our lively forums!
www.gomanga.com

OMAKE

The following pages are Melvin Calingo's tryout pages for Destiny's Hand and shows the earliest incarnations of the characters.

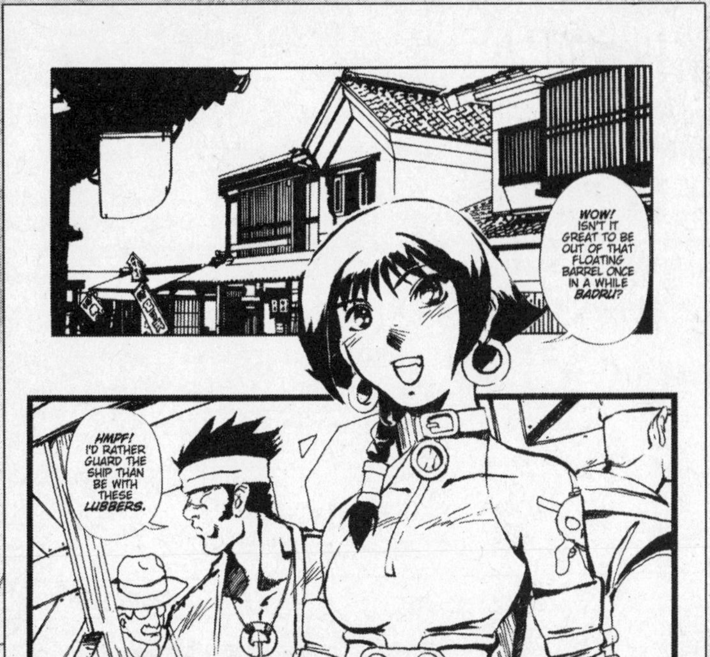
WOW! ISN'T IT GREAT TO BE OUT OF THAT FLOATING BARREL ONCE IN A WHILE BADRU?
HMPF! I'D RATHER GUARD THE SHIP THAN BE WITH THESE LUBBERS.
CREAK

"At this point in the production, only Olivia's character design was finalized (her having shorts came much later). This was also the first time I drew Badru (even before the actual character designs.)"

- Melvin C.

Based on N&C's description of Badru, I njured up a character who'd probably be obbish but downright loyal... kinda like a rate version of Alfred from Batman. The final rsion of Badru turned out to be the silent, -nonsense, bodyguard-type... my favorite nong the crew! (after Olivia of course.)

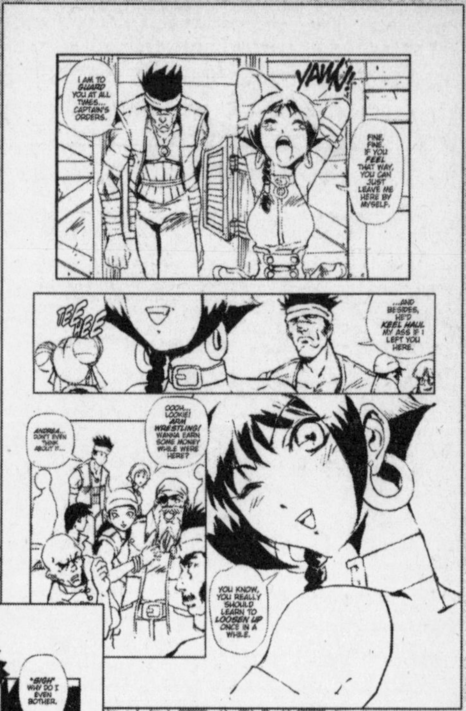
YANK!
FINE, FINE. IF YOU FEEL THAT WAY, YOU CAN JUST LEAVE ME HERE BY MYSELF.
I AM TO GUARD YOU AT ALL TIMES... CAPTAIN'S ORDERS.
...AND BESIDES, HE'D KEEL HAUL MY ASS IF I LEFT YOU HERE.
TEE HEE
YOU KNOW, YOU REALLY SHOULD LEARN TO LOOSEN UP ONCE IN A WHILE.
OOOH... LOOKIE! ARM WRESTLING! WANNA EARN SOME MONEY WHILE WE'RE HERE?
ANDREA... DON'T EVEN THINK ABOUT IT...

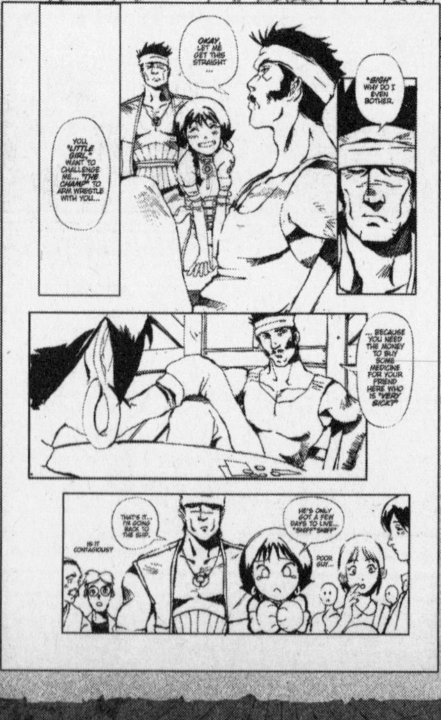
SIGH WHY DO I EVEN BOTHER.
OKAY, LET ME GET THIS STRAIGHT...
YOU, "LITTLE GIRL," WANT TO CHALLENGE ME... "THE CHAMP" TO ARM WRESTLE WITH YOU...
...BECAUSE YOU NEED THE MONEY TO BUY SOME MEDICINE FOR YOUR FRIEND HERE WHO IS "VERY SICK?"
HE'S ONLY GOT A FEW DAYS TO LIVE... *SNIFF* SNIFF
THAT'S IT... I'M GOING BACK TO THE SHIP.
POOR GUY...
IS IT CONTAGIOUS?

Here, she tricks the guy into arm wrestling with her because she says Badru's really sick and only has a few days to live. Badru doesn't like this one bit.

OMAKE

At first, I thought of Olivia as a childish pirate girl who'd use her charms more than her wits to get her way. In the book, she's far more mature and would choose finesse over charm any day.

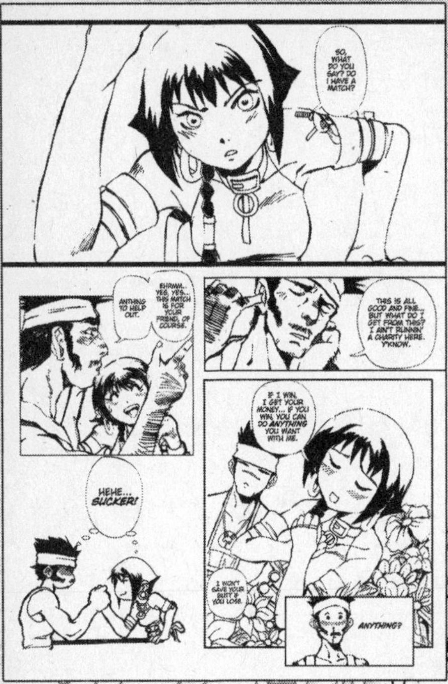

SO, WHAT DO YOU SAY? DO I HAVE A MATCH?
THIS IS ALL GOOD AND FINE... BUT WHAT DO I GET FROM THIS? I AIN'T RUNNIN' A CHARITY HERE. Y'KNOW.
EHRMM... YES, YES... THIS MATCH IS FOR YOUR FRIEND, OF COURSE.
ANTHING TO HELP OUT.
IF I WIN, I GET YOUR MONEY... IF YOU WIN, YOU CAN DO *ANYTHING* YOU WANT WITH ME.
I WON'T SAVE YOUR BUTT IF YOU LOSE.
ANYTHING?
HEHE... SUCKER!

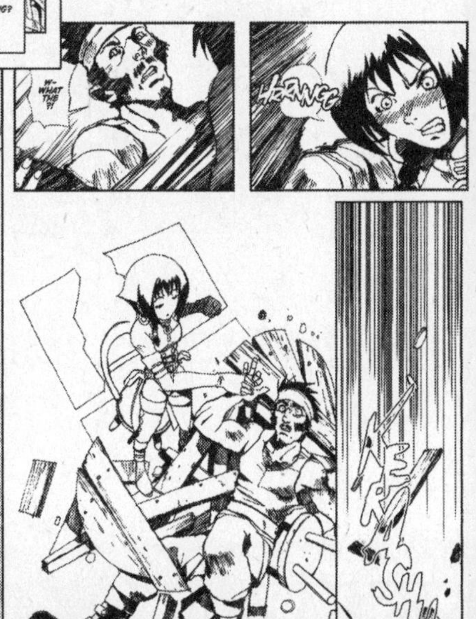

W-WHAT THE ?!

Yup she's strong. It's probably a manga exaggeration, but it gets the point across. Read chapter 1 again and see how she kicks the cabin door into splinters!

THE END

YOU'RE READING THE WRONG WAY

This is the last page of
Destiny's Hand Volume 1.

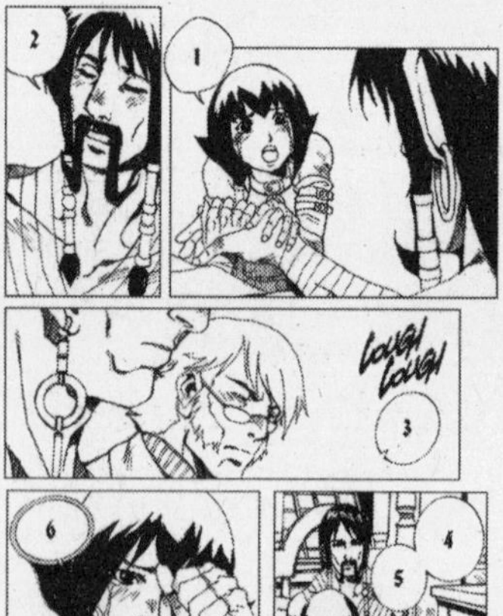
1
2
COUGH COUGH
3
4
5
6

This book reads from right to left, Japanese style. To read from the beginning, flip the book over to the other side, start with the top right panel, and take it from there.

If this is your first time reading manga, just follow the diagram. It may seem backwards at first, but you'll get used to it! Have fun!